DECISIVE BATTLES OF WORLD WAR II

DECISIVE BATTLES OF WORLD WAR II

Edited by Brigadier Peter Young

GALLERY BOOKS
An imprint of W.H. Smith Publishers Inc.
112 Madison Avenue
New York, New York 10016

Published by Gallery Books
A Division of W H Smith Publishers Inc.
112 Madison Avenue
New York, New York 10016

Produced by
Brompton Books Corp.
15 Sherwood Place
Greenwich, CT 06830

ISBN 0-8317-2158-8

Printed in Hong Kong

10 9 8 7 6 5 4 3 2 1

Page 1: The crew of the carrier USS *Yorktown* attempt to
prevent the vessel from sinking after a Japanese air attack,
the Battle of Midway, June 1942.
Pages 2-3: German infantry prepare to advance against a
Russian position in Stalingrad's factory district. A self-
propelled gun is moving forward to support the attack.
Pages 4-5: Working under German fire, British troops
attempt to recover a damaged Crusader tank in the
Western Desert.

Contents

Introduction

Put two military historians together and ask them to list their choice of the major battles of the Second World War and in general terms there would be considerable agreement. However, there would be perhaps some disagreement if these two military historians came from different national backgrounds. A German military historian, for example, asked to choose between the battles of Stalingrad and El Alamein would undoubtedly select the former, on the grounds that it was a truly decisive battle for Germany and the Soviet Union in the war's main theater of operations. Today perhaps, a British military historian would objectively agree that this was a correct choice. Yet at the same time, El Alamein was of considerable importance to British and western strategy. The Axis forces were turned back from the gates of Cairo – this was a significant victory in terms of proving to the Americans that the British could win battles on land and in raising the morale of British civilians and soldiers. Thanks to Montgomery's great skill at raising the fighting abilities of the Eighth Army, his soldiers learnt that Rommel was not invincible.

Selecting decisive battles always involves making value judgments about the nature of war and history. The battles included in this volume have been chosen because they were recognized at the time as being important, and

whatever the fashion in historical interpretation, are still considered so today. In this volume there is a balance between land, sea and air operations, and between the different theaters of war. Strictly speaking some of these battles should be viewed as campaigns because of their duration and intensity. Even specific battles such as Imphal or Cassino took place over several weeks, even months, while others such as the Battle of the Atlantic or Singapore involved a number of engagements which eventually, taken together, resulted in a decisive outcome.

The accounts selected here have been written by participants, some of whom, like Montgomery, Chuikov and Guderian, held senior command appointments, while others, like Tsuji, were senior staff officers. In general their literary works are subjective and biased, written after the event to demonstrate the importance of their role in the battle or campaign. There are also considerable differences in style and interpretation, even between generals of the same army. Compare the rather formal style of Montgomery with the more self-effacing one of Slim, who, furthermore, writes in a flowing, enjoyable manner reflecting his excellent command of the English language.

None of these accounts is a fully accurate and objective analysis of the battle described. The

Right: The crew of the light carrier USS *Princeton* abandon ship after the vessel was hit by a bomb during the Battle of the Sibuyan Sea, Leyte Gulf, 24 October 1944. A subsequent internal explosion sank the carrier and damaged the cruiser *Birmingham*, seen here alongside the *Princeton*.

Below right: A half-submerged Sherman, waterproofed and fitted with exhaust vents, lies on Omaha Beach, a victim of rough seas during the opening hours of Operation Overlord, June 1944.

Below: Smiling German infantry pose for the camera in front of an overturned US truck – a picture taken on the first day of the Battle of the Bulge.

authors were intimately involved in the action
and by act of omission do not necessarily detail
every decision and action taken. Each is one
man's view of a battle, one that does not make
use of all the operational, administrative and
tactical information available. Few of them
even hint at the importance of the work undertaken to break and listen to the enemy's coded
signal traffic. Personal rivalries between commanders are barely mentioned; nor are the
unfortunate inter-Allied squabbles which at
times threatened to overturn their common
military objectives.

Equally, few of these accounts dwell on the
'loneliness of command,' that hackneyed
phrase which sums up the immense strain that
any senior military commander bears in war.
Each commander was responsible for the planning of a major battle on which depended not
only the lives of his own troops but the very
existence of his country. Many of them fought
as young officers during the First World War,
and although as senior officers in the Second
World War they were not placed in positions of
personal danger, death was an ever-present
companion. Few of these commanders were
'armchair generals.' All of them were conscious
of the need to be seen and heard by their troops.
One attribute all these men had in common
during the war was that quality of command,
both mental and physical, that Field Marshal
Wavell rated so highly – robustness.

Blitzkrieg 1940

by Heinz Guderian

The Blitzkrieg of 1940 is for the student of military affairs one of the most rewarding in the whole History of the Art of War. In this chapter one of the great pioneers of armoured warfare and one of the best of Hitler's generals, describes his part in the campaign that cut the Allied array in two and came within an ace of cutting off the British Expeditionary Force. Guderian served in von Rundstedt's Army Group A. There can be little question that he is an honest witness, but he is not infallible. He blames Hitler for stopping the German armour before Dunkirk. It is certain, however, that although Hitler approved of the order it was actually given by von Rundstedt on 24 May. Guderian underestimates, moreover, the delaying effect of the defence of Calais. The repulse of von Bock's Army Group B by the B.E.F. in the Ypres-Comines battle (26-28 May) finds no mention in Guderian's pages, but that is scarcely surprising, since he was not himself directly concerned.   EDITOR

Chronology

1940

10 May	Germans invade Holland, Belgium and Luxembourg.
14 May	Surrender of Dutch Army, Germans cross the Meuse.
19 May	General Weygand replaces General Gamelin as French C.-in-C.
20 May	German panzers reach the Channel coast at Abbeville.
21 May	British counterattack at Arras.
24 May	Von Rundstedt halts his armour.
25 May	Fall of Boulogne.
26-28 May	Battle of Ypres-Comines.
27 May	Calais is taken.
27 May- 4 June	Dunkirk.
28 May	Surrender of Belgium.
14 June	Fall of Paris.
22 June	France accepts Hitler's terms.

These pages: The remains of a bridge in the Dutch town of Zutphen lie in the River Ijssel, blown by retreating troops of the Dutch Army in May 1940.

Preparations for the Campaign

Before embarking on the campaign against the Western Powers – which we would gladly have avoided – we carefully evaluated the lessons learned in Poland. These proved that the Light Divisions were an anomalous mixture, a discovery which did not take me by surprise. It was therefore ordered that they be changed into panzer divisions, bearing the numbers 6 to 9. The motorized infantry divisions had turned out to be too large and unwieldy. They were made smaller by the removal of one of their infantry regiments. The very urgent business of re-equipping the tank regiments with Panzers III and IV went forward only slowly, partially owing to the limited production capacity of the industry, but also because of a tendency by the Army High Command to hoard the new tanks.

I was given command of a few panzer divisions and the Infantry Regiment 'Gross Deutschland' for training purposes. Apart from this I was mainly occupied with plans and appreciations for the future operations in the West.

The Army High Command, spurred on by Hitler to mount an offensive, was intending to use, once again, the so-called 'Schlieffen Plan' of 1914. It is true that this had the advantage of simplicity, though hardly the charm of novelty.

Colonel-General Heinz Guderian
(1888-1954)

The son of a military family, he was commissioned into the 10th Hanoverian Jäger Battalion in 1907. In 1913 he was at the Kriegsakademie and throughout the First World War he served as a Staff Officer, except for a single tour of duty as a battalion commander on the Western Front (1917). After the war he served in the Freikorps on the Eastern Front and in several Staff appointments, chiefly in the Motorized Troops directorate, Germany's cover organization for armoured development. In 1927 he was promoted Major, and in 1933 Colonel. In 1934 he was appointed Chief of Staff to the Panzer Command, in 1935 G.O.C., 2 Panzer Command, and in 1938 (as lieutenant-general) XVI Army Corps. In the same year he was promoted General, and appointed Chief of Mobile Troops. He commanded XIX Corps in Poland (1939) and in the West (1940), then commanded a Panzer Group and was promoted Colonel-General. In 1941 he became commander of 2 Panzer Army which he led in Russia until removed (December 1941) thanks to the enmity of Field-Marshal von Kluge. After a period in retirement he was made Inspector-General of Armoured Troops, and after the Bomb Plot, Chief of the General Staff. After frequent disagreements with the Führer, he was dismissed on the grounds of ill-health on 28 March 1945. At the surrender he became a prisoner of the Americans.

Thoughts therefore soon turned to alternative solutions. One day in November Manstein asked me to come to see him and outlined his ideas on the subject to me; these involved a strong tank thrust through southern Belgium and Luxembourg towards Sedan, a breakthrough of the prolongation of the Maginot Line in that area and a consequent splitting in two of the whole French front. He asked me to examine this plan of his from the point of view of a tank man. After a lengthy study of maps and making use of my own memories of the terrain from the First World War, I was able to assure Manstein that the operation he had planned could in fact be carried out. The only condition I attached was that a sufficient number of armoured and motorized divisions must be employed, if possible all of them.

Manstein thereupon wrote a memorandum which, with the approval and signature of Colonel-General von Rundstedt, was sent to the Army High Command on the 4 December 1939. There it was by no means joyfully received. To start with, the High Command only wanted to use one or two panzer divisions for the attack through Arlon. I held such a force to be too weak and therefore pointless. Any subdivision of our already weak tank forces would have been the greatest mistake that we could make. But it was precisely this that the High Command was intent on doing. Manstein became insistent and by so doing aroused such animosity in the High Command that he was appointed commanding general of an Infantry Corps. He requested that he be at least given a Panzer Corps: his request was not granted. As a result our finest operational brain took the field as commander of a corps in the third wave of the attack, though it was largely thanks to his brilliant initiative that the operation was to be such an outstanding success. His successor with Colonel-General von Rundstedt was the more prosaic General von Sodenstern.

Meanwhile an aeroplane accident compelled our masters to abandon the Schlieffen Plan. A Luftwaffe officer-courier who, contrary to standing orders, was flying by night with important papers containing references to the proposed Schlieffen Plan operation, crossed the Belgian frontier and was compelled to make a forced landing on Belgian soil. It is not known whether he had succeeded in destroying his papers. In any case it had to be assumed that the Belgians, and probably also the French and British, knew all about our proposed operation.

Apart from this, when Manstein reported to Hitler on assuming command of his corps, he took the opportunity to express his views on the forthcoming operations. This resulted in the Manstein Plan now becoming the object of

Below: A column of British soldiers marches through a village in northern France during the winter of 1939-40. This period became known as the 'Phony War,' due to the lack of military activity on the Western Front. But while the British and French just waited, the Germans prepared to launch a Blitzkrieg attack through the Ardennes to the north of the Maginot Line.

serious study: a war game that took place at Koblenz on 7 February 1940, seemed to me decisive in its favour. During the course of this map exercise I proposed that on the fifth day of the campaign an attack be made with strong armoured and motorized forces to force a crossing of the Meuse near Sedan with the objective of achieving a break-through which would then be expanded towards Amiens. The Chief of the Army General Staff, Halder, who was present, pronounced these ideas 'senseless'. He envisaged tank forces reaching the Meuse and even securing bridgeheads across it, and then waiting for the infantry armies to catch up; after this a 'unified attack' would be launched, which would not be mounted before the ninth or tenth day of the campaign. He called this *'einen rangierten Gesamtangriff'* ('a properly marshalled attack in mass'). I contradicted him strongly and repeated that the essential was that we use all the available limited offensive power of our armour in one surprise blow at one decisive point; to drive a wedge so deep and wide that we need not worry about our flanks; and then immediately to exploit any successes gained without bothering to wait for the infantry corps.

Guderian goes on to explain why he looked forward to the pending operations with such confidence. He describes at some length the development of armoured vehicle warfare and their restoration of the power of the offensive. He shows that the Germans were fully aware that the French High Command was wedded to outworn ideas: 'so far as the French were concerned the German leadership could safely rely on the defence of France being systematically based on fortifications'.

On 14 February another war game took place at Mayan, the headquarters of Colonel-General List's Twelfth Army; again Halder was present and once again the battle for the Meuse crossing

Below: Armed with an antiquated M1914 Hotchkiss machine gun, French troops scan the skies for sight of German aircraft, January 1940.

was the subject under study. The main questions that were put to me boiled down to this; could the panzer divisions attempt to force a river crossing on their own, or should they not rather wait until the infantry had caught up with them: in the latter case, should they take part in the initial river crossing or should this be left to the infantry? This last solution was impossible in view of the difficult terrain in the Ardennes north of the Meuse. The whole tone grew more and more depressing until at last General von Wietersheim – whose motorized XIV Army Corps was supposed to follow behind mine – and I eventually declared that in these circumstances we would have no confidence in the leadership of the operation. We declared that the proposed employment of the armour was incorrect and that in the event of its commitment in this fashion a crisis must arise.

The situation became even tenser when it became clear that not even Colonel-General von Rundstedt had any clear idea about the potentialities of tanks, and declared himself in favour of the more cautious solution. Now was the time when we needed Manstein!

There was endless discussion and worry about how the many armoured units should be commanded. After much chopping and changing it was decided that General von Kleist, who up to now had not shown himself particularly well disposed to the armoured force, should be placed in command. When it was at last settled that in any case my Panzer Corps should form the van of the attack through the Ardennes, I settled down busily to train my generals and

staff officers for their forthcoming tasks. I was given the 1st, 2nd and 10th Panzer Divisions, the Infantry Regiment Gross-Deutschland, and a quantity of corps troops, including a mortar battalion. With the exception of Infantry Regiment 'G.D.' I knew my troops well both from peace and war and I had unbounded faith in their ability. Now I had the opportunity to prepare them for their hard task ahead, in whose successful outcome nobody at that time actually believed, with the exception of Hitler, Manstein and myself. The struggle to get our ideas accepted had proved exhausting in the extreme. I was in need of a little rest, and was granted short leave in the second half of March.

Before that, however, a conference took

Above: Members of the Allied High Command during the days prior to the German attack of May 1940 (from left to right) – General Ironside, Winston Churchill, General Gamelin, the French commander of Allied land forces, Field Marshal Lord Gort, the commander of the British Expeditionary Force, and General Georges.

Below: British troops erect an anti-tank barrier on the Amiens road.

place attended by the army and army group commanders of Army Group A, accompanied by General von Kleist and myself, in the Reich Chancellery. Hitler was there. Each of us generals outlined what his task was and how he intended to carry it out. I was the last to speak. My task was as follows: on the day ordered I would cross the Luxembourg frontier, drive through Southern Belgium towards Sedan, cross the Meuse and establish a bridgehead on the far side so that the infantry corps following behind could get across. I explained briefly that my corps would advance through Luxembourg and Southern Belgium in three columns; I reckoned on reaching the Belgian frontier posts on the first day and I hoped to break through them on that same day: on the second day I would advance as far as Neufchâteau; on the third day I would reach Bouillon and cross the Semois; on the fourth day I would arrive at the Meuse; on the fifth day I would cross it. By the evening of the fifth day I hoped to have established a bridgehead on the far bank. Hitler asked: 'And then what are you going to do?' He was the first person who had thought to ask me this vital question. I replied: 'Unless I receive orders to the contary, I intend on the next day to continue my advance westwards. The supreme leadership must decide whether my objective is to be Amiens or Paris. In my opinion the correct course is to drive past Amiens to the English Channel.' Hitler nodded and said nothing more. Only General Busch, who commanded the Sixteenth Army on my left, cried out: 'Well, I don't think you'll cross the river in the first place!' Hitler, the tension visible in his face, looked at me to see what I would reply. I said: 'There's no need for you to do so, in any case.' Hitler made no comment.

I never received any further orders as to what I was to do once the bridgehead over the Meuse was captured. All my decisions, until I reached the Atlantic seaboard at Abbeville, were taken by me and me alone. The Supreme Command's influence on my actions was merely restrictive throughout.

In order to establish a sound basis for co-operation as quickly as possible, I had invited the airmen to my planning exercises and I also took part in an air exercise that General Lörzer organized. The principal matter discussed was the Meuse crossing. After detailed study we agreed that the air force could best be employed in giving the ground forces continuous support during the crossing; that meant no concentrated attack by bombers and dive-bombers, but rather, from the very beginning of the crossing and throughout the whole operation, perpetual attacks and threats of attack against the enemy batteries in open emplacements; this should force the enemy gunners to take cover both from the bombs that were dropped and from the bombs that they expected to be

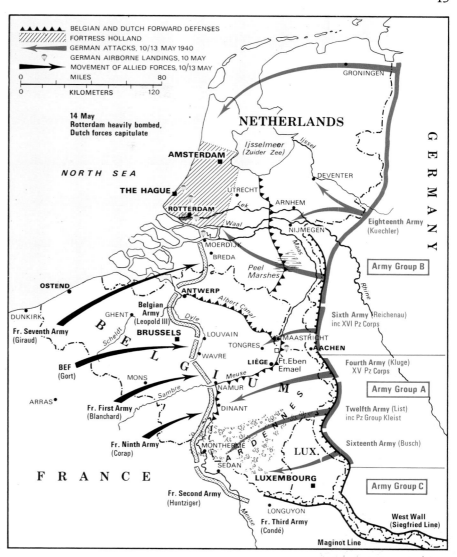

dropped. The time schedules for these attacks, together with the targets, were marked on a map.

Shortly before the operation was due to start it was decided, in accordance with Göring's wish, that a battalion of Infantry Regiment 'G.D.' be loaded in 'Stork' aircraft and landed, on the first morning of the attack, behind the Belgians at Witry, west of Martelange, with the aim of spreading alarm among their frontier defence force.

For the rapid thrust through Luxembourg and southern Belgium, the three panzer divisions of the corps were drawn up in line. In the centre was the 1st Panzer Division, with behind it the corps artillery, the corps headquarters and the mass of our anti-aircraft artillery; here, to start with, was to be our point of main effort. On the right of the 1st Panzer was the 2nd Panzer Division: on its left the 10th Panzer Division and Infantry Regiment 'G.D.' The 1st Panzer Division was commanded by General Kirchner, the 2nd by General Veiel, and the 10th by General Schaal. I knew all three of them well. I had complete trust in their competence and reliability. They knew my views and shared my belief that once armoured formations are out on the loose they must be given the green

Above: The opening moves of the Battle of France – the Allies cautiously advance into Belgium, while two German army groups cross the Meuse near Sedan.

Left: German paratroops make a surprise drop near Rotterdam, May 1940. The daring employment of paratroops to capture key positions within the Dutch defenses – considered to be among the strongest in the world – created a very deep impression on the British and Americans who then began raising their own parachute-equipped troops.

light to the very end of the road. In our case this was – the Channel! That was a clear inspiration to every one of our soldiers, and he could follow it even though he might receive no orders for long periods of time once the attack was launched.

The Break-through to the Channel

We were alerted at 13.30 hrs. on 9 May 1940. I left Koblenz at 16.00 hrs. and arrived at my corps headquarters, the Sonnenhof near Bitberg, that evening. The troops, as ordered, were drawn up along the frontier between Vianden and Echternach.

At 05.30 hrs. I crossed the Luxembourg frontier with the 1st Panzer Division near Wallendorf and headed for Martelange. By the evening of that first day the advance guard of the division was already through the Belgian frontier defences and had established contact with the airborne troops of Infantry Regiment 'G.D.' but had not been able to advance deep into Belgium owing to extensive road-demolitions which could not be by-passed in that mountainous terrain. The roads were to be cleared during the night. The 2nd Panzer Division was fighting near Strainchamps, while the 10th Panzer Division, advancing through Habay-la-Neuve and Étalle, was in contact with French units (the 2nd Cavalry Division and the 3rd Colonial Infantry Division). Corps headquarters was established at Rambruch, west of Martelange.

In the morning of the 11th the demolitions and minefields along the Belgian frontier were broken through. Towards noon the 1st Panzer

Division began to move forward. With its tanks leading, it headed towards the fortifications on either side of Neufchâteau, which were held by the Belgian *Chasseurs Ardennais*, withdrawn from the frontier, and by French cavalry. After a short fight, with only light casualties, the enemy positions were broken and Neufchâteau taken. 1st Panzer Division immediately drove on, took Bertrix, and as dusk was falling reached Bouillon, but the French managed to hold that town throughout the night. The other two divisions had advanced exactly according to plan in the face of only slight opposition. The 2nd Panzer Division took Libramont. The 10th Panzer Division had had a few casualties near Habay-la-Neuve; the commander of Rifle Regiment 69, Lieutenant-Colonel Ehlermann, had fallen on 10 May near Sante-Marie.

During the night of the 10th-11th, Panzer Group von Kleist, which was in control of the operation, ordered the 10th Panzer Division on the left flank to change direction at once and move on Longwy, since French cavalry were reported to be advancing from that direction. I asked for the cancellation of these orders; the detachment of one-third of my force to meet the hypothetical threat of enemy cavalry would endanger the success of the Meuse crossing and therefore the whole operation. In order to anticipate any difficulties that might be engendered by this curious fear of hostile cavalry, I ordered 10th Panzer Division to move along a parallel road north of its previous line of advance and to go through Rulles towards the sector of the Semois between Cugnon and Mortehan. The advance went on. The immediate danger of a halt and a change of direction was passed. The

Below: General Gerd von Rundstedt, the veteran commander of Army Group A that had been assigned the spearhead role in the great Blitzkrieg offensive of May-June 1940. Although on the retired list when war broke out in 1939, von Rundstedt proved to be receptive to the new theories of armored warfare specialists like Guderian and Rommel.

Panzer Group finally agreed to this. The French cavalry did not in fact appear.

Infantry Regiment 'G.D.' was withdrawn into corps reserve at Saint-Médard. Corps headquarters spent the night in Neufchâteau.

On Whitsun, 12 May, at 05.00 hrs. I drove with my staff through Bertrix-Fays les Veneurs-Bellevaux to Bouillon against which town the 1st Rifle Regiment under Lieutenant-Colonel Balck launched an attack at 07.45 hrs., which soon carried its objective. The French had blown the bridges over the Semois, but the stream was fordable for tanks at a number of points. The divisional engineers began the immediate construction of a new bridge. After I had satisfied myself concerning the measures taken I followed the tanks across the stream in the direction of Sedan, but mined roads compelled me to return to Bouillon. Here, in the southern part of the town, I experienced an enemy air attack for the first time; they were after 1st Panzer Division's bridge. Luckily the bridge remained undamaged, but a few houses were set on fire.

I now drove through the woods to 10th Panzer Division, which had crossed the Semois in the sector Cugnon-Herbeumont. When I reached their road of advance I witnessed an attack by the Reconnaissance Battalion on the frontier defences; the riflemen advanced immediately behind the reconnaissance unit, with the brave brigade commander, Colonel Fischer, at their head, followed closely by the divisional commander, General Schaal. The steady way the division moved forward under the command of its officers was an impressive sight. The defensive positions in the woods

were soon captured; the advance through La Chapelle towards Bazeilles-Balan continued. I could return without anxiety to my corps headquarters at Bouillon.

Colonel Nehring, my Chief of Staff, had meanwhile established himself in the Hotel Panorama, from whose windows there was a splendid view over the valley of the Semois. In the office that we shared my desk was in an alcove much decorated by trophies of the chase.

We went to work. Suddenly there was a series of explosions in rapid succession; another air attack. As though that were not enough, an engineer supply column, carrying fuses, explosives, mines and hand grenades, caught fire and there was one detonation after the other. A boar's head, attached to the wall immediately above my desk, broke loose and missed me by a hair's breadth; the other trophies came tumbling down and the fine window in front of which I was seated was smashed to smithereens and splinters of glass whistled about my ears. It had in fact become very unpleasant where we were and we decided to move elsewhere. We chose a small hotel to the north of Bouillon which had served as regimental headquarters for the 1st Panzer Regiment. When we went to look at it the commander of our air support, General von Stutterheim, who happened to be present, warned me that it was very exposed. Even while we were talking a squadron of Belgian planes appeared and bombed the bivouacs of the tank regiment. Our casualties were negligible, but we were now prepared to listen to Stutterheim's advice; we then moved farther north, to the next village along, Bellevaux-Noirefontaine.

Above left: Testimony to the French failure to anticipate the potential of the tank – a battered pill-box on the Maginot Line. This fortified system was simply by-passed by the German panzer divisions and left for the follow-up troops to reduce at their leisure.

Above: Junkers Ju 87 Stuka dive-bombers on their way to attack French positions on the River Meuse. The German ground forces called them their 'aerial artillery' and they played an important role in the air-ground co-operation that was vital to the Blitzkrieg 'philosophy.'

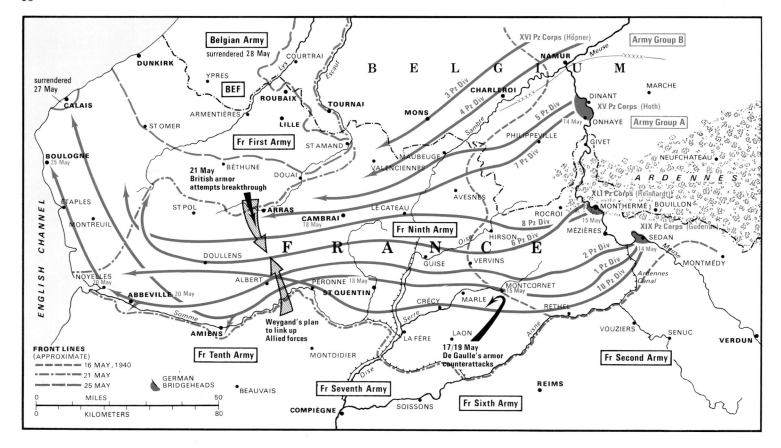

Belgian Army
surrendered 28 May

surrendered
27 May

XVI Pz Corps (Höpner)
Army Group B
XXXXX

XV Pz Corps (Hoth)
Army Group A

XLI Pz Corps (Reinhardt)
XIX Pz Corps (Guderian)

BEF

Fr First Army

21 May
British armor
attempts breakthrough

Fr Ninth Army

Weygand's plan
to link up
Allied forces

ENGLISH CHANNEL

FRANCE

17/19 May
De Gaulle's armor
counterattacks

FRONT LINES
(APPROXIMATE)
— 16 MAY, 1940
—·— 21 MAY
— — 25 MAY

GERMAN
BRIDGEHEADS

Fr Tenth Army

Fr Second Army

0   MILES   50
0   KILOMETERS   80

Fr Seventh Army

Fr Sixth Army

Above: The famous
'panzer corridor,' made
possible by the rapidity of
the German advance.
Once the Germans had
reached the Channel
coast, the Allied armies
were cut in two, the
German victory all but
complete.

Before this second move could be carried out a Fieseler-Stork aeroplane appeared to fetch me to General von Kleist's headquarters for orders. The order I received was to attack across the Meuse on the next day, 13 May, at 16.00 hrs. My 1st and 10th Panzer Divisions should be in position by that time, but the 2nd Panzer Division, which had run into difficulties along the Semois, would certainly not be. I reported this fact, which was of importance in view of the weakness of our attacking force. General von Kleist would not modify his orders, however, and I felt obliged to admit that there were probably advantages in thrusting forwards immediately without waiting for all our troops to be ready. A further order was far less pleasant. Unaware of the arrangements I had come to with Lörzer, General von Kleist and the air force General Sperrle had decided on a mass bombing attack, to be co-ordinated with the beginning of the artillery preparation. My whole attack plan was thus placed in jeopardy, since if such an attack were carried out the long-drawn-out neutralization of the enemy batteries could no longer be achieved. I argued strongly against this and asked that my original plan, on which the whole attack was founded, be followed. General von Kleist refused this request too, and I flew back in the Fieseler-Stork, with a new pilot, to my corps headquarters. The young man maintained he knew exactly where the landing strip from which I had set off was located, but he could not find it in the fading light and the next thing I knew we were on the other side of the Meuse, flying in a slow and unarmed plane over the French positions. An unpleasant moment. I gave my pilot emphatic orders to turn north and find my landing strip; we just made it.

Back at corps headquarters I settled down at once to drawing up orders. In view of the very short time at our disposal, we were forced to take the orders used in the war games at Koblenz from our files and after changing the dates and times, issue these as the orders for the attack. They were perfectly fitted to the reality of the situation. The only change that had to be made was that at Koblenz we had imagined the attack going in at 10.00 instead of 16.00 hrs. 1st and 10th Panzer Divisions copied this procedure and so the issuing of orders was an agreeably quick and simple business.

By the evening of 12 May the 1st and 10th Panzer Divisions had occupied the northern bank of the Meuse and had captured the historic city and fortress of Sedan. The night was spent in making final preparations for the assault and in moving the Corps and Panzer Group artillery into position. The point of main effort lay in the sector of the 1st Panzer Division, which was reinforced by the Infantry Regiment 'G.D.', the corps artillery and the heavy artillery battalions of the two flanking divisions. When judging the achievements of the two flanking divisions on the following day, this weakening of their artillery strength must be borne in mind.

The transfer of corps headquarters to La Chapelle was ordered for 13 May.

In the morning I first visited the headquarters of the 1st Panzer Division to see how far advanced their preparations were: then, driving across partially mined ground, which my staff drivers cleared, and under artillery fire put down by the French defence from the far bank, I went on to the 2nd Panzer Division at Sugny. The head of the division had reached the French frontier. At midday I returned to my corps headquarters, by now installed at La Chapelle.

At 15.30 hrs. I went through French shell fire to an advanced artillery O.P. of 10th Panzer Division in order personally to observe the effects of my artillery and of the Luftwaffe's contribution. At 16.00 hrs. the battle began with a display of artillery fire which, to me, at least, seemed magnificent. Tensely I waited for the air force. It arrived punctually but my astonishment was great to see only a few squadrons of bombers and dive-bombers, under fighter cover; they adopted the tactics which Lörzer and I had agreed on during our war games. Had General von Kleist changed his mind, or had the new orders for the attack not got through to the squadrons in time? In any event the flyers were doing exactly what I believed to be most advantageous for our attack and I sighed with relief.

I was now anxious to take part in the assault across the Meuse by the riflemen. The actual ferrying must be nearly over by now, so I went to St Menges and from there to Floing, which was the proposed crossing-place of 1st Panzer Division. I went over in the first assault boat. On the far bank I found the efficient and brave commander of the 1st Rifle Regiment, Lieutenant-Colonel Balck, together with his staff. He greeted me cheerfully with the cry: 'Joy riding in canoes on the Meuse is forbidden.' I had in

fact used those words myself in one of the exercises that we had had in preparation for this operation, since the attitude of some of the younger officers had struck me as rather too light-hearted. I now realized that they had judged the situation correctly.

The attack by the 1st Rifle Regiment and by Infantry Regiment 'G.D.' was developing as though it were being carried out on manoeuvres. The French artillery was almost paralysed by the unceasing threat of attack by Stukas and bombers. The concrete emplacements along the Meuse had been put out of action by our anti-tank and anti-aircraft artillery, and the enemy machine-gunners were forced to keep down by the fire of our heavy weapons and artillery. Despite the completely open nature of the ground, our casualties remained light. By the time night fell a considerable penetration of the enemy's defences had been made. The troops had been ordered to keep up the attack without pause throughout

Above: A crashed Junkers Ju 52, shot down over Holland while carrying German paratroops. Despite losses such as these, German casualties remained surprisingly light during the course of the campaign.

Left: Dutch gunners make ready a 100mm field gun hidden in a prepared position along the German line of advance into Holland. The Dutch were only able to offer token resistance, however, so overwhelming was the momentum of the German advance.

the night, and I could rely on this important order being obeyed. By 23.00 hrs. they had captured Cheveuges and part of the Bois de la Marfée to the west of Wadelincourt and had reached the French main line of defence. Pleased and proud of what I had seen, I returned to my corps headquarters in the Bois de la Garenne, arriving at La Chapelle just in time for another air attack, and settled down to study the reports from the flanks.

Only the advance elements of the 2nd Panzer Division, the Reconnaissance Battalion and the Motor-cycle Battalion together with the heavy artillery, had been in action. With such few troops they had not succeeded in forcing a crossing. The whole of 1st Panzer Division's Rifle Brigade was over on the left bank of the Meuse by now: the division's tanks and artillery were ready to follow just as soon as a bridge could be thrown across. The 10th Panzer Division had crossed the river and established a small bridgehead on the far side; owing to lack of artillery support this division had had a hard day. Flanking fire from the Maginot Line south of Douzy-Carignan had been particularly worrying. The next morning, however, should bring relief both to them and to the 2nd Panzer Division. The corps heavy anti-aircraft was to be brought up to the near bank of the river during the night, since from the 14th no more support could be expected from the Luftwaffe, which was to be employed elsewhere.

During the night I telephoned Lörzer to inquire what the reason was for the change in the plan of air support which had contributed so markedly to our success. I learned that Sperrle's order had in fact arrived too late to be passed on to the squadrons and that Lörzer had

Above: Employing scaling ladders and inflatable pontoon sections, German infantry make their way across the River Meuse. Once this barrier was crossed the French melted away, leaving a fatal gap in the Allied line – one which Guderian's panzers were quick to exploit.

Left: Panzer IIs and 38ts, supported by a variety of transports, wait for the order to advance through the Ardennes.

therefore quite correctly made no modifications to the existing plan. I then sent a signal to Busch, who during the Hitler conference in Berlin had questioned my ability to cross the Meuse, informing him of my troops' success; he sent me a very cordial reply. Finally I thanked my colleagues on my staff for their devoted help.

Early on 14 May the brave 1st Panzer Division signalled that they had managed to increase their penetration considerably during the night and were now through Chémery. So off to Chémery I went. On the banks of the Meuse were thousands of prisoners. At Chémery the commander of the 1st Panzer Division was giving orders to his subordinate commanders and I listened while he did so. There was a report of strong French armoured forces moving up, and he sent the tanks of 1st Panzer Division into the attack towards Stonne to head them off; then I returned to the Meuse bridge, where I had arranged for my command staff to await me, and ordered that 2nd Panzer Brigade move across the river immediately behind the 1st, so that there would be sufficient armour available on the far side to meet the French attack when it came in. This attack was stopped at Bulson with the destruction of 50 more tanks. Infantry Regiment 'G.D.' took Bulson and advanced from there on Villers-Maisoncelle. Unfortunately shortly after my departure German dive-bombers attacked our troop concentration in Chémery, which caused us heavy casualties.

Meanwhile the 2nd Panzer Division had crossed the Meuse near Donchéry and was engaged in fighting its way up the southern bank. I drove there to see how they were getting on and found the responsible commanders, Colonels von Vaerst and von Prittwitz, at the head of their troops, so I was able to return to the Meuse. There was now a most violent air attack by the enemy. The extremely brave French and English pilots did not succeed in knocking out the bridges, despite the heavy casualties that they suffered. Our anti-aircraft gunners proved themselves on this day, and shot superbly. By evening they calculated that they had accounted for 150 enemy aeroplanes. The regimental commander, Colonel von Hippel, later received the Knight's Cross for this.

Meanwhile the 2nd Panzer Brigade continued to cross the river in uninterrupted flow. Towards midday, to our general delight, the Army Group commander, Colonel-General von Rundstedt, arrived to have a look at the situation for himself. I reported our position to him in the very middle of the bridge, while an air-raid was actually in progress. He asked drily: 'Is it always like this here?' I could reply with a clear conscience that it was. He then spoke a few deeply felt words in appreciation of the achievements of our gallant soldiers.

Once again to the 1st Panzer Division, where

Above: The battle-weary crew of a Czech 35t take a break from the rapid advance toward Paris and the Channel coast.

I found the divisional commander accompanied by his first general staff officer, Major Wenck; I asked him whether his whole division could be turned westwards or whether a flank guard should be left facing south on the east bank of the Ardennes Canal. Wenck saw fit to interject a somewhat slangy expression of mine 'Klotzen, nicht Kleckern'(the sense of it being to strike concentrated, not dispersed – it might be translated roughly as 'Boot 'em, don't spatter 'em'), and that really answered my question. 1st and 2nd Panzer Divisions received orders immediately to change direction with all their forces, to cross the Ardennes Canal, and to head west with the objective of breaking clear through the French defences. That I might co-ordinate the movements of the two divisions I next went to the command post of the 2nd Panzer Division, which was in the Château Rocan, on the heights above Donchéry. From that vantage-point a good view could be obtained over the ground across which 2nd Panzer Division had advanced and attacked on the 13 and 14 May. I was surprised that the French long-range artillery in the Maginot Line and its westerly extension had not laid down heavier fire and caused us more trouble during our advance. At this moment, as I looked at the ground we had come over, the success of our attack struck me as almost a miracle.

In the afternoon I returned to my headquarters to arrange for the co-ordination of my divisions for the 15 May. Immediately north of my corps was XLI Army Corps (Reinhardt), which had originally been following behind me and which, since the 12th, had been committed on the right of XIX Army Corps in the direction of Mézières Charleville. On the 13th this corps had forced a crossing of the Meuse (at Monthermé) and was making a fighting advance westwards. General von Wietersheim's XIV Army Corps was now in my immediate rear and must soon reach the Meuse.

By evening the 1st Panzer Division had strong elements across the Ardennes Canal and had taken Singly and Vendresse despite strenuous enemy resistance. The tanks of the 10th

Panzer Division had crossed the line Maison-celle-Raucourt-et-Flabas, while the bulk of the division had reached the high ground south of Bulson-Thélonne, where they had captured more than 40 guns.

The principal task of XIX Army Corps had been to secure the dominating heights around Stonne, thus depriving the enemy of any chance of breaking into our bridgehead, and assuring the formations that were moving up behind us a safe river crossing. The attack on the heights had involved the Infantry Regiment 'G.D.' and the 10th Panzer Division in heavy fighting on the 14th. The village of Stonne had changed hands several times. On the 15th these attacks were to be carried through to a success-ful conclusion.

At 04.00 hrs. on 15 May I met General von Wietersheim at my corps headquarters to dis-cuss with him the relief by his troops of my units now in the Meuse bridgehead south of Sedan. After briefly summarizing the situation we set off together for the headquarters of the 10th Panzer Division near Bulson. General Schaal was forward with his troops. The first general staff officer of the division, the excellent Lieutenant-Colonel Freiherr von Liebenstein, explained the difficulties of the situation and answered patiently the many detailed questions of the general who was to take over from us. Finally we agreed that, for the duration of the relief, 10th Panzer Division and the Infantry Regiment 'G.D.' would be placed under com-mand of XIV Army Corps until such time as units of that corps could take over from them. So I found my command limited, for the next few days, to the 1st and 2nd Panzer Divisions.

The 10th Panzer Division, with the Infantry Regiment 'G.D.' under command, was ordered to cover the southern flank of XIX Army Corps along the line Ardennes Canal-the high ground by Stonne-the bend in the Meuse south of Ville-montry. In the course of 15 May it was already being strengthened by the advance units of the 29th (Motorized) Infantry Division.

From the headquarters of the 10th Panzer Division I drove to the headquarters of the Infantry Regiment 'G.D.' in Stonne. A French attack was actually in progress when I arrived and I could not find anyone. A certain nervous tension was noticeable, but finally the positions were held. I then went to my new corps head-quarters, which was in a small wood near Sapogne on the southern bank of the Meuse.

Contrary to expectations the night was one of confusion, not owing to the activity of the enemy but on account of command difficulties with our superiors. Panzer Group von Kleist ordered a halt to all further advance and to any extension of the bridgehead. I neither would nor could agree to these orders, which involved the sacrifice of the element of surprise we had gained and of the whole initial success that we had achieved. I therefore got in touch, personally, first with the Chief of Staff of the Panzer Group, Colonel Zeitzler, and since this

Above: The aftermath of the German raid on Rotterdam – the rubble of the city center has been cleared away to reveal the undamaged buildings which stand in stark contrast to the empty grid-pattern of streets without houses.

was not enough with General von Kleist himself, and requested that the order to stop be cancelled. The conversation became very heated and we repeated our various arguments several times. Finally, General von Kleist approved of the advance being continued for another twenty-four hours so that sufficient space be acquired for the infantry corps that were following. I had finally had to mention the Hentzsch Mission and thus remind him of the 'Miracle of the Marne', a reminder that was no doubt not very well received by the Panzer Group.

I was pleased to have retained my freedom of movement when, early on 16 May, I went to the headquarters of the 1st Panzer Division. I drove through Vendresse to Ormont. The situation at the front was not yet clear. All that was known was that there had been heavy fighting during the night in the neighbourhood of Bouvellemont. So on to Bouvellemont. In the main street of the burning village I found the regimental commander, Lieutenant-Colonel Balck, and let him describe the events of the previous night to me. The troops were overtired, having had no real rest since 9 May. Ammunition was running low. The men in the front line were falling asleep in their slit trenches. Balck himself, in wind jacket and with a knotty stick in his hand, told me that the capture of the village had only succeeded because, when his officers complained against the continuation of the attack, he had replied: 'In that case I'll take the place on my own!' and had moved off. His men had thereupon followed him. His dirty face and his red-rimmed eyes showed that he had spent a hard day and a sleepless night. For his doings on that day he was to receive the Knight's Cross. His opponents – a good Norman infantry division and a brigade of Spahis – had fought bravely. The enemy's machine-guns were still firing into the village street, but for some time now there had been no artillery fire and Balck shared my opinion that resistance was almost over.

Now on the previous day we had captured a French order, originating if I am not mistaken from General Gamelin himself, which contained the words: 'The torrent of German tanks must finally be stopped!' This order had strengthened me in my conviction that the attack must be pressed forward with all possible strength, since the defensive capabilities of the French were obviously causing their high command serious anxiety. This was no time for hesitancy, still less for calling a halt.

I sent for the troops by companies and read them the captured order, making plain its significance and the importance of continuing the attack at once. I thanked them for their achievements to date and told them that they must now strike with all their power to complete our victory. I then ordered them to return to their vehicles and to continue the advance.

The fog of war that had confused us soon lifted. We were in the open now, with results that were rapidly to be seen. In Poix-Terron I found the first general staff officer of the 2nd Panzer Division, told him what the position was and drove on to Novion-Porcien and from there to Montcornet. On this drive I passed an advancing column of the 1st Panzer Division. The men were wide awake now and aware that we had achieved a complete victory, a breakthrough. They cheered and shouted remarks which often could only be heard by the staff officers in the second car: 'Well done, old boy' and 'There's our old man', and 'Did you see him? That was hurrying Heinz', and so on. All this was indicative.

In the market-place of Montcornet I found General Kempff, the commander of the 6th Panzer Division of the Corps Reinhardt, whose troops, after crossing the Meuse, had arrived in this town at the same moment as my own. Now roads had to be allotted among the three panzer divisions – the 6th, 2nd and 1st – which were pouring through the town in their headlong drive towards the west. Since the Panzer Group had laid down no boundary between the two corps, we soon agreed on one among ourselves and ordered the advance to go on until the last drop of petrol was used up. My foremost units reached Marle and Dercy (over 40 miles from that morning's starting-point, and 55 miles from Sedan).

Meanwhile I told the men who were with me to go through the houses on the market-place. Within a few minutes they had collected several hundred prisoners, Frenchmen from various units, whose amazement at our being there was plain to see on their faces. An enemy tank company, which tried to enter the town from the southwest, was taken prisoner. It belonged to

Below: A British motorcycle reconnaissance team advances through a French village prior to crossing the frontier into Belgium. The British Expeditionary Force was a largely mechanized army, superior in this respect to the infantry divisions of the German armed forces.

22

General de Gaulle's division, of whose presence in the area north of Laon we had already heard. We set up our corps headquarters in the little village of Soize, east of Montcornet. I was in contact with the staffs of the 1st and 2nd Panzer Divisions. The Panzer Group was informed by wireless of the day's events and I announced my intention of continuing the pursuit on 17 May.

After our splendid success on 16 May and the simultaneous victory won by XLI Army Corps, it did not occur to me that my superiors could possibly still hold the same views as before, nor that they would not be satisfied with simply holding the bridgehead we had established across the Meuse while awaiting the arrival of the infantry corps. I was completely filled with the ideas that I had expressed during our conference with Hitler in March, that is to say to complete our break-through and not to stop until we had reached the English Channel. It certainly never occurred to me that Hitler himself, who had approved the boldest aspects of the Manstein plan and had not uttered a word against my proposals concerning exploitation of the break-through, would now be the one to be frightened by his temerity and would order our advance to be stopped at once. Here I was making a great mistake, as I was to discover on the following morning.

Early on 17 May I received a message from the Panzer Group: the advance was to be halted at once and I was personally to report to General von Kleist, who would come to see me at my airstrip at 07.00 hrs. He was there punctually and, without even wishing me a good morning, began in very violent terms to berate me for having disobeyed orders. He did not see fit to waste a word of praise on the performance of the troops. When the first storm was passed, and he had stopped to draw breath, I asked that I might be relieved of my command. General von Kleist was momentarily taken aback, but then he nodded and ordered me to hand over my command to the most senior general of my corps. And that was the end of our conversation. I returned to my corps headquarters and asked General Veiel to come to see me, that I might hand over to him.

I then sent a message to Army Group von Rundstedt by wireless in which I said that after I had handed over my command at noon, I would be flying to the Army Group headquarters to make a report on what had happened. I received an answer almost at once: I was to remain at my headquarters and await the arrival of Colonel-General List, who was in command of the Twelfth Army that was following behind us and who had been instructed to clear this matter up. Until the arrival of Colonel-General List all units were to be ordered to remain where they were. Major Wenck, who came to receive these orders, was shot at by a French tank while returning to his division and was wounded in the foot. General

Left: British transport vehicles move through a Belgian town to bring up supplies in a vain attempt to halt the German offensive.

Veiel now appeared and I explained the situation to him. Early that afternoon Colonel-General List arrived and asked me at once what on earth was going on here. Acting on instructions from Colonel-General von Rundstedt he informed me that I would not resign my command and explained that the order to halt the advance came from the Army High Command (the OKH) and therefore must be obeyed. He quite understood my reasons, however, for wishing to go on with the advance and there-

Below: Surrounded by sandbags, a British two-pounder anti-tank gun is set up for battle in the Belgian city of Louvain, brutally destroyed by the Germans in 1914 and soon to suffer the horrors of world war for a second time.

fore, with the Army Group's approval, he ordered: 'Reconnaissance in force to be carried out. Corps headquarters must in all circumstances remain where it is, so that it may be easily reached.' This was at least something, and I was grateful to Colonel-General List for what he had done. I asked him to clear up the misunderstanding between General von Kleist and myself. Then I set the 'reconnaissance in force' in motion. Corps headquarters remained at its old location in Soize; a wire was laid from there to my advanced headquarters, so that I need not communicate with my staff by wireless and my orders could therefore not be monitored by the wireless intercept units of the OKH and the OKW.

Before receiving the order to halt early on the 17th, 1st Panzer Division had taken Ribémont on the Oise and Crécy on the Serre. The advanced units of 10th Panzer Division, released from the area south of Sedan, had reached Fraillicourt and Saulces-Monclin. On the evening of 17 May a bridgehead was satisfactorily established across the Oise near Moy (15 miles from Dercy and 70 miles from Sedan).

At 09.00 hrs. on 18 May the 2nd Panzer Division reached St Quentin. On its left the 1st Panzer Division was also across the Oise, advancing on Péronne. Early on the 19th the 1st Panzer Division succeeded in forcing a bridgehead across the Somme near this town. Several French staffs, who had arrived at Péronne in an attempt to find out what was happening, were captured.

Advanced corps headquarters moved to Villers-le-Sec.

On 19 May we crossed the old Somme battlefield of the First World War. Until now we had been advancing north of the Aisne, the Serre and the Somme, and those rivers had served to guard our open left flank, which was also covered by reconnaissance troops, anti-tank units and combat engineers. The danger from this flank was slight; we knew about the French 4th Armoured Division, a new formation under General de Gaulle, which had been reported on 16 May and had first appeared, as already stated, at Montcornet. During the next few days de Gaulle stayed with us and on the 19th a few of his tanks succeeded in penetrating to within a mile of my advanced headquarters in Holnon wood. The headquarters had only some 20 mm anti-aircraft guns for protection, and I passed a few uncomfortable hours until at last the threatening visitors moved off in another direction. Also we were aware of the existence of a French reserve army, some eight infantry divisions strong, which was being set up in the Paris area. We did not imagine that General Frere would advance against us so long as we kept on moving ourselves. According to the basic French formula, he would wait until he had exact information about his enemy's position before doing anything. So we had to keep him guessing; this could best be done by continuing to push on.

By the evening of 19 May XIX Army Corps had reached the line Cambrai-Péronne-Ham. 10th Panzer Division took over the protection of our increasingly extended left flank, relieving the units of 1st Panzer Division, which had previously been engaged on this task. During

Below: German artillerymen load a field gun as part of a bombardment of Allied positions in Belgium.

the night of the 19th-20th corps headquarters moved forward to Marleville. On this day the corps at last received its freedom of movement once again, with the authorization to move on Amiens as from the 20th. 10th Panzer Division was now entrusted with the defence of our left flank as far as Corbie, to the east of Amiens. Its previous sector was taken over by the 29th (Motorized) Infantry Division. 1st Panzer Division was to advance towards Amiens and to establish a bridgehead on the south bank of the Somme with all speed. 2nd Panzer Division was ordered to move through Albert to Abbeville, there to seize another bridgehead across the Somme and to clean up any enemy troops in the area between Abbeville and the sea. The boundary between the 2nd and 1st Panzer Division was fixed as Combles-Longueval-Pozières-Varennes-Puchevillers-Canaples-Flixécourt-the Somme.

Defensive sectors along the Somme were:

2nd Panzer Division: the mouth of the Somme to Flixécourt (exclusive).

1st Panzer Division: Flixécourt to the junction of the Avre and the Somme (east of Amiens).

10th Panzer Division: the Avre-Somme junction to Péronne.

I reckoned that the 1st Panzer Division should be in a position to attack Amiens at about 09.00 hrs. I therefore ordered my car for 05.00 hrs., since I wished to participate in this historic event. My officers maintained that this was too early and suggested a later start, but I stuck to my original schedule and was proved right.

When I reached the northern outskirts of Amiens at 08.45 hrs. on 20 May, 1st Panzer Division was just moving into the attack. On my way there I had visited Péronne to make sure that the 10th Panzer Division was in position and there heard, in very strong terms, how 1st Panzer Division had been relieved. It seems that the units of 1st Panzer Division which were holding the bridgehead had not waited for the relieving force to arrive before pulling out, because the officer in charge, Lieutenant-Colonel Balck, had feared that otherwise he would be late for the attack on Amiens, which he regarded as more important than the holding of the bridgehead. His successor, Colonel Landgraf, was extremely angry at such casual behaviour and even more infuriated by Balck's answer to his remonstrances: 'If we lose it you can always take it again. I had to capture it in the first place, didn't I?' Luckily the enemy allowed Landgraf sufficient time to reoccupy the empty ground without having to fight for it. I drove around Albert, which was still held by the enemy, and passed endless columns of refugees on my way to Amiens.

1st Panzer Division's attack went well, and by about noon we had taken the city and forced a bridgehead to a depth of some four miles. I had a quick look over the ground we had seized and also the city with its beautiful cathedral, before hurrying back to Albert where I expected to find the 2nd Panzer Division. I met the columns of my advancing troops and had to drive through crowds of fleeing refugees. I also ran into a number of enemy vehicles which, thick with dust, had joined the German columns and hoped in this fashion to reach Paris and avoid being taken prisoner.

In Albert I found General Veiel. The 2nd Panzer Division had captured an English artillery battery drawn up on the barrack square and equipped only with training ammunition, since nobody had reckoned on our appearance that day. Prisoners of all nationalities filled the market-place and the adjoining streets. 2nd Panzer Division was almost out of fuel and were therefore proposing to stop where they were but they were soon disillusioned. I ordered them to advance at once to Abbeville and by 19.00 hrs they had reached this objective, passing through Doullens-Bernaville-Baumetz-Saint Riquier. Once there, a bombing attack by a few enemy bombers caused them a certain discomfort. After visiting the nimble commander of the 2nd Panzer Brigade, Colonel von Prittwitz, to make sure he understood about advancing on Abbeville, I made my way to Querrieu, to the northeast of Amiens, which was the new location of my corps headquarters. Here we were attacked by our own aeroplanes. It was perhaps an unfriendly action on our part, but our flak opened fire and brought down one of the careless machines. The crew of two floated down by parachute and were unpleasantly surprised to find me waiting for them on the ground. When the more disagreeable part of our conversation was over, I fortified the two young men with a glass of champagne. Unfortunately the destroyed machine was a brand-new reconnaissance plane.

During that night the Spitta Battalion of the 2nd Panzer Division passed through Noyelles and was thus the first German unit to reach the Atlantic coast.

On the evening of this remarkable day we did not know in what direction our advance should continue; nor had Panzer Group von Kleist received any instructions concerning the further prosecution of our offensive. So 21 May was wasted while we waited for orders. I spent the day visiting Abbeville and our crossings and bridgeheads over the Somme. On the way I asked my men how they had enjoyed the operations to date. 'Not bad,' said an Austrian of the 2nd Panzer Division, 'but we wasted two whole days.' Unfortunately he was right.

The Capture of the Channel Ports

On 21 May I received orders to continue to advance in a northerly direction with the capture of the Channel Ports as objective. I wanted the 10th Panzer Division to advance on Dunkirk by way of Hesdin and St Omer, the 1st Panzer Division to move on Calais and the 2nd on Boulogne. But I had to abandon this plan since the 10th Panzer Division was withdrawn from my command by an order of the Panzer Group dated 22 May, 06.00 hrs., and was held back as Panzer Group reserve. So when the advance began on the 22nd the only divisions I

commanded were the 1st and 2nd Panzer. My request that I be allowed to continue in control of all three of my divisions in order quickly to capture the channel ports was unfortunately refused. As a result the immediate move of the 10th Panzer Division on Dunkirk could not now be carried out. It was with a heavy heart that I changed my plan. 1st Panzer Division, together with Infantry Regiment 'G.D.', which had meanwhile arrived from Sedan, was to go by Samer-Desvres-Calais, while the 2nd Panzer Division moved along the coast to Boulogne.

On 21 May a noteworthy event occurred to the north of us: English tanks attempted to break through in the direction of Paris. At Arras they came up against the SS Division *Totenkopf*, which had not been in action before and which showed signs of panic. The English did not succeed in breaking through, but they did make a considerable impression on the staff of Panzer Group von Kleist, which suddenly became remarkably nervous. Subordinate units, however, were not infected by this. On 21

Above: A French gun team brings up a shell for loading into a field gun. Tied to outdated concepts of infantry-artillery co-operation, the French artillery arm failed in its role of slowing the German offensive.

Below: A German prime-mover half-track trundles past an anti-tank obstacle – hastily erected, easily dismantled – while heading westward into France in May 1940.

May the 8th Panzer Division of the XLI Army Corps reached Hesdin while the 6th Panzer Division of the same corps took Boisle.

Our new advance began early on 22 May. At 08.00 hrs. the Authie was crossed in a northerly direction. Neither the 1st nor the 2nd Panzer Division could move in full strength since units of both divisions, and particularly of the 2nd, had to be left behind to secure our Somme bridgeheads until such time as they could be relieved by General von Wietersheim's XIV Army Corps which was following after us in the same role as at Sedan.

In the afternoon of the 22nd there was fierce fighting at Desvres, Samer and to the south of Boulogne. Our opponents were mostly Frenchmen, but included a number of English and Belgian units and even an occasional Dutchman. Their resistance was broken. But the enemy air force was very active, bombing us and firing their guns at us too, while we saw little of our own Luftwaffe. The bases from which our planes were operating were now a long way away and could not be moved forward with sufficient speed. All the same, we managed to force a way into Boulogne.

Corps headquarters was moved to Recques. The 10th Panzer Division was now once again placed under my command. I decided to move the 1st Panzer Division, which was already close to Calais, on to Dunkirk at once, while the 10th Panzer Division, advancing from Doullens through Samer, replaced it in front of Calais. There was no particular urgency about capturing this port. At midnight I sent my orders to the 1st Panzer Division by wireless: 'Assemble

north of the Canche by 07.00 hrs. 23 May, as 10th Panzer Division is following up behind you. 2nd Panzer Division has fought its way into Boulogne. 1st Panzer Division to move at once to line Audruicq-Ardes-Calais and then swing eastwards to advance east through Bourbourgville-Gravelines to Bergues and Dunkirk. 10th Panzer Division will be to the south. Carry out instructions on receipt of code-word "Eastwards advance". Move off 10.00 hrs.'

Early on the 23rd I supplemented these instructions with a wireless order. 'Eastwards advance 10.00 hrs. Attack south of Calais towards St Pierre-Brouck and Gravelines.'

On 23 May the 1st Panzer Division set off towards Gravelines against strong resistance, while the 2nd Panzer Division was involved in heavy fighting in and around Boulogne. The attack on the town itself assumed a curious form, since for some time neither our tanks nor our guns managed to penetrate the old town walls. By the use of a ladder from the kitchen of a nearby house, and with the powerful assistance of an 88mm flak gun, a breach was at last made in the wall near the cathedral and an entry forced into the town itself. There was fighting in the harbour area, during the course of which a tank managed to sink one British motor torpedo boat and damage several others.

On 24 May the 1st Panzer Division reached the Aa Canal between Holque and the coast and secured bridgeheads across it at Holque, St Pierre-Brouck, St Nicholas and Bourbourgville; the 2nd Panzer Division cleared up Boulogne; the bulk of the 10th Panzer Division reached the line Desvres-Samer.

Above: German troops advance in open order across the countryside of northeastern France.

The SS Division *Leibstandarte 'Adolf Hitler'* was now placed under my corps command. I ordered this division to advance on Watten, thus giving more power to 1st Panzer Division's drive on Dunkirk. The 2nd Panzer Division was ordered to withdraw all the troops it could spare from Boulogne and to send them off too in the direction of Watten. The 10th Panzer Division encircled Calais and prepared to attack the old sea fortress. I visited the division during the afternoon and ordered it to advance carefully, so as to avoid casualties. On 25 May it was to be reinforced by the heavy artillery that was no longer needed at Boulogne.

Reinhardt's XLI Army Corps had meanwhile secured a bridgehead over the Aa at St Omer.

Hitler's Momentous Order to Stop

On this day (the 24th) the Supreme Command intervened in the operations in progress, with results which were to have a most disastrous influence on the whole future course of the war. *Hitler ordered the left wing to stop on the Aa.* It was forbidden to cross that stream. We were not informed of the reason for this. The order contained the words: 'Dunkirk is to be left to the Luftwaffe. Should the capture of Calais prove difficult, this port too is to be left to the Luftwaffe.' (I quote here from memory.) We were utterly speechless. But since we were not informed of the reasons for this order, it was difficult to argue against it. The panzer divisions were therefore instructed: 'Hold the line of the canal. Make use of the period of rest for general recuperation.'

Fierce enemy air activity met little opposition from our air force.

Early on 25 May I went to Watten to visit the *Leibstandarte* and to make sure that they were obeying the order to halt. When I arrived there I found the *Leibstandarte* engaged in crossing the Aa. On the far bank was Mont Watten, a height of only some 235 feet, but that was enough in this flat marshland to dominate the whole surrounding countryside. On top of the hillock, among the ruins of an old castle, I found the divisional commander, Sepp Dietrich. When I asked why he was disobeying orders, he replied that the enemy on Mont Watten could 'look right down the throat' of anybody on the far bank of the canal. Sepp Deitrich had therefore decided on 24 May to take it on his own initiative. The *Leibstandarte* and the Infantry Regiment 'G.D.' on its left were now continuing their advance in the direction of Wormhoudt and Bergues. In view of the success that they were having I approved the decision taken by the commander on the spot and made up my mind to order the 2nd Panzer Division to move up in their support.

On this day we completed the capture of Boulogne. 10th Panzer Division was fighting outside the Calais citadel. When a demand that he surrender was addressed to the English commandant, Brigadier Nicholson sent the laconic reply: 'The answer is no, as it is the British Army's duty to fight as well as it is the German's.' So we had to take it by assault.

On 26 May the 10th Panzer Division captured Calais. At noon I was at the divisional headquarters and according to the orders I had received I asked Schaal whether he wanted to leave Calais to the Luftwaffe. He replied that he did not, since he did not believe that our bombs would be effective against the thick walls and earthworks of the old fortifications. Furthermore, if the Luftwaffe were to attack them it would mean that he would have to withdraw his troops from their advanced positions on the edge of the citadel, which would then have to be captured all over again. I was bound to agree with this. At 16.45 hrs. the English surrendered. We took 20,000 prisoners, including 3-4,000 British, the remainder being French, Belgian and Dutch, of whom the majority had not wanted to go on fighting and whom the English had therefore locked up in cellars.

In Calais, for the first time since 17 May, I met General von Kleist, who expressed his appreciation for the achievements of my troops.

Below: The shrinking perimeter around the port of Dunkirk.

On this day we attempted once again to attack towards Dunkirk and to close the ring about that sea fortress. But renewed orders to halt arrived. We were stopped within sight of Dunkirk! We watched the Luftwaffe attack. We also saw the armada of great and little ships by means of which the British were evacuating their forces.

General von Wietersheim appeared at my headquarters during the course of the day to discuss with me arrangements for the relief of XIX Army Corps by his XIV Army Corps. The advanced division of this corps, the 20th (Motorized) Infantry Division, was placed under my command. I put it in on the right of the *Leibstandarte 'Adolf Hitler'*. Before this discussion was over, a small incident occurred. The commander of the *Leibstandarte*, Sepp Dietrich, while driving from the front came under machine-gun fire from a party of Englishmen who were still holding out in a solitary house behind our lines. They set his car on fire and compelled him and his companions to take shelter in the ditch. Dietrich and his adjutant crawled into a large drain pipe where the ditch ran under a crossroad, and in order to protect himself from the burning petrol of his car covered his face and hands with damp mud. A wireless truck following his command car signalled for help and we were able to send part of the 3rd Panzer Regiment of the 2nd Panzer Division, whose sector this was, to get him out of his unpleasant predicament. He soon appeared at my headquarters covered from head to foot in mud and had to accept some very ribald comment on our part.

It was not until the afternoon of 26 May that Hitler gave permission for the advance on Dunkirk to be resumed. By then it was too late to achieve a great victory.

The corps was sent into the attack during the night of the 26th-27th. The 20th (Motorized) Infantry Division with the *Leibstandarte 'Adolf Hitler'* and the Infantry regiment 'G.D.' under command and reinforced by heavy artillery, was given Wormhoudt as its objective. 1st Panzer Division on its left was ordered to push forward, with the point of main effort its right wing, in accordance with the progress that that attack should make.

The Infantry Regiment 'G.D.' received useful support from the 4th Panzer Brigade of the 10th Panzer Division and secured its objective, the high ground Crochte-Pitgam. The Armoured Reconnaissance Battalion of the 1st Panzer Division took Brouckerque.

Heavy enemy movement of transport ships from Dunkirk was observed.

On 28 May we reached Wormhoudt and Bourbourgville. On the 29th Gravelines fell to the 1st Panzer Division. But the capture of Dunkirk was after all completed without us. On 29 May XIX Corps was relieved by XIV Corps.

The operation would have been completed very much more quickly if Supreme Headquarters had not kept ordering XIX Army Corps to stop and thus hindered its rapid and successful advance. What the future course of the war would have been if we had succeeded at that time in taking the British Expeditionary Force prisoner at Dunkirk, it is now impossible to guess. In any event a military victory on that scale would have offered a great chance to capable diplomats. Unfortunately the opportunity was wasted owing to Hitler's nervousness. The reason he subsequently gave for holding back

Left: Panzers advance northward, beginning to squeeze the Allies back to the beach-head around Dunkirk.

my corps – that the ground in Flanders with its many ditches and canals was not suited to tanks – was a poor one.

On 26 May I was anxious to express my gratitude to the brave troops under my command. This took the form of the following corps order:

Soldiers of the XIX Army Corps!

For seventeen days we have been fighting in Belgium and France. We have covered a good 400 miles since crossing the German border: we have reached the Channel coast and the Atlantic Ocean. On the way here you have thrust through the Belgian fortifications, forced a passage of the Meuse, broken the Maginot Line extension in the memorable Battle of Sedan, captured the important heights at Stonne and then, without a halt, fought your way through St Quentin and Péronne to the lower Somme at Amiens and Abbeville. You have set the crown on our achievements by the capture of the Channel Coast and of the sea fortresses at Boulogne and Calais.

I asked you to go without sleep for 48 hours. You have gone for 17 days. I compelled you to accept risks to your flanks and rear. You never faltered.

With masterly self-confidence and believing in the fulfilment of your mission, you carried out every order with devotion.

Germany is proud of her Panzer Divisions and I am happy to be your commander.

We remember our fallen comrades with honour and respect, sure in the knowledge that their sacrifice was not in vain.

Now we shall arm ourselves for new deeds.

For Germany and for our leader, Adolf Hitler!
signed, GUDERIAN

A short passage is here omitted. In it Guderian gives his opinion that Hitler not von Rundstedt halted the German armour. Although Hitler agreed with von Rundstedt's action he did not originate it. Guderian goes on to state that the defence of Calais 'had no influence on the development of events outside Dunkirk'. In fact the garrisons of Boulogne and Calais held two of Guderian's three armoured divisions and gave the British III Corps time to move west and cover the rear of the B.E.F. withdrawing to Dunkirk.

In Flanders I received news that my elder son had been wounded, though mercifully the wound was not mortal. My second son was decorated in France with the Iron Cross, both First and Second Class. Despite being in action with an armoured reconnaissance battalion, he had survived all his engagements unhurt.

In the second phase of the campaign, which Guderian calls 'The Break-through to the Swiss Border', he commanded a Panzer Group. This phase was very much less exacting than the break-through to the Channel coast, for the bulk of the French armoured and motorized strength had already been destroyed. Even so, thanks in the main to conflicting orders, the commander needed all his energy. He describes a typical episode.

On 13 June I first visited the Reinhardt Corps and its 6th and 8th Panzer Divisions which were still engaged in battle with the enemy forces from Verdun and the Argonnes. Towards evening I set off to find the headquarters of the 1st Panzer Division, which had reached the Rhine-Marne Canal near Étrépy. XXXIX Army Corps had ordered the division not to cross this canal. I knew nothing of this order; nor would I have approved it if I had. Outside Étrépy I found Balck, the inexhaustible commander of the leading elements of 1st Panzer Division, and asked him whether he had secured the bridge over the canal. He replied that he had. I asked him if he had also established a bridgehead on the far side. After a pause he answered that he had done that too. His reticence surprised me. Was it possible, I asked, to drive over to his bridgehead by car? Looking at me with deep distrust, he rather timidly said that it was. So over we went. In the bridgehead I found a capital engineer officer, Lieutenant Weber, who had risked his life to prevent the demolition of the bridge, and the

Above: A long column of French troops stands in line on the dockside at Dunkirk. Although many French soldiers were captured when the Germans finally broke through the Allied lines, many escaped to Britain. Of the total of 338,226 men evacuated from Dunkirk some 112,000 were French.

Below: A German motorcycle combination roars through a burning French town during the final stages of the Battle of France, the phase when the German divisions turned from the Channel coast to deal with the remnants of the French Army south of the River Somme.

commander of the rifle battalion which had formed the bridgehead, a Captain Eckinger. I was delighted to be able to decorate these two brave officers with the Iron Cross, First Class, on the spot. I then asked Balck why he had not pushed farther forward; it was only then I learned of XXXIX Army Corps' order to stop. This was the explanation of Balck's extraordinary reticence; he had already gone farther than he should and he expected me to reprimand him for doing so.

By 17 June Guderian was on the Swiss frontier.

. . .We sent a message to supreme headquarters informing them that we had reached the Swiss border at Pontarlier, to which Hitler signalled back: 'Your signal based on an error. Assume you mean Pontailler-sur-Saône.' My reply, 'No error. Am myself in Pontarlier on Swiss border,' finally satisfied the distrustful OKW.

There was some French resistance even after Pétain's Cabinet began negotiations (16 June). On the 19th Guderian's men had . . . a certain amount of trouble with the Eastern Belfort forts, but finally these too surrendered. 1st Panzer Division stormed the heights of Belchen and the Ballon de Servance and at about midnight captured Le Tillot. The 2nd Panzer Division took Fort Rupt on the Moselle. The advance through the Vosges was carried out on a broad front. The infantry divisions of I Army Corps, advancing towards Épinal from the north, had to be halted, since the roads were already overloaded with panzer troops and the arrival of infantry formations as well would have brought all movement to a standstill. The infantry complained loudly at Army Group headquarters about what they regarded as this ill-treatment; they too wanted to have a go at the enemy. I sent my operations officer, Major Bayerlein, with all speed by aeroplane to Colonel-General Ritter von Leeb, since I wished the Army Group commander to know my reasons for halting the infantry. Bayerlein arrived just in time to prevent any further unpleasantness.

The headquarters of the Panzer Group was now moved to the resort town of Plombières, an old spa well known to the Romans. We spent three very agreeable days there.

The collapse of the French was complete. On 20 June Cornimonet fell and on the 21st Bussang in the Vosges. The 2nd Panzer Division reached St Ame and Tholy, the 29th (Motorized) Infantry Division Delle and Belfort. We took 150,000 prisoners. Arguments had developed between the generals of Army Group C concerning the numbers of prisoners captured by their respective troops; which prisoners belonged to whom? Colonel-General Ritter von Leeb had to sit in judgement like Solomon. He allotted the figure of 150,000 to me and added

the flattering comment that had it not been for the encircling movement of my Panzer Group through Belfort and Épinal the totals for all units would have been considerably smaller.

Since the crossing of the Aisne the Panzer Group had taken in all approximately 250,000 prisoners besides an incalculable quantity of equipment of all sorts.

On 22 June the French Government agreed to an armistice. We were not immediately informed of its conditions. On the 23rd I drove through the Vosges, by way of Schlucht and Kaysesberg, to visit General Dollman in his headquarters at Colmar. I saw once again the town in which I had spent my happy childhood.

My staff was moved to Besançon where we lived at first in a hotel, afterwards moving into the building which had previously housed the French area command. Now that the fighting was over I had the opportunity to thank my generals and general staff officers for their superb performance. Our work together had been marred by no misunderstandings whatever. The brave soldiers had carried out their very heavy duties with the greatest devotion. They could well be proud of their recent achievements.

On 30 June I said farewell to them with the following order of the day:

Group Guderian.   Besançon 30.6.40

At this moment, when Group Guderian is about to be dissolved, I want to express to all commands, and units who are about to depart for fresh tasks, my very best wishes.

The victorious advance from the Aisne to the Swiss border and the Vosges will go down in history as an heroic example of a break-through by mobile troops.

I thank you for what you have done. It has been the finest fulfilment of my labours and struggles of more than a decade's duration.

On to fresh tasks, with the same spirit and the same success, until the final victory of Greater Germany is complete!

Heil dem Führer!

signed, GUDERIAN

Below: Savoring their moment of triumph, German motorized troops drive through the streets of Paris in an enormous victory celebration. The Arc de Triomphe is in the background, acting as an ironic affirmation of this greatest of German successes.

At the beginning of July my Panzer Group was dissolved, some divisions returning to Germany while others were moved to the Paris area. The staff also went to Paris. We were supposed to organize a great parade at which the Führer was to have been present; fortunately this never took place.

While in Paris I visited Versailles and Fontainebleau, the latter a wonderful old castle full of historical memories and beautiful objects. I was particularly interested by the Napoleonic Museum at Malmaison. The aged and dignified director was kind enough to show me around himself, and I had a most instructive and interesting conversation about the great Corsican with that scholarly historian. Needless to say I visited all the sights of Paris, so far as military conditions permitted. I stayed first at the Hotel Lancaster: later I was given very comfortable quarters in a private house in the fashionable Bois de Boulogne.

My stay in Paris was interrupted by the Reichstag session of 19 July at which I, as well as the majority of other general officers, was ordered to be present. Here Hitler announced my promotion to Colonel-General.

Since the parade was not to take place, there was no point in the staff of the Panzer Group remaining in Paris. We were, therefore, transferred to Berlin in early August, where we enjoyed a period of leisure and relaxation which was very welcome.

Below: The panzer advance southward into France only confirmed the German victory, for with a few notable exceptions the French armies had little fight left in them. On 22 June 1940 armistice terms were agreed.

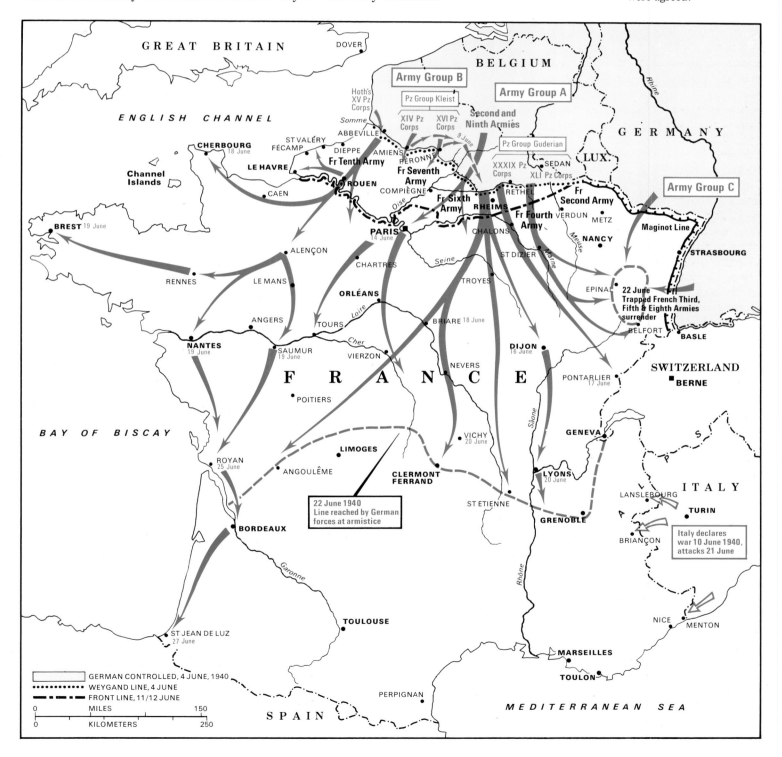

The Battle of Britain

by Adolf Galland

After the fall of France there were those among the German High Command who expected that Great Britain would sue for peace. Finding that this was not her intention the German High Command gave orders to the *Luftwaffe* designed to pave the way for invasion. Two phases were foreseen.

(1) The interdiction of the Channel to merchant shipping, to be carried out in conjunction with German naval forces, by means of attacks on convoys, the destruction of harbour facilities, and the sowing of mines in harbour areas and the approaches thereto.

(2) The destruction of the Royal Air Force.

Two air fleets under Field-Marshals Kesselring (Second) and Sperrle (Third) took part in the attack. They had at their command:

1,300	fighters (Messerschmitt 109)
180	fighter-bombers (Messerschmitt 110)
1,350	bombers (Heinkel 111, Junkers 88 and Dornier 17)
2,830	

To oppose them Fighter Command (Air Vice-Marshal Sir Hugh Dowding) had 55 squadrons, including six of night-fighters (Blenheims). The majority of the 600-700 British planes were Hurricanes, but about one-fifth were Spitfires, and two squadrons were Defiants. By 29 September the British strength had risen to 59 squadrons, including eight of night-fighters.

The battle began with German attacks on merchant convoys in the Channel on 10 July. On 7 September the Germans made their first mass attack on London. The *Luftwaffe* suffered heavy casualties during the days that followed and by the end of the month the Battle of Britain was at an end. It had been a very near thing, and had the Germans concentrated on the destruction of the RAF and its bases, instead of switching to attacks on cities, the end might have been very different.

On 12 October Hitler cancelled Operation Sealion. The struggle had cost the *Luftwaffe* 1,733 aircraft and the RAF 915. In the first three months of the Blitz 12,696 Londoners had been killed. EDITOR

These pages: The weapon that allowed the RAF to match the Luftwaffe's Me 109, the Supermarine Spitfire. This formation is flying at a cruising speed of 300mph in line abreast at a height of around 6,000 feet.

The first year of the war confirmed to a certain degree the strategical concept of the German *Luftwaffe*, in which the fighter arm represented a *quantité négligeable*. In Poland as well as in France a greater part of the enemy air force had been destroyed on the ground, a minor part only in the air. Meanwhile, it had become obvious that the *Luftwaffe* would not have a walk-over against the RAF. At the opening of the battle it showed, as it had done previously during the air battles of the French campaign, that the British had a fighter arm which was numerically stronger and better controlled because of their lead in the field of radar. With regard to crews and fighting spirit it was absolutely first class.

Already in the second phase of the Battle of Britain, therefore, the German fighters were allotted a task that exceeded the operational limits fixed for them inside the German *Luftwaffe*. They were to defeat the British fighters in large-scale battle in order to win the total air supremacy necessary for the bombers which were to follow up the attack.

During the midsummer weeks in 1940 the 2nd and 3rd Air Fleets were concentrated on the

---

Lt-General Adolf Galland
(1911-)

Son of the Graf von Westerholt's bailiff, Galland joined a Gliding Club, and by the age of 19 was a qualified pilot, who had distinguished himself in competitions.

In 1931 Galland was at the flying school in Brunswick where he studied to become a pilot in Lufthansa. Germany was at the time rebuilding her *Luftwaffe* and Udet sent many pilots, Galland amongst them, to Italy to be trained as fighter pilots.

At the beginning of 1934 he was invited to join the new *Luftwaffe*; on 15 February he began his basic training at the Grenadier Barracks in Dresden and was commissioned in October.

In 1936 Galland was posted with the 'Condor Legion' to Spain and here he stayed for 15 months, gaining much useful experience.

Czechoslovakia, Poland and France followed and when France fell Galland was promoted Major and awarded the Knight's Cross of the Iron Cross. Galland's squadron moved to the airfield of St Omer and prepared for the next phase, the destruction of the RAF.

At the end of the war Galland, though now a Lieutenant-General, was commanding an élite squadron (JV 44) of Me 262 jet-fighters. 'Most of them,' he writes, 'had been in action since the first day of the war, and all had been wounded, all bore the scars of war and displayed the highest medals. The Knight's Cross was, so to speak, the badge of our unit.' With them he fought on to the bitter end. As the first of General Devers' tanks neared Salzburg airfield, on 3 May 1945, his jet-fighters went up in flames.

Channel Coast. My wing, the 3rd JG26, was stationed on a well-camouflaged airfield near Guines. Contrary to all expectations, the concentration of these forces incidentally took place without interference from enemy aircraft. The British seemed to be concentrating their forces on defence.

Establishing our aircraft in these positions brought to an end the first phase of the Battle of Britain on 24 July 1940. Up to then the action of the *Luftwaffe* had been directed against the Navy and merchant shipping. Already soon after the beginning of the war isolated attacks without fighter support had been made from northwest Germany and from Norway, after the occupation of that country, on British warships and the northern English ports. For these actions the twin-engined dive-bomber Ju 88 was particularly suitable, but it was not available in sufficient numbers and its successes were limited. The sensational sinking of the aircraft-carrier *Ark Royal* turned out to be an error caused by a misread report, which was unfortunately only found out after the alleged feat had been considerably exploited by propaganda. On Hitler's special orders, we were not allowed to attack the battleship *Repulse*, which was lying in dry-dock, because at that time he was still anxious to avoid in all circumstanes the dropping of bombs on English soil. The *Luftwaffe* were to concentrate exclusively on military and maritime targets. Simultaneously, intensive reconnaissance supplied the information for essential military objectives in the British Isles.

With the opening of the Western Campaign the attack by the *Luftwaffe* on British merchant shipping was intensified. It acted in co-operation with the German Navy, hoping to cut off

Above: Adolf Galland, a great fighter ace but also a thoughtful tactician of aerial warfare.

Below: Sitting beneath the wing of a Heinkel He 111 medium bomber, German aircrew eat a hasty meal between operational sorties.

the supply lines for the British troops, who had now entered into a shooting war with Germany. Neither the bombing attacks, with or without fighter cover, against British supply ships mainly off the east coast of England, nor the mining of ports brought any telling success. The forces employed were too small, as the bulk of the *Luftwaffe* was still tied down in the French campaign.

When this was brought to a victorious end, the first tentative plans for an invasion of England, the so-called Operation Sealion, were prepared. They received only dilatory attention as long as the British reply to Hitler's last peace offer of 19 July 1940 was still in abeyance.

The second phase of the Battle of Britain, lasting from 24 July to 8 August 1940, was essentially a fighter battle. On its opening day I was with my wing for the first time in action over England. Over the Thames Estuary we got involved in a heavy scrap with Spitfires, which were screening a convoy. Together with the Staff Flight, I selected one formation as our prey, and we made a surprise attack from a favourably higher altitude. I glued myself to the tail of the plane flying outside on the left flank and when, during a right-handed turn, I managed to get in a long burst, the Spitfire went down almost vertically. I followed it until the cockpit cover came flying towards me and the pilot bailed out, then followed him down until he crashed into the water. His parachute had failed to open.

The modern Vickers Supermarine Spitfires were slower than our planes by about 10 to 15 mph, but could perform steeper and tighter turns. The older Hawker Hurricane, which was at that time still frequently used by the British,

compared badly with our Me 109 as regards speed and rate of climb. Our armament and ammunition were also undoubtedly better. Another advantage was that our engines had injection pumps instead of the carburettors used by the British, and therefore did not conk out through lack of acceleration in critical moments during combat. The British fighters usually tried to shake off pursuit by a half-roll or half-roll on top of a loop while we simply went straight for them, with wide-open throttle and eyes bulging out of their sockets.

During this first action we lost two aircraft. That was bad, although we had three kills. We were no longer in doubt that the RAF would prove a most formidable opponent.

Above: A German sailor inspects the progress of a steamer towing landing craft toward the Channel ports, part of the build-up for Operation Sealion, the planned invasion of England.

Left: An oil storage plant belches forth distinctive black smoke after being hit in a German raid against shore installations on the Thames Estuary.

A Battle for Life and Death

The German fighter squadrons on the Channel were from now on in continuous action. Two or three sorties daily was the rule, and the briefing read: 'Free chase over southeast England.' The physical as well as the mental strain on the pilots was considerable. The ground personnel and the planes themselves were taxed to the limit.

After the take-off, the formations used to assemble in the coastal area, still over land, at an altitude of 15,000 to 18,000 feet, in order to climb to between 21,000 and 24,000 feet when crossing the English coast. In an attempt to outclimb the opponent, our dog-fights occurred at ever-increasing altitudes. My highest combat at that time took place at 25,000 feet, but at 27,000 feet and more – close to the lower limits of the stratosphere – one could usually see the vapour trails of German or British fighters.

It used to take us roughly half an hour from take-off to crossing the English coast at the narrowest point of the Channel. Having a tactical flying time of only eighty minutes, we therefore had about twenty minutes to complete our task, and this fact limited the distance of penetration. German fighter squadrons based on the Pas de Calais and on the Cotentin pensinsula could barely cover the southeastern parts of the British Isles, circles drawn from these two bases at an operational range of 125 miles overlapping approximately in the London area. Everything beyond was practically out of our reach. This was the most acute weakness of our offensive. An operating radius of 125 miles was sufficient for local defence, but not enough for such tasks as were now demanded of us.

In the Battle of Britain a powerful air force was to be used strategically on a big scale for the first time in the history of warfare. The bomber is the vehicle of strategic warfare. It is therefore amazing that the opening of the battle was not allotted to it, but to fighters, which previously had only been regarded as a tactical weapon. It was assumed that the appearance of German fighter squadrons over England would draw the British fighters into the area within our range, where they would be destroyed, beaten, or at least decimated in large-scale air battles. Although only a small portion of the English homeland was covered by the operational range of our fighters, it was hoped in this way to achieve air supremacy, or at least sufficient superiority in the air over the whole of the British Isles to expose it to the attack of the German bomber force.

Things turned out differently. Our fighter formations took off. The first air battles took place as expected and according to plan. Because of German superiority, these attacks,

had they been continued, would certainly have achieved the attempted goal, but the British fighters were recalled from the area long before this goal was reached. The weakened squadrons of the RAF left their bases near the coast and used them only for emergency landings or to refuel. Concentrated in a belt around London in readiness for our bomber attacks, they thus evaded the attack *in* the air in order to encounter more effectively the attack *from* the air which would logically follow. The German fighters found themselves in a similar predicament to a dog on a chain which wants to attack the foe, but cannot harm him because of his limited orbit.

As long as the enemy kept well back, our task could not be accomplished. Rather aptly, we called the few bombers and Stukas which from now onwards accompanied our roving expeditions 'decoy ducks'. Only with bombers was the war from the air over England a possibility, and to prevent such a development was the decisive aim of the British Command. To this end the RAF called out the fighters again, but the German hope of attracting them into annihilating combats was never realized.

In the opening encounters the British were at a considerable disadvantage because of their close formation. Since the Spanish Civil War we had introduced the wide-open combat formation, in which great intervals were kept between the smaller single formations and groups, each of which flew at a different altitude. This offered a number of valuable advantages: greater air coverage, relief for the individual pilot, who could not concentrate more on the enemy than on keeping formation, freedom of initiative right down to the smallest unit without loss of collective strength, reduced vulnerability as compared to close formation,

Below: An Me 110 fighter-bomber flies over shipping in the English Channel. Originally intended to act as an ordinary fighter, the Me 110 proved to be hopelessly outclassed by the Spitfires and Hurricanes of RAF Fighter Command and was later withdrawn from day service.

and, most important of all, better vision. The first rule of all air combat is to see the opponent first. Like the hunter who stalks his prey and manoeuvres himself unnoticed into the most favourable position for the kill, the fighter in the opening of a dog-fight must detect the opponent as early as possible in order to attain a superior position for the attack. The British quickly realized the superiority of our combat formation and readjusted their own. At first they introduced the so-called 'Charlies' – two flanking planes following in the rear of the main formation and flying slightly higher and further out on a weaving course. Finally, they adopted our combat formation entirely. Since then, without any fundamental change, it has been accepted throughout the world. Werner Mölders was greatly responsible for these tactical developments.

From the very beginning the British had an extraordinary advantage which we would never overcome throughout the entire war: radar and fighter control. For us and for our command this was a surprise, and a very bitter one. Britain possessed a closely knit radar network conforming to the highest technical standards of the day which provided Fighter Command with the most detailed data imaginable. Thus the British fighter was guided all the way from take-off to his correct position for attack on the German formations.

We had nothing of the kind. In the application of radiolocation technique, the enemy was far in advance of us. It was not that British science and technics were superior – on the contrary, the first success of radar must be recorded on the German side. On 18 December, after the RAF had previously tried in vain to attack Wilhelmshaven on 4 September 1939 – the day following the British declaration of war – a British bomber formation approached the German Bight, making for the same target. An experimental Freya radar set sighted their approach in time for German fighters to intercept and practically destroy the enemy task force, which flew without fighter protection. After this defensive success, thanks to timely radiolocation, the British bombers never returned without fighter protection.

There could be no more singular proof of the importance of high-frequency technique for defence against air attacks, but since the German Command was largely preoccupied with offensive plans, not enough attention was given to it. The possibility of an Allied air attack on the Reich was at that time unthinkable. For the time being, therefore, we were content to erect a few Freya sets along the German and later along the Dutch, Belgian and French coasts; they had a range of 75 miles, but gave no altitude reading.

Under the serious threat for Britain arising from the German victory in France – no one described it more forcibly than Churchill in his

memoirs – the British command concentrated desperately on the development and perfection of radar. Its success was outstanding. Our planes were already detected over the Pas de Calais while they were still assembling and were never allowed to escape the radar eye. Each of our movements was projected almost faultlessly on the screens in the British Fighter Control centres and, as a result, Fighter Command was able to direct its forces to the most favourable position at the most propitious time.

In the battle we had to rely on our own human eyes. The British fighter pilots could depend on the radar eye, which was far more reliable and had a longer range. When we made contact with the enemy our briefings were already three hours old; the British only as many seconds old – the time it took to assess the latest position by means of radar to the transmission of attacking orders from Fighter Control to the already airborne force.

Of further outstanding advantage to the British was the fact that our attacks, especially those of the bombers, were of sheer necessity

Above: Known in the *Luftwaffe* as the 'flying pencil' the Dornier Do 17 was distinguished by its streamlined shape. Alongside the Heinkel He 111 the Dornier was a mainstay of the *Luftwaffe*'s medium bombing force.

Below: The unmistakable sight of an oil tanker on fire – the black pall of smoke would be visible for many miles, attracting enemy aircraft and U-boats like wasps to a jam pot.

Left: England's Channel
ports were early victims of
German attacks in 1940.
Here Portsmouth harbor
is the target of a bombing
raid; a direct hit has been
scored on dock
installations (top right of
photograph) while
splashes in the harbor
proper indicate misses.

directed against the central concentration of the
British defence. We were not in a position to
seek out soft spots in this defence or to change
our approach and to attack now from this direction, now from that, as the allies did later in
their air offensive against the Reich. For us
there was only a frontal attack against the
superbly organized defence of the British Isles,
conducted with great determination.

Added to this, the RAF was fighting over its
own country. Pilots who baled out could go into
action again almost immediately, whereas ours
were taken prisoner. Damaged British planes
could sometimes still reach their base or make
an emergency landing, while for us engine
trouble or fuel shortage could mean a total loss.

Morale, too, and the emotions played a great
part. The desperate seriousness of the situation
apparently aroused all the energies of this hardy
and historically conscious people, whose arms
in consequence were directed towards one goal;
to repulse the German invaders at any price!

Thus, during the first weeks of our air offensive it was already apparent that in spite of our
good bag of enemy planes, this was not the way

to achieve air superiority. The German Command, which in any case lacked clarity in its
aims, grew more uncertain. The order came for
low-level attacks on English fighter bases – a
difficult and costly undertaking. The sites were
well protected by a host of heavy and light A.A.
guns, and we also met with a novel defence:
aerial cables, fired by rockets during our attack,
which descended slowly on parachutes, protecting the lower air regions above the targets.
The planes themselves were magnificently
camouflaged, so that our efforts were out of
proportion to the number of effectively destroyed enemy planes.

During this time we provided fighter cover
for the attacks by bomber formations and Stukas on shipping and convoys. We could not
miss the splendid opportunity of continuously
attacking the convoys, so important to Britain's
subsistence, under the protection of the German fighter squadrons stationed on the Channel coast. Here the slow speed of the Ju 87
turned out to be a great drawback. Owing to the
speed-reducing effect of the externally sus-
pended bomb-load, she only reached 150

Below: Air Marshal Sir
Hugh Dowding,
commander of Fighter
Command during 1940.
Dowding was both an able
and popular leader, and
his handling of Fighter
Command's scarce
resources during the
Battle of Britain was
exemplary.

m.p.h. when diving, and as the required altitude for the dive was between 10,000 to 15,000 feet, these Stukas attracted Spitfires and Hurricanes as honey attracts flies. The necessary fighter protection for such sorties was considerable and the task of the pilots fraught with great difficulties. The British soon realized that the Stukas, once they peeled out of formation to dive singly on to their target, were practically defenceless until they had reassembled. We made numerous attempts to counteract this shortcoming. With our greater speed, it was impossible to follow the Stukas into the dive without a dive-brake; equally impossible was the idea of providing fighter cover on all different levels between the start of the dive and the pull-out. The losses of Ju 87s rose from sortie to sortie.

We fighter pilots were blamed. The Stuka was regarded as the egg of Columbus by the German Air Command. It was not born in the eyrie of the German eagle, for Udet and other experts had brought it over from the New World. This type had been developed in the USA as a small, handy light bomber suitable for pin-point attacks. The idea of the Stuka was taken up in Germany with enthusiasm because it promised the greatest success with a minimum expenditure of material and man-power. Single precision attacks on pin-pointed targets instead of mass attacks on large areas became the motto of German bomber strategy; the greatest effect was to be achieved with the smallest expenditure of material. This demand was imperative owing to the situation of German raw materials – a situation which would become dangerous in the event of a long war. Major-General Jeschonnek, who was then the *Luftwaffe* Chief-of-Staff, was a keen champion of this idea. In spring, 1939, he said to his colleagues of the *Luftwaffe*: 'We must save more – not money, but material.'

Only the Stuka seemed to solve this problem. Thus originated the Ju 87, which had contributed considerably to the successful Blitzkrieg in Poland and France, although in actual fact it encountered little opposition. Right until the end of the war, it proved repeatedly its value as a tactical weapon in support of an army, especially against tanks. In the Battle of Britain it proved disastrous.

This did not deter the German Command from continuing with the idea of the Stuka. The accompanying fighter pilots were blamed for the painfully high losses, although the limitations of the Stuka in action were obvious enough in the Battle of Britain. The fighter pilots were blamed, not the designers, who continued to base their entire production of medium and heavy bombers on the Stuka idea. They not only went on to produce a twin-engined Stuka, the Ju 88, and the Do 217, but demanded full diving performance from all subsequent types of bombers, including the

four-engined He 177, which entailed high stability, the fitting of dive-brakes, automatic pull-out apparatus, Stuka target-sighters, etc. Because of this blockheadedness – one cannot call it anything else – the development and production of the German long-range bomber were seriously delayed. I shall refer later to this very serious problem.

The next phase, which started on 8 August and was the third in the Battle of Britain, had several objects in view. When the fighter force failed to achieve air supremacy, the bomber force was ordered to attack British fighter bases and to bomb aircraft and motor industries. While, in particular, Portsmouth, Portland and numerous targets on the British East Coast were bombed, attacks on convoys and the free chase of the fighters continued.

The bombing attacks on the British fighter bases did not achieve the expected success. Apart from the fact that it was purely coincidental if the respective fighter squadrons were grounded at the time of the attack, the quantity of bombs dropped on each target was by no means sufficient. Runways and buildings were usually only slightly damaged and could generally be repaired overnight. At *Luftwaffe* HQ, however, somebody took the reports of the bombers of Stuka squadrons in one hand and a thick blue pencil in the other and crossed the squadron or base in question off the tactical map. It did not exist any more – in any case, not on paper. Reports of fighter and other pilots regarding numbers of enemy planes shot down were also exaggerated, as happens on both sides during large-scale air battles. Thus it came about that one day, according to the calculations in Berlin, there were no more British fighters, while we were supposed to have achieved a certain superiority, but were far from achieving air supremacy. One of the main reasons for this was that the short range of the Me 109 allowed only little penetration and in consequence also reduced the range of the bombers.

With additional tanks which could be released and discarded after use, a device

Above: WAAF controllers plot the course of German intruders based on information provided by the chain of radar stations and specially trained observers in southern England. The controllers would then direct the appropriate RAF squadrons to intercept the enemy bombers.

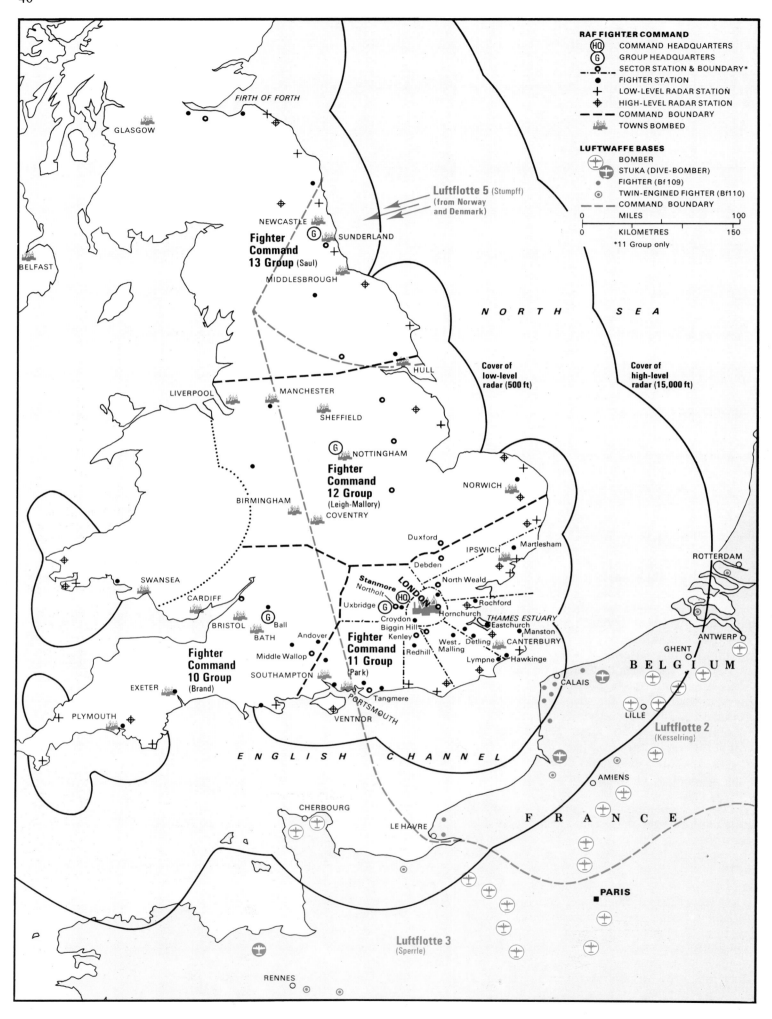

RAF FIGHTER COMMAND
- (HQ) COMMAND HEADQUARTERS
- (G) GROUP HEADQUARTERS
- SECTOR STATION & BOUNDARY*
- FIGHTER STATION
- LOW-LEVEL RADAR STATION
- HIGH-LEVEL RADAR STATION
- COMMAND BOUNDARY
- TOWNS BOMBED

LUFTWAFFE BASES
- BOMBER
- STUKA (DIVE-BOMBER)
- FIGHTER (Bf 109)
- TWIN-ENGINED FIGHTER (Bf110)
- COMMAND BOUNDARY

MILES 0 — 100
KILOMETRES 0 — 150
*11 Group only

FIRTH OF FORTH

GLASGOW

BELFAST

Luftflotte 5 (Stumpff)
(from Norway and Denmark)

NEWCASTLE
Fighter Command 13 Group (Saul)
SUNDERLAND
MIDDLESBROUGH

NORTH SEA

HULL
Cover of low-level radar (500 ft)
Cover of high-level radar (15,000 ft)

LIVERPOOL
MANCHESTER
SHEFFIELD
NOTTINGHAM
Fighter Command 12 Group (Leigh-Mallory)
NORWICH
BIRMINGHAM
COVENTRY
Duxford
IPSWICH
Martlesham
Debden
ROTTERDAM

Stanmore (HQ)
Northolt
LONDON
North Weald
Uxbridge (G)
Rochford
SWANSEA
CARDIFF
Croydon
Hornchurch
THAMES ESTUARY
ANTWERP
BRISTOL
Ball
BATH
Biggin Hill
Kenley
Eastchurch
Manston
GHENT
Andover
Redhill
West Malling
Detling
CANTERBURY
B E L G I U M
Middle Wallop
SOUTHAMPTON
Fighter Command 11 Group (Park)
Lympne
Hawkinge
CALAIS
Luftflotte 2 (Kesselring)
Fighter Command 10 Group (Brand)
Tangmere
PORTSMOUTH
LILLE
EXETER
VENTNOR
PLYMOUTH

E N G L I S H   C H A N N E L

AMIENS

CHERBOURG
LE HAVRE
F R A N C E

PARIS

Luftflotte 3 (Sperrle)

RENNES

employed later by both sides and one which we had already tried successfully in Spain, our range could have been extended by 125 to 200 miles. At that time this would have been just the decisive extension of our penetration. As it was, we ran daily into British defences, breaking through now and then, with considerable loss to ourselves, but without substantially approaching our final goal.

Failure to achieve any noticeable success, constantly changing orders betraying lack of purpose and obvious misjudgment of the situation by the Command, and unjustified accusations had a most demoralizing effect on us fighter pilots, who were already overtaxed by physical and mental strain. We complained of the leadership, the bombers, the Stukas, and were dissatisfied with ourselves. We saw one comrade after the other, old and tested brothers in combat, vanish from our ranks. Not a day passed without a place remaining empty at the mess table. New faces appeared and became familiar, until one day these too would disappear, shot down in the Battle of Britain.

In those days I often met my younger brother Wilhelm, who was an aide-de-camp in an A.A. training camp, also on the Channel coast. The youngest of the family, Paul, was training as a fighter pilot. Fritz, the eldest, contemplated a changeover from A.A. to fighters, and Wilhelm too soon decided to join us. In the end we were all four fighter pilots, and three of us often flew together in the same group. At that time I expressed my conviction to Wilhelm quite openly that things could not go on much longer as they were. You could count on your fingers when your turn would come. The logic of the theory of probabilities showed us incontestably that one's number was up after so many sorties. For some it was sooner; for some later.

The reproaches from higher quarters became more unbearable. We had the impression that whatever we did we were bound to be in the wrong. Fighter protection created many problems, which had to be solved in action. As in Spain, the bomber pilots preferred close screening, in which their formation was surrounded by pairs of fighters pursuing a zigzag course. Obviously, the proximity and the visible presence of the protective fighters gave the bomber pilots a greater sense of security. However, this was a faulty conclusion, because a fighter can only carry out this purely defensive task by taking the initiative in the offensive. He must never wait until he is attacked, because then he loses the chance of acting. The fighter must seek battle in the air, must find his opponent, attack him and shoot him down. The bomber must avoid such fights, and he has to act defensively in order to fulfil his task: war from the air. In co-operation between bomber and fighter, these two fundamentally different mentalities obviously clash. The words of Richthofen expressed during the First World

War, summarizing the task of the fighters, often came to our lips. Fundamentally, they are still valid today: 'The fighter pilots have to rove in the area allotted to them in any way they like and when they spot an enemy they attack and shoot him down; anything else is rubbish.'

We fighter pilots certainly preferred the 'free chase during the approach and over the target area'. This in fact gives the greatest relief and the best protection for the bomber force, although not perhaps a direct sense of security. A compromise between these two possibilities was 'extended protection', in which the fighters still flew in invisible contact with the bombers, but were allowed to attack any enemy fighter which drew near to the main force.

In addition to this, we introduced 'Fighter Reception': fighter squadrons or wings which sometimes went right up to the English coast to

Left: An RAF
reconnaissance
photograph indicating the
presence of German
invasion barges in French
Channel ports.

meet the often broken-up and battered formations on their return journey and protected them from pursuing enemy fighters. The Sea Rescue Service was carried out with boats and flying-boats under fighter protection, with the aim of saving parachuted airmen or crews from 'ditched' aircraft. This service was a boon, for it rescued many German and British pilots, even from the Thames Estuary.

It was of great interest to me after the war, in conversation with British or American airmen, to discover that they had been troubled with identical problems regarding long-range fighter protection.

What we went through in 1940 they experienced in the years 1943 to 1945 during the large-scale daylight raids on the Reich. The points of view expressed by the fighter pilots as well as by the bomber pilots of both sides were identical.

This protective role should actually have been allotted to the more suitable Me 110, a machine specially created for tasks which fighters were not up to on account of their small radius. But soon it was clear that the Me 110 was even less suited to this than the 109. Often they could not escape the British fighters except by forming a defensive circle for their getaway, or else we had to come to their aid and free them. In the end it came to the point that we even had

to give protection to the pursuit planes – a really farcical situation. It would have been much better to take the Me 110 out of service altogether – a difficult decision which was made only much later, after heavy losses had been incurred.

After something like a month of action on the Channel coast neither the situation nor our mood was particularly rosy. It was then that I was ordered to attend a war conference at Karinhall. I flew to Berlin and was taken from there by a staff car to Göring's estate in the most beautiful part of the March of Brandenburg. Germany presented a picture of peaceful serenity, the war having hardly made any difference to the daily life at home, while those who were not yet called up earned good money, and the wives of servicemen received generous subsidies. Money circulated freely; theatres, cinemas and places of amusement were crowded. No, the war had not even touched the outer husk of German life.

Was one to take this as a bad or a good omen? The I-could-not-care-less attitude at home and the general lack of interest in the war did not please me. I had come straight out of a battle for life and death, the brunt of which so far had been borne by the fighter force. Naturally, we had no insight into the ramifications of the war, but we guessed fairly accurately that the battle

Below: Heinkel He 111
medium bombers fly
through light cloud while
assembling into battle
formation over northern
France.

we were fighting on the Channel was of decisive importance to the continuance and final outcome of the struggle. We were aware that it needed a tremendous concentration of strength in order to emerge victoriously, and we felt that our own strength was being overtaxed. The colossus of this Second World War seemed to be like a pyramid turned upside down, balancing on its apex, not knowing which way to lean. And for the moment the whole burden of the war rested on a few hundred German fighter pilots on the Channel coast. Did not their number sink into insignificance, like a dot, in comparison with the millions of men under arms in Germany? Emotions are often illogical. Naturally, neither the Army divisions which led a peaceful life in occupied territories or in garrison at home, nor those happy and carefree crowds bent on amusement, could have been of any help to us in the fight against the RAF. And yet this contrast had a deeply depressing effect on me.

The frame of mind of those in the High Command and other offices was optimistic. In the cultured and luxurious atmosphere of Karinhall one felt out of place with one's small troubles and scruples amongst all the self-assured, confident, and yet understanding and helpful generals and General Staff officers. After a general discussion of the situation Göring drew Mölders and myself into a lengthy conversation. It opened with our being invested with the Gold Pilot Medal with jewels and by an appreciation of our successes. But after this ceremony the Reichsmarschall let us know quite plainly that he was not satisfied to date with the performance of the fighter force, particularly with the execution of fighter protection, and energetically called for greater efforts. He also had his own plan for reviving the alleged lack of aggression on the part of the fighters. To this end he wanted to introduce radically younger blood into the command of the fighter force.

At the beginning of the war all commanding officers were elderly men who had already seen service in the First World War. During the Western offensive it had already been obvious that they were neither physically nor mentally equal to the high demands aviation made upon them, and most of them had, therefore, been released. As the next step, Göring wanted to put young and successful pilots in command of the fighter groups. He started with Mölders and myself, and promoted us to group commodores.

I was not at all satisfied with this, and said to Göring openly: 'My wing is a pleasure to me and the responsibility sufficient; I am also scared of being tied to the ground and of not seeing enough action.' 'Don't worry,' said Göring. He then explained that the main idea of his new measure was that the groups should be led in the air by the commodore himself, who could only be the most successful pilot of the entire unit.

Could such a revolutionary measure be imposed upon military tradition? Young fighter-pilot officers, well tested in solo fights and in the leadership of small formations, would come quickly and unconventionally into high-ranking and responsible positions. One or two failures were only to be expected. However, during the course of this, in increasingly difficult fight, it was proved that the leader of a figher group only received full recognition if he asked nothing from his men that he was not prepared to do himself. Fighter Command was the first branch of the Air Force to introduce younger men into the leader corps. Two years later, Bomber Command followed suit after overcoming the greatest resistance.

I did not entirely believe Göring's promise that I should see just as much flying, and was

Below: RAF pilots race toward their Hurricane fighters in response to the 'scramble' call. British success in the battle relied heavily upon such quick-response techniques, so that the 'bombers did not get through.'

suspicious and annoyed. When he asked us finally if we had any request to make, I said: 'Yes, Herr Reichsmarschall: to remain a wing commander.' This was turned down.

On our journey back to Berlin, Mölders and I naturally discussed all that had been said. Mölders had a splendid record of successfully destroyed enemy aircraft, and the figure had mounted since the Battle of the Western Wall, during the offensive against France, and now over England. He was the ace of all the German fighter pilots. Wieck, Balthasar and I followed him at some distance in constant rivalry. Brilliant though Mölders was as a fighter, his actual abilities and ambitions lay more in the field of tactics and organization. He did not approve at all of my opposition to Göring's plan, which suited his wishes and inclinations perfectly. He alluded to the great fighter pair of the First World War, Richthofen and Bölcke, the former of whom was the more successful fighter, while the latter was – at least for the development of fighters as a weapon – the more important tactician. 'Well,' he said indignantly at last, 'as far as I am concerned, you can be the Richthofen of the *Luftwaffe*. I prefer one day to be its Bölcke.' He certainly would have been, too, had his death not torn him away from his activities.

A fortnight later we met the Reichsmarschall again. This time he came to visit us on the coast. The large-scale attacks of the bombers were imminent, and the air supremacy necessary for them had not been achieved to the degree expected. The British fighter force was wounded, it was true, but not beaten. And our pursuit Stuka and fighter force had naturally suffered grievous losses in material, personnel and morale. The uncertainty about the continuation of the air offensive reflected itself down to the last pilot. Göring refused to understand that his *Luftwaffe*, this shining and so far successful sword, threatened to turn blunt in his hand. He believed there was not enough fighting spirit and a lack of confidence in ultimate victory. By personally taking a hand, he hoped to get the best out of us.

To my mind, he went about it the wrong way. He had nothing but reproaches for the fighter force, and he expressed his dissatisfaction in the harshest terms. The theme of fighter protection was chewed over again and again. Göring clearly represented the point of view of the bombers and demanded close and rigid protection. The bomber, he said, was more important than record bag figures. I tried to point out that the Me 109 was superior in the attack and not so suitable for purely defensive purposes as the Spitfire, which, although a little slower, was much more manoeuvrable. He rejected my objection. We received many more harsh words. Finally, as his time ran short, he grew more amiable and asked what were the requirements for our squadrons. Mölders asked for a series of Me 109s with more powerful engines. The request was granted. 'And you?' Göring turned to me. I did not hesitate long. 'I should like an outfit of Spitfires for my group.' After blurting this out, I had rather a shock, for it was not really meant that way. Of course, fundamentally I preferred our Me 109 to the Spitfire, but I was unbelievably vexed at the lack of understanding and the stubbornness with which the command gave us orders we could not execute – or only incompletely – as a result of many shortcomings for which we were not to blame. Such brazen-faced impudence made even Göring speechless. He stamped off, growling as he went.

Below left and below: The Germans prepare for the next phase of the battle – *Bomben auf Engeland*. A Heinkel He 111 (left) is bombed up prior to its mission over southern England while an Me 109 pilot (right) has his parachute harness adjusted before taking off to act as an escort for the bombers.

'Bombs on England'
('Bomben auf En-ge-land')

In those days all the loudspeakers of the 'Greater German Reich' from Aachen to Tilsit, from Flensburg to Innsbruck, and from the Army stations of most of the occupied countries, blared out the song, 'Bomben auf En-ge-land'. By beating the big drum in strong and martial rhythm and blending it with the roar of aircraft, they expected a mass psychological effect. We pilots could not stand this song from the very start.

Moreover, during the first and second phase of the Battle of Britain there could be no question as yet of 'Bombs on England'. Only with the third phase did bombers appear over England to assist the fighters in the battle for air supremacy. Until then they had concentrated on shipping targets. This third phase of the Battle of Britain was fought between 8 August and 7 September 1940. In this action the bombers returned to the task allocated to them by Douhet: the enemy air force must be wiped out while still grounded. Douhet, however, envisaged for this task waves and waves of bombers, darkening the sky with their multitudes. He would have been gravely disappointed to see the realization of his strategic dream as it was put into practice over England.

Unfortunately, the English defence profited once more by the limited range of the German fighters. In effect, the actual battle sector over Britain represented not even a tenth of the total area of the island. In the remaining nine-tenths the RAF could build aircraft, train pilots, form new squadrons and build up reserves almost without interference, and these forces could then be sent into the very limited front, mainly the sector around London. Churchill describes in his memoirs the difficult situation of the British faced by a superior German fighter force, especially with regard to personnel, at the beginning of the Battle of Britain. The situation was only saved by concentrating all resources on the replacement of losses. All these efforts would have been of no avail had the whole island been the battlefield instead of this restricted tenth.

This unfortunate state of affairs could only have been changed effectively by an efficient German long-range bomber. If such machines could have carried the war from the air to the north, northwest and west coasts, and into all corners of Britain, then the process of replenishing the already damaged RAF could have been prevented or at least hampered. Furthermore, it would have forced the British defence to spread out. Instead of this, it could only concentrate on the narrow sector against which we carried out a frontal attack.

The *Luftwaffe*, alas! had no heavy strategic bombers. General Wever, their champion, had demanded them energetically, and the German aircraft industry had delivered him a whole series of good designs. The choice at last fell on the He 177, a four-engined aircraft in which two combined engines each drove a four-bladed airscrew. Hitler, who often showed an amazingly correct intuitive judgment, especially in questions of engine technics, raised his doubts about such a combination from the start. He proved to be right. This combination became the source of technical hitches, which – combined with other reasons – delayed the mass production of the He 177 for about three years. Incidentally, Hitler, acting on his correct judgment, later assumed the right to interfere in the technical development of the *Luftwaffe*, sometimes in a way which proved disastrous. But more of this later.

In any case, the long-distance bomber was not available in 1940. Not until Dönitz became Commander-in-Chief of the Navy and demanded aircraft with a longer range for the protection of his U-boats was the He 177 once more seriously considered. She went into service for the first time on the supply lines to Stalingrad in the winter of 1942-3, when, contrary to her original purpose, she was used as a troop-carrier. Even on this run considerable technical faults came to light. On the death of Wever the development of a long-range strategic bomber force was stopped. It was considered sufficient

Below: The cutting edge of Fighter Command – a Hurricane and Spitfire (foreground). As Spitfires had the superior performance of the two aircraft, they were usually allocated the role of attacking the German fighters while the slower Hurricanes concentrated on the enemy bomber force.

to have Stukas and a large fleet of twin-engined medium-range bombers. Jeschonnek, who after Kesselring and Stumpf became the fourth *Luftwaffe* Chief of Staff, gave his specifications for a long-range twin-engined fast bomber as follows: 2,500-lb. bomb load, 600 miles range, and a speed of 435 mph. His demands were held up because of the impressive initial successes at the beginning of the war and because Hitler's dislike of a war with England made any new developments appear as of secondary importance.

We therefore had to get used to the fact that our offensive could only be directed against a small and extraordinarily well-defended sector of the British Isles. But this sector included the capital, the heart of the British Empire, London. The densely populated city on the Thames was of exceptional military importance as the brain and nerve centre of the British High Command, as a port and as a centre for armament and distribution. The fact that London was within the range of day-bombing attacks with fighter cover, however inefficient and disadvantageous the German offensive was, must be regarded as one of the positive sides of our offensive.

We fighter pilots, discouraged by a task which was beyond our strength, were therefore looking forward impatiently and excitedly to the start of the bomber attacks. We believed that only then would the British fighters leave their dens and be forced to give us open battle.

The Commander-in-Chief appeared once more at the Channel to be on the spot and to give the order for the beginning of the operation in person. When on the afternoon of 7 September the German squadrons assembled over the Channel coast – bombers, Stukas, fighters, destroyers, more than 1,000 aircraft in strength – and set course for London, each of the participants realized the importance of the hour. The fourth phase of the Battle of Britain had started.

Today it is easy to smile at the expectations we nursed in those days as to the possible effect of such an attack. With two or three times the number of bombers carrying five times the bomb-load, with improved bombsights and perfected methods of attack, the Allies could not destroy nor even completely paralyse a city like Berlin. The step which we then took was leading us into unknown territory.

During the first of the thirty-eight large-scale raids on London the targets were confined to

Above left: An He 111 flies over the River Thames in the heart of London's dockland – the docks in the Isle of Dogs can be clearly seen on the right of the photograph.

Above: The remains of a street in Coventry following the German raid of November 1940. London was the main target for the bombers but other centers of strategic importance were also chosen for special attention.

London installations and oil depots on the Thames. Only later were the raids extended to targets in the London area. We used 150-, 750-, 1,250- and very rarely 2,500-lb. high-explosive bombs. In contrast to these, the Allies later used bombs up to 10 tons. The bomb-load was between 2,500 and 4,500 lb. per aircraft and the total weight of bombs released in each attack was about 500 tons. The later practice of saturation bombing as employed by the Allies in their raids on the Reich could not be achieved with the means at our disposal. Moreover, the bombs dropped were scattered over many single targets.

The raiding unit was generally one bomber wing, of between fifty and eighty planes, protected by a fighter wing. In the beginning of the fourth phase our total strength was about 400 to 500 bombers and 200 Stukas. Protection was given by about 500 fighters and 200 destroyers. The enemy, according to German calculations at the time, had not much more than 200 front-line aircraft.

The assembly of the bombers and fighters took place in the vicinity of our fighter bases over some landmark on the coast at a predetermined altitude and zero hour. It happened more than once that the bombers arrived late. As a result, the fighters joined another bomber formation which had already met its fighter escort and thus flew doubly protected, while the belated formation had either to turn back or make an unescorted raid which usually resulted in heavy losses. Radio or radar guidance for such an assembly was not yet available, and even our intercom did not work most of the time. These difficulties increased with the deterioration of the weather in the autumn, and finally assumed the proportions of a tragedy.

All formations had to take the shortest route to London because the escorting fighters had a reserve of only ten minutes' combat time. Large-scale decoy manoeuvres or circumnavigation of the British A.A. zone were therefore impossible. The A.A. barrage round London was of considerable strength and concentration, and seriously hampered the target approach of the bombers. The balloon barrage over and around the capital made low-level attacks and dive-bombing impossible. The bulk of the British fighters were sent up to encounter the German raiders just before they reached their target. I know of no instance in which they managed to prevent the bombers reaching their target, but they inflicted heavy losses on both them and on the German escort fighters.

The types of bombers used were He 111, Do 17, Ju 87 and Ju 88. They had all been put into service long before the outbreak of the war, the He 111 and the Do 17 having been already used in the Spanish War. Even the Ju 88, sometimes called the 'Wonder Bomber', had risen to fame in 1938 by putting up a world speed record. Exposed to the vigorous modern British defence and to new conditions, a great number of insufficiencies came to light with regard to these planes. In addition to many other shortcomings, all types showed that they were not sufficiently armed for defence. The existing armament was of morale value alone.

Below: Once the German bomber offensive got underway – the 'Blitz' as it became known – so the civil population went underground. Here people of southeast London bed down for the night in a specially prepared shelter.

The A.A. batteries concentrated round London and their accurate fire, sometimes directed from fighter planes, forced the German bomber formations higher and higher. In this way they exceeded their best operational altitude and became even slower.

The Ju 87 squadrons already had to be taken out of service after the first large-scale attacks on London. The losses of the bombers were high enough, but the Stuka losses could not be supported. Their pinpoint accuracy lost its effect because of the interference on the part of the defence. They changed over at last to dropping their load in horizontal flight, but in this way they were less efficient as bombers and more susceptible to the enemy's defence. The High Command of the *Luftwaffe* therefore gave orders that in future they were only to be used for attacks on convoys and targets in the coastal regions. The renunciation of such a weapon of attack, from which it had expected so much, was certainly no easy decision for the German command.

Nor did the destroyer units last through this phase of the battle. In view of their losses and previously recognized failings, the High Command converted a proportion of them into fast bombers for use in the next phase of the battle. It was deplorable that these units were created, so to speak, at the expense of the fighters, and their failure indirectly caused a weakening of the fighter arm.

Any encounter with British fighters called for maximum effort. One day on my way back from London, I spotted a squadron of twelve Hurricanes north of Rochester. Attacking from 2,500 feet above them and behind, I shot like an arrow between the flights and from ramming distance fired on one of the aircraft in the rear line of the formation, tearing large pieces of metal out of the plane. At the last moment I pulled my nose up and leaped over her, then flew right through the centre of the enemy's formation. It was not a pleasant sensation. Again I fired my cannon and machine gun into one of the Hurricanes from close range. Luckily, the British had had a similar or even bigger fright than I. No one attacked me. As I broke off I saw two parachutes open below the aircraft of the broken formation.

It was not as simple as this with another Hurricane I shot down west of Dungeness. I had damaged her so badly that she was on fire and ought to have been a dead loss. Yet she did not crash, but glided down in gentle curves. My flight companions and I attacked her three times without a final result. As I flew close alongside the flying wreck, by now thoroughly riddled, with smoke belching from her, from a distance of a few yards I saw the dead pilot sitting in his shattered cockpit, while his aircraft spiralled slowly to the ground as though piloted by a ghostly hand.

I can only express the highest admiration for the British fighter pilots, who, although technically at a disadvantage, fought bravely and indefatigably. They undoubtedly saved their country in this crucial hour.

The short range of the Me 109 became more and more of a disadvantage. During a single sortie of my group we lost twelve fighter planes, not by enemy action, but simply because after two hours' flying time the bombers we were escorting had not yet reached the mainland on their return journey. Five of these fighters managed to make a pancake landing on the French shore with their last drop of fuel; seven of them landed in the 'drink'.

It turned out that a forced landing on the water was preferable to a parachute descent into the sea. After touching down on the water, the plane remained afloat for between forty and sixty seconds – just about long enough for the pilot to unstrap himself and scramble out. The lucky ones were fished out of the 'drink' by the tireless Air Sea Rescue Service. 'Mae West,' rubber dinghy, coloured flare-bag, Verey pistol and other useful trifles may have weighed the pilot down like a Father Christmas, but they turned out to be excellent accessories.

I made my fortieth kill over the Thames Estuary on 24 September. Our group was in the best of spirits, for the JG26 'Schlageter' had already made a name for itself in the Battle of

Below: Two Dornier Do 17 bombers fly over fires started by a previous bombing run over the Royal Victoria Docks and the Silvertown region of West Ham, London, on 7 September 1940.

Britain and no difference was made between my own successes and the group's. I was the third member of all the armed forces – after Dietl and Mölders – to receive the Oak Leaves to the Knight's Cross. Apart from the Grand Cross, which was reserved solely for the Reichsmarschall, this was the highest military award in those days. It did not worry me a great deal that I was grounded at the same time; things would be arranged somehow. I had been ordered to Berlin for the investiture.

Hitler received me in the new Reich Chancellery. It was the second time I sat opposite him. On the first occasion, after my return from Spain with the Condor Legion, our meeting had been in the form of a collective reception, but now I was alone with him. Our conversation was a lengthy one. I expressed my great admiration for our enemy across the water. I was embittered by several insidious and false representations and commentaries by the Press and on the radio which had referred to the RAF in a condescending and presumptuous tone. Although I was expecting contradiction or anger from Hitler when I gave him a different picture, he did not interrupt me, nor did he try to change the subject, but nodded repeatedly and said that my description confirmed his

beliefs. He too had the greatest respect for the Anglo-Saxon race. It had made it all the more difficult for him, he said, to decide on waging this life-and-death struggle which could only end with the total destruction of one or the other. He called it a world historical tragedy and said that it had been impossible to avoid this war, despite all his sincere and desperate attempts. If we won the war, a vacuum would be created by the destruction of Great Britain which it would be impossible to fill.

In most convincing terms, Hitler expressed not only his sympathy for the English race, but also his admiration for the class of political and industrial leaders which down the ages had developed on a much broader basis than anything that had so far existed in Germany. In their political development, favoured by different circumstances, the English were a hundred years ahead of us. All the virtues an eminent race had developed over long periods became manifest during critical phases in its history, as that which England was going through then. He regretted that he had not managed to bring the English and the German people together, in spite of a promising start.

I must admit that I was highly impressed by the Führer's words at the time. He had man-

Above: Bert Hardy's famous photograph of St Paul's Cathedral emerging unscathed from the fire and smoke of the Blitz. The picture came to be seen as a symbol of Britain's refusal to be cowed by the might of the German war machine.

50

Left: As the German offensive faltered so the *Luftwaffe* took to bombing London by night. It was the easy option. Although much damage was done and many civilians killed, it was a tacit admission of failure, the Germans accepting the fact that they could no longer mount daylight raids in the face of Fighter Command's resistance.

aged to take the wind out of my sails. I no longer felt bitter.

At the Air Ministry a *Luftwaffe* liaison officer attached to the Ministry of Propaganda greeted me with the embarrassing news that representatives of the foreign Press were waiting to interview me. It did not suit me at all, but it could not be avoided. What I had already heard from German propaganda about the war-front was not to my liking, as I have already mentioned, and I had no intention of speaking now in the same vein. My answers were tape-recorded and the Ministry made me a present of the recording later. The last time I played them was on the day I was taken prisoner, and I noted that I had no desire to take one word back, nor did I wish that they had remained unsaid. Some time later a US Interrogation Officer began his conversation with the remark: 'We are old

acquaintances. I have interviewed you before.' It was in the Theatersaal of the Ministry of Propaganda in the Wilhelmsplatz, Berlin.

From Berlin I flew to see Göring in East Prussia and at the gate of the Reichsjägerhof in the Rominterheide met Mölders. As Commander of the 51st Fighter Group, also based on the Channel, he had received the Oak Leaves three days before myself for his fortieth kill. He was in a hurry to get back to his station, but to his annoyance had been detained until now by Hitler and Göring. The obligation to defend your title as the most successful fighter pilot in the world was still taken very seriously. After a hurried farewell, he called to me: 'Fatty promised me he would detain you at least as long as he did me. And by the way, good luck with the stag I missed.'

The Reichsjägerhof was a log cabin made of

Below left: At the height of the Blitz, 'roof spotters' monitor the spread of fires from German incendiary bombs.

Below: Southeast England's first line of defense during the Battle of Britain – a four-inch anti-aircraft gun on the Channel coast is readied for action.

huge tree trunks, with a thatched roof jutting far over the eaves. Göring came out of the house to meet me, wearing a green suede hunting jacket over a silk blouse with long, puffed sleeves, high hunting boots, and in his belt a hunting knife in the shape of an old Germanic sword. He was in the best of humour. Both the disagreeable memory of our last meeting and his worries about the *Luftwaffe* in the Battle of Britain seemed to have been spirited away. We could hear the stags out on the heath: it was their rutting time.

After congratulating me, he said that he had a special treat in store for me: permission to hunt one of the royal stags which were usually reserved for him, a so-called 'Reichsjägermeister' stag. He knew them all and each one had a name; he watched over them, and was loath to part with one of them. 'I promised Mölders,' Göring said, 'to keep you here at least three days, so you've got plenty of time.' That night no mention was made either of the war in general or the Battle of Britain in particular.

Next morning at ten o'clock I had bagged my stag: it was really a royal beast, the stag of a lifetime. There was no further reason to prolong my stay at the Reichsjägerhof.

Yet Göring kept his promise to Mölders and did not let me go. In the afternoon the latest front-line reports from Air Fleets 2 and 3 were brought to him. They were devastating. During a raid on London exceptionally high losses had been sustained.

Göring was shattered. He simply could not explain how the increasingly painful losses of bombers came about, and I assured him that, in spite of the heavy losses we were inflicting on the enemy fighters, no decisive decrease in their number or in their fighting efficiency was noticeable. At the great altitudes where aerial combats took place it was only possible in rare cases to follow the possible victim down to its final crash in order to verify the kill. Even if the German figures of enemy aircraft destroyed were perhaps over-estimated, the fact that their fighter strength obviously did not diminish could only be accounted for in this way: England, by a great concentration of energy, was making up her losses in the peaceful ninetenths of her territory.

The achievements of a nation determined to assert itself would be exemplified a few years later by the Germans.

When, after this conversation, I asked Göring to allow me to rejoin my group, he had no objection. I flew back to the Channel. I had to make a forced landing over Pomerania, and in the train, as I continued my journey, the stag caused more of a sensation than the Oak Leaves to my Knight's Cross. My fellow passengers insisted that the stag's head stank to heaven, or that it was dangerous to travel with the 'horns' unprotected. A few hunters opened their eyes in astonishment. All of them were right.

Left: Before the war most military theorists considered civilian morale to be easily susceptible to the effects of a bombing offensive. They were wrong, for in almost all cases morale improved under aerial attack – as this photograph suggests.

Below: Men of a bomb disposal unit successfully defuse and remove a 4,000-lb bomb from a garden in south London. Bombs of this size were rare, however, most being of the smaller incendiary type.

Matapan

by Viscount Cunningham of Hyndhope

In the spring of 1941 Admiral Cunningham's Mediterranean Fleet was based on Alexandria. Its aims were twofold; firstly, to protect British convoys on their way to Malta and the Western Desert, and, secondly, to destroy Axis convoys on their way to the same theatre. Essentially the British Navy dominated the Mediterranean, for since the attack by the Fleet Air Arm on Taranto in November 1940 the Italians had skulked in their ports, refusing every challenge to come out and fight.

In the south, in the Western Desert, the position was somewhat similar, with General O'Connor's troops forcing the Italians rapidly backwards. However, the arrival of Rommel in February with a crack German division altered the situation. On the other Mediterranean front, in Greece, the Greek Army had dealt the Italians a crippling blow. The chances were that Hitler would soon lose patience with his bungling ally, Mussolini, and that a German army, capable of breaking the Allies' thinly held line, would be dispatched to this front.

With the threat of a reverse on both fronts it became essential for the navy to maintain its superiority at sea. The Italians had been struck heavy blows at Taranto and Genoa but, in general, the British fleet could only watch and wait, hoping the enemy might emerge for long enough to be forced into battle.

An increase in radio traffic from 25 March onwards and the stepping up of air reconnaissance in the area of Greece and Crete, and over Alexandria, suggested a possible sortie by the Italian Fleet. There were three possible courses open to it:

1. An attack on vulnerable Allied troop and supply convoys supporting the army in Greece.

2. To cover Axis troop convoys taking reinforcements to the Dodecanese.

3 A diversion to cover landings in Greece or Cyrenaica, or even Malta.

Of these the most likely seemed to be the first. Therefore, when, on 27 March, three Italian cruisers and a destroyer were sighted steering roughly towards Crete, there seemed a distinct possibility that the rest of the Italian fleet might be out.

EDITOR

These pages: The *Fiume* fires her main armament in a pre-war exercise. The Italian dictator, Benito Mussolini, hoped to make the Mediterranean an 'Italian lake' but before this dream could be realized he would have to eliminate the Royal Navy.

By the third week in March 1941, we knew that the German attack upon Greece could not be much longer delayed. Moreover, from 25 March onwards it was observed that there was a noticeable increase in the enemy's air reconnaissance to the south and west of Greece and Crete, with daily attempts to reconnoitre the harbour at Alexandria. The unusual persistence with which the movements of the Mediterranean Fleet were being watched caused us to believe that some important operation by the Italian fleet might also be intended.

There were various courses of action open to the enemy. They might attack our vulnerable and lightly escorted convoys carrying troops and stores to Greece. They might intend to cover a convoy of their own taking reinforcements to the Dodecanese. It was possible, too, that the Italian fleet might create a diversion to cover a landing in Greece or Cyrenaica, or even an all-out attack upon Malta. Of these possibilities, the first, the attack upon our convoy route to Greece, probably south of Crete, was the most likely.

To prevent this our most obvious course was to have the battlefleet to the area west of Crete. However, it was practically certain that we

should be shadowed and reported by the enemy's air reconnaissance, in which event the Italian fleet would merely defer its operation until we were forced to return to Alexandria to refuel. If we were to have a fair chance of intercepting the Italians we needed tolerably accurate information that they were actually at sea, while it was desirable that we should leave during the early part of the night to avoid being located by aircraft till next morning. If our departure from Alexandria could be kept secret, so much the better. The movements of our convoys in and out of the Aegean were also perfectly well-known to the enemy, so to raise no suspicion it was necessary that their movements should appear normal, while at the same time they must not be exposed to attack.

During the morning of the 27th, one of the flying-boats from Malta reported a force of three Italian cruisers and a destroyer 80 miles east of the southeastern corner of Sicily steering to the southeastward, roughly in the direction of Crete. The visibility being bad, the flying-boat could not shadow. There was considerable discussion between my staff and myself as to what the sighting of this Italian cruiser squadron really meant. For cruisers to be in that posi-

Below: A victim of the devastating power of naval aviation, the Italian battleship *Littorio* was sunk at her moorings after the Swordfish attack on Taranto. The vessel sustained three torpedo hits.

Admiral of the Fleet Viscount Cunningham of Hyndhope, KG, GCB, OM, DSO (1883-1963)

The son of an Edinburgh professor, he joined the Royal Navy in 1897 as a cadet and served with the Naval Brigade in the South African War. From 1911 to 1918 he commanded the destroyer *Scorpion*, serving with distinction in the Gallipoli campaign and in the Dover Patrol.

Between 1918 and 1938 he commanded the battleship *Rodney*, the Mediterranean destroyer flotillas and finally, as a Vice-Admiral, the Mediterranean battle-cruiser squadron. In November 1938 he became Deputy Chief of Naval Staff, but was, the following year, re-appointed to the Mediterranean as Commander-in-Chief, in preparation for the coming war with Germany.

As C.-in-C. Admiral Cunningham ordered the Fleet Air Arm attack on Taranto in November 1940, which crippled half the Italian Battle-Fleet. In April 1941, after the Battle of Cape Matapan, he organized the evacuation of the British Army from Greece and Crete. Both operations were successful, although lack of air support caused very severe naval losses.

Admiral Cunningham left the Mediterranean in the spring of 1942, to go to America before, in November, becoming the Naval C.-in-C. for the Allied assault on North Africa. In February 1943 he returned as C.-in-C. Mediterranean in time to receive the surrender of the Italian fleet. Eight months later he returned to Britain as First Sea Lord, the position which he retained until the end of the war. In June 1945 he retired, after almost fifty years in the Navy, renowned as one of the navy's finest commanders.

tion and steering that particular course seemed to indicate that some of the Italian heavy ships were also in that neighbourhood, and our lightly escorted convoys to Greece were certainly a tempting bait.

It so happened that on 27 March only one convoy was at sea. Bound for Piraeus with troops it was to the southward of Crete. It was ordered to steam on until dark, and then to reverse its course. A southbound convoy from Piraeus was directed not to sail.

I myself was inclined to think that the Italians would not dare to try anything. Later on we noticed some unusual Italian wireless activity, which finally decided us to go to sea after dark and to place the battle-fleet between the enemy and where he supposed our convoys must be. At the same time I bet Commander Power, the Staff Officer, Operations, the sum of ten shillings that we would see nothing of the enemy.

It was fortunate we made up our minds to proceed after nightfall, for at noon and again in the late afternoon the enemy air reconnaissance over Alexandria must have reported a very peaceful-looking fleet lying at its moorings.

I also arranged a little private cover plan of my own. We were aware that the Japanese consul at Alexandria was in the habit of reporting any fleet movements that he observed, though whether or not his information reached the enemy in time to be of any importance to them was another matter. I decided to bluff this gentleman, so went ashore to play golf carrying an obvious suit-case as though I intended to spend the night ashore. The Japanese consul spent most of his afternoons on the golf links. He was unmistakable, indeed a remarkable sight, short and squat, with a southern aspect of such vast and elephantine proportions when he bent over to putt that the irreverent Chief of Staff had nicknamed him 'The blunt end of the Axis'.

This little plot worked as intended. Retrieving my suit-case, I returned to the *Warspite* after dark and the fleet sailed at 7 p.m.

What the Japanese consul thought and did when he saw the empty harbour next morning was no affair of mine.

While leaving harbour the *Warspite* went too close to a mud-bank, which filled the condensers with mud. This had consequences later, as our speed was reputed to be reduced to 20

Below: A reconnaissance photograph taken on the day after the attack. Partially submerged and leaking oil is a Cavour-class battleship (center of picture), probably the *Conte di Cavour*.

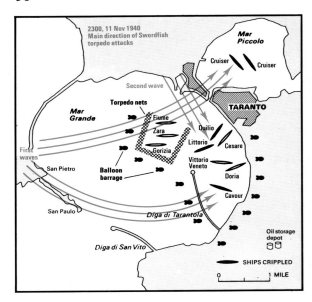

knots. The night was uneventful as we steamed on to the northwestward at that speed. The *Warspite, Barham, Valiant* and *Formidable* were in company, screened by the destroyers *Jervis, Janus, Nubian, Mohawk, Stuart, Greyhound, Griffin, Hotspur* and *Havock*.

As I have said, the one convoy at sea in the danger area had been ordered to reverse its course at nightfall. Vice-Admiral Pridham-Wippell in the *Orion* with the *Ajax, Perth* and *Gloucester,* and the destroyers, *Ilex, Hasty, Hereward* and *Vendetta,* all of which had been operating in the Aegean, were ordered to be southwest of Gavdo Island at daylight on 28 March.

A dawn air search was flown off from the *Formidable,* and at about 7.40 a.m. one of these aircraft reported four cruisers and some destroyers not far off the position where our four cruisers were supposed to be, so naturally we took them for Vice-Admiral Pridham-Wippell's force. However, just before 8.30, Pridham-Wippell himself reported three enemy cruisers and destroyers to the northward of him. This made it clear that the enemy fleet was at sea, so I cheerfully paid up my ten shillings.

The situation, however, was confused, and it was difficult to estimate from the aircraft reports just how many different enemy forces had been sighted. One report mentioned

Above left: The heavily fortified harbor of Taranto.

Above: Despite its antiquated appearance, the Swordfish formed the basis of the Fleet Air Arm's torpedo-bomber force during the early part of the war.

Below: HMS *Warspite,* flagship of the British fleet in the Mediterranean. A veteran of the First World War – she had fought at Jutland.

'battleships', and it seemed natural enough to us that the Italian cruiser squadrons should be supported by a battle-squadron. On the other hand, we could not be certain. Italian cruisers had constantly been confused with battleships in previous reconnaissance reports.

Pridham-Wippell's cruisers were estimated to be about 90 miles ahead of us, so we increased to the *Warspite*'s full speed, which at the time was no more than 22 knots because of the condenser trouble. Meanwhile Pridham-Wippell had recognized the enemy cruisers he had in sight as ships armed with 8-inch guns. As he wrote: 'Knowing that vessels of that class could outrange my squadron and that, having superior speed, they could choose the range, I decided to try to draw them towards our own battle-fleet and carrier.'

The Italian cruisers followed him, and at 8.12 opened fire at a range of nearly 13 miles. It was accurate to start with and seemed to be concentrated on the *Gloucester*, which 'snaked the line' to avoid being hit. At 8.29, when the range had dropped by about a mile, the *Gloucester* opened fire with three salvoes from her 6-inch guns, all of which fell short. The enemy altered course to the westward, and at 8.55 ceased firing. Pridham-Wippell sighted an enemy battleship to the northward, which immediately opened an accurate fire at a range of 16 miles. Our cruisers turned away under cover of a smokescreen and ran for it at full speed; but had a very unpleasant time, being closely straddled by 15-inch projectiles.

To us in the *Warspite* the situation did not look so good. We knew that the 'Littorio' class battleships were capable of 31 knots, and the night before, because of engine trouble, the *Gloucester* had reported herself capable of no more than 24. There was also another strong enemy cruiser squadron to the northward of Pridham-Wippell. However, the sight of an enemy battleship had somehow increased the *Gloucester*'s speed to 30 knots.

Something had to be done, and the *Valiant* was ordered to go on at her utmost speed to support Vice-Admiral Pridham-Wippell. It had always been my intention to hold back the air torpedo striking force until the enemy battle-fleet was close enough to ensure that if one of their ships were hit, our battle-fleet would be certain of overtaking and destroying her. But in this emergency my hand was forced. The striking force was already in the air, and I ordered the *Formidable* to send them in. Their attack relieved the pressure on Pridham-Wippell; but had the unfortunate effect of causing the enemy battleship to turn away and make off while still some 80 miles distant. This meant there was no chance of bringing her to action during daylight, if at all.

Meanwhile the low speed of the *Warspite* was causing me much annoyance. I knew that the Commander (E) was sick ashore; but was aware that the Fleet Engineer Officer, Engineer Captain B. J. H. Wilkinson was on board. So I sent for him and told him to do something about it. He went below, and in a short time I was grat-

Below: Holding onto Malta was central to British strategy in the Mediterranean, and so its defense was a major priority. Here Rear-Admiral AJ Power (third from right) poses with his escort captains after the successful arrival of a supply convoy to the beleaguered island.

ified to see that the *Valiant*, which had been coming up at full speed from astern, was no longer gaining. We pressed on together.

At this time further considerable delay was caused by the fact that the wind was in the east, from astern. This meant we had to make periodical turns in that direction to allow the *Formidable* to work her aircraft. However, at 11.30 it became so essential for us to hurry on to Pridham-Wippell's support, that the *Formidable* quickly dropped astern, and it was with some anxiety that we saw her attacked by torpedo-bombers. Our relief can be imagined when she successfully avoided the torpedoes.

At about noon the air-striking force returned and reported one probable hit on the battleship, which was the *Vittorio Veneto*. A few minutes later a Royal Air Force flying-boat reported a further enemy force consisting of two 'Cavour' class battleships and some further 8-inch cruisers. The battleship attacked by the Fleet Air Arm was alone except for a destroyer screen; but there was another force of cruisers 20 miles to the southeastward of her. The air reports showed that all the enemy forces were retiring to the westward.

We sighted our own cruisers at 12.30, and the *Formidable* was ordered to fly off a second striking force to attack the *Vittorio Veneto*, then roughly 65 miles ahead.

We settled down to a chase, and it was clear enough that it would be a long one and without reward unless the *Vittorio Veneto* was damaged and slowed up by our aircraft attacks. The pursuit was made even longer as speed had to be reduced to 22 knots to allow the *Formidable* and the *Barham* to keep up. But we had one providential piece of good fortune. The easterly wind dropped and it became flat calm with occasional light airs from the westward, which meant that the *Formidable* could carry out all her flying operations from her station in the line.

Just after 3 p.m. one of our aircraft reported the *Vittorio Veneto* still about 65 miles ahead and still steering to the westward. The second air-striking force went in to the attack, to report three hits and that the *Vittorio Veneto*'s speed was down to 8 knots. This excellent news was unduly optimistic, for an hour later our quarry was still 60 miles ahead and going 12-15 knots, which meant she could not be overhauled before dark. A small force of Fleet Air Arm Swordfish from the airfield at Maleme in Crete had also attacked one of the cruiser squadrons and reported a possible hit, while in the course of the afternoon Royal Air Force bombers from Greece came into action with bombing attacks. No ship was hit; but there were several near misses. The attacks gave the enemy a good fright, and were particularly welcome to us, giving the Italians a dose of the medicine we had been enduring for months.

It now became necessary to establish surface touch with the enemy, so at 4.44 p.m. Vice-Admiral Pridham-Wippell was ordered to press on at full speed and get into visual touch with the retreating enemy. The destroyers *Nubian* and *Mohawk* were also sent ahead to form a visual signal link between Pridham-Wippell's cruisers and the battle-fleet. The situation was still very confused, for as the afternoon wore on we continued to receive reports showing another enemy force containing battleships to the northwest of the *Vittorio Veneto*. These reports, as we discovered later, were incorrect. The force referred to consisted entirely of cruisers. No other battleship was out.

We now had to signal some plan for the night which was coming on, and decided to form a striking force of eight destroyers under Captain Philip Mack of the *Jervis*. If the cruisers made contact with the *Vittorio Veneto* the destroyers would be sent in to attack, and if necessary we should follow it up with the battleships. If the cruisers failed to make contact, I intended to work round to the north and northwest and try

Below: The Hero-class destroyer HMS *Hotspur* sets out to sea on a routine patrol. The destroyer was a highly versatile craft, capable of acting both as a convoy escort and of supporting the line-of-battle ships in fleet actions such as Matapan.

and catch the *Vittorio Veneto* at daylight next morning. In the meanwhile the *Formidable* was ordered to send in a third aircraft torpedo attack at dusk.

But we needed a clear picture, and at 5.45 the *Warspite* catapulted her own aircraft with the Commander-in-Chief's observer, Lieutenant-Commander A. S. Bolt on board, to try and clarify the situation. By 6.30 we had the first of a series of reports from this highly trained and experienced officer which quickly told us what we needed. The *Vittorio Veneto* was 45 miles from the *Warspite* and making good about 15 knots to the westward. The Italian fleet had concentrated into a bunch, with the battleship in the middle with two columns of ships on each side of her, one of the destroyers and the other of cruisers, with a destroyer screen ahead. From other air reports we still heard of the other force of battleships and eight-inch cruisers to the northwestward.

At about 7.30, by which time it was nearly dark, the third striking force of Swordfish went into attack, and at the same time Pridham-Wippell reported the enemy ships about nine miles to the northwest. A little later the striking force reported probable hits, though there was no definite information that the battleship had been hit again.

Now came the difficult moment of deciding what to do. I was fairly well convinced that having got so far it would be foolish not to make every effort to complete the *Vittorio Veneto*'s destruction. At the same time it appeared to us that the Italian Admiral must have been fully aware of our position. He had numerous cruisers and destroyers in company, and any British Admiral in his position would not have hesitated to use every destroyer he had, backed up by all his cruisers fitted with torpedo tubes, for attacks upon the pursuing fleet. Some of my staff argued that it would be unwise to charge blindly after the retreating enemy with our

three heavy ships, and the *Formidable* also on our hands, to run the risk of ships being crippled, and to find ourselves within easy range of the enemy dive-bombers at daylight. I paid respectful attention to this opinion, and as the discussion happened to coincide with my time for dinner I told them I would have my evening meal and would see how I felt afterwards.

My morale was reasonably high when I returned to the bridge, and I ordered the destroyer striking force off to find and attack the enemy. We settled down to a steady pursuit with some doubts in our minds as to how the four destroyers remaining in the battle-fleet would deal with the enemy destroyer attacks if the Italians decided to make them. At this stage the enemy fleet was estimated to be 33 miles ahead making good about 15 knots.

Vice-Admiral Pridham-Wippell with his cruisers also had his perplexities. To gain contact with the *Vittorio Veneto*, closely guarded by three cruiser squadrons and some eleven destroyers, was indeed a problem, particularly as Pridham-Wippell must keep his four ships concentrated in readiness for instant action. In the event he never made contact.

At 9.11 we received Pridham-Wippell's report that an unknown ship lying stopped five miles to port of him had been located by radar. We went on after the enemy's fleet, and altered course slightly to port to close the stopped ship. The *Warspite* was not fitted with radar; but at 10.10 the *Valiant* reported that her instruments had picked up what was apparently the same ship six miles on her port bow. She was a large ship. The *Valiant* gave her length as more than 600 feet.

Our hopes ran high. This might be the *Vittorio Veneto*. The course of the battle-fleet was altered to 40 degrees to port together to close. We were already at action stations with our main armament ready. Our guns were trained on the correct bearing.

Below: The ill-fated heavy cruisers *Fiume*, *Pola* and *Zara* pictured at their berths in the naval harbor at Naples in 1938. All three were sunk at close range by the heavy guns of the British battle squadron at Matapan.

Left: HMS *Valiant* looses off a salvo of 15-inch shells from one of her three-gun turrets. Following *Valiant* in line ahead are *Barham* and *Warspite*, the battleships at Cunningham's disposal for the Battle of Matapan.

Below: Italian capital ships head out to sea on one of their infrequent sorties into the Mediterranean. Such expeditions were fraught with danger and at Matapan ended in disaster.

Rear-Admiral Willis was not out with us. Commodore Edelsten, the new Chief of Staff, had come to gain experience. And a quarter of an hour later, at 10.25, when he was searching the horizon on the starboard bow with his glasses, he calmly reported that he saw two large cruisers with a smaller one ahead of them crossing the bows of the battle-fleet from starboard to port. I looked through my glasses, and there they were. Commander Power, an ex-submarine officer and an abnormal expert at recognizing the silhouettes of enemy warships at a glance, pronounced them to be two 'Zara' class 8-inch gun cruisers with a smaller cruiser ahead.

Using short-range wireless the battle-fleet was turned back into line ahead. With Edelsten and the staff I had gone to the upper bridge, the captain's, where I had a clear all-round view. I shall never forget the next few minutes. In the dead silence, a silence that could almost be felt, one heard only the voices of the gun-control personnel putting the guns on to the new target. One heard the orders repeated in the director tower behind and above the bridge. Looking forward, one saw the turrets swing and steady when the 15-inch guns pointed at the enemy cruisers. Never in the whole of my life have I experienced a more thrilling moment than when I heard a calm voice from the director tower – 'Director layer sees the target'; sure sign that the guns were ready and that his finger was itching on the trigger. The enemy was a range of no more than 3,800 yards – point-blank.

It must have been the Fleet Gunnery Officer,

Commander Geoffrey Barnard, who gave the final order to open fire. One heard the 'ting-ting-ting' of the firing gongs. Then came the great orange flash and the violent shudder as the six big guns bearing were fired simultaneously. At the very same instant the destroyer *Greyhound*, on the screen, switched her searchlight on to one of the enemy cruisers, showing her momentarily up as a silvery-blue shape in the darkness. Our searchlights shone out with the first salvo, and provided full illumination for what was a ghastly sight. Full in the beam I saw our six great projectiles flying through the air. Five out of the six hit a few feet below the level of the cruiser's upper deck and burst with splashes of brilliant flame. The Italians were quite unprepared. Their guns were trained fore and aft. They were helplessly shattered before they could put up any resistance. In the midst of all this there was one milder diversion. Captain Douglas Fisher, the captain of the *Warspite*, was a gunnery officer of note. When he saw the first salvo hit he was heard to say in a voice of wondering surprise: 'Good Lord! We've hit her!'

The *Valiant*, astern of us, had opened fire at the same time. She also had found her target, and when the *Warspite* shifted to the other cruiser I watched the *Valiant* pounding her ship to bits. Her rapidity of fire astonished me. Never would I have believed it possible with these heavy guns. The *Formidable* had hauled out of the line to starboard; but astern of the *Valiant* and *Barham* was also heavily engaged.

The plight of the Italian cruisers was indescribable. One saw whole turrets and masses of other heavy debris whirling through the air and splashing into the sea, and in a short time the ships themselves were nothing but glowing torches and on fire from stem to stern. The

whole action lasted no more than a few minutes.

Our searchlights were still on, and just after 10.30 three Italian destroyers, which had apparently been following their cruisers, were seen coming in on our port bow. They turned, and one was seen to fire torpedoes, so the battle-fleet was turned 90 degrees together to starboard to avoid them. Our destroyers were engaging, and the whole party was inextricably mixed up. The *Warspite* fired both 15-inch and six-inch at the enemy. To my horror I saw one of our destroyers, the *Havock*, straddled by our fire, and in my mind wrote her off as a loss. The *Formidable* also had an escape. When action was joined she hauled out to starboard at full speed, a night battle being no place for a carrier. When she was about five miles away she was caught in the beam of the *Warspite*'s searchlight

Above: Admiral Sir Andrew Cunningham, the British Commander-in-Chief in the Mediterranean, considered by many naval historians to have been Britain's finest fighting sailor of the Second World War.

Below: The Battle of Matapan was a complex running action which saw the Italian fleet attempting to escape the British battle squadron, comprising three heavy units, an aircraft carrier and destroyers under the dynamic leadership of Admiral AB Cunningham.

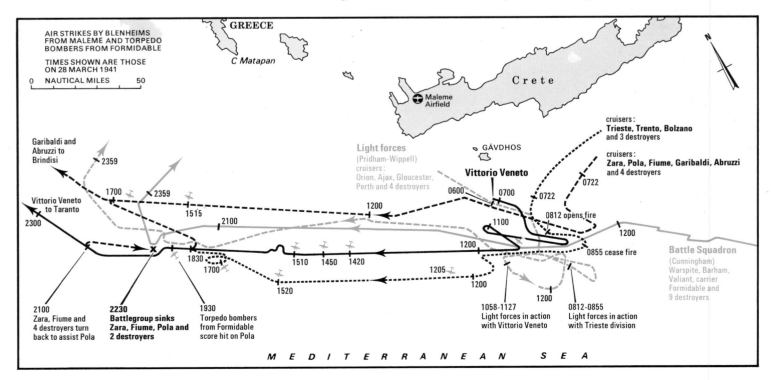

AIR STRIKES BY BLENHEIMS FROM MALEME AND TORPEDO BOMBERS FROM FORMIDABLE

TIMES SHOWN ARE THOSE ON 28 MARCH 1941

0 NAUTICAL MILES 50

GREECE

C Matapan

Crete

Maleme Airfield

GÁVDHOS

Light forces (Pridham-Wippell) cruisers: Orion, Ajax, Gloucester, Perth and 4 destroyers

Vittorio Veneto

cruisers: **Trieste, Trento, Bolzano** and 3 destroyers

cruisers: **Zara, Pola, Fiume, Garibaldi, Abruzzi** and 4 destroyers

Garibaldi and Abruzzi to Brindisi

2359

1700   2359

Vittorio Veneto to Taranto

2300   1515   2100

1830   1700

1510 1450 1420

1520

0600   0700   0722   0722

1200

0812 opens fire

1100   1200

1200   0855 cease fire

1205   1200   1200

Battle Squadron (Cunningham) Warspite, Barham, Valiant, carrier Formidable and 9 destroyers

2100 Zara, Fiume and 4 destroyers turn back to assist Pola

2230 Battlegroup sinks Zara, Fiume, Pola and 2 destroyers

1930 Torpedo bombers from Formidable score hit on Pola

1058-1127 Light forces in action with Vittorio Veneto

0812-0855 Light forces in action with Trieste division

M E D I T E R R A N E A N   S E A

sweeping on the disengaged side in case further enemy ships were present. We heard the six-inch control officer of the starboard battery get his guns on to her, and were only just in time to stop him from opening fire.

The four destroyers, *Stuart*, Captain H. M. L. Waller, Royal Australian Navy; *Greyhound*, Commander W. R. Marshall-A'Deane; *Havock*, Lieutenant G. R. G. Watkins; and *Griffin*, Lieutenant-Commander J. Lee-Barber, in company with the battle-fleet, were then ordered to finish off the enemy cruisers, while the battle-fleet collected the *Formidable* and withdrew to the northward to keep out of their way. According to their own reports the destroyers' movements were difficult to follow; but they had a wild night and sank at least one other enemy destroyer.

At 10.45 we saw very heavy gunfire, with star-shell and tracer, to the southwestward. Since none of our ships was on that bearing it seemed to us that either the Italians were engaging each other, or that the destroyers of our striking force might be going in to attack. Just after 11 p.m. I made a signal ordering all forces not engaged in sinking the enemy to withdraw to the northeastward. The objects of what I now believe to have been an ill-considered signal were to give our destroyers who were mopping up a free hand to attack any sizeable ship they saw, and to facilitate the assembly of the fleet next morning. The message was qualified by an order to Captain Mack and his eight destroyers of the striking force, now some 20 miles ahead, not to withdraw until he had attacked. However, it had the unfortunate effect of causing Vice-Admiral Pridham-Wippell to cease his efforts to gain contact with the *Vittorio Veneto*.

Just after midnight the *Havock*, after torpedoing a destroyer and finishing her off by gunfire, reported herself in contact with a battleship near the position where we had been in action. The battleship was Captain Mack's main objective, and the *Havock*'s report brought Mack's destroyer striking force back hot-foot from their position nearly 60 miles to the westward. An hour later, however, the *Havock* amended her report to say that it was not a battleship she had sighted, but an 8-inch cruiser. Soon after 3 a.m. she sent a further message reporting herself close to the *Pola*, and, as all her torpedoes had been fired, Watkins asked whether – 'to board or blow off her stern with depth-charges'.

The *Havock* had already been joined by the *Greyhound* and *Griffin*, and when Captain Mack

Above: The Italian battleship *Vittorio Veneto* fires a broadside. Although the ship escaped destruction at Matapan, carrier-borne aircraft did score one torpedo hit which forced her to reduce speed to 19 knots.

Below: A detachment of anti-aircraft gunners watch the arrival of a convoy into Malta's Grand Harbour.

arrived he took the *Jervis* alongside the *Pola*. That ship was in a state of indescribable confusion. Panic-stricken men were leaping over the side. On the crowded quarterdeck, littered with clothing, personal belongings and bottles, many of the sailors were drunk. There was no order or discipline of any sort, and the officers were powerless to enforce it. Having taken off the crew Mack sank the ship with torpedoes. The *Pola*, of course, was the vessel reported by Pridham-Wippell and the *Valiant* between 9 and 10 the night before as lying stopped on the port side of our fleet's line of advance. She had not been under gunfire or fired a gun; but had been torpedoed and completely crippled by one of the aircraft from the *Formidable* during the dusk attack.

Her sinking at 4.10 a.m. was the final act of the night's proceedings.

Reconnaissance at dawn by the *Formidable*'s aircraft, with others from Greece and Crete, failed to discover any trace of the enemy to the westward. As we discovered afterwards, the *Vittorio Veneto* had been able to increase speed and get clear away during the night.

As daylight came on 29 March our cruisers and destroyers were in sight making for the rendezvous with the battle-fleet. Feeling fairly certain in our minds that the *Warspite* had sunk a destroyer in the mêlée the night before, we eagerly counted them. To our inexpressible relief all twelve destroyers were present. My heart was glad again.

It was a fine morning. We steamed back to the scene of the battle to find a calm sea covered with a film of oil, and strewn with boats, rafts and wreckage, with many floating corpses. All the destroyers we could spare were detached to save what life was possible. In all, counting the men from the *Pola*, British ships rescued 900, though some died later. In the midst of this work of mercy, however, the attentions of some German Ju 88s pointed the fact that it was unwise to dally in an area where we were exposed to heavy air attack. So we were compelled to proceed to the eastward, leaving some hundreds of Italians unrescued. We did the best we could for them by signalling their exact position to the Italian Admiralty. They sent out the hospital ship *Gradisca*, which eventually saved another 160.

An unfortunate mistake in ciphering prevented a Greek destroyer flotilla from being present at the action, in which I feel sure they would have played a gallant part. They were sent through the Corinth Canal to Argostoli with commendable promptitude; but arrived too late for the battle, though they picked up another 110 Italians.

The fleet was subjected to the expected air attack during the afternoon of 29 March. Though broken up by the *Formidable*'s fighters it was fairly heavy; the *Formidable* herself being close-missed by several heavy bombs. We reached Alexandria without further incident in the early evening of Sunday, 30 March. On 1 April I caused a special Thanksgiving Service to be held on board all ships for our success off Cape Matapan.

Shortly afterwards I was visited by the

Patriarch of the Orthodox Greek Church at Alexandria who offered us his congratulations on the victory which he described not only as a great deliverance; but also a manifestation of God's Power, for which he and his Church offered thanks to Almighty God. After his return to the City he presented the fleet with a sacred icon of St Nicholas, the patron saint of sailors and travellers, which was placed in the Chapel precincts of the *Warspite*.

Although the *Vittorio Veneto* had escaped, we had sunk the three 10,000-ton, 8-inch gun cruisers *Zara*, *Pola* and *Fiume*, together with the 1,500-ton destroyers *Alfieri* and *Carducci*. The Italian loss in personnel was about 2,400 officers and men, most of them being caused by our devastating bombardment at close range. The *Fiume* received two 15-inch broadsides from the *Warspite*, one from the *Valiant*, and five from the *Barham*. The effect of those six- or eight-gun salvoes of shell, each weighing nearly a ton, cannot be described.

There was considerable jubilation in the fleet at Alexandria. Our sailors felt, and rightly, that they had something back for the days of continual bombing they had endured during their repeated excursions to sea in the Mediterranean.

At Matapan our casualties were happily very light, for we lost only one aircraft with its crew.

Once again, before closing this account of the battle, I must pay a tribute to the magnificent work of the Fleet Air Arm. To quote from my despatch in the *London Gazette* of 31 July 1947:

. . . whatever the result, the gallantry and perseverance of the aircraft crews and the smooth efficiency of deck and ground crews in HMS *Formidable* and at Maleme are deserving of high praise. An example of the spirit of these young officers is the case of Lieutenant F. M. A. Torrens Spence, Royal Navy, who, rather than be left out, flew with the only available aircraft and torpedo from Elsusis to Maleme and in spite of reconnaissance difficulties and bad communications arranged his own reconnaissance and finally took off with a second aircraft in company and took part in the dusk attack.

Looking back on the engagement which is now officially known as the Battle of Matapan, I am conscious of several things which might have been done better. However, calm reflection in an armchair in the full knowledge of what actually happened is a very different matter to conducting an operation from the bridge of a ship at night in the presence of the enemy. Instant and momentous decisions have to be made in a matter of seconds. With fast-moving ships at close quarters and the roar of heavy gunfire, clear thinking is not easy. In no other circumstances than in a night action at sea does the fog of war so completely descend to blind one to a true realization of what is happening.

Nevertheless, we could claim substantial results. Those three heavy Italian cruisers with their eight-inch guns were armoured against six-inch gunfire and always a threat against our smaller and more lightly armed ships. More important still, the supine and inactive attitude of the Italian fleet during our subsequent evacuations of Greece and Crete was directly attributable to the rough handling they had received at Matapan. Had the enemy's surface ships intervened in those operations, our already difficult task would have been well nigh impossible.

Admiral Angelo Iachino was in command of the Italian fleet with his flag in the *Vittorio Veneto*. I have read his account of the operation and the night battle, and there is no doubt that he was badly served by his air reconnaissance.

Below: A Bristol Beaufighter of the RAF's Desert Air Force. In the Mediterranean theater of operations command of the air was of the greatest importance – both over land and sea.

This is surprising to us who know how efficient the Italian reconnaissance had been on many other occasions. However, as Admiral Iachino says, the Italian naval co-operation with the air in the tactical field was very imperfect.

It appears that they were relying upon German aircraft reports before the battle, and as the weather was by no means unfavourable it is not easy to understand why their reconnaissance failed. At 9 a.m. on 28 March German aircraft from the Aegean had actually reported one aircraft-carrier, two battleships, nine cruisers and fourteen destroyers in such and such a position at 7.45. This actually was our fleet, which up to that time Admiral Iachino had thought was still safely at Alexandria. However, on plotting the position given, the Admiral convinced himself that his Aegean reconnaissance had mistaken the British fleet for his own, and signalled Rhodes to this effect. He does not seem to have become aware that the British battle-fleet was at sea until later.

On the evening of the 28th, when the *Pola* was damaged by our air attack, Admiral Iachino's information led him to believe that the nearest British battleship was 90 miles astern of him, something over four hours' steaming. With this in mind his decision to detach the *Zara* and the *Fiume* to help the crippled *Pola* cannot be questioned. He was originally urged to send destroyers; but finally decided that only a Flag Officer, Rear-Admiral Carlo Cateneo in the *Zara*, who did not survive, could take the responsibility of deciding whether the *Pola* should be taken in tow, or abandoned and sunk.

Instead of being 90 miles astern, the British battle-fleet was roughly half that distance.

The result we know.

Admiral Iachino's book also discloses an extraordinary state of unpreparedness in the technique of night fighting on the part of the Italian Navy. They had not visualized a night action between heavy ships and did not keep their heavy guns manned, which accounts for the turrets of the *Zara* and *Fiume* being trained fore and aft when we first sighted them. They had good ships, good guns and torpedoes, flashless ammunition and much else; but even their newest ships lacked the radar which had served us so well, while in the art of night fighting in heavy ships they were no further advanced than we had been at the Battle of Jutland twenty-five years before.

Admiral Iachino's reception at the hands of the Chief of the Italian Naval Staff, Admiral Riccardi, was chilly. Mussolini, on the other hand, was not unfriendly, and listened with patience to Iachino's complaints about the reconnaissance. The outcome of that interview, and of Matapan, strengthened the Italian resolve to build aircraft-carriers to provide the Navy with its own reconnaissance. I seem to remember that Italy had an uncompleted aircraft-carrier at the time of her surrender in September 1943.

Above: The cloud of dust and smoke indicates a hit against buildings in Valetta, Malta's capital city. At the height of the conflict in the Mediterranean, Malta became one of the most heavily bombed places in the world. As a tribute to the steadfast determination of the Maltese people in the face of Axis attacks, the whole island was subsequently awarded the George Cross.

Singapore

by Masanobu Tsuji

On 15 February 1942 Lt.-General A. E. Percival surrendered Singapore and some 85,000 British, Australian and Indian troops, of whom about 15,000 were non-combatants. It has fallen to me to comment on this episode before and I do not wish to alter one word of what I wrote in *World War 1939-45*.

'In Britain's long military annals there is no more dismal chapter than the fall of Singapore. It is a sort of anthology of all that is worst in British military history. It is a tale of complacency, unpreparedness, and weakness, relieved only by isolated tactical successes and the firmness of a handful of units and individuals. Defeat is something not unknown in the history of any martial race. But seldom indeed has an army capitulated to one which it actually outnumbered. Lt.-General Yamashita and his men had, from the tactical point of view, literally run rings round the defenders. Once more in this war the better balanced force had won. Yamashita may have had fewer soldiers, but he had air and sea power.'

It is difficult to understand a disaster of this sort without looking at it from the enemy's point of view. This Colonel Tsuji's work allows us to do.

He writes with an engaging candour, and it is refreshing to find the Japanese, who, for a time, were regarded almost as supermen, subject to human failings as was the 'weak-willed Konie divisional commander'.

Hampered by *bouches inutiles* and with a totally inadequate fighter force Percival, although he outnumbered General Yamashita, had a well-nigh impossible task on his hands. An appendix to Colonel Tsuji's book gives the breakdown of the forces at the former's disposal during the battle.

THE BRITISH GARRISON IN MALAYA. The garrison in Malaya comprised: 9th Indian Division (2 brigades); 18th British Division (3 brigades); and 12th, 28th, 44th, and 45th Indian Brigades – a total of 13 brigades. In addition, Singapore fortress troops on the island consisted of two Malayan brigades.

The British official history of the campaign (*The War Against Japan,* vol. 1; HMSO, 1956) states on p. 473 that the total British casualties in Malaya were 138,708 (of whom more than 130,000 were prisoners of war). With the exception of the relatively small number who escaped or were evacuated, this figure represents the strength of the British and Commonwealth forces in Malaya.   EDITOR

Chronology

1941

7 Dec.	Japanese attack Pearl Harbor.
8 Dec.	Japanese invade Malaya.
10 Dec.	Sinking of HMSs *Repulse* and *Prince of Wales.*
	Japanese invade the Philippines.
11 Dec.	Japanese repulsed at Wake Island.
17 Dec.	Japanese invade Sarawak.
23 Dec.	Capture of Wake Island.
26 Dec.	Fall of Hong Kong.

1942

2 Jan.	Japanese take Manila.
3 Jan.	Japanese invade Borneo.
10 Jan.	Fall of Kuala Lumpur.
21 Jan.	Japanese land in New Guinea and the Solomons.
8 Feb.	The Japanese cross the straits to Singapore Island.
15 Feb.	Surrender of Singapore.

1945

3 Sep.	British reoccupy Singapore.
7 Dec.	Execution of Yamashita.

These pages: Led by a sword-carrying officer, a squad of Japanese marines advances past a wrecked British aircraft on Singapore's Tengah airfield, early February 1942.

The Pivot

Singapore was Britain's pivotal point in the domination of Asia. It was the eastern gate for the defence of India and also the northern gate for the defence of Australia. It was the axis of the steamship route from Europe to the Orient, north to Hong Kong and through to Shanghai, and to the treasures of the Dutch East Indies to the south and east. Through these two arteries alone, during a period of many years, Britain controlled the Pacific Ocean.

The young and spirited empire-builder, Sir Stamford Raffles, controlling a few troops, landed in the territory and hoisted the Union Jack on 29 January 1819. By 6 February, by skilful diplomatic measures, he pacified Lamon the Mohammedan king of Johore with barely 650,000 dollars, thus acquiring a perpetual lease. He then set to work to establish a commercial port. Singapore, at that time a village with barely a hundred and fifty or a hundred and sixty people, was a desolate savage jungle with nothing more than barbarian villages scattered here and there. Then in 1824 the whole island was formally transferred to the British East India Company.

In 1923, two years after the Washington Conference had solved the problem of abolition of the Anglo-Japanese Alliance, Britain commenced strengthening the defence of the island. The Washington Agreement restricted expansion of the Japanese Navy, but permitted Britain to proceed with a plan for the fortification of Singapore at an estimated cost of many millions of pounds sterling, the project to be completed over ten years, while at the same time the defence of other countries outside the limits of this area was skilfully restricted. In 1938 with completion of the large floating dock and the King George VI graving dock, Singapore became a first-class modern fortress, one of the four great fortresses of the world, ranking with Gibraltar, Pearl Harbor, and Malta. It was ready for use and the British went so far as to boast of its magnificence and power.

Colonel Masanobu Tsuji

Colonel Masanobu Tsuji was the chief of the planning staff, who devised the 70-day campaign which brought about the conquest of Malaya and the fall of Singapore. He was Director of Military Operations, 25th Japanese Army, during the operations in which his plan was successfully executed.

When Japan surrendered Colonel Tsuji evaded arrest and for three years wandered about Asia, until, hearing that he was cleared of all charges against him, he ventured to return home. He described his adventures in another book, *Underground Escape*. He later became a Member of The Diet of Japan.

With the outbreak of the China Incident in 1937 the policies of Britain and Japan became sharply pitted against each other in eastern Asia. Britain established her East Asia army headquarters in Singapore under supreme command of General Pownall, planned the unification of the local volunteer forces, consolidated the defences with Australian and Indian soldiers, and, with the assistance of America, reinforced her military preparations in epoch-making fashion just prior to the outbreak of hostilities, when the Japanese-American conference was at its peak and tension at its highest.

Britain's boast that Singapore was an impregnable fortress, and her attempted coercion of Japan by dispatching to Singapore the two great and efficient battleships *Repulse* and *Prince of Wales*, were things that remain fresh even now in the memory of the people of Japan.

Singapore was naturally easy to defend, and with consolidation of its equipment could be shaped into an impregnable fortress. Facing the sea coast a battery of 15-inch guns was installed which dominated the eastern mouth of Johore Strait and protected the vast military barracks at Changi. The fortress was constructed in steel and concrete, and the world's greatest guns

Below: The beginnings of the Japanese conquest of the Malayan peninsula – units of the Twenty-fifth Army land at Singora, 8 December 1941.

directed their forbidding muzzles towards the sea front. The military aerodromes of Tengah, Kallang, Seletar, and Sembawang were good bases of operation for a large air force, and in Seletar naval harbour two great docks were installed which could easily take in 50,000-ton battleships.

The British boasted about the huge graving dock, the King George VI, which was 1,000 feet long, 130 feet wide, and 35 feet deep. About 900,000 cubic yards of cement were used in its construction. The floating dock, little if at all inferior in capacity, was constructed in England and towed out to Singapore in two separate pieces. It had an overall length of 1,000 feet, an overall width of 300 feet, and was anchored in a mooring place 70 feet in depth. About 1,500,000 tons of fuel oil, sufficient to maintain the whole of the British Fleet, and to provide for any emergency, was stored in a number of huge storage tanks. The fortress took nearly ten years to build, cost over ten million pounds sterling, and was completed in February 1938.

At the opening ceremony of this great naval port a threatening attitude to Japan's southward advance was revealed by the attendance of battleships of every nation of the British-

American Allied camp. In the spring of 1937 a plan to equip completely and to consolidate the fleets of both hemispheres was introduced into the British Parliament. But, as this work was not yet completed, it was a case of having 'the chicken house ready but no chickens'.

In this great fortress, which Britain boasted could never be captured by attack from the sea, there was however an important weak point. As already stated, the rear defences in the region of Johore Province were incomplete. This resulted from a defect in the organization of the fortress, or rather from a defect in the plan of military operations.

In other words, to land in southern Thailand, brave the intense heat and the long distance of 1,100 kilometres, and advance through dense jungle, was probably deemed an impossibility by what seemed to the British common-sense judgement. A Japanese Army contemplating such operations in an emergency, would, it appeared, in view of the long distance overland, have to labour for perhaps more than a year to reach Singapore from Thailand. It was not difficult to imagine that the British would complete fortification of the landward front.

Above: Aided by a comrade, a Japanese infantryman leaves a naval transport *en route* for the northeastern shores of Malaya.

In barely fifty-five days, however, the Japanese Army overwhelmed Malaya, carrying everything before it, and during the campaign the British, not being gods, were never certain of our whereabouts.

According to Mr Churchill's memoirs, Singapore's rear defences (the Johore front) were believed to be in readiness. This was accepted by everyone as a matter of course.

On the morning of 19 January, from a telegram from General Wavell, Mr Churchill for the first time heard not only that there were no permanent fortifications for the rear defence of Singapore, but also that since the outbreak of hostilities, especially since the Japanese had been building up strength in the southern part of Indo-China, the lack of rear fortifications had not even been considered or discussed by any commanding officer in Singapore. The suggestion had not even been made that field-operation fortifications should be constructed on the landward side of the island.

It seems inconceivable that the British in Singapore should neglect even to report the truth of the non-existence of rear defences. In the circumstances Mr Churchill's rebuke was quite proper. Among the commanding officers in the Malayan theatre there was not one who had a tithe of the enthusiasm and feeling of responsibility of Mr Churchill. This however was to be considered the unexpected good fortune of the Japanese Army.

Considerations of space have compelled me to omit Colonel Tsuji's interesting account of the planning for the assault on Singapore. Since the operation went more or less according to plan, this is, perhaps, justifiable.

Above: HMS *Repulse* leaves Singapore harbor on 8 December 1941. Part of the Royal Navy's Force Z, the *Repulse* was sunk two days later after an attack by land-based Japanese torpedo-bombers.

Below: A column of lightly armed Japanese troops advances inland from Singora during the first stages of the campaign in Malaya.

To the Heights of the Imperial Palace

In deciding the position from which Army Headquarters would exercise supreme command of the battle to decide the destiny of Japan and the emancipation of Asia, there were many aspects to be considered. But, notwithstanding the risks involved, we chose the heights of the Imperial Palace. It was an obvious target for enemy planes, but it possessed such outstanding advantages for observation and signal communication that we decided this was where our Headquarters should be.

The Sultan of Johore who had built the Imperial Palace regardless of expense, boasted of its beauty and majestic appearance. It stood on the heights on the north side of Johore Strait looking down on Singapore Island. It was within easy range of the enemy artillery, and at times even machine-gun bullets came flying past, for the enemy lines were not more than two kilometres distant. From the palace the naval port of Seletar lay beneath one's eyes, and Tengah aerodrome appeared as if it could be grasped in the hand. It was on our infantry front line and it was also our forward artillery observation post.

There was reasonable and genuine opposition to the occupation of the palace as Army Headquarters. Many believed that it was too exposed to enemy fire for use by the Army, and divisional headquarters felt strongly that the Army had stolen a march on them. It was however the only position from which the Army Commander could have a close view of the whole battle line from the crossing of Johore Strait to the capture of the heights of Bukit Timah, and the spiritual effect alone of being able to see every detail of the battle was of sufficient importance to override all opposition, which was strong even among members of the staff.

The Army Commander's decision however ended all discussions, and the minimum number of staff personnel necessary pushed forward to the palace while the rest remained in the rear in the rubber jungle. Although the palace stood in an exposed position the unanimous opinion was, 'Anyhow, if we are to die, will not the heights of the Imperial Palace be a suitable place?'

Standing on an excellent lawn the red-brick and green-tiled building, of whose splendid appearance the Sultan was so proud, was perfectly visible to the enemy. Shells sometimes fell on the lawns, turning up the earth and leaving craters like pitted pock scars. At the eastern end of the building there was a five-storey observation tower, with a narrow spiral iron ladder leading to the top where there was a four-and-a-half mat room, glassed in on all sides. It gave the impression of a small castle tower.

A warship has a steel conning-tower, but here we had a glass-covered battle command post. Struck by stray enemy bullets several of the glass windows were smashed, but although not constructed for the purpose the building was strong and powerful. We decided to use the glass-enclosed room for the military operations room, and for about a week we were practically confined there making preparations for the attack. With field glasses the movements of even individual men over on the enemy side of the strait could be clearly seen.

In this observation post was drafted the Army Commander's first telegram: 'I, this whole day, pushing forward the command post to the heights of the Johore Imperial Palace, will observe directly the strenuous efforts of every divisional commander. (Signed) Lieutenant-General Yamashita.' Thus under hostile shellfire Army Headquarters gave silent encouragement to the officers and men of the whole Army.

Normally there are numerous arrivals at and departures from Army Headquarters, and many people disregard the regulations laid down for the preservation of concealment and privacy. In this place, however, there was no traffic, for visitors to Headquarters came at the risk of their lives from enemy fire. The staff practically lived on dry bread and tinned food, and on no account was any cooking allowed at the Headquarters. While we lived together at the Army Artillery Unit Observation Post enemy shells sometimes flew over the heights, but the glass-covered observation room towering in the sky was practically a safety zone. When the enemy surrendered we inquired, 'Why did you not shell the heights of the Imperial Palace?' The reply was, 'It was not thought that under any circumstances such a distinct building would be used as Army Headquarters.' Up to the last it was the most suitable military operations command post, and our use of it completely surprised the enemy.

Above: The battleship *Prince of Wales* prepares to sail from Singapore. Lack of effective air protection was to seal the fate of the ship on 10 December.

Distressing Preparations

Concealment of the plan was absolutely necessary. The main Army forces and vehicles of all descriptions except the patrols, the guards and the staff necessary for the preparation for crossing the strait were protected from enemy observation by the rubber jungle in a position suitably isolated from Johore Strait.

In accordance with the plans all inhabitants within approximately 20 kilometres of the strait were evacuated; enemy transmitters and signal staff were difficult to distinguish from the civil population. We had to avoid killing innocent people by fire and sword. The columns of refugees, removed from the houses in which they had lived for so many years, irrespective of age or sex, with their personal possessions over their shoulders, moved out slowly. Five- and six-year-old girls, with quart bottles of drinking water hanging from their shoulders, pulled along by their mothers' hands, were jostled along in a long line. Seeing them trudging barefoot along the hot asphalt roads, thinking of one's own children left behind in the Fatherland, it was difficult to view this as a matter of military necessity, but there was no alternative but to avert our faces and steel our hearts against compassion, knowing that the hardships of the refugeees would be over in a short time, and in the meantime to help as many as possible by giving them transport in empty trucks that were returning northwards.

In about a week every detachment working almost to exhaustion had completed preparations. The principal task of carrying out an accurate artillery survey, amending existing defects on our maps and exactly plotting enemy positions on them, was satisfactorily carried out. Other things which had to be undertaken were determination of the necessary data for the artillery ranges and accumulation of ammunition to complete the full quantity required per gun, preparations by the engineers for crossing the strait, the overhaul of boat equipment (an important matter), and cutting down jungle and opening up roads from troop concentration points to the water's edge.

The crippled Staff Officer Hongo (railways), Staff Officer Kato (ammunition supplies), Staff Officer Kera (boat preparations), Staff Officers Asaeda and Kunitake (attack preparations of each division) and Staff Officer Sugita (intelligence), all watching the enemy movements and giving full attention to their tasks, had not a moment's leisure. Worthy of special mention are the engineers and the railway unit, which so far had repaired 1,100 kilometres of road and railway that had been badly damaged by the retreating enemy up to the boundary of Johore State. This had been completed by the end of January, and within another week the full requirement of ammunition per gun had been completed. The work was completed as the result of a supreme effort, the spirit of which permeated all the troops on the extensive lines of communication.

Motor traffic reached the limits of congestion thrusting forward with ammunition for every Army division and every artillery unit to positions near the front line, at the northern extremity of Johore Strait. In all probability nearly three thousand motor vehicles were in use. The central and sea-coast roads were re-

Left: Mortally wounded by strikes from Japanese torpedo-bombers, the *Prince of Wales* settles in the water. Her crew attempt to abandon ship, but the loss of life was heavy.

stricted to outward and return journeys respectively, and in Skudai in the south movement was permitted only by night. Traffic was very strictly controlled since violation of the rules laid down could obstruct the preparations of the whole Army. Control, however, was not easy.

The commander of the Tank Brigade organized all movement of motor vehicles, which was kept in order by numerous traffic-control squads. A surprising amount of labour was saved by the engineers' preparations for crossing the strait. Selected officers, non-commissioned officers and men supervised by day and night the work carried on at the water's edge inside the jungle, warding off attacks by crocodiles, watching enemy movements on the opposite shore, hourly and systematically investigating the condition of the constantly changing tidal currents, and measuring the depth of the water at as many points as possible. One party reconnoitred for the presence of obstacles on the opposite shore in order to indicate secretly the road to be followed by the main forces moving into position.

The fuel stored in Singapore was a quantity equivalent to six months' supply for the whole British Fleet. If, after we commenced the channel crossing, the enemy deliberately and without warning opened the oil-feed pipes on to the streams inside the island and on to the waters of the strait and then ignited it, the battlefield would be transformed into a sea of fire. From the commencement of the operation this possibility had greatly worried General Yamashita, who, during his visit to Germany, had been told of such an occurrence by a German general. Staff officers repeatedly experimented with

drums of oil thrown into the water of a small pond behind our lines, and on the smooth water it certainly appeared possible the surface of the water could be set afire. On the Johore Strait, however, with the rise and fall of tide and the strong current, it would not be easy to cover the whole surface with oil, so we did not consider seriously how to cope with the situation; nevertheless, to lessen the possibility of the enemy's attempting to set the waters of the strait afire, the oil tanks were immediately attacked and destroyed by heavy artillery bombardment. The whole island was hidden in black smoke, which hampered us to a great extent, for it prevented observation of the fall of our shells either from the ground or from the air.

One problem was to protect our main forces crossing the strait from attack by enemy gunboats. This duty was given to the right wing of the 18th Division. One section of artillery was

Above: In an attempt to stem the tide of the Japanese advance in Malaya Indian troops move into action; local villagers look on with little interest.

Left: Japanese infantry negotiate a river crossing. Bicycles, each able to transport a man and his equipment, allowed the Japanese to move with great speed during the runaway advance on Singapore.

located in concealed positions at the water's
edge, and laid its guns to fire low across the surface so that they could secure direct hits on any
small craft crossing their line of fire; and large
rafts were built with which to block the
entrance to the strait and obstruct any vessels
attempting to enter it. All preparations were
completed in about a week. The hardships experienced by officers and men during this preparatory period were not less than those of the
battlefield.

Army orders demanded that all preparations
should be complete by noon of 7 February, but
except for the artillery no reports that preparations had been completed had been received
by that time. In reply to urgent telephone calls
the divisions answered, 'We will finish without
fail by the evening of the 7th.'

The Army Commander, however, after
mature consideration, decided to postpone the
attack for one day. No division, of course, made
any comment on this decision, but there is little
doubt they were all very pleased at the extra
time given them. The postponement was
typical of General Yamashita's consideration
for those under his orders, which marked him
as a commander of outstanding qualities.

All preparations having been completed and
reconnaissance reports synthesized without
necessitating any alteration whatever in the
Army plan, everything was now ready for the
attack. The commander of the Konoe Imperial
Guards Division, who had been directed to
carry out a demonstration on X – 1 day and to
cross Johore Strait in the rear of the 5th Division on X + 1 day and evening, was, however,
not satisfied. He wanted his division in the
attack, and suggested to the Army Commander
the desirability of amending one section of
Army orders, which were on the point of being
issued, to enable him to do so.

General Yamashita revised his orders accordingly, and this matter later gave rise to serious
problems.

A Demonstration to Mislead the Enemy

The Konoe Division had been ordered to contain the exhausted enemy at the eastern end of
Singapore Island by a strong demonstration,
and they carried out this task thoroughly, in a
manner befitting the reputation of the division.
The divisional staff planned that on X – 1 day
and night (7 February) a section of the division
would attack and occupy Ubin Island, an important strategic point 200 or 300 metres high
closely overlooking Changi Fortress and Seletar
Naval Base. The whole island is virtually a
rocky mountain, and originally produced baux-
ite. Since 1940 the British had been making
strenuous efforts to complete its fortifications
and the island had been a prohibited area to all
except those working there. Owing to the deep

mud surrounding it, landing on its shores could
be expected to be difficult.

The Konoe Division staff officers were confident of the ability of their troops to capture the
island, but for the attack they required twenty
collapsible motor launches, all of which had
been allocated for the main attack on Singapore
Island.

Although the whole Army admired the
Konoe Imperial Guards for the manner in
which they had carried out the duties assigned
them, they had a reputation for occasionally
taking pride in defying Army orders.

Early in the evening of 7 February I drove to
the Division Headquarters, then to the headquarters of the crossing detachment. They took
twenty collapsible launches, and silently carried them on their shoulders through the jungle
to the water, where they set them and started
the engines – praying their high-pitched noise
would not be heard by the enemy. Each boat

Above: A light howitzer, a
weapon that could be
carried by a handful of
men, blazes away at a
British target. Plunging
fire was particularly useful
in the rugged terrain of
Malaya.

Below: Japanese troops
abandon their bicycles to
attack a British position
on the outskirts of the
town of Alor Star, 12
December 1941.

carried eight men and all crossed three times to Ubin Island, taking over in all about four hundred officers and men. At the time my feelings about these men was that if they drew upon themselves a heavy enemy attack it would considerably assist the main landings on Singapore Island. A few shells came over and a red signal flare was fired, but the resistance was unexpectedly light and Ubin Island was successfully occupied without any enemy reaction as time passed. During the evening two mountain guns were landed on the island.

From the morning of 8 February all thirty-six field guns of the Konoe Division, twelve infantry guns, and four heavy guns concentrated heavy fire on Changi Fortress. They fired from an extended front. In general it is the practice to put a battery (four guns) fairly close together for purposes of command, but on this occasion our guns were scattered in ones and twos through the rubber jungle where they could not be observed by the enemy, who would probably be hoodwinked into believing that each gun position was a separate battery.

Effective air reconnaissance by the enemy of our positions in the rubber jungle was practically an impossibility. They could judge our gun positions only by the reports of the firing.

The enemy appeared surprised at our bombardment and reacted strongly with artillery several times our strength. About noon the enemy fire became intense, but it did extraordinary little damage except to the innocent rubber-trees, the trunks of which were torn to shreds and the branches thrown in all directions. In this war were they to be regarded as something without blood and life?

Notwithstanding the very heavy bombardment poured on the jungle there were no casualties among the officers and men of the Konoe Division deployed there. At four o'clock in the afternoon I made my way back to the Imperial Palace with the welcome news of the successful

beginning of the battle for the occupation of Singapore.

On the evening of X day (8 February), the 5th and 18th divisions assembled on the secret jungle roads which had been prepared and the units advanced to the water's edge, where they immediately commenced preparations for crossing the strait. Right up to the last this movement was concealed in the deep jungle of the rubber forest.

At the appointed time our artillery opened fire. The guns were spread over the elevated ground around Johore Bahru. The pivot of the battle for Singapore was the Causeway across the Johore Strait, which runs on through the heart of Singapore Island. As our guns had occupied positions which were almost perfectly concealed, from which they could shell both sides of the Causeway, they could not have been better placed for the battle.

After our shells had set fire to the oil-tanks, black smoke covered Singapore Island and prevented observation of the fall of our shells, and our gunners therefore for the greater part of the time had to fire by the map, basing their aim on the accurate topographic surveys made during the preparatory period.

It was difficult to understand why the palace was not destroyed by shellfire, but it appeared as if the British were reluctant to destroy such a magnificent building. Strangely enough, throughout the bombardment the pivotal assembly points of the 5th and 18th divisions remained quiet with apparently only a very few guns firing in their direction.

Mr Churchill's memoirs state that on the morning of 8 February, a patrol boat reported that the Japanese Army was concentrating in the rubber jungle to the northwest of Singapore Island and apparently intending to attack there. Of course it cannot be assumed that an accurate idea of military strength can be obtained from the sea looking through thick jungle. Occasion-

Below: Covered by their fellows, three infantrymen make a cautious advance through a rubber plantation on the road to Singapore.

ally however enemy fighter planes flew over very low above the rubber-trees and one of them was shot down. Some of these planes however may have observed our larger troop concentrations.

In view of the general situation our main forces were deployed on the front east of the Causeway – that is to say, on the front of the Imperial Guards Division.

The disposition of Lieutenant-General Percival's forces was eloquent testimony of the importance he placed on this sector, which he defended with the full strength of his 3rd Army Corps (9th, 11th and 18th divisions). The sector west of the Causeway was defended by troops of the 8th Australian Division.

It seems in fact that our plans worked better than we had thought they would. The demonstration by the Konoe Division in their capture of Ubin Island obtained better results than we expected in attracting the enemy's attention to the eastern sector, and in this respect the distinguished service of the Konoe Division must be acknowledged.

The Blue Signal Flares

After concealment in the jungle for about a week, the 5th and 18th divisions, without even paying their respects to the sun, began to move on the evening of 8 February. While they had been assembling in the jungle fifty small motor boats and a hundred collapsible launches had been prepared for each division. These were now given their final inspection and were then carried on the shoulders of the troops for several kilometres along the jungle roads to the

water's edge – a task which was by no means easy under the circumstances.

When our infantry and engineers arrived at their selected positions at the water's edge at 11 o'clock at night the whole of our artillery opened fire on the enemy pillboxes, trenches, and wire entanglements defending the Singapore side of the strait. Our barrage covered the whole shore of the strait in order to make it difficult for the enemy to judge the points at which our main attack would be launched. This was the first time the enemy had experienced the full power of our artillery. Four hundred and forty guns were in action and the field guns fired two hundred rounds per gun during the night and the heavy guns one hundred rounds, and every gun was right on its target. Wire entanglements were everywhere cut, pillboxes destroyed and trenches blown in; machine guns at the water's edge were almost completely silenced.

The troops of both divisions who were in the first wave of the attack, roughly four thousand men, went aboard three hundred boats at 12 midnight on 8 February as arranged. The sound of the boats' engines was drowned by the noise of our bombardment. As our boats touched the opposite shore our star shells shed a faint light over the scene. Silently the men jumped out of the boats, sinking up to their loins in the mud of the shore; but they forced their way through the mud, mangrove roots, and broken wire entanglements protecting the enemy position, and rushed their trenches and pillboxes. Our bombardment had forced the enemy troops to keep down in their trenches and shelters, and it enabled our men to get among them before they

Left: A triumphant column of Japanese infantry marches by the remains of a brace of British Bren-gun carriers. The devastation of the surrounding houses testifies to the forcefulness of the attack on Singapore.

had recovered from the effects of the shellfire.

In the Army Command Post at the Imperial Palace there was an atmosphere of tension, but nobody was doubtful of victory. Everything which the staff had to do had been done to the limit of human ability, and there was nothing more to do now except await the result. The issue, victory or defeat, would soon be decided.

From the glass door of the palace tower, as one looked down on Johore Strait and at the blaze of fire on both sides, one gained but little idea of the progress of the battle. There was no difference in the sound of our own shells and the enemy's. The boom of artillery, the crash of explosives, the flashes of guns and the red lotus flames of fires enveloped the whole of Singapore Island.

At ten minutes past midnight on the morning of the 9 February first of all on the 5th Division front, and shortly after on that of the 18th Division, blue flares were fired high in the sky, signifying that the landing had been accomplished as planned. At the Army Command Post not one man, Army Commander or staff officers, could speak. The moonlight shone dimly on tears flowing down all our cheeks. The second

line of a unit crossing the strait about half an hour after midnight arrived on the enemy shore and ran into heavy machine-gun fire, which we could hear from the Command Post together with the din of the battle as our infantry gradually extended over the whole front.

Throughout the operations in Malaya the Yokoyama Regiment of Engineers, which served continuously with the 5th Division, had given distinguished service unsurpassed in the whole Army. They had fought with the infantry and repaired roads and bridges at unprecedented speed. At the crossing of Johore Strait they upheld their splendid record. For their attack on Singapore they handled approximately one hundred collapsible motor launches in which they crossed Johore Strait under heavy enemy fire carrying infantry to the assault again and again – three, four times – continuing throughout the night under the increasing enemy barrage.

One of the boat commanders, Troop Leader Lance-Corporal Yamamoto, standing at the bow of a raft made of three launches lashed together, was continually drenched with spray thrown up by enemy shells hitting the water around the

Above: A bridge destroyed by the retreating British proves little obstacle to the advancing Japanese; a makeshift crossing of planks allows troops to reach the opposite bank.

boats. While fully loaded with men of the second line of assault troops, a shell burst on the gunwale of one of the launches composing the raft, killed the two other coxswains and severely damaged their boats. Yamamoto was the only man left capable of handling the launches, which had fifty men aboard. He landed them on the enemy shore and then collapsed like a falling tree. When the squad commander of the troops lifted him in his arms he saw his lungs protruding through his ribs. Yamamoto had said nothing about his wound until he landed the troops in his charge, and while the squad commander still held him in his arms he said, 'Long live the Emperor! I am indebted to you for your kind assistance. Excuse me for going a step ahead of you.' And so saying he breathed his last.

When both Yamamoto's neighbouring coxswains were killed the fifty men in the launches felt they would be unable to land without their coxswains and that therefore they too must die, but Yamamoto's miraculous endurance despite his wound enabled them all to land safely. In consequence of his bravery the Yokayama Engineer Regiment was awarded a letter of commendation as a unit and Troop Leader Lance-Corporal Yamamoto was posthumously awarded an individual letter of commendation; a proclamation was issued to the whole Army announcing that he had been promoted.

The achievements of the 18th Division were in no way inferior to those of the 5th. The section of artillery which had been placed to fire across the surface of the water was quicky in action, and sank one enemy gunboat which attempted to interfere with the passage of our troops across the strait.

The first crossing, at the same time as that of the 5th Division, was successful, but the men in the second line had to fight from the moment they landed on the enemy shore, and the enemy resisted stubbornly all night.

The Koike Engineer Regiment was responsible for transporting the troops of the 18th Division across the strait. In the soundness of their preparations and in their fighting capacity they were quite the equal of the Yokoyama Regiment. During the week of preparation prior to the crossing they had reconnoitred in the jungle at the water's edge in order to observe closely the British positions on the island side. In particular they had located their machine-gun posts on the flank of our attack, and made important and valuable observations on the tides and the state of the enemy shore which were of great assistance when it came to landing our assault forces.

Sergeant Hisamitsu Fukui was leader of the squad who carried out this work, and when the movement across the strait began he commanded the boats carrying the first group of troops and landed them at a weak spot in the enemy position which he had discovered on his previous reconnaissance.

Having crossed the strait twice and successfully landed all the troops he carried, Sergeant Fukui was severely wounded by machine-gun fire, but nevertheless continued to stand bravely at the bow of his boat, and waving the control flag brought his flotilla back to the Johore side, on reaching which he collapsed and died. For his distinguished service Sergeant Hisamitsu Fukui also received an individual posthumous letter of commendation.

By dawn on 9 February, as the sun began to peep from behind the black smoke, the whole of the infantry of both divisions – the 5th and the 18th – and part of the artillery had already landed on the enemy shore. From the high ground of the Imperial Palace the troops could be seen threading their way through the low rubber-trees, sweeping away the remnants of the enemy and attacking Tengah aerodrome. Although enemy planes had been flying the previous evening there were none to be seen on this

morning. As enemy positions were seized the Rising Sun flag was hoisted over them and our artillery was asked to lengthen its range. Black smoke rose high and thick from the burning oil-storage tanks, but in some places it hung in low clouds. Here and there in the front line of our infantry enemy armoured cars were on fire.

At sunset on the 9th, after the Konoe Imperial Guards Division reported having forced a passage across the strait on their sector, the Army Commander and most of his staff officers, on a raft made of three boats lashed together, crossed the strait in the 5th Division sector. The enemy artillery, behaving as if it was trying to block the passage after our troops had crossed, continued to shell the channel heavily. But before dawn the shelling of the strait had subsided, and the peace and beauty of the moon on the water was in extraordinary contrast to the tumult of the shellfire and the gruesome casualties of a few hours earlier.

Watching the Konoe Division crossing near the Kranji River one saw the water glowing redly; it was as bright as day. Immediately the question arose: Had the enemy flooded the strait with petroleum and set fire to it? For an answer we had to wait for news from the Konoe Division.

As General Yamashita climbed the low cliff on the enemy side of the strait, a group of European prisoners of war watched him curiously. They were our first living sign of our success in the battle. At last we had set foot on a corner of Singapore.

The Only Mistake

It was dawn on the 10th. The Army Command Post on Singapore Island had been established, and connected by telephone and submarine cable with the Imperial Palace on Bukit Serene. The main strength of the Army staff was still on the Johore side of the strait directing the cross-

ing of the tanks, heavy guns, and ammunition to Singapore Island. All reports indicated that on all fronts the forcing of the strait has proceeded without a hitch. The front lines of the 5th and 18th Divisions had already taken possession of Tengah aerodrome, and were now consolidating on the western side and preparing for an attack on fortified positions on the heights of Bukit Timah.

In a tent in the rubber forest on the north side of Tengah aerodrome, the Army Commander, General Yamashita, was eating a breakfast of dry bread when suddenly Staff Officer Kera rushed in, steam rising from his bald head. Usually a jovial, smiling man, this officer now agitatedly reported that halfway through the previous evening the Konoe Division commander, looking pale and angry, had come to Army Headquarters at the Imperial Palace with his chief of staff and shouted, 'The Konoe Divi-

Above: Japanese bicycle troops head through the suburbs of Johore Bahru in January 1942. The city was evacuated by the British on the 31st.

Below: Japanese infantry charge down one of Johore Bahru's main thoroughfares in pursuit of the retreating British. Singapore island became the Twenty-fifth Army's next objective in the lightning campaign.

sion, just as they commenced to cross the strait near the Causeway, became caught in petroleum to which the enemy set fire. The front-line regiment was enveloped in fire while on the water and was almost annihilated. The leader of the Kobayashi Infantry Regiment was seen swimming in a sea of fire and his fate is unknown. This disaster is Army's responsibility! Reckless forcing of a passage without adequate preparation caused unnecessary casualties. For what reason have the Konoe Division been allowed to make such a crossing? Such an occurrence is most surprising and regrettable.'

Originally, Army orders for the assault on Singapore grouped the Konoe Division as the second line, but the commander of that division emphatically demanded a modification of the orders because of his fervent desire to attack shoulder to shoulder with the other two divisions, and the Army Commander acceded to his request.

Rightly or wrongly, all action by Army is the responsibility of Army HQ. But the responsibility for such changes must rest upon those demanding them.

General Yamashita, who was not easily perturbed, inquired about the annihilation of the regiment, and his face changed colour.

Presently a Konoe Division staff officer dejectedly put in an appearance. Turning and facing him I asked, 'When one regiment was annihilated by the enemy's flooding the water with burning petroleum, how did it become known?' The staff officer replied, 'One of the engineers who made the crossing with the Kobayashi Regiment survived and returned to report.'

'You great fool!' I thundered out in my rage. 'When your front line crossed the strait was there not even one staff officer with them? One man from the engineers brings back a report without verification and you swallow it whole and become frenzied. Return to your troops, have another look at the battle, and come back and report the facts. Remember your division asked for Army orders to be amended. Can't you carry them out when they are altered in the way that you requested?'

Did not this episode show the true nature of the Konoe Division, which boasted of its long tradition? When asked how the division was to be used subsequently in the battle I coldly replied, 'There is no reason for any further change in Army orders. We can take Singapore with the 5th and 18th divisions.' Then General Yamashita remarked in a very loud voice to the Konoe Division staff officer, 'Return at once to your divisional commander and tell him the Konoe Division can do as it pleases in this battle.' The weak-willed Konoe divisional commander who had demanded a change of Army orders so that he might thrust his division into the first line of the attack could scarcely have

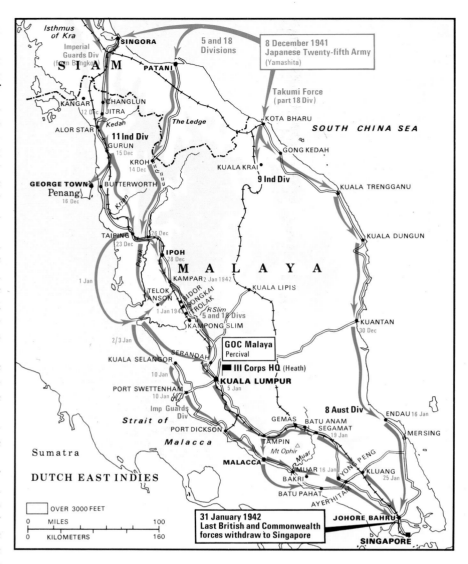

dreamed he would receive such scathing criticism in the middle of a decisive battle.

During the afternoon of that day there came a telephone call from Headquarters at the Imperial Palace: 'The Konoe Division's report this morning was a mistake. At the time we verified the situation, the division's front line, after trifling losses, was in the midst of an attack on the enemy's position on the southern side of the Causeway. The division commander reports to the Army Commander that he will this evening carry out a further advance on the Causeway sector.'

Above: The Japanese conquest of Malaya, showing the rapid advance on Singapore, the supposedly impregnable 'Gibraltar of the East.'

Below: Japanese tankettes and supporting infantry wait for orders to cross the causeway leading from Johore Bahru to Singapore.

Slaughter on Bukit Timah

Bukit Timah is a strategic point in Singapore Island situated about seven and a half English miles northwest of the city with an altitude of 177 metres. It is the highest point in the island. Its name is composed of two Malay words – *Bukit*, mountain, *Timah*, tin – and its meaning is therefore 'Tin Mountain'. At its base there were roughly three hundred dwellings, and also rubber factories, racecourses, golf clubs, and so on, together with large army storage warehouses established by the British. On its northeastern slope was situated a reservoir, the source of water supply for Singapore's one million citizens. According to our intelligence reports this strategic point appeared to be strongly fortified with concrete positions.

Considering the situation seriously it appeared we would have to wait for the advance of our heavy guns before we could take this position by storm. It was, however, of the utmost importance that no opportunity for reorganization be given the enemy, and the idea of capturing the heights of Bukit Timah in the initial attack on the fortress had been constantly in our minds; in view of the manner in which the battle had developed it was decided to make an immediate assault.

We were disgusted with the unseemly behaviour of the Konoe Division, so now, without even making a rough estimate of the position, we decided to capture the heights with the 5th and 18th divisions only.

Observing the progress in the battle of both divisions we advanced on foot to the south. The small number of enemy aeroplanes which had failed to escape had been abandoned by their owners, and they looked lonely standing on the runway of Tengah aerodrome.

I entered the British barracks. Fresh bread and soup were still on the dining tables and clothing and suitcases belonging to the troops were lying around. 'Good heavens!' I thought. 'There is no doubt they were considerably agitated when they escaped.' From this we knew that our successful forcing of the strait by our whole Army had not been expected by the enemy and had come as a complete surprise to them.

Astonished by the state of affairs revealed by our inspection of the barracks, we came to our senses, however, and realized we still had to capture Bukit Timah heights and the reservoir. We instinctively felt now that to launch an immediate attack might be stupid and that it would be wiser to wait for the arrival of our heavy artillery batteries.

Suddenly a violent rain squall swept over the battlefield, soaking us with rain and washing us clean of sweat. Happily, together with soldiers of the 18th Division, we hurried through the rubber jungle to the front line. After a while we noticed one another's faces. We all looked like

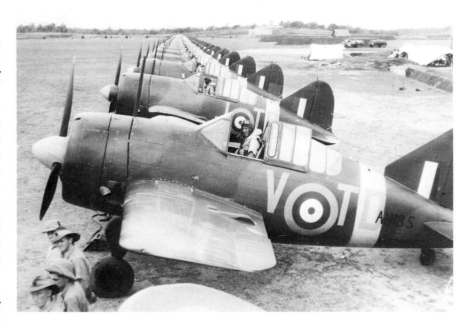

Negroes. 'I say, look at your faces, they are black as ink,' called the troops. 'Yours too, Mr Staff Officer. Ha, ha, ha!' laughed the soldiers. None of us had noticed the blackening of our faces. Soot from the burning oil-tanks had been falling on the leaves of the rubber-trees for several days, and the heavy rain washed it off on to the troops as they passed beneath, turning their skins and their uniforms as jet black as an Army service coat. Queer as we were in colour we continued to grope our way to the 18th Division while trying to shelter from the rain in the rubber-trees.

The divisional commander, his Chief of Staff, and Staff Officer Hashimoto were listening silently to the reports of the guns. They greeted us with: 'Congratulations! Many thanks for your trouble.' Looking closely at Lieutenant-General Mutaguchi I saw bloodstains on the left shoulder of his coat surrounding a small hole where evidently a bullet had penetrated. 'Ah, sir, you are wounded,' I said. 'Be silent,' he replied. 'The truth is that while our boats were crossing the Johore Strait the third time I was hit by one of the enemy machine-guns which still remained in action. While we suffered no damage during the first landing, during the second and third landings the enemy kept on firing even as they were retreating.'

Staff Officer Hashimoto, who was close by, supplemented his divisional commander's story. 'During the first landing,' he said, 'it appears that our bombardment kept the enemy troops well down in the bottom of their trenches, but during the second and third landings, manning their parapets they resisted splendidly. At Headquarters they broke through and attacked a pillbox we had occupied, and Staff Officer Ino lost both legs in a hand-grenade explosion. Wasn't he unlucky? The divisional commander was wounded and another staff officer received a bomb wound. It was a desperate fight while it lasted . . . The

Above: Buffalo fighters of the RAF's No 453 Squadron lined up for inspection on Sembawang airfield. Slow and lacking maneuverability, the Buffalo proved to be no match for the Japanese Zeros.

divisional commander says what about the Army plan? We're still under shellfire and our artillery has not yet crossed the strait. We're in a quandary, I tell you!'

The divisional commander's expression was full of anxiety, and I understood the difficult position quite well, but when one remembered the obvious confusion of the enemy at Tengah aerodrome it gave one confidence that our sudden surprise attack had been perfectly carried out.

The Army Commander wished to attack Bukit Heights almost immediately, before the enemy came to life again and reorganized. As there were no guns to support the attack it would have to be made that night with the bayonet. The only comment by the 18th Division commander and his staff officers was, 'If the Army Commander thinks it should be done we will make a full-strength surprise attack tonight with our divisional commander in the lead. The attack should be made this evening before the enemy has had time to rally.' It was a comment that expressed the high morale of the division.

Going to the 5th Division we asked for their opinion. After Lieutenant-General Matsui had been told the views of the Army Comander and of Lieutenant-General Mutaguchi he replied, 'If Mutaguchi can do it, so can I. My division will make the attack without artillery support.'

Both divisions thus agreed to make the night attack. As the results proved, the decision was thoroughly sound. The attack was perfectly successful. When I left Army Headquarters I was ordered by General Yamashita to conduct each division's action in accordance with its conditions.

At that time I had no data on which to decide whether we should make a night attack, or re-

Left: Lieutenant-General Arthur Percival (1887-1966) served in France before being posted to the Far East to take charge of the British forces in Malaya. After the fall of Singapore he was interned in Manchuria but was released in time to see the formal surrender of the Japanese on the USS *Missouri* in 1945.

sume the attack after our heavy guns had crossed the strait. Whether because of the Konoe Division's feint attack, or for other reasons, the enemy's main forces still faced the Konoe Division on the Seletar Harbour-Changi Fortress sector, and the 8th Australian Division was defending on a broad front. The key Bukit Timah position was almost vacant. In the barracks of Tengah aerodrome I got the idea of surprising this vacant nest.

The plan provided for the 5th Division to attack with their full strength on the north side of the Chua Chu Kang road and the 18th Divi-

Below: The calm before the storm – Australian troops line up to receive their midday rations. Many of these men were destined to become prisoners of the Japanese.

sion with their full strength on the south side of the road with the crest of Bukit Timah heights as the objective. The advance commenced at dark and throughout the night of 10th-11th the battle zone was in an extreme of tumult.

Army Headquarters, from which orders were issued to both divisions for the night attack, consisting of about forty persons including the Army Commander, moved to a position in a fortified enemy anti-aircraft-gun position at the edge of the jungle to the south of Tengah aerodrome.

Apparently the enemy had hastily constructed the position at the outbreak of hostilities. It consisted of a single barrack building around which was a trench surrounded by barbed-wire entanglements. It was a key position discharging two functions simultaneously, protecting the aerodrome against both ground and air attack.

On the evening of 10 February, and throughout the night, enemy gunfire raged at its most extreme intensity over the whole island. We believed that Ulu Pandan Fortress was being defended with roughly one brigade, but the 18th Division bypassed the enemy there and pressed forward in its attack on Bukit Timah heights, which the 5th Division, having moved slightly to one side, were assaulting from the direction of the Causeway.

At midnight, while I was half dozing and half listening to the artillery fire, my reverie was suddenly destroyed by indications of a strong force crawling around the perimeter of Headquarters. We knew there were remnants of the enemy still straggling in each sector, but we had not one reserve soldier at Headquarters. The Army Commander had insisted that every available man was required by the divisions engaged in the assault.

Suddenly there was a violent explosion and the barrack building shook. The smashing of windows set up a frightful din. It appeared that a number of enemy troops making an outflanking movement had fired a trench mortar into our Headquarters. As I have said, the Headquarters staff, including the Army Commander, numbered no more than forty men. A certain senior staff officer said, 'I say, can't you get some reserves quickly? Even one company from both divisions.' Silently, and not appearing to listen, I pretended to snore. Shaking my bed he said a second time, 'I say, do something quickly. We will be all right with one company.' Of necessity I then got up, but I rejected his proposal out of hand, telling him that both divisional commanders were leading their men in the night attack, and were too busy to be bothered with such a request. Again this staff officer asked, 'Can't we get some troops from one of the divisions? Isn't it unreasonable and rash to risk damage to Headquarters? Do you want to get us all killed?'

I replied, 'We are behind trenches and wire entanglements and have twenty sentries on guard. They are enough. I don't mind if the enemy do retreat past us.' Shortly afterwards we heard the senior adjutant giving orders to the sentries.

Since the beginning of the assault, Headquarters had been enveloped in an atmosphere of tension, aggravated by the possibility of enemy trench mortars dropping bombs on the barrack building. I exchanged glances with Staff Officer Asaeda and we both broke into a smile; in a calm state of mind we waited for the confusion to die down.

With the approach of dawn of the 11th the threat to Headquarters passed away. To begin with, a reassuring message, 'Have seized Bukit Timah', arrived from the 18th Division, and there was soon a similar report from the 5th Division; both reports were brought by dispatch officers on foot. The morning sun rose peacefully over the island battlefield on Kigensetsu, the anniversary of the coronation of the Emperor Jimmu.

Welcoming the Kigen Festival

As I have previously stated, the capture of Bukit Timah heights was prearranged to the day. So also was the period which we had determined for the surrender of the enemy general. Up to Kigensetsu we had dreamed of the surrender of Singapore, and now the dream promised to become reality. Pinned down by the throat the enemy would perhaps accept our advice to surrender, but we did not know. With such a hopeful observation, our note advising capitulation, drafted by Staff Officer Sugita, was dropped from the air behind the enemy lines. It read as follows:

Below: Members of the Singapore Volunteer Corps prepare to defend the island; their enthusiasm could not compensate for a lack of training and out-moded equipment.

The Japanese Commander to the British Commander.

In a spirit of chivalry we have the honour of advising your surrender. Your Army, founded on the traditional spirit of Great Britain, is defending Singapore, which is completely isolated, and raising the fame of Great Britain by the utmost exertions and heroic fighting. I disclose my respect from my inmost feelings. Nevertheless the war situation is already determined and in the meantime the surrender of Singapore is imminent. From now on resistance is futile and merely increases the danger to the million civilian inhabitants without good reason, exposing them to infliction of pain by fire and sword. Furthermore we do not feel you will increase the fame of the British Army by further resistance. From first to last our counsel is that Your Excellency will cease to think of meaningless resistance, and from now on, yielding to our advice, promptly and immediately will suspend the action extending over the whole British battlefront. It is expected that you will take measures to dispatch an Army messenger as stated below. If on the contrary you continue resistance as previously, it will be difficult to bear with patience from a humanitarian point of view, and inevitably we must continue an intense attack against Singapore. Ending this advice we show respect towards Your Excellency.

1. The Army messenger's route of advance shall be by the Bukit Timah road.
2. The Army messenger, hoisting a white flag as well as the British flag, will be escorted by a number of soldiers as a protection.

(Signed) Japan's Army Commander,
Lieutenant-General Tomoyuki Yamashita.

Enemy anti-aircraft guns greeted our aeroplanes with a fierce barrage. Managing to avoid the fire a reconnaissance plane, clearly showing the Japanese markings, dropped a signalling communication tube containing the surrender advice on the outskirts of Singapore city. The long streamers of red and white fluttered in the wind as the tube descended. A signal was then sent to Imperial General Headquarters and General Headquarters by Army Headquarters. 'The Japanese Army, having stormed and captured Bukit Timah heights, has advised the surrender of Singapore city upon which we look down.'

After passing the night within sound of the enemy guns, which prevented sleep, the next morning, accompanied by an orderly, I examined the progress of the battle in the Bukit Timah sector. We hurried along the main road in a small enemy car which had been captured. When we reached the southeast extremity of Tengah aerodrome, we found that bombs or heavy-calibre shells were blowing large holes in the roadway. As the firing was intense our engineers had not yet commenced repairs. Abandoning the car the orderly and I continued on foot. Just at that moment there was a shellburst which shocked our eardrums, while the blast jarred our spines. The flash seared my eyes, and I was thrown into the roadside ditch. In my agitation I thrust myself into an earthenware drainage pipe. The heavy shelling continued – one discharge – two discharges. Up to this moment I had had no experience of such heavy projectiles, which tore holes in the ground 15 or 16 metres in diameter and four or five metres deep. They were probably 15- or 16-inch fortress guns which had been swung round 180 degrees to fire over the ground instead of over the water out to sea, and they were apparently attempting a demolition bombardment of Tengah aerodrome and the main road in the area.

Crouching like a crab inside the earthen pipe I imagined what would happen if a shell fell on me. It did not appear as if anything of myself would be left. I had landed on the island with the intention of dying, but unconsciously I drew myself further into the pipe. The shells were frightful. However, after getting to know the firing interval of the heavy guns, I raised my body, which was covered with mud and dust, and unseen by anyone began to crawl out of the pipe.

After the debris of one explosion had fallen there was an interval of several minutes until the next shell landed. I escaped the first – the second – but still felt no guarantee of security; but at last I scrambled out of the danger zone. I rose to my feet, at the same time clearing away spiders' webs from my head. 'It was fine, nobody was looking,' I said to myself, and felt ashamed.

We arrived at a three-forked road. It being almost immediately after the assault our own and enemy wounded were lying where they had fallen, mingled with each other, unattended to and groaning. Enemy motor cars and trucks which had been destroyed blocked the road in all directions and it was difficult to pass easily through them.

Reaching General Matsui's Headquarters in an enemy air-raid shelter I congratulated him,

Below: Scenes of devastation in central Singapore following a Japanese bombing raid. Firefighters attempt to control the spread of the blaze.

and together we rushed up hurriedly to the crest of Bukit Timah heights. The soldiers of the 18th and 5th divisions were mixed together, as reorganization had not yet commenced. From the atmosphere of the battlefield it did not appear as if the enemy were likely to surrender immediately. I peeped out over the front from our advanced line. The villages of Bukit Timah were being completely wiped out by shellfire; a soldier showed his face from inside a drainpipe where he was chewing a piece of dry bread. Recalling my own position but a short time ago I smiled wryly.

As noon approached the enemy bombardment increased and a large force of enemy soldiers surged up the heights like a tidal wave under cover of the barrage. They were supported by armoured cars. It appeared as if the British were staking everything on a counter-attack. 'This is gallantry, is it not?' I said to myself, and involuntarily I was lost in admiration for them.

According to our bearings it was believed the 18th Division was separated from the 5th Division by a deep valley. A hand-to-hand struggle could be seen proceeding on the 18th Division front. I said to myself, 'We cannot keep on in this way. Before long we will have to move out of Army Headquarters. We must get the heavy

guns and tanks across the strait to support our troops.'

Hurriedly I returned to Headquarters.

Owing to the clumsy work of the Konoe Division the Causeway had not yet been re-opened to traffic, and the Engineer Regiment was now ordered to set every available man to work to complete repairs notwithstanding enemy action. While waiting for the work to be completed, all the boats were assembled and some tanks, ammunition, and artillery were ferried across the strait during the day, but it

Above: A plume of thick smoke rises from a timber yard in Singapore's dock area. The Japanese raids threatened to destroy the British ability to resist a sustained ground attack.

Below: A British anti-aircraft gun blasts away at a Japanese bomber formation on its way to attack the island's main port facilities.

was not until evening that Army Headquarters moved up the mountain halfway between Tengah aerodrome and Bukit Timah heights. There they were directly behind the front-line troops where the observation was good and they were well protected. We had to be prepared for heavy shelling by the enemy as soon as their presence became known.

From the divisional staff officers in charge of operations we obtained by telephone frequent and detailed reports of the progress of both divisions in the battle. The 5th and 18th divisions, competing with each other for supremacy, appeared somewhat exhausted after the day's fighting. The Konoe Division was now the only chessman we still had to play. When told, 'The Konoe Division can do as it pleases', they kept good countenance, and the whole division had passed the evening of 10 February with the enemy still on the heights of Mandai in front of them. The Konoe Division had scarcely appeared to be moving. They were now ordered to advance without a moment's loss of time on the eastern side of the reservoir and strike at the enemy's flank in the midst of their counter-attack on Bukit Timah. This was the key to the solution of the difficult strategical position of the other two divisions.

The assistant commandant staff officer at Army Headquarters jumped into a car and personally attempted to hasten the movement of the Konoe Division, but without effect. The Army Chief of Staff repeatedly visited them, but I regret to say the petulant Konoe Division Headquarters showed no disposition to help the other divisions in their emergency. Those divisions, however, maintained the battle and grasped the opportunity to further greatly distinguish themselves despite their difficulties, while the Konoe Division, who had been told to do as they pleased, were having to be coaxed and cajoled like cross children. Unable to do anything about it our affable Chief of Staff and

the strategic specialist assistant commandant appeared angry and embarrassed, and we spent the evening of Kigensetsu, on the anniversary of which we wished to secure the surrender of Singapore, in an uncomfortable atmosphere. I accompanied these two officers on another visit to Konoe Division Headquarters. On arrival there I said to Staff Officer Asaeda, 'Hello, Asaeda! Will you please bring me the seniority list?' 'What?' said he. 'The seniority list?' He was a quick-witted man, but on this occasion appeared completely taken aback. 'Oh, it's a trivial matter,' I said. 'Matsui, Mutaguchi, and Nishimura, our three lieutenant-generals, are Army graduates of the same year; if by any chance someone has to take command of the Army let us investigate the position.' Listening by my side our Army Chief of Staff and the assistant commandant assumed expressions of profound thoughtfulness.

Above: Japanese infantry advance under cover of smoke billowing from a burning oil refinery.

Below: Two British infantrymen watch the distant jungle for signs of the Japanese attackers.

During the night enemy heavy shells fell through the roof of the Army operations section and two or three of the signals staff were wounded by fragments of tiles. A certain staff officer, rudely awakened from a nap, agitatedly ran out clasping his pillow in his hands calling, 'Hey! This place is getting too dangerous. How about moving Headquarters a little to the rear for safety's sake?' 'By heavens no!' I replied. 'If we have to die, let us die together in the front line. We'll never get another such opportunity.'

Throughout the fighting there was a youth at Headquarters who all the time went calmly on with his work. His name was Morita, and he was eighteen years old. He was an excellent and pleasant-mannered mess steward. He boiled water under the eaves and did his other jobs, looking out in the intervals between shells; without any chance of glory or promotion he went on with his work, a genuinely unspoiled youth. It seems to me that as human beings grow older they hold life more precious, and avarice emerges in conformity with class advancement. Even though one's remaining days are short there is always a lingering desire for the insignificant life that remains.

The 5th Division attack on the reservoir sector at dawn on 12 February was driven home by sheer weight of numbers and the cooperation of the flight groups. The enemy had ceased to think of Bukit Timah heights, and it was natural that they should defend desperately the heights around the circumference of the reservoir – their last lifeline. All their serviceable guns were concentrated on the area and they seemed to be using up all the ammunition in their magazines. The fire on the position was of great intensity.

Also co-operating with the 5th Division was the full strength of the Tank Brigade and all our heavy guns as they came across the strait.

Realizing that this was a battle to finish the British Army defending Singapore, we poured all our fighting strength into the battle line. It was a battle in which the fame and honour of both armies – no, more of both countries – were at stake. For five days the life-and-death struggle had continued.

The 18th Division, which had to act in concert with the 5th in this action, moved along the sea coast and drove a strong wedge into the enemy's left wing. The Konoe Division at last began to move, and by a detour from the north of the reservoir penetrated the flank of the enemy's main force. Thus was the general trend of the battle determined.

The flight group heavily attacked an enemy convoy attempting to escape by sea. Together with the Navy it had in the last fifteen days attacked and sunk in the waters around Singapore about eighty large and small British ships. Some of these events are recorded in Mr Churchill's memoirs.

Our Army was now deployed over the whole front and the strategic position seemed to reach a climax when we received a signal from General Headquarters. 'On 15th February an officer attached to the Court of the Emperor will be dispatched to the battlefield. We can postpone the visit if the progress of your Army's operations makes it desirable to do so. We wish to hear your opinion.'

There were some who said, 'Let us welcome him,' and others who argued, 'We must postpone the visit of the Emperor's envoy for a little while'; and so opinions were divided into two camps.

Once previously during the China Incident I had been in a similar position when conducting military operations in Shansi together with the Itagaki group. During a bitterly contested battle for the reduction of Taiyuan Sheng, on 7 November, Shidei, the aide-de-camp to the Emperor, arrived on the battlefield. I immediately began to think of the reduction of the mountain stronghold Yen Hsi Shan.

After a general discussion we unanimously resolved: 'On the 15th day of February the enemy will positively surrender to the power of the august Emperor.' We drafted these words as a telegram of welcome to the Emperor's envoy.

On the evening of 14 February the Konoe Division completed repairs to the Causeway and pushed forward. Our heavy guns moved in rapid succession to positions on the heights to the east of the reservoir. For the first time our whole Army was across Johore Strait and concentrated on Singapore Island.

The True Spirit

On the morning of 15 February I was called to the telephone by Staff Officer Hashimoto, the Officer-in-Charge of Operations of the 18th Division. 'Today,' he said happily, 'the division will attack with its full strength towards

Above: A carefully sited ambush pays dividends – a two-pounder anti-tank gun deals with the leading vehicle of a Japanese armored column.

Keppel Barracks. Will you be good enough to look at our position?' I answered briefly, 'I will start immediately.' I had been out to the 5th Division so often as to have almost become a nuisance, but I had not yet been to the 18th Division.

All my work at Headquarters had been completed. Today without fail we must take Singapore in order to welcome the officer attached to the Emperor's Court. I made preparations to set out, and, accompanied by an orderly, and moving in the intervals between enemy shellfire, drove out towards the coast road by car, intending to call in person at 18th Division Headquarters.

Changing the plan, however, we drove straight through to the front-line headquarters of the Koba Regiment, which overlooked the enemy position, but was also under enemy observation so that the movement of even one Japanese soldier brought down concentrated shellfire on the position.

The regimental commander, with the regimental colours beside him, was crouching for shelter in what I thought was a narrow firing trench, but which I subsequently found out was an octopus trap. He was watching the enemy position and, raising his bald head only, directing his subordinates.

Every time a shell exploded they pulled their heads like snails down into the octopus trap. They were in the midst of preparations for an attack at 2 p.m., which had been ordered by their division. The front-line battalion commander was Major Kojiro Ito, an officer of the same period as myself. The artillery with which he was to co-operate in the attack was a battalion of mountain artillery under command of Lieutenant-Colonel Kusido and eight heavy mortars under command of Lieutenant-Colonel Tanaka. These officers were my seniors by one year. On the right-hand side of the Koba Regiment was the Oku Regiment, in the same stage of preparation for the attack. Both headquarters were about two or three hundred yards from the enemy front line, and under the bombardment we were powerless to do anything.

After roughly a week of fighting since we crossed Johore Strait the ammunition accumulated for the assault on Singapore Island was nearly exhausted. We had barely a hundred rounds per gun left for our field guns, and less for our heavy guns. With this small ammunition supply it was impossible to keep down enemy fire by counter-battery operations.

Our only standby was Colonel Tanaka's 40-centimetre (16-inch) mortars. For mobility these were taken apart and loaded on handcarts, and at night placed in position in the front-line firing trench. Their shells, brought forward by the same means, thoroughly inspected and overhauled, were loaded and fired upon the enemy in Keppel Barracks at the rate of about one round every ten minutes.

The enemy were apparently resting while waiting for our attack. The Ito Battalion decided to launch an attack, and like men rising from their graves the men began to emerge from their trenches. Immediately a large number of British guns directed an intense barrage on the position. It seemed as if everyone on the battlefield would be suffocated by the dust and smoke from the bursting shells.

Takeda, the divisional chief of staff, who had come forward to direct the attack, came reluctantly to the conclusion that it was a sheer impossibility to proceed with it owing to the fact that the troops were exhausted by previous operations and the violent bombardment by the enemy. Arms and legs were flying through the air and heads scattered everywhere. Twisting my body like a crab and hiding my head behind an old tree I wished to myself that I had a steel helmet. A soldier, edging close to me, took off his own and put it on my head. We were complete strangers to each other. 'Mr Staff Officer,' he said, 'it is dangerous to be without a steel helmet. Please wear this one.' I thanked him and returned it to him, but he did not put it on his head again. I was deeply moved by the spirit of self-sacrifice of this soldier with whom I had not even a nodding acquaintance.

The regimental headquarters trench became shallower every time a shell exploded close to it. Frequently we were half buried. At last, carrying the regimental colours, we moved out of the trench and sought shelter behind the brick wall of a wrecked house, to which we clung like geckos. A soldier beside me had his head blown off, and blood was scattered everywhere. Two of his comrades stood up holding a blanket.

Below: A crewman of a Japanese tankette calls for help to extricate his vehicle from deep mud.

'How will this do for a coffin?' asked one. They wrapped the corpse in the blanket and carried it on their shoulders to an abandoned trench about 20 yards in the rear. The regimental adjutant called to them, 'It's too dangerous to bury him now. You'll be wiped out by a shell. Do it later.' Undeterred, the two men carried on with their self-appointed task. Several times they were enveloped in the smoke and dust of bursting shells and we thought they had been killed, but after the smoke of each explosion cleared away they were to be seen still digging. It was an act of madness. Finally they finished digging the grave, laid the corpse in it and filled it in again. Taking two or three pieces of bread from a haversack they laid them on the head of the grave and sprinkled water on it from a water-bottle. Then, taking off their helmets they made a profound bow to the comrade they had just buried, and calmly walked back to the front line.

It had been decided to carry on with the attack and the troops had just commenced to move out of the trenches. There was no time to inquire about the names of the men who had shown such reverence for their dead comrade. In all probability they were soldiers of the Ito Battalion. I was so impressed by their sense of duty to a fallen comrade that I felt as though I had worshipped in the presence of the Revered Gods. The regimental commander who saw the incident was similarly affected.

The furious bombardment eased off about four o'clock in the afternoon and moved away from the Ito Battalion. I started homewards thinking, 'If the enemy resists in this manner he probably contemplates fighting from house to house and it will take more time to capture the fortress. Our artillery ammunition is almost exhausted. We will have to concentrate on a new plan.' Tired and heavy-footed, my orderly and I moved back along the road by which we had come that morning.

Just prior to the assault Major Matoba, who had been attached to the operations section at Army Headquarters, was transferred as battalion commander of the Oku Regiment. During the day's fighting he had been shot through the chest. I met him as he was being carried, blood-stained, on a stretcher to the rear. Putting my mouth to his ear to rouse him I said, 'Hello, Major Matoba! Here is a gift of wine bestowed by the Emperor,' and poured the water from my flask into his mouth. I knew that giving a wounded man a drink was prohibited, but thought the major was near his end and that the water would be a drink in the hour of death. He had been completely unconscious, but he opened his eyes and said faintly, 'The Imperial gift cup,' and with an effort swallowed the last few drops of water in the flask. He did not die, and subsequently made a miraculous recovery.

We left our car concealed under the shade of a tree. Returning to the spot we found that it had been blown up and only a few fragments were left. It was the third car I had had destroyed by shellfire. Proceeding on foot we arrived at 18th Division Headquarters, where I explained the strategic position minutely to the divisional commander, Lieutenant-General Mutaguchi. As I was leaving Staff Officer Hashimoto pulled my sleeve and whispered, 'Just a moment, sir, just a moment!' When out of earshot of the divisional commander he said in a low voice, 'The Old Man says he wants to go up to the front line again and will not listen to us. Will you do something to stop him?'

I said to the general, 'I think at the present time Your Excellency should remain in the background. The shellfire is very heavy and the way to the front line dangerous, and moreover your subordinate commanders in the front line who are doing their utmost will think you have come to the front line to spur them to further effort when really they can do no more. Your presence there will only increase their difficulties. Please wait until night.' And with these words I sought to prevent him from taking an unnecessary risk.

'Mr Tsuji,' he said, 'I do not wish to go to the front line to supervise the actions of my regimental commanders. But it is possible that in tonight's attack they will both be killed and I wish to shake hands with them before they die. I would not think of going to the front with the cold-hearted intention of supervising my subordinates. That is not the action to be expected of a divisional commander.' He then firmly shook hands with me, and his staff officers sighed with relief.

There were strong bonds of affection throughout the 18th Division. Not only were the rough Kyushu coalminers physically strong, but they showed an extraordinarily deep sense of loyalty to their comrades and officers irrespective of rank. The sympathetic general who wished to shake hands with his battalion commanders, and the two soldiers burying a dead friend under a hail of shells, typified the spirit of the division, the men of which put forth their utmost energy in action, and, forgetting home and self, strengthened their spirit a thousandfold, and charged willingly into the jaws of death, showing the high morale of the Japanese Army which fought in Malaya.

As my pen comes thus far in narrating these records of the Malayan campaign, I close my eyes and look back upon that time. The years have passed quickly since those days, which I cannot now think of without deep emotion, when I consider the changes which have occurred. Ah! Indeed in Malaya one saw and shared the true spirit of the Army.

During my interval of penance, which involved denial of all connection with the defeated Army of the Fatherland and the shame of travelling incognito for several years, I could not forget, even though I tried, the spirit of the comrades with whom I had fought in the Malayan campaign.

The numerous and disgusting later breaches of military discipline must be considered in comparison with the far more numerous fine and noble actions on the battlefield. Beside them any discreditable actions will in time be swept into oblivion.

On the battlefields of Malaya where we conquered, courage and comradeship were the spirit of the Army.

As regards the opposite side, could it not be that in their defeat some shamelessness and corruption were also concealed?

Conscious of the nation's eternal life, and of the large number of departed spirits who have fallen like heroes – the deceased of the family, the husband, the father, the child – who were offered as sacrifices, and who are now neglected because of defeat and ruthlessly abandoned, one must believe there will come into existence a new Japan yearning for enlightenment.

Above: Japanese armor pushes across the causeway from Johore Bahru to Singapore.

Every morning and evening, as we bow before the *ihai* of our deceased blood relations, the tears that cannot be kept back will be a denial of the trust and sincerity of human beings and a weak resistance to a cold-hearted society unless we have faith in the love of country and patriotism which still exists in spite of defeat.

Hoisting the White Flag

As the day was gradually drawing to a close, I sorrowfully said farewell to Staff Officer Hashimoto, who was leaving Headquarters. I began to walk down the hill when I was called to answer an excited call on the telephone. Putting the receiver to my ear I said, 'What is the matter? Is it urgent at this time of day?' Trembling with excitement the voice of my dear friend Staff Officer Hayashi answered, 'The enemy has surrendered! Has surrendered!'

Unconsciously dropping the receiver I thought, 'Ah! Seventy days of fighting . . . Keppel Barracks and the death struggle . . . Jitra's bloody battle.' Like a magic lantern it all flashed before my mind. How would the heart of the nation be when this news came over the radio? It seemed a dream. Only a few moments ago we were engaged in a life-and-death struggle. 'Perhaps I am dreaming,' I thought. I pinched the flesh of my thigh hard through my trousers. I was certainly awake and in my right senses. It was no dream. From several places in the firing line cheering voices rose in the air. Then, originating in some corner, the Japanese National Anthem, *Kimi Ga Yo*, spread in a wave over the battlefields.

During the day on the 5th Division front the battle had raged as violently as in the Keppel Barracks area. Our front line had only been able to advance to the southern end of the reservoir. The troops had never before been under such heavy shellfire, from which the front-line trenches afforded very little shelter. The division had attacked from the main-road sector supported by the full strength of the 'Tiger's Cub' Tank Brigade, but the troops were finally brought to a standstill at half past three in the afternoon. Then suddenly, ahead of the front line which was renewing its assault along the central highway, there appeared a white flag.

Major Wylde, an English staff officer, came bearing the flag of truce.

Like lightning this was reported to Bukit Timah headquarters. Immediately on receiving the news Staff Officer Sugita, in charge of intelligence, who was in a plaster cast because of a broken collar-bone, was taken by car to the front line, where he personally delivered to the bearer of the flag of truce documents which had been prepared in anticipation at our Army Headquarters. The British staff officer at once returned to Singapore with them to enable the British commander of the fortress to consider our proposals.

The first proposal was that the two Army Commanders should meet at 1800 hours on 15 February. The second demanded that the British Army should promptly suspend resistance and disarm. The others dealt with administrative matters, including the surrender of Allied nationals and the release of Japanese prisoners.

The streamlined motor car with the Union Jack and the white flag crossing each other stopped in front of the Ford car factory north of the three-pronged Bukit Timah road. The British Commander, Lieutenant-General Percival, accompanied by Brigadier Torrens, Brigadier Newbigging (Deputy Adjutant-General) and Major Wylde, were led to the place of interview by Staff Officer Sugita. General Yamashita, who was roughly five minutes behind time, entered followed by his staff officers, exchanged handshakes, and took his seat. How did the English general feel surrendering to his enemy after defeat? The faces of the four English officers were pale and their eyes bloodshot. General Yamashita indicated to General Percival a document written in English, saying, 'I wish you to answer these questions very briefly.'

The questions and answers were:

'Does the British Army surrender unconditionally?' – 'Yes.'

'Are there any Japanese prisoners of war?' – 'Not even one man.'

Left: Japanese sappers look on as a supply column crosses the causeway to Singapore. Its partial destruction by the British did not halt the Japanese advance.

Left: The victor Yamashita (center) views the fruits of his triumph in February 1942.

'Are there any Japanese men held prisoner?' – 'All Japanese civilian prisoners have been sent to India. The guarantee of their position is being entrusted to the Government of that country.'

'Do you agree to this document unconditionally?' – 'Please wait until tomorrow morning for the answer.'

'Then, in that case, up till tomorrow morning we will continue the attack. Is that all right, or do you consent immediately to unconditional surrender?' – 'Yes.'

'Well, then, there will be a cessation of hostilities from 10 p.m. Japanese time. The British Army, using a thousand men as a police force, will please maintain order. In case of any violation of these terms a full-scale attack on Singapore will commence immediately.'

Below: Japanese troops pose for the camera with their captives. Despite their somewhat apprehensive smiles, the British troops could not disguise the scale of the defeat.

General Percival then said, 'I wish to receive a guarantee of the safety of the lives of the English and Australians who remain in the city.'

'You may be sure of that. Please rest assured. I shall positively guarantee it.'

In this way the curtain dropped on the campaign for the occupation of Singapore. Even more dramatic was the arrival at that time of the Emperor's military aide-de-camp at Bukit Timah. In 1819, one hundred and twenty-three years earlier, Stamford Raffles had landed on this island. Everything that Great Britain had since built up here in the Far East had now been beaten to a standstill.

After General Percival had gone, escorted by the beaming General Mutaguchi and others, we returned to Army Headquarters, where the customary rites and ceremonies were performed. When we had left Headquarters on this same morning, maps and documents had been spread all over the operations room. Now they were neatly stacked in order. On a table covered with white woven material were set out dried cuttlefish, excellent chestnuts, and wine, the gifts of the Emperor. Someone without our knowledge had made the preparations.

By both the Army Commander and Army Chief of Staff we were hospitably entertained. General Yamashita said, 'You have done a good job. Thank you very much. From now on you can drink *sake* whenever you like.'

Remembering the fighting of nearly a hundred days all present raised their full wine cups, and, worshipping from a distance and facing the northeast, they drank a silent toast. The cheerful voice of the Army Commander at that moment became charged with feeling, and hot tears flowed into his wine cup.

Since my appointment to the 25th Army as Staff Officer in Charge of Operations, I had vowed to the Gods to abstain from wine and tobacco until my cherished wish was accomplished. We had expected that on this day we would drink until our glasses were 'bottoms up'. But what actually happened was that we could not enjoy our wine or eat our delicacies. They tasted bitter and seemed to choke one's throat because of the three thousand several hundred seniors, colleagues, and soldiers with whom we could not share this day's joy. Thinking of the feelings of the families of the dead men caused the wine to be bitter tonic indeed.

Major Take-no-Uchi, a great swordsman, who had fallen in Bangkok on the first day of fighting, had been a heavy drinker. I quietly raised my glass of *sake* to his memory. 'Forgive me, Take-no-Uchi, why did you not wait until Bukit Timah? I am the only one left.'

That night, after finishing drafting the telegram planned to be sent to Imperial Headquarters and to the whole Army, I fell into the sleep of the dead. A year of fatigue it seems had set everybody dozing off at the same time. The

following morning, all concerned, having taken a bath, escorted the Emperor's aide-de-camp to deliver to the troops the Imperial Rescript that had been received by telegram from Imperial Headquarters.

The Imperial Rescript
Throughout the campaign in Malaya the Army and Navy, in close and appropriate association, have carried out difficult and dangerous sea convoys, transport duties, and military landing operations. Officers and men, risking malaria, and enduring intense heat, have struck violently at the enemy, engaged in unremitting pursuit at lightning speed, destroyed his powerful army, and captured Singapore. As a consequence Britain's base of operations in the Far East is overthrown and annihilated.

I deeply approve of this.

Thus for Japan the curtain fell brilliantly on the struggle for the capture of Singapore, the great undertaking of the century.

Now let us calculate the results:
1. The military strength of the Japanese and British armies was respectively about one to two.
2. The principal gains were:
    (a) Roughly 100,000 prisoners of war, of whom about 50,000 were white soldiers.
    (b) Roughly 740 guns.
    (c) More than 2,500 machine-guns.
    (d) About 65,000 rifles and other small arms.
    (e) About 1,000 locomotives and railway trucks.
    (f) About 200 armoured cars.
    (g) Ten light aeroplanes.
    (h) Several thousand motor cars and trucks.
3. In the final battle for Singapore, from the crossing of Johore Strait until the enemy surrender, our Army casualties were:
    (a) Killed in action, 1,714 officers and men.
    (b) Wounded, 3,378 officers and men.
    (c) Total casualties in the final battle, 5,092.
4. Total casualties in the Malayan campaign from the landing at Singora to the surrender of Singapore were:
    Killed in action, 3,507 officers and men.
    Wounded in action, 6,150 officers and men.
5. The number of enemy casualties is not clear, but they were at least nearly three times our losses.

Above: A pair of Japanese medium tanks control a major road junction outside the Cathay building in Singapore. A combat photographer (foreground) records the scene for posterity.

Rushing the Camera

On the occasion of the meeting of Generals Yamashita and Percival the enemy general said, 'This evening, as there will be great confusion in the city, if by any chance the Japanese Army should make a triumphal entry into the fortress, it will be impossible to guarantee that unforeseen happenings will not occur. Please wait until tomorrow morning.'

'Yes. That will be so,' agreed General Yamashita, acceding to General Percival's request.

On the morning of 16 February it had to be confirmed whether the order of their commander would be acceptable to the hundred thousand British troops in the fortress.

With Staff Officers Okamura and Kawajima, who came from Imperial Headquarters as liaison officers for the whole Army, I hurried into the city in a car from which a large Japanese flag, stained and dishevelled, was flying.

Passing shell craters, burnt-out cars and trucks, and other traces of the recent severe fighting, we entered Singapore city.

For the whole Japanese Army we conducted the first triumphal entry into the fortress. The first thing in the city to strike the eye was the waves of men in khaki uniforms. Many of them still carried their rifles, walking about and nibbling bread. Groups of them were squatting on the road smoking, talking and shouting in rather loud voices. Strangely enough, however, there was an expression of resignation such as is shown by the losers in fierce sporting contests.

Taking out a well-worn camera for the first time, I photographed the surging crowd. Suddenly from all quarters white and black soldiers rushed up around the car, shouting, according to the interpreter, 'Please take a photo of everyone!' When I inquired why they all wanted their photographs taken, the nonchalant answer was, 'Your photographs will be sent to Japan, and from there to world newspapers immediately. Our wives and families will see the photographs and know their husbands and sons have survived.'

The British soldiers looked like men who had finished their work by contract at a suitable salary, and were now taking a rest free from the anxiety of the battlefield. They even bowed courteously to us Japanese whom they hated.

The English storehouses and dwellings were swallowed in waves of looting Chinese and Malays. Even the women and children were all mobilized like thieves at a fire. The inhabitants, who were to be pitied, were today giving vent to the feelings of hostility that more than a hundred years of coercion had aroused, and each was struggling to get to the front and take by force an indemnity several times the value of his losses during the war. The wretched nations without an Imperial Rescript on which to base their conduct!

At Far Eastern British Headquarters, which were firmly closed, two sentries stood, still holding rifles. Their faces showed resentment. With due solemnity they opened the gate. Only a few British subordinate officers remained behind, and there was no agitation or confusion anywhere. Inside and outside the Headquarters building had been neatly cleaned and swept. I climbed on to the roof of the four-storey building. On Bukit Timah heights the Japanese flag fluttered in the breeze as if ruling the whole island. Black smoke with occasional bursts of flame from the burning oil-tanks covered half the island.

We patrolled the changing city. Groups of plundering people, guarding their loot, were everywhere beginning bloody quarrels, and it was obvious that if we did not take action quickly our administration of the city would become extremely difficult.

A part only of one of our units, under the command of Major-General Kawamura, was chosen with care to perform guard duties at the danger points. It immediately set about maintaining order in the city. The rest of the Army remained firmly on the outskirts. Even officers were strictly prohibited from entering the fortress without an Army order. This was the basis of the maintenance of military discipline after the cessation of hostilities.

General Yamashita decided against a triumphal entry into Singapore and instead held a ceremonial commemoration service for the dead (20 February) before pushing on into Sumatra.

Immediately after the capture of Singapore the establishment of the Shonan Shinto Shrine was discussed. A site was chosen in the virgin forest on the reservoir heights which had been the centre of the battle for the conquest of the British fortress.

Officers and men of the Japanese Army and a group of prisoners of war set to work with picks and shovels, and in a spirit transcending both gratitude and revenge they rendered service to the Gods.

When we commenced building the memorial to our war dead on Bukit Timah heights, a tower was also erected for the purpose of holding requiem masses for the British officers and men who had fallen in the fighting. Although small it was built by the hands of the Japanese Army which had conquered. It was a new symbol – a substitute for the bronze statue in Singapore of Raffles, which had been removed.

When we entered Singapore we were surprised to see that the aerodromes, harbour, and city had not been destroyed by the enemy. Seizing a junior enemy officer we questioned him. 'Why did you not destroy Singapore?' we asked. 'Because we will return again,' he replied. Again we asked, 'Don't you believe Britain is beaten in this war?' He replied, 'We

Above: A Japanese victory parade passes in front of Singapore's Raffles Hotel.

Right: The victory march continues – Japanese troops advance by Singapore's General Post Office. The fall of Singapore was the greatest British defeat of the war.

may be defeated ninety-nine times, but in the final round we will be all right – we will win that.' This one junior officer prisoner of war spoke with the voice and the belief of the whole Anglo-Saxon nation.

A little more than three and a half years later the curtain fell on the Japanese Army's government of Malaya – the seventh in the country's history. Smeared with the blood of young officers and men who gave their lives for their country on Bukit Timah heights, the Shonan Shinto Shrine changed to smoke in the blast of an explosive charge. The bronze statue of Raffles appeared on its pedestal for the second time; but without anyone knowing the reason, its colour appears to have faded. Judging from its expression it may be that it had lost confidence in the principle of government by force.

In military operations we conquered splendidly, but in the war we were severely defeated. But, as if by magic, India, Pakistan, Ceylon, Burma, the Dutch East Indies, and the Philippine Islands one after another gained independence overnight. The reduction of Singapore was indeed the hinge of fate for the peoples of Asia.

Midway

by Mitsuo Fuchida and Masatake Okumiya

The American victory in the Battle of the Coral Sea had turned the tide in the Pacific. They were no longer on the defensive. This was the first sea battle in which the opposing fleets never had a glimpse of each other. All the damage had been done by aircraft. In this new era of sea warfare the Americans were already getting the upper hand. But the battle had been a fantastic chapter of accidents and blunders.

On 5 May the Japanese ordered the occupation of Midway Island and the Western Aleutians, and mounted the biggest operation ever fought by their navy. Warships and auxiliaries involved numbered 162. By taking Midway the Japanese hoped to secure a base from which to bomb Pearl Harbor. The Aleutians were to form part of the 'ribbon defence' by which they intended to consolidate their conquests.

Against Admiral Isoroku Yamamoto's armada, Admiral Chester W. Nimitz (CINCPAC) could muster three carriers, under Rear Admiral Frank Jack Fletcher. One of these, *Yorktown*, severely damaged in the Coral Sea battle had been repaired at Pearl Harbor in *two* days, an operation which, in peacetime, would have taken 90! Vice-Admiral Chuichi Nagumo's Pearl Harbor Striking Force consisted of four big carriers, but since the Americans had the 'unsinkable aircraft carrier' of Midway Island itself, the odds were not altogether unequal. Moreover, they had broken the Japanese naval code.

Nagumo's carriers approached Midway unseen under the cover of heavy cloud. A Catalina sighted the Midway Occupation Force on 3 June, but island-based aircraft only succeeded in hitting one oiler early on the 4th.

Nagumo began the day with a dawn air attack by 108 of his 201 planes. The rest were armed with bombs and torpedoes, in case American ships should put in an appearance.

At 0630 the Japanese struck Midway and did a good deal of damage, though the runways were not put out of action. The Americans lost 15 fighters, but shot down or damaged about 35 enemy planes.

Meanwhile Midway-based bombers were on their way to the Japanese carriers, and Rear-Admiral Spruance, with the carriers *Enterprise* and *Hornet*, was searching for two Japanese carriers which a Catalina from Midway had reported moving southeast.

At 0700 Spruance, when he was an estimated 175 miles from the enemy, ordered an all-out strike (116 planes). Nagumo, who did not expect to find American carriers in the vicinity of Midway, had sent out only a few reconnaissance planes, and these had spotted nothing. At 0700 hearing that Midway required a second attack, Nagumo ordered his 93 reserve aircraft to be rearmed with incendiary and fragmentation bombs.

Fifteen minutes later one of his scout planes reported 10 American ships to the northeast, where, according to his calculations no such force should be. For a *mauvais quart d'heure* he pondered this problem, and then decided to rearm his reserve aircraft with torpedoes. 'Order; counter-order; disorder' is a hoary military gibe. Planes now began to return from Midway adding to the confusion.

Nagumo turned east-northeast (0905) to search for the reported American Task Force. The result of this was that the fighters and dive-bombers from *Hornet* missed him. But her 15 torpedo-bombers did sight him. Attacking without fighter cover only one survived the Zekes and anti-aircraft fire. The torpedo-bombers of *Enterprise* and *Yorktown* were no more successful. When at 1024 their attack ended only eight of their Devastators were left, and not a single hit had been scored. Professor Samuel Eliot Morison, the Official Historian of US Naval Operations, writes: 'For about one

These pages: The USS *Yorktown*, part of Rear Admiral Frank Fletcher's Task Force 17 during the Battle of Midway, finally succumbs to Japanese attacks, 4 June 1942.

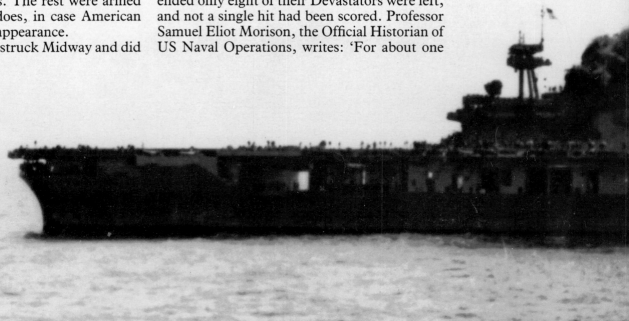

hundred seconds the Japanese were certain they had won the Battle of Midway, and the war.'

At 1026 *Enterprise*'s 37 dive-bombers swooped down to change the course of the war. The sacrifice of the torpedo-bombers had not been in vain, for the Zekes that had destroyed them had not time to climb to meet the new menace. Aboard the carriers the Japanese were still changing the armament of their planes. The flagship *Akagi* received two bombs and Nagumo was compelled to shift his flag to the cruiser *Nagara*. *Soryu* was hit three times and afterwards sunk by the US submarine *Nautilus*. *Kaga* was set aflame by four hits. The swift series of disasters left Nagumo only one carrier, the *Hiryu*. He now sent 40 planes to attack the *Yorktown*. Only seven got through, but they scored hits with three bombs and two torpedoes (1445). Fletcher, like his opponent, was compelled to transfer to a cruiser, the *Astoria*. He had, however, ordered a search for the remaining enemy carrier, and at 1700 24 planes from the *Enterprise* – ten being 'refugees' from the *Yorktown* – dived down on the *Hiryu*, scored four hits, and sent her to the bottom.

The loss of all his four fast carriers compelled Yamamoto to withdraw.

The Japanese still had five carriers, including one big one, besides six on the stocks or under repair. The Americans still had three large carriers in the Pacific, besides 13 more building, as well as 15 escort carriers. Since the Japanese could not possibly match their opponent's rate of construction, it is evident that the Battle of Midway, which completely changed the balance of forces in the Pacific, was a decisive one. It cost the Americans the *Yorktown* and 147 planes. Coming less than six months after Pearl Harbor it was an astonishing feat.   EDITOR

Chronology

1941

7 Dec.	Pearl Harbor.
26 Dec.	Surrender of Hong Kong.

1942

15 Feb.	Surrender of Singapore.
27 Feb.	Battle of the Java Sea.
9 March	Fall of Rangoon.
3 May	Japanese occupy Tulagi, unopposed.
4 May	*Yorktown*'s aircraft bomb Tulagi.
6 May	Surrender of Corregidor.
7 May	*Shoho* sunk.
8 May	Climax of Battle of the Coral Sea.
3 June	Japanese bomb Dutch Harbor.
4 June	Battle of Midway.
7 June	Japanese occupy Attu and Kiska.

Five Fateful Minutes

As our fighters ran out of ammunition during the fierce battle they returned to the carriers for replenishment, but few ran low on fuel. Service crews cheered the returning pilots, patted them on the shoulder and shouted words of encouragement. As soon as a plane was ready again the pilot nodded, pushed forward the throttle, and roared back into the sky. This scene was repeated time and again as the desperate air struggle continued.

Preparations for a counter-strike against the enemy had continued on board our four carriers throughout the enemy torpedo attacks. One after another, planes were hoisted from the hangar and quickly arranged on the flight deck. There was no time to lose. At 1020 Admiral Nagumo gave the order to launch when ready. On *Akagi*'s flight deck all planes were in position with engines warming up. The big ship began turning into the wind. Within five minutes all her planes would be launched.

Five minutes! Who would have dreamed that the tide of battle would shift completely in that brief interval of time?

Visibility was good. Clouds were gathering at about three thousand metres, however, and though there were occasional breaks, they afforded good concealment for approaching enemy planes. At 1024 the order to start launching came from the bridge by voice-tube. The Air Officer flapped a white flag, and the first Zero fighter gathered speed and whizzed off the deck. At that instant a lookout screamed: 'Hell-Divers!' I looked up to see three black enemy planes plummeting towards our ship. Some of our machine-guns managed to fire a few frantic bursts at them, but it was too late. The plump silhouettes of the American Dauntless dive-bombers quickly grew larger, and then a number of black objects suddenly floated eerily from their wings. Bombs! Down they came straight towards me! I fell intuitively to the deck and crawled behind the shelter of a command post mantelet.

The terrifying scream of the dive-bombers reached me first, followed by the crashing explosion of a direct hit. There was a blinding flash and then a second explosion, much louder than the first. I was shaken by a weird blast of warm air. There was still another shock, but less severe, apparently a near-miss. There followed a startling quiet as the barking of guns suddenly ceased. I got up and looked at the sky. The enemy planes were already gone from sight.

The attackers had got in unimpeded because our fighters, which had engaged the preceding wave of torpedo planes only a few moments earlier, had not yet had time to regain altitude. Consequently, it may be said that the American dive-bombers' success was made possible by the earlier martyrdom of their torpedo planes. Also, our carriers had no time to evade because clouds hid the enemy's approach until he dived down to the attack. We had been caught flat-footed in the most vulnerable condition possible – decks loaded with planes armed and fuelled for an attack.

Looking about, I was horrified at the destruction that had been wrought in a matter of seconds. There was a huge hole in the flight deck just behind the amidship elevator. The elevator itself, twisted like molten glass, was dropping into the hangar. Deck plates reeled upwards in grotesque configurations. Planes stood tail up, belching livid flame and jet-black smoke. Reluctant tears streamed down my cheeks as I watched the fires spread, and I was terrified at the prospect of induced explosions which would surely doom the ship. I heard Masuda yelling, 'Inside! Get inside! Everybody who isn't working! Get inside!'

Unable to help, I staggered down a ladder

Above: Vice-Admiral Chuichi Nagumo (1887-1944) led the attack on Pearl Harbor and commanded the Japanese First Carrier Striking Force at Midway.

Right: An aerial view of the US Navy's base at Pearl Harbor.

Below: An episode during the Battle of the Coral Sea, May 1942 – the *Shoho* is attacked by aircraft from the *Lexington* and *Yorktown*. The *Shoho* was the first Japanese carrier to be sunk in the Second World War.

Mitsuo Fuchida

Former Captain, Imperial Japanese Navy
The principal author, Captain Fuchida, was an outstanding officer in the Naval Air Force. At the outbreak of war he was senior air wing commander in the Carrier Task Force, which was actually the main striking strength of the Japanese Fleet. In this capacity he led the air assault on Pearl Harbor as well as subsequent air-strikes by the same task force. In every operation he performed brilliantly and capably. Captain Fuchida was present at the Midway battle from start to finish onboard aircraft carrier *Akagi*, flag-ship of the Nagumo Force. Immediately afterward he was transferred to the Naval War College as an instructor, with the special assignment of studying and making a report on the battle using all available records, official and private. This he did. Later in the war he served as Air Operations Officer in Combined Fleet Headquarters.

He was wounded at Midway.

Masatake Okumiya
Former Commander, Imperial Japanese Navy

Commander Masatake Okumiya, who collaborated with Captain Fuchida in writing the present chapter, observed the Midway battle from a different vantage point. He was in the light carrier *Ryujo*, flagship of the Second Task Force, which operated in the Aleutians area as the northern prong of the offensive. Later, as a staff officer of the sole carrier division to survive the Midway débâcle, he had access to all the detailed action reports concerning the battle and made a painstaking study of them. Towards the end of the war he was assigned to the Naval General Staff, where he enjoyed ready access to all operational records and reports.

These biographical notes are taken from the introduction which Admiral Nobutake Kondo wrote for their book.

and into the ready room. It was already jammed with badly burned victims from the hangar deck. A new explosion was followed quickly by several more, each causing the bridge structure to tremble. Smoke from the burning hangar gushed through passageways and into the bridge and ready room, forcing us to seek other refuge. Climbing back to the bridge, I could see that *Kaga* and *Soryu* had also been hit and were giving off heavy columns of black smoke. The scene was horrible to behold.

Akagi had taken two direct hits, one on the after rim of the amidship elevator, the other on the rear guard on the port side of the flight deck. Normally, neither would have been fatal to the giant carrier, but induced explosions of fuel and munitions devasted whole sections of the ship, shaking the bridge and filling the air with deadly splinters. As fire spread among the planes lined up wing to wing on the after flight deck, their torpedoes began to explode, making it impossible to bring the fires under control. The entire hangar area was a blazing inferno, and the flames moved swiftly towards the bridge.

Because of the spreading fire, our general loss of combat efficiency, and especially the sev-erance of external communication facilities, Nagumo's Chief of Staff, Rear-Admiral

Kusaka, urged that the flag be transferred at once to the light cruiser *Nagara*. Admiral Nagumo gave only a half-hearted nod, but Kusaka patiently continued his entreaty: 'Sir, most of our ships are still intact. You must com-mand them.'

The situation demanded immediate action,

Above: The *Yorktown* heads for Midway.

Below: The complex Japanese naval moves prior to the attack on Midway involved eight different task forces.

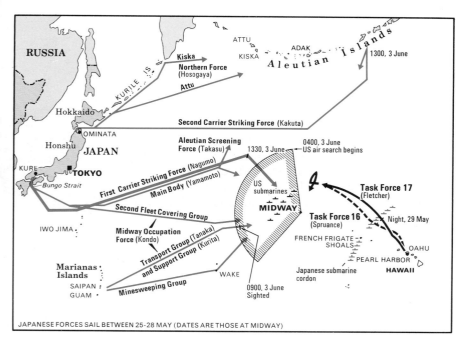

but Admiral Nagumo was reluctant to leave his beloved flagship. Most of all he was loath to leave behind the officers and men of *Akagi*, with whom he had shared every joy and sorrow of the war. With tears in his eyes, Captain Aoki spoke up: 'Admiral, I will take care of the ship. Please, we all implore you, shift your flag to *Nagara* and resume command of the Force.'

At this moment Lieutenant-Commander Nishibayashi, the Flag Secretary, came up and reported to Kusaka: 'All passages below are on fire, sir. The only means of escape is by rope from the forward window of the bridge down to the deck, then by the outboard passage to the anchor deck. *Nagara*'s boat will come alongside the anchor deck port, and you can reach it by rope ladder.'

Kusaka made a final plea to Admiral Nagumo to leave the doomed ship. At last, convinced that there was no possibility of maintaining command from *Akagi*, Nagumo bade the Captain goodbye and climbed from the bridge window with the aid of Nishibayashi. The Chief of Staff and other staff and headquarters officers followed. The time was 1046.

On the bridge there remained only Captain Aoki, his Navigator, the Air Officer, a few ratings, and myself. Aoki was trying desperately to get in touch with the engine room. The Chief Navigator was struggling to see if anything could be done to regain rudder control. The others were gathered on the anchor deck fighting the raging fire as best they could. But the unchecked flames were already licking at the bridge. Hammock mantelets around the bridge structure were beginning to burn. The Air Officer looked back at me and said,

'Fushida, we won't be able to stay on the bridge much longer, you'd better get to the anchor deck before it is too late.'

In my condition this was no easy task. Helped by some sailors, I managed to get out of the bridge window and slid down the already smouldering rope to the gun deck. There I was still ten feet above the flight deck. The connecting monkey ladder was red hot, as was the iron plate on which I stood. There was nothing to do but jump, which I did. At the same moment another explosion occurred in the hangar, and the resultant blast sent me sprawling. Luckily the deck on which I landed was not yet afire, for the force of the fall knocked me out momentarily. Returning to consciousness, I struggled to rise to my feet, but both of my ankles were broken.

Crewmen finally came to my assistance and took me to the anchor deck, which was already jammed. There I was strapped into a bamboo stretcher and lowered to a boat which carried me, along with other wounded, to the light cruiser *Nagara*. The transfer of Nagumo's staff and of the wounded was completed at 1130. The cruiser got under way, flying Admiral Nagumo's flag at her mast.

Meanwhile, efforts to bring *Akagi*'s fires under control continued, but is became increasingly obvious that this was impossible. As the ship came to a halt, her bow was still pointed into the wind, and pilots and crew had retreated to the anchor deck to escape the flames, which were reaching down to the lower hangar deck.

When the dynamos went out, the ship was deprived not only of illumination but of pumps for combating the conflagration as well. The fireproof hangar doors had been destroyed, and in this dire emergency even the chemical fire extinguishers failed to work.

The valiant crew located several hand

Above: A Japanese carrier circles to avoid the attentions of US dive-bombers at Midway.

Left: The *Yorktown* under attack by aircraft from the *Hiryu*. Despite ferocious anti-aircraft fire, the Japanese pilots scored several hits on the carrier.

Below: Raizo Tanaka commanded the Japanese Transport Group during the Battle of Midway. His vessels were detailed to protect the troops earmarked for the occupation of Midway island.

pumps, brought them to the anchor deck and managed to force water through long hoses into the lower hangar and the decks below. Firefighting parties, wearing gas masks, carried cumbersome pieces of equipment and fought the flames courageously. But every induced explosion overhead penetrated to the deck below, injuring men and interrupting their desperate efforts. Stepping over fallen comrades, another damage-control party would dash in to continue the struggle, only to be mowed down by the next explosion. Corpsmen and volunteers carried out dead and wounded from the lower first-aid station, which was jammed with injured men. Doctors and surgeons worked like machines.

The engine rooms were still undamaged, but fires in the middle deck sections had cut off all communication between the bridge and the lower levels of the ship. Despite this the explosions, shocks and crashes above, plus the telegraph indicator which had rung up 'Stop', told the engine-room crews in the bowels of the ship that something must be wrong. Still, as long as the engines were undamaged and full propulsive power was available they had no choice but to stay at General Quarters. Repeated efforts were made to communicate with the bridge, but every channel of contact, including the numerous auxiliary ones, had been knocked out.

The intensity of the spreading fires increased until the heat-laden air invaded the ship's lowest sections through the intakes, and men working there began falling from suffocation. In a desperate effort to save his men, the Chief Engineer, Commander K. Tampo, made his way up through the flaming decks until he was able to get a message to the Captain reporting conditions below. An order was promptly given for all men in the engine spaces to come up on deck. But it was too late. The orderly who tried to carry the order down through the blazing hell

never returned, and not a man escaped from the engine room.

As the number of dead and wounded increased and the fires got further out of control, Captain Aoki finally decided at 1800 that the ship must be abandoned. The injured were lowered into boats and cutters sent alongside by the screening destroyers. Many uninjured men leapt into the sea and swam away from the stricken ship. Destroyers *Arashi* and *Nowaki* picked up all survivors. When the rescue work was completed, Captain Aoki radioed to Admiral Nagumo at 1920 from one of the destroyers,

Above: The crew of the *Yorktown* abandon ship as destroyers wait nearby to pick up survivors.

Below: Bloodied but unbowed, US anti-aircraft gunners on a carrier stand ready to repel another attack by Japanese aircraft.

asking permission to sink the crippled carrier. This inquiry was monitored by the Combined Fleet flagship, whence Admiral Yamamoto dispatched an order at 2225 to delay the carrier's disposition. Upon receipt of this instruction, the Captain returned to his carrier alone. He reached the anchor deck, which was still free from fire, and there lashed himself to an anchor to await the end.

Meanwhile, uncontrollable fires continued to rage throughout *Kaga*'s length, and finally, at 1640, Commander Amagai gave the order to abandon ship. Survivors were transferred to the two destroyers standing by. Two hours later the conflagration subsided enough to enable Commander Amagai to lead a damage-control party back on board in the hope of saving the ship. Their valiant efforts proved futile, however, and they again withdrew. The once crack carrier, now a burning hulk, was wrenched by two terrific explosions before sinking into the depths at 1925, in position 30° 20′ N, 170° 17′ W. In this battle eight hundred men of *Kaga*'s crew, one-third of her complement, were lost.

Soryu, the third victim of the enemy dive-bombing attack, received one hit fewer than *Kaga*, but the devastation was just as great. When the attack broke, deck parties were busily preparing the carrier's planes for take-off, and their first awareness of the onslaught came when great flashes of fire were seen sprouting from *Kaga*, some distance off to port, followed by explosions and tremendous columns of black smoke. Eyes instinctively looked skyward just in time to see a spear of thirteen American planes plummeting down on *Soryu*. It was 1025.

Three hits were scored in as many minutes. The first blasted the flight deck in front of the forward elevator, and the next two straddled the amidship elevator, completely wrecking the deck and spreading fire to petrol tanks and munition storage rooms. By 1030 the ship was transformed into a hell of smoke and flames, and induced explosions followed shortly.

In the next ten minutes the main engines stopped, the steering system went out, and fire mains were destroyed. Crewmen, forced by the flames to leave their posts, had just arrived on deck when a mighty explosion blasted many of them into the water. Within twenty minutes of the first bomb hit the ship was such a mass of fire that Captain Ryusaku Yanagimoto ordered 'Abandon ship!' Many men jumped into the water to escape the searing flames and were picked up by destroyers *Hamakaze* and *Isokaze*. Others made more orderly transfers to the destroyers.

It was soon discovered, however, that Captain Yanagimoto had remained on the bridge of the blazing carrier. No ship commander in the Japanese Navy was more beloved by his men. His popularity was such that whenever he was

going to address the assembled crew, they would gather an hour or more in advance to ensure getting a place up front. Now, they were determined to rescue him at all costs.

Chief Petty Officer Abe, a Navy wrestling champion, was chosen to return and rescue the Captain, because it had been decided to bring him to safety by force if he refused to come willingly. When Abe climbed to *Soryu*'s bridge he found Captain Yanagimoto standing there motionless, sword in hand, gazing resolutely towards the ship's bow. Stepping forward, Abe said, 'Captain, I have come on behalf of all your men to take you to safety. They are waiting for you. Please come with me to the destroyer, sir.'

When this entreaty met with silence, Abe guessed the Captain's thoughts and started towards him with the intention of carrying him bodily to the waiting boat. But the sheer strength of will and determination of his grim-faced commander stopped him short. He turned tearfully away, and as he left the bridge he heard Captain Yanagimoto calmly singing *Kimigayo*, the national anthem.

At 1913, while her survivors watched from the nearby destroyers, *Soryu* finally disappeared into a watery grave, carrying with her 718 men, including her Captain. The position of the sinking was 30° 38′ N, 179° 13′ W.

Not one of the many observers who witnessed the last hours of this great carrier saw any sign of an enemy submarine or of submarine torpedoes. There was a succession of explosions in the carrier before she sank, but these were so unquestionably induced explosions that they could not have been mistaken for anything else. It seems beyond doubt, therefore, that American accounts which credit US submarine *Nautilus* with delivering the *coup de grâce* to *Soryu* have confused her with *Kaga*. Nor, as already related, did the submarine attack on *Kaga* contribute in any way to her sinking.

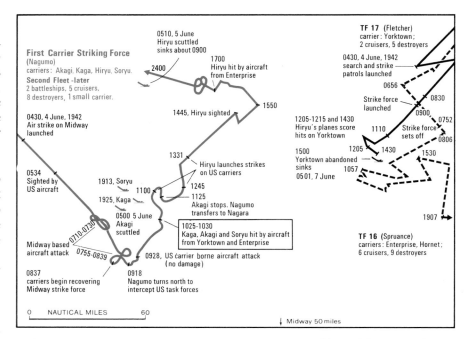

Above: The Battle of Midway, showing the moves of the rival fleets, the attacks that led to the loss of four Japanese carriers and the destruction of Task Force 17's *Yorktown*.

Finale

On 7 June, 'with no enemy in sight and his ships in need of fuel', Yamamoto called off his vain pursuit and retired towards the homeland.

Mogami, in the meantime, had continued westward in her effort to lure the enemy. Through the untiring efforts of her crew, a speed of twenty knots was achieved by 1515 despite the heavy bomb damage she sustained and the loss of her bow. She was fortunate that no enemy planes had appeared since *Mikuma*'s sinking, and she was able to creep out of the very jaws of death, the last Japanese warship to come clear of enemy attacks in the Midway battle. Kondo's force finally rendezvoused with the crippled *Mogami* and provided escort to Truk.

Further American attempts to hit the retreating Japanese Fleet this day were made by 26 B-17s from Midway, but the foul weather thwarted these efforts and no contacts were made. Alert to the possibility of attack by planes based on Wake Island, the enemy carriers also gave up the chase, and the action was over.

Thus fell the curtain on a spectacular and historic battle. Japan's sole consolation for the defeat lay in the minuscule success of having captured two Aleutian bases. The northern operations, resumed after their earlier cancellation, had progressed smoothly and led to the occupation of the islands of Attu and Kiska on 7 June. But these unimportant acquisitions were small compensation for the devastating fleet losses suffered to the south, and in the end they were to bog us down still deeper in the quicksands of defeat.

The catastrophe of Midway definitely marked the turning of the tide in the Pacific war, and thenceforward that tide bore Japan inexorably on towards final capitulation.

Left: Members of the USS *Yorktown* walk cautiously over the sloping deck of the carrier. The ship was finally sunk by the Japanese submarine I-168 on 7 June.

Below: The heavy cruiser *Mogami* lies dead in the water on 6 June. Dive-bombers from the USS *Enterprise* caught the ship after it had collided with another Japanese vessel.

El Alamein

by Viscount Montgomery of Alamein

No battle is ever lost till the general in command thinks so. If I had not stood firm and insisted that my plan would be carried through, we would not have won at Alamein. Montgomery

To read the works of some of the pundits who have written about this great turning point of the Second World War, one would think that it could have been won by any *bon général ordinaire*. The pundits in question are not themselves men who have exercised high command in the field, and some of them have fought all their battles in the peaceful seclusion of their studies. Historians of this sort depend for the success of their work on the provocative and interested comments of generals whose careers did not long survive the arrival of General Montgomery in the Desert.

It is true that the Allies outnumbered the Axis forces at El Alamein. The balance of force was something like two to one in Montgomery's favour. Even so there are those who believe that one cannot look for success in attack with less than a superiority of three to one.

The Eighth Army, experienced through it was – in disaster as well as triumph – had suffered some 80,000 casualties since its formation, and in the nature of things was less well-trained than it should have been when Montgomery assumed command. Both as divisional and corps commander he had proved himself a great trainer of men, and beyond question the way in which he prepared for the battle was of

These pages: Silhouetted against the setting sun, a Vickers machine-gun crew prepares for action. During the opening barrage at Alamein, tracer rounds from machine guns guided the mine-clearing parties across no man's land.

paramount importance. This was not simply a question of the planning and of the Deception Plan. His orders on Morale, Leadership, Secrecy, Grouping and the operation instructions which he delivered in his address to all officers down to battalion commanders, set the tone for the great fight in which, as he put it, the Eighth Army would 'hit the enemy for "six", right out of North Africa'. It has been the lot of the present writer to command a unit in three of Field-Marshal Montgomery's campaigns. His detractors point to various blemishes, real or imagined, on his military or personal character. Some think him unduly cautious, others consider him unduly severe to deserving generals who failed at some time or another. The soldiers Montgomery commanded never thought it remotely possible that they would be beaten. This seems to me to be rather more important than the plaintive jealousy of lesser men.

If, for once, a British general managed to get his army across the start line with a numerical superiority over the enemy, this should be a matter for praise rather than complaint!

EDITOR

Chronology

1942

1 July	Rommel's advance held up at El Alamein.
13 Aug.	Montgomery assumes command of the Eighth Army.
30 Aug.-	
7 Sept.	Battle of Alam Halfa.
23 Sept.-	
25 Oct.	Rommel on leave.
6 Oct.	Montgomery changes his plan.
23 Oct.-	
4 Nov.	Battle of El Alamein.
8 Nov.	British take Tobruk.
20 Nov.	Capture of Benghazi.
24 Nov.	Rommel halts at El Agheila.

1943

(4 Jan.	Japanese begin to evacuate Guadalcanal. Turning point of Pacific War.)
23 Jan.	Eighth Army enters Tripoli.
(2 Feb.	Germans surrender at Stalingrad.)
12 May	Battle of Tunis ends. End of fighting in North Africa.

Preparations for the Battle of El Alamein

The Battle of Alam Halfa had interfered with our preparations for the formation of a reserve corps, and had caused us some delay. As soon as the situation had been restored, however, no time was lost in continuing with our plans.

10th Corps (General Lumsden) was to consist of 1st Armoured Division, 10th Armoured Division (including an armoured brigade under command). This Corps was concentrated for training and re-equipment in the rear areas. 2nd New Zealand Division was relieved in the line by 44th Division, whose positions at Alam Halfa were taken over by 51st Division, recently arrived from the United Kingdom.

Field-Marshal Viscount Montgomery of Alamein, KG, GCB, DSO
(1887-1976)

The son of a Bishop, Montgomery was educated at St Paul's and the RMC Sandhurst. He joined the Royal Warwickshire Regiment in 1908, and served with distinction on the Western Front during the First World War, winning the DSO. In 1931 he commanded the 1st Battalion and by 1938 had risen to the rank of Major-General in command of the 8th Infantry Division in Palestine during the Arab Rebellion. Within a year he had been invalided home, but recovered in time to command the 3rd Division in the BEF.

After Dunkirk he commanded V Corps, then XII Corps until, in 1942, he became C.-in-C. South East Command, before being given command of the Eighth Army, on the death of General 'Strafer' Gott, the Army commander designate. Taking over from General Sir Claude Auchinleck he completely revitalized the battle-weary army with his new and ruthless approach. After his victories in Africa, Montgomery took the Eighth Army on to Sicily and Italy.

After the Battle of the Sangro he returned home for the invasion of Europe. In the Normandy landings (6 June 1944) he commanded all troops, both British and American. Later he commanded the northern half of the Allied advance (21st Army Group) up until the German surrender of 4 May 1945.

After the war Field-Marshal Montgomery became Commander of the British Army of Occupation and Military Governor of the British Zone in Germany. In June 1946 he became CIGS and in the same year was created Viscount of Hindhead. From 1948 until 1951 he was Chairman of the Western Europe Commanders-in-Chief Committee before finally becoming Deputy Supreme Allied Commander, Europe. He retired in 1958. His publications include: *Ten Chapters*, 1946; *Forward to Victory*, 1946; *Normandy to the Baltic*, 1947; *Forward from Victory*, 1948; *El Alamein to the River Sangro*, 1948; *Memoirs*, 1958; *An Approach to Sanity: A Study of East-West Relations*, 1959; *The Path to Leadership*, 1961; *Three Continents*, 1962.

My policy at this stage was to build up the Army on three basic fundamentals: leadership, equipment and training. By early October I was satisfied with the leadership aspect; my subordinate commanders were sound, and I had every confidence in them.

The equipment situation improved rapidly; Sherman tanks, sent to us at the personal instigation of President Roosevelt, started arriving in the Delta from America in August, and were issued to 10th Corps. In the Sherman we had at last a match for the German tanks. We had moreover a great weight of artillery and there was plenty of ammunition.

My great anxiety was that the state of training was still not good, and it was becoming clear that I would have to be very careful to ensure that units and formations were not given tasks which would be beyond their capabilities. I would have to stage-manage the forthcoming battle in such a way that the troops would be able to do what was demanded of them, and I must not be too ambitious in my demands.

During this period of preparation, I was working out the plan for the Battle of Alamein. It was because of shortcomings in the standard of training in the Army that I had to alter, early in October, the whole conception of how I intended to fight the battle.

The Battle of El Alamein, 23 October 1942

Major considerations affecting the plan

Full moon was on 24 October. A full moon was essential for the operation, since there was no open flank, and we had to make gaps in the minefields and to blow a hole through the enemy's defensive system during the night. The earliest therefore that we could mount the offensive was on the night 23/24 October.

The enemy had made good use of the lull after his abortive attack, to strengthen and deepen his defences. In the northern sector he had three belts of defended localities and minefields and any attack by us was intended to lose both force and direction within this system itself. In the south, the defences were not so highly organized, but were sited to canalize any penetration we might make. In general the minefields alone extended to some 5,000 to 9,000 yards in depth. The enemy positions were held by one German and five Italian divisions, together with a German parachute brigade; detached German infantry elements were used to stiffen the Italian sectors. In reserve in the north were the 15th Panzer and Italian Littorio Armoured Divisions, and further to the rear, on the coast, was 90th Light Division. In reserve in the south there were 21st Panzer and

the Ariete Armoured Divisions. On the Egyptian frontier stood the Pistoia Division.

It was extremely difficult to achieve any form of surprise. It seemed impossible to conceal from the enemy that we meant to launch an attack. At best we could deceive him about the direction of our main thrusts and the date by which we would be ready to begin.

The plan

In planning the Battle of Alamein the main difficulties confronting us were three: first, the problem of blowing a hole in the enemy positions; secondly, the dispatch of a Corps strong in armour through the hole into enemy territory; and lastly, the development of operations so as to destroy the Axis forces.

In September I had been working on the idea of attacking the enemy simultaneously on both flanks – the main attack being made in the north by 30th Corps (General Leese). This operation would force a gap across the enemy's defensive system through which 10th Corps would pass. 10th Corps would position itself on ground of its own choosing astride the enemy supply routes; the enemy armour would deploy against it, and be destroyed: probably piecemeal, as I hoped to keep it dispersed as long as possible. The attack of 13th Corps (General Horrocks) in the south would draw off enemy armour to that flank, and thus weaken the opposition to 10th Corps.

As I have mentioned already, early in October I changed the conception of how I would fight the battle, because I was not satisfied that we were capable of achieving success in a plan so ambitious.

It had been generally accepted that the plan in a modern battle should aim first at destroying the enemy's armour, and that once this had been accomplished, the unarmoured portion of

Above left: An Afrika Korps armored column, including several Panzer IIIs mounting short-barreled 5cm guns, moves toward El Alamein in the summer of 1942.

Above: A map showing the German right-hook at the Battle of Alam Halfa (31 August–7 September 1942). The engagement marked Montgomery's debut in the Western Desert and saw the Axis drive into Egypt halted.

Left: A British 25-pounder opens fire on the German forces attempting to turn the Eighth Army's southern flank at Alam Halfa.

his army would be dealt with readily. I decided to reverse this concept and to destroy first the unarmoured formations. While doing this I would hold off the armoured divisions, which would be tackled subsequently. In broad terms, the fighting elements of Rommel's army comprised holding troops (mostly unarmoured) who manned defences and guarded essential areas of ground; and mobile troops (mostly armoured) whose role was offensive. The mobile troops were used to deliver counter-attacks during defensive periods, and to form the spearhead of advance in the offensive. If the holding troops could be destroyed the enemy would be unable to secure ground vital to the action of his armoured forces; these would be denied firm bases from which to manoeuvre and within which to refurbish, and their supply routes would lie open to interruption. In these circumstances the armoured forces would be forced to withdraw or perish.

My idea therefore was to aim first at the methodical destruction of the infantry divisions holding the enemy's defensive system. This would be accomplished by means of a 'crumbling' process, carefully organized from a series of firm bases: an operation within the capabilities of my troops. For success, the method depended on holding off the enemy's armour while the 'crumbling' battle, designed to gain a foothold in the enemy's defences, should achieve complete success, so that the enemy infantry might be attacked from the flank and rear.

The enemy's armour would obviously not sit still and watch the gradual destruction of the infantry; it would be launched into counter-attacks. If I could position my armour beyond the area of the 'crumbling' operations, on ground of its own choosing, the enemy tanks would have to attack in conditions favourable to us, and could be held off. The minefields, particularly those west of the main Axis positions, would restrict the approaches available to those enemy tanks which might try to counter-attack our assaulting units while they were dealing with the defending infantry. If the approaches themselves were closed by our own tanks in position, we would be able to proceed relentlessly with our plans.

My orders for the battle, issued on 6 October, provided for three attacks.

The main thrust of 30th Corps in the north was to be made on a front of four divisions, with the task of forcing two corridors through the enemy's minefields. 10th Corps was to pass through these corridors.

In the south, 13 Corps was to mount two operations: one east of Gebel Kalakh and Qaret el Khadim, the other further south directed on Himeimat and the Taqa feature.

13th and 30th Corps having broken into the enemy's defences were to undertake the methodical destruction of the troops holding the forward positions.

10th Corps had as its ultimate task the destruction of the enemy armour, and was to be manoeuvred so as to prevent enemy interference with 30th Corps operations; it would assist, as opportunity offered, in the 'crumbling' process.

The role of 13th Corps was primarily to mislead the enemy into believing that our main thrust was being delivered in the south, and to contain enemy forces there: particularly 21st Panzer Division. 7th Armoured Division was available for the operation, but I ordered that it was to be kept intact on the southern flank, in order to preserve balanced dispositions throughout the front. I made it clear that the attack was not to be pressed if heavy casualties were likely to result.

Below: *Bersaglieri*, considered the elite of the Italian Army, trudge forward to Alamein. The Italians were destined to absorb much of the opening British attacks at Alamein.

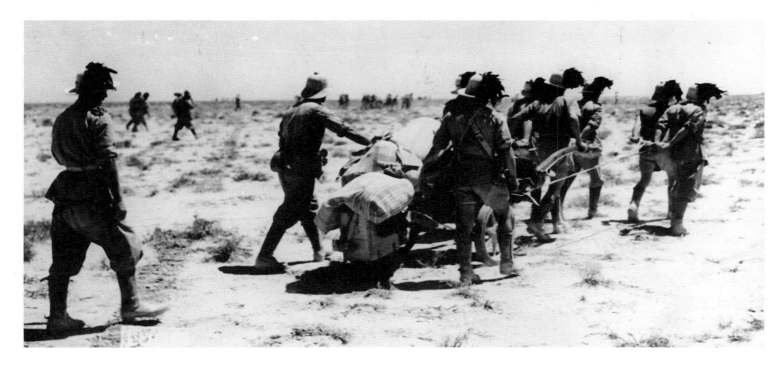

My orders emphasized that it was vital to retain the initiative and to keep up sustained pressure on the enemy. The troops were to take advantage of any weakening and were to avoid any long pauses which might give the enemy time to recover his balance.

The break-in operation was to be facilitated by a very heavy counter-battery plan, the effect of which was to be strengthened by switching the whole of the bomber effort onto the artillery areas as soon as the battle began. I realized that following the break-in, a real dog-fight would ensue. I was confident that our resources were sufficient to withstand the strain which this would impose. The essentials of the battle would be the retention of the initiative, the maintenance of pressure on the enemy, and the preservation of balance so that it would be unnecessary to react to the enemy's thrusts.

The Royal Air Force plan of operations began with the winning of the air battle before the attack opened. Having obtained ascendancy over the German Air Force, the whole of the air effort was to be available to co-operate intimately in the land battle.

The cover plan

The cover plan for the battle was worked out in August and September. It aimed at misleading the enemy about the direction of the main thrusts and the date of our readiness for the attack.

The basis of 'visual deception' was the preservation of a constant density of vehicles throughout the zone of operations, so that the enemy would be denied the inferences made from the changes disclosed in day-to-day air photographs. By means of pooled transport resources (enlarged by the reduction of divisional holdings) and by the construction of large numbers of dummy lorries, the layout and density of vehicles required for the assault in the northern sector was established on the ground as early as 1 October. During the period of forward concentration of 51st and 2nd New Zealand Divisions and 10th Corps, the substitute transport was replaced at night by the operational transport of the divisions concerned. Guns, limbers, and quads of reinforcing artillery units were dealt with in a similar way. The rear areas whence these units and formations came were maintained at their full vehicle quota by the erection of dummies as the real transport moved out. Dumps were concealed by elaborate camouflage and by stacking stores to resemble vehicles. A month before the attack, slit trenches were dug, in which (when the time came) the assaulting infantry could be concealed.

Meanwhile active measures were employed to cause the enemy to believe the main blow would be delivered in the south. A dummy pipeline was started late in September, and progress into the work was timed to indicate its

completion by the first week in November; dummy dumps were also made working to a similar date. Headquarters 8th Armoured Division was used to assist, with its wireless network, the notion that armoured forces were moving to the southern flank.

Final preparations for the offensive

An essential feature of my plan was that every commander in the Army, down to the rank of Lieutenant-Colonel, should know from me personally how I proposed to fight the battle, what issues depended on it, and what were the main difficulties we were likely to encounter. I toured the Army addressing the officers.

On 21 and 22 October, the battle was explained to the troops by their officers.

I was determined that the soldiers should go into the battle having been worked up into a great state of enthusiasm, and realizing fully what was expected of them.

Heavy and sustained air attacks against the Axis air forces and land communications reached a crescendo on 22 October. The degree of air superiority thus achieved was such that throughout 23 October our aircraft maintained continuous fighter patrols over enemy landing grounds without interference.

Concentration in the forward assembly areas was completed during the night 22/23 October, and by first light all formations were dug in and camouflaged. The assaulting infantry spent the day of 23 October unobserved in the slits dug in front of our foremost positions, and it was clear from the absence of shelling of our positions that we would indeed achieve tactical surprise.

The stage was set. During the morning my personal message was read out to all ranks:

'The Battle which is now about to begin will be one of the decisive battles of history. It will be the turning point of the war . . . The Lord mighty in battle will give us victory.'

With these words the Eighth Army was launched into battle.

Above: Part of Montgomery's elaborate deception measures designed to mislead the Axis forces at Alamein as to the true strength of the Eighth Army – a Crusader tank disguised by a canvas and wood frame to look like a truck.

The 'break-in' 23-24 October 1942

Operations 23/24 October

The night of 23 October was still and clear. At 2140 hours in the bright moonlight, the Eighth Army artillery opened on located enemy batteries. Over a thousand field and medium guns were employed, and the effect was terrific.

At 2200 hours fire was switched to the enemy's foremost positions, and the assaulting divisions of 13th and 30th Corps advanced to the attack.

In the north, the four divisions of 30th Corps attacked in line. 9th Australian and 51st Divisions, responsible for forcing the northern corridor through the minefields, attacked west from their positions just north of Miteiriya ridge; the New Zealanders and South Africans thrust in a south-southwesterly direction onto the ridge itself, and were to establish the southern corridor. At the same time 4th Indian Division carried out a strong raid against enemy positions on the western end of Ruweisat ridge, and in the extreme north an Australian brigade made a feint attack between Tel el Eisa and the sea.

Heavy fighting continued all night against stiffening resistance, but by 0530 hours most of the final objectives had been reached. The two corridors had been pushed through the main minefield belts and supporting weapons of the infantry were moving forward. 9th Armoured Brigade (2nd New Zealand Division) was also reported to be progressing well through the southern corridor.

Behind the division of 30th Corps, 1st and 10th Armoured Divisions of 10th Corps crossed their start line at 0200 hours and made for the northern and southern routes respectively. Both formations, however, got behind schedule. 1st Armoured Division was delayed because a strong enemy locality held up 51st Division. When 10th Armoured Division came up to the Miteiriya ridge, enemy artillery and anti-tank gun fire prohibited its progress. 9th Armoured Brigade of 2nd New Zealand Division got forward to the ridge, but met further minefields and also heavy anti-tank gun fire. The armour remained behind the Miteiriya feature and engaged the enemy at long range. 15th Panzer Division delivered a series of minor attacks which were beaten off with considerable casualties to the enemy tanks.

Meanwhile in 13th Corps sector to the south, an operation was mounted by 7th Armoured and 44th Divisions with the object of forcing two gaps in the minefields north of Himeimat. At the same time 1st Fighting French Brigade attacked Hunter's Plateau.

The attempt to breach the western field failed after being hung up by scattered mines between the two major belts. 13th Corps therefore resorted to 'crumbling' action between the belts during 24 October and achieved valuable results. The French took their objective, but soft sand delayed their supporting weapons, and they were driven back by a counter-attack delivered by the Kiel Group – a German armoured column.

Situation on 24 October

In the north we had successfully broken into the enemy positions and secured a good bridgehead. But attempts to pass the armour into the open and to the west of the Axis defensive system had been unsuccessful.

My plan was now to force 1st and 10th Armoured Divisions into the open as quickly as possible, and to commence 'crumbling' operations to the southwest by 2nd New Zealand Division. I also ordered a strong raid westwards from the Ruweisat ridge by 30th Corps and completion of the gaps through the southern minefield by 13th Corps.

Below: A 25-pounder in action, part of the massive preliminary barrage employed by Montgomery to smash the Axis positions at Alamein and cover the first advances of the infantry.

Left: A youthful veteran of the Afrika Korps enjoys a break from building the extensive defenses created to blunt the Eighth Army's 'crumbling' attacks in the first stages of Operation Lightfoot, Montgomery's plan to crush the Axis forces at Alamein.

Far left: General Bernard Law Montgomery (1887-1976) took charge of the Eighth Army in August 1942, halted the Afrika Korps at Alam Halfa and then dealt a body-blow to Axis ambitions in North Africa at Second Alamein.

Below: A painting depicting the beginning of the Eighth Army's attack on the night of 23 October. Parties of Royal Engineers clear paths through the Axis minefields for Montgomery's infantry and armor.

The 'dog-fight' 24-30 October 1942

Operations 24/25 October

The attack on the north corridor axis was resumed by 1st Armoured Division and 51st Division at 1500 hours on 24 October. My orders were very firm and produced good results; by 1800 hours 2nd Armoured Brigade (1st Armoured Division) had broken out from the western minefield, and was taking up positions beyond.

On the southern corridor axis, 10th Armoured Division, supported by 30th Corps artillery, renewed its attack at 2200 hours. During the night reports showed that the operation was not making progress. I feared that my plan for getting this formation through the mine belt was in danger of failure and at 0400 hours, 25 October, I issued orders that it must and would get forward. By 0800 hours, the leading armoured brigade was reported in position, 2,000 yards west of the minefield area, and in touch with 1st Armoured Division on its right. The leading regiment of the other armoured brigade of the division had also cleared the enemy's main position.

Meanwhile 9th Armoured Brigade of 2nd New Zealand Division was clear of the corridor, and was operating southwest according to plan.

During 25 October, 15th Panzer Division again made a series of counter-attacks, including one near Kidney ridge in which about 100 tanks were used. Our armour was not in position, but our anti-tank guns repulsed these attacks with heavy casualties to the enemy.

In the 13th Corps area, 44th Division renewed its efforts to gap the minefields during the night 24/25 October and was successful. A small bridgehead was formed and 4th Light Armoured Brigade was passed through. Scattered mines and an anti-tank gun screen were encountered, however, and it was apparent that heavy casualties would be sustained if the attack were pressed home. On the morning of 25 October, I authorized 13th Corps to break off this action, in accordance with my policy of maintaining 7th Armoured Division at effective fighting strength. It was essential to maintain the balance of the Army, and as long as 21st Panzer Division was in the south, I required an

Right: The plan of attack at Alamein. The corridors for the infantry and armor of 10th Corps are clearly visible.

Below: Surrounded by primed shells, the crew of a British 5.5in medium field gun pounds a distant target.

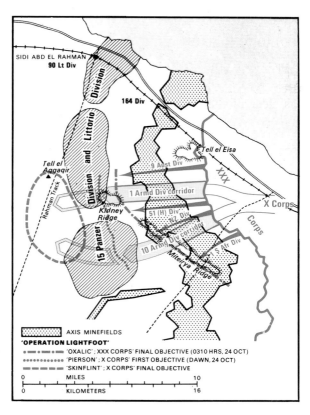

AXIS MINEFIELDS

'OPERATION LIGHTFOOT'

━ ∙ ━ ∙ ━ 'OXALIC'; XXX CORPS' FINAL OBJECTIVE (0310 HRS, 24 OCT)
∙∙∙∙∙∙∙∙∙∙ 'PIERSON'; X CORPS' FIRST OBJECTIVE (DAWN, 24 OCT)
━ ━ ━ ━ 'SKINFLINT'; X CORPS' FINAL OBJECTIVE

0   MILES   10
0   KILOMETERS   16

armoured division in 13th Corps: and its presence there assisted materially in keeping enemy armour in the south.

On 25 October, 50th Division mounted an attack in the Munassib area. This was not pressed and soon petered out in face of thick wire and anti-personnel mines.

Situation on 25 October

We had now thrust our armour out into positions where it was well placed to meet the enemy tanks and inflict on them heavy casualties. It could function as I had intended, and as long as the enemy attacked us, particularly in isolated and piecemeal fashion, I was well content with the action so far.

In the south 13th Corps was maintaining the threat well.

My major consideration was now the 'crumbling' process of wearing down the enemy's infantry in the north. It became clear that 2nd New Zealand Division's move southwest would be a most costly undertaking, and at midday on 25 October I decided to abandon it and to switch the main 'crumbling' action to the Australian sector. I gave orders for 9th Australian Division to attack north towards the sea, with the object of destroying the German forces in the coastal salient which had been created by our break-in battle. In conjunction with this attack, I provided for operations to be developed westwards by 1st Armoured Division from its position in the bridgehead. If 1st Armoured Division could make progress to the west, the opportunity might come to pass its armoured brigade through to the Rahman track; it could then get behind the enemy holding the salient. In the following days I was constantly considering the problem of establishing armour in the Rahman area, since it was the key to the system of enemy supply routes in rear.

In switching the main 'crumbling' process so radically I hoped to gain surprise and to take a heavy toll of the enemy.

Operations night 25/26 October and 26 October

The Australian attack on the night 25/26 October was completely successful. The Germans suffered some 300 casualties.

1st Armoured Division, however, failed to make any progress to the west in its operations in the Kidney ridge sector.

On 26 October, 1st South African Division and 2nd New Zealand Division advanced about 1,000 yards, thus gaining more depth in front of the Miteiriya ridge. The same night, 7th Motor Brigade established itself on Kidney ridge.

Below: The first fruits of the Allied victory at Alamein – dejected Axis prisoners head to the rear and captivity.

Situation 26 October

I spent the day in detailed consideration of the situation, and it was from this date onwards that plans were evolved culminating in the final break-out operation which was launched on the night 1/2 November.

My tank state showed over 800 runners, and the ammunition situation was sound. But a note of caution was imposed in my planning. The assaulting divisions had suffered considerable casualties, and there was a lack of replacements for the depleted New Zealand and South African Divisions.

The infantry divisions had, according to plan, carried out slow and methodical improvement of their positions by a series of carefully co-ordinated attacks on narrow fronts with limited objectives. In this they had taken heavy toll of the hostile infantry. 30th Corps was now, however, in need of a short pause for much-needed reorganization.

The armoured divisions were forward in positions from which heavy casualties had been caused to the enemy armour.

The momentum of the attack, however, was diminishing and 10th Corps had not broken out into open country. The enemy had withdrawn troops and guns from his forward positions in anticipation of our offensive, and we had therefore found him in greater depth than had been expected. Our break-in area was still ringed by a strong anti-tank screen, and attempts to pierce it had been unsuccessful.

Above: A troop of Crusader tanks awaits the order to break through the Axis line. Heavy losses, stubborn resistance and a degree of disagreement between the Eighth Army's commanders forced Montgomery to reorganize his attack at Alamein. The operation, codenamed Supercharge, commenced at the end of October.

Left: The crew of a six-pounder anti-tank gun takes cover during an Axis bombardment. A potent weapon, the gun was capable of dealing with any of the Axis armored vehicles at Alamein.

By evening on 26 October I had decided to regroup, in order to create fresh reserves for further offensive action. The next phase would be in the north again, as I had been impressed with the results of the Australian attack on the night 25/26 October. If I could get behind the enemy holding the coastal salient, I would annihilate or capture a strong force of Germans and perhaps open up the operation along the coastal axis. The first stage of regrouping was the reversion of 2nd New Zealand Division into reserve. Its sector was taken over by 1st South African Division, which was relieved in turn by 4th Indian Division. The latter I placed under 13th Corps.

Operations 27 and 28 October

Throughout 27 October the enemy launched heavy armoured counter-attacks against Kidney ridge. These attacks were put in by both 15th and 21st Panzer Divisions, the latter having moved north during the previous night. The enemy was repulsed in all cases, and suffered very heavy losses. 1st Armoured Division alone knocked out nearly fifty German tanks in this engagement.

On 28 October the enemy made a prolonged reconnaissance of Kidney ridge, probing for soft spots while the two German Panzer Divisions waited in the rear. In the evening they began to concentrate for attack, but the Desert Air Force intervened with such effect that the enemy was defeated before he completed his forming-up.

Situation on 27 and 28 October

On 27 October, I developed my plan for breaking out in the northern sector.

I gave orders for 9th Australian Division to launch a heavy attack northwards on the night 28/29 October.

I intended to destroy the enemy coastal salient, and then drive 30th Corps westwards along the road and railway route to Sidi Abd el Rahman. Holding off the enemy armour, our tanks would operate to the south.

The situation in the south was such that I decided that 13th Corps should become primarily defensive. Every endeavour was to be made by means of patrols and artillery action to prolong the enemy's anxiety in this sector, but no further major operations would be staged there. 21st Panzer Division had been contained in the south until the night of 26 October, and our infantry had inflicted heavy casualties on the enemy. 13th Corps had successfully fulfilled its role.

I now ordered the second stage of regrouping. 7th Armoured Division (with a brigade of 44th Division), a brigade of 50th Division and the Greek Brigade, were to be sent up to the northern sector from 13th Corps; and, to release

troops for the forthcoming Australian attack, a brigade of 51st Division relieved 20th Australian Brigade. 1st Armoured Division needed a pause for reorganization, and since it was clear that the whole German Afrika Korps was now facing the northern corridor, I turned the sector over to the defensive, and withdrew 1st Armoured Division and 24th Armoured Brigade into reserve.

New Zealand Division was selected to lead the drive westwards, and since it was now in strength, I arranged for the brigades from 13th Corps to be available to work with it and keep it at operational strength.

In this way regrouping of the Army was undertaken, and I was soon to have a strong reserve force ready to stage the break-out and to deliver the knock-out blow.

Operations night 28/29, 29 and 30 October

The Australian attack on night 28/29 October made good progress and about 200 prisoners were taken. A narrow wedge was driven into the enemy's positions, reaching almost to the road between Sidi Abd el Rahman and Tel el Eisa. On the right of the attack very strong opposition and extensive minefields were encountered round Thompson's Post, which was the bastion of the enemy's coastal salient.

During 29 October, and again early on 30 October, repeated counter-attacks by tanks and infantry were hurled against the Australians in the wedge, but they held on and retained the ground won.

Situation 29 and 30 October

I learnt during the morning of 29 October that 90th Light Division had moved into the Sidi Abd el Rahman area. This was very significant, for it showed that Rommel was reacting to the

Below: A column of weary German prisoners heads away from the battlefield. The British victory at Alamein ripped the heart out of the Afrika Korps.

threat in the north and had probably guessed my intention of striking west along the road and rail axis.

As a result I modified my plan for the break-out by moving the axis of the westwards drive further to the south, so that the blow would fall mainly on the Italians.

9th Australian Division would resume its threat northwards to the sea on the night 30/31 October. This would prepare the way for the break-out to the west by confirming the enemy's fears in the extreme north. Above all it would probably ensure that 90th Light Division remained about Sidi Abd el Rahman.

On night 31 October/1 November (subsequently postponed 24 hours) 2nd New Zealand Division thrusting due west would blow a new gap through the enemy positions just north of the existing northern corridor. Through this gap 10th Corps would pass out into the open desert with 1st, 7th and 10th Armoured Divisions and two armoured car regiments. The armoured divisions were to destroy the German Afrika Korps and the armoured cars were to operate on the enemy supply routes to intensify the enemy's administrative difficulties – particularly his shortage of petrol. To this operation I gave the name 'Supercharge'.

'Supercharge' was to get us out into the open country and to lead to the disintegration of Rommel's forces in Egypt. We had got to bring the enemy's armour to battle and get astride his lines of communication. 2nd New Zealand Division's task involved a penetration of some 6,000 yards on a 4,000-yard front, and I made it clear that should 30th Corps fail to reach its final objectives, *the armoured divisions of 10th Corps were to fight their way through.*

The change of thrust line of 'Supercharge' to the south proved most fortunate. I learnt on 1 November that 21st Panzer Division had joined 90th Light Division in the Rahman area, so that

the road and railway axis was very strongly covered. Rommel was playing into my hands, for the bulk of his German forces were now concentrated on the coast, leaving the Italians to hold the more southerly sectors. I could drive a blow between the Germans and Italians and concentrate on destroying the former.

Above: A headline from the *Daily Mirror* tells the story of Alamein. The battle did much to improve the morale of the British public and made Montgomery a national hero.

Left: Blazing German trucks, victims of an attack by aircraft of the British Desert Air Force. Powerful air cover prevented the Axis forces from mounting a co-ordinated riposte to the Eighth Army's thrusts.

Right: A British Grant tank heads out into open country. Although the vehicle suffered from a high profile, its armor and 75mm side-mounted gun made it an effective counter to the Panzer IIIs and IVs of the German 15th and 21st Panzer Divisions.

The 'break-out' 31 October–4 November 1942

Operations 31 October to 3 November

The thrust north started again on the night 30/31 October as planned. The Australians succeeded in crossing the coast road and pushed forward to the sea and then turned eastwards. The Panzer Grenadiers of 164th Division were thus trapped, and the enemy launched a number of furious counter-attacks to free them. Towards evening some German tanks from the west succeeded in joining the defenders of Thompson's Post, and eventually the majority of the Germans fought their way out. But the enemy suffered very severe casualties in this action.

At 0100 hours, 2 November, 'Supercharge' began and the assaulting troops advanced behind a creeping barrage.

151st and 152nd Infantry Brigades attacked on the main frontage, under command of 2nd New Zealand Division. Subsidiary attacks were staged to extend the base of the salient.

9th Armoured Brigade was to pass through the infantry on its final objective and form a bridgehead beyond the track running south from Sidi Abd el Rahman. 1st and 7th Armoured Divisions (and later 10th Armoured Division) were to debouch from this bridgehead, together with the two armoured car regiments detailed for raids deep in the enemy rear.

The operation achieved great success. The new corridor was established and 9th Armoured Brigade reached the Rahman track just before light. The Royals swung southwest and reached open country, and were followed later by 4th South African Armoured Car Regiment which had been considerably delayed in breaking out.

As it became light 9th Armoured Brigade ran into a formidable anti-tank gun screen and during the day suffered over seventy-five per cent casualties. It hung on tenaciously, inflicting losses on the enemy, and its action was instrumental in holding the bridgehead. 1st Armoured Division, too, became involved near Tel el Aqqaqir, and a fierce armoured battle ensued in which both sides had losses.

In the afternoon 51st Division extended the salient to the south, and at night 7th Motor Brigade attacked to the west of the Rahman track.

On 3 November, the Desert Air Force reported heavy traffic moving westwards on the coast road, but the enemy anti-tank gun screen held, and 1st Armoured Division was still unable to pierce it.

Below: The course of the Battle of Alamein. After heavy fighting around Kidney and Miteiriya ridges, 10th Corps' armor broke through the Axis positions during the first days of November.

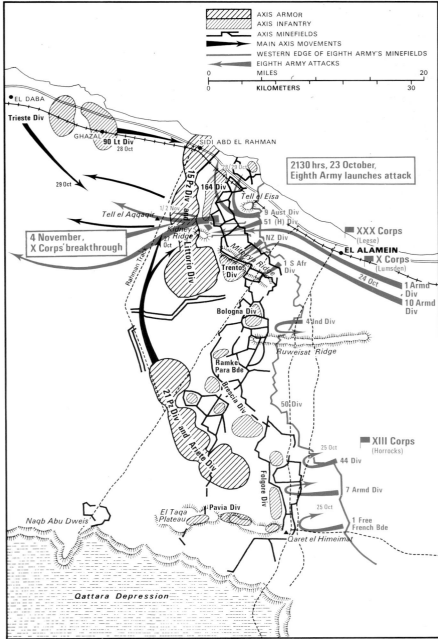

Situation 3 November

It was now clear that the enemy contemplated a withdrawal, but would have difficulty in getting his troops away owing to shortage of transport and fuel. And so I expected that he would try and hold me off while his evacuation of the Alamein positions proceeded, but I made plans to complete the break-out and get behind him.

I ordered an attack to the south of Tel el Aqqaqir, with the object of outflanking the anti-tank gun screen which was hemming us in.

Operations on night 3/4 and 4 November

On the night 3/4 November, 51st Division and a brigade from 4th Indian Division launched a very speedily mounted thrust which reached the Rahman track south of Tel el Aqqaqir on a front of over four miles. My intention was to break through the southern sector of the enemy's anti-tank gun screen which was preventing our penetration; the enemy was not in very great depth in the area and once a gap had been made the way would be clear for our armour to pass out into the open desert, outflanking the stronger resistance to the north. Very great credit is due to the formations which organized this attack in an extremely short time and carried it through successfully, for by the morning of 4 November the enemy screen had been forced back and reformed facing southeast covering the coast road. The armoured divisions and New Zealanders were set in motion. The Battle of El Alamein had been won. Everywhere the enemy was in full retreat.

The pursuit from El Alamein

I planned to cut off the retreating enemy by swinging north to cut the coast road at the bottlenecks of Fuka and Matruh. 2nd New Zealand Division was ordered to Fuka, and 10th Corps to Matruh.

Meanwhile, to the south of the break-out area, 13th Corps formed mobile columns which raced westwards to round up the Italians, four of whose divisions had been left without transport and with very little food or water.

The Desert Air Force operated at maximum intensity and took every advantage of the exceptional targets which the fleeing enemy presented.

During 4 November 10th Corps encountered the remnants of the enemy armour south of Ghazal. 2nd New Zealand Division by-passed these rearguards to the south, but on 5 November had a sharp engagement near Fuka; during the afternoon 4th Light Armoured Brigade broke through the opposition and swung in to the road.

On 5 November I regrouped for the pursuit. 10th Corps (1st and 7th Armoured and 2nd New Zealand Divisions) was to lead the chase. 30th Corps I positioned between Matruh and Alamein, and to 13th Corps I assigned the task of clearing up the battlefield.

By nightfall 6 November, advanced troops were nearing the Matruh-Charing Cross area, where I hoped to cut off a considerable body of the enemy survivors.

Heavy rains interfered with my plans. On 7 November the force was bogged in the desert, with its petrol and supplies held up some miles behind. 1st Armoured Division failed to reach Charing Cross and delay was experienced on the coast in clearing the enemy rearguards at Matruh. The enemy made good use of this respite of some twenty-four hours to retrieve some of his troops and transport, which fled along the coast road, and the long pursuit of the Afrika Korps and the Italians to their El Agheila position began in earnest.

Some reflections on the battle of El Alamein

The Axis forces in North Africa had sustained a crushing defeat, and indeed only the rain on 6 and 7 November saved them from complete annihilation. Four crack German divisions and eight Italian divisions had ceased to exist as effective fighting formations.

30,000 prisoners were taken.

A great number of enemy tanks had been destroyed, and the quantity of guns, transport, aircraft and stores of all kinds captured or destroyed was immense.

The battle had conformed to the pattern anticipated. The break-in, or battle for position, had given us the tactical advantage; the dog-fight which followed reduced the enemy's strength and resources to a degree which left him unable to withstand the final knock-out blow. The dog-fight demanded rapid regrouping of forces to create reserves available for switching the axis of operations as the situation required; in this way the initiative was retained, and the battle swung to its desired end.

Tactical surprise was an important factor; the break-in operation achieved it completely, for the enemy had expected our main thrust in the south. In the final thrust again the enemy was deceived; he had prepared for it in the extreme north, and concentrated his German troops to meet it. It was delivered against the Italians, two miles south of the German flank.

The most critical time in the battle was 26 and 27 October. Fighting was intense but the momentum of our attacks was diminishing. It was then that I started drawing divisions into reserve, ready for the final operation. At the time this gave to some the impression that I had decided that we could not break through the enemy and was giving up; but I would say that when you find a commander drawing troops into reserve at a critical moment of the battle, it probably means he is about to win it.

It was always clear in my mind that once a commander defeated his enemy in battle, everything else would be added unto him. The great hazard at El Alamein was whether the enemy would stand and fight it out. He did; he was decisively defeated; the rest was relatively easy. In the previous desert campaigns, Rommel had never been decisively defeated in battle; he had been forced to withdraw, but not because of decisive defeat. There was now a fundamental difference in the problem of the future conduct of the Desert War.

This . . . was a basic consideration in my plans to ensure that there would never be another Axis recovery and re-entry into Egypt.

Left: German prisoners await transportation to the rear. Rommel lost over 20,000 men, 1,000 guns and an estimated 450 tanks in the battle.

Below left: Lieutenant-General Sir Leslie Morshead (1889-1959), commander of the Australian 9th Division. A somewhat difficult character, he was known to some as 'Ming the Merciless.' However, his epic defense of Tobruk in 1941 remains one of the outstanding events of the desert campaign.

Below: A pair of Crusader tanks lead the pursuit of the Afrika Korps along the North African coast. Bad weather and a poorly co-ordinated operation allowed part of Rommel's battered command to escape to fight another day.

Stalingrad

by Vasili I. Chuikov

The Russian counter-offensive in the winter of 1941-42 drove back the Germans along much of the 1,200-mile front. Still Hitler compelled his generals to hang on, and enhanced his reputation as a 'military genius' when they managed to do so. With 3,000,000 men at his command he was confident of securing the vital oil supplies in the Caucasus and taking Stalingrad.

A Russian offensive round Kharkov, though eventually held, delayed the Germans for a month, and when they began their advance, progress was not as swift as had been hoped. Chuikov's description of the improving Russian tactics must in part account for this failure.

Stalingrad, a city of half a million inhabitants was reduced to rubble by the *Luftwaffe,* and the initial German assault left 45,000 Russians clinging to four narrow bridgeheads along the banks of the Volga.

General Friedrich Paulus, the commander of the German Sixth Army, was a Hessian officer, aged 52. Guderian described him as 'the finest type of brilliantly clever, conscientious, hardworking, original and talented General Staff Officer'. Not an inspiring leader perhaps, but if the Germans failed before Stalingrad it was not so much that they lacked their old dash, but that the Russians, now extremely well commanded, displayed an admirable resolution and tenacity. As Antony Brett-James wrote:

'That the Sixth Army did its utmost to capture . . . the city is shown by the fact that General Gurtiev's Siberian Division defending the Red October factory was subjected to over 100 assaults in the course of a month, and on one day alone German tanks tried 23 times to oust the tenacious defenders.'

In November Hitler tempted Providence by declaring to the 'old comrades' of the Nazi Party that he was now master of the city. But early that month the temperature fell sharply

These pages: A Russian mortar section trudges through the ruins of Stalingrad after the surrender of the German Sixth Army, February 1943.

and ice appeared on the Volga. The end, though long delayed, was now perhaps inevitable. Von Manstein made a desperate effort to relieve Paulus but in vain, and on 31 January the latter surrendered.

This catastrophe cost Hitler 20 German and two Rumanian divisions. The losses included 1,500 tanks, 6,000 guns, 60,000 vehicles, and 91,000 men, of whom perhaps 6,000 lived to tell the tale.

Göring's promise to supply the Sixth Army from the air had proved as empty as his claims that the *Luftwaffe* could prevent the evacuation of the BEF from Dunkirk, and that no Allied bomb would ever fall on Berlin.

General von Mellenthin commented that 'the tactical conduct of the battle by the Russians was on a high level'. It is this aspect that gives Chuikov's account its peculiar interest.

EDITOR

Chronology

1940
22 June	Germans invade Russia.
18 Sept.	Fall of Kiev.
6 Oct.	Germans attack Moscow.
Oct.	Leningrad beleaguered.
7 Nov.	Stalin's Holy Russia speech.
6 Dec.	Zhukov counter attacks.
14 Dec.	Germans retreat on the Moscow front.

1942
Mid-Feb.	End of Russian winter offensive.
28 June	Germans take Sevastopol.
23 July	Fall of Rostov.
6 Sept.	Germans halted at Stalingrad.
9 Sept.	Hitler assumes command of Army Group A.
19/21 Nov.	Stalingrad encircled.
16 Dec.	Italian Eighth Army broken on the Don.
19 Dec.	Fourth Panzer Army within 35 miles of Stalingrad.
28 Dec.	Von Manstein orders the withdrawal of Fourth Panzer Army.

1943
3 Jan.	Germans retreat from the Caucasus.
14 Jan.	Russians attack on the Don. Hungarian Second Army disintegrates.
31 Jan.	Paulus surrenders at Stalingrad.

Baptism of Fire

'For us there is no
land across the Volga!'

*In his first battle of the Second World War (25-27
July) Chuikov made a close study of German tactics. He was not particularly impressed.*

Observing how the Germans carried out their artillery preparations against the 229th Infantry Division's sector, I saw the weak points in their tactics. In strength and organization this artillery preparation was weak. Artillery and mortar attacks were not co-ordinated or in depth, but only against the main line of defence. I saw no broad manoeuvre with artillery cover in the dynamic of battle.

When I was a student at the Frunze Academy I studied many battles and German operations on the Western Front in the First World War. I knew the views of the German generals about the role of artillery in future war (for example, the views of von Bernhardi). In the first days of the battle on the Don, therefore, I was expecting close combined operations between the enemy's artillery and ground forces, a precise organization of the artillery barrage, a lightning-fast manoeuvre of shell and wheel. But this was not the case. I encountered the far-from-new method of slow wearing-down, trench by trench.

If at this time we had had a deeper defence structure (not five, but all ten battalions) and bigger anti-tank reserves, we could have not only beaten off the attack, but soundly thrashed the enemy.

The German tanks did not go into action without infantry and air support. On the battlefield there was no evidence of the 'prowess' of German tank crews, their courage and speed in action, about which foreign newspapers had written. The reverse was true, in fact – they operated sluggishly, extemely cautiously and indecisively.

The German infantry was strong in automatic fire, but I saw no rapid movement or resolute attack on the battlefield. When advancing, the German infantry frequently fired into thin air.

Marshal Vasili Ivanovitch Chuikov
(1900-)

When the Germans invaded the Soviet Union Chuikov was in China, serving as military attaché and chief military adviser to Chiang Kai-shek. Recalled to Moscow (March 1942) he was appointed Acting Commander of the reserve army training in the Tula region (May). In July his army, renamed the 64th Army, was transferred to the Don where the Russians were under severe pressure. He was in action against the Germans for the first time on 26 July.

On 12 September he was appointed Commander of the 62nd Army.

On 27 July, when one regiment of the 112th Division counter-attacked at Novomaksimovski Farm, the enemy's infantry did not engage battle at all and retreated. Only on the next day, when tank units had come up, did it fight for the positions it had abandoned without battle the previous day.

The German forward positions, particularly at night, were beautifully visible, being marked by machine-gun fire, tracer bullets, often fired into empty space, and different coloured rockets. It seemed as if the Germans were either afraid of the dark or were bored without the crackle of machine-guns and the light of tracer bullets.

Any enemy troop manoeuvre could be clearly followed by the columns of motor vehicles moving across the steppe with their headlights on.

The enemy's air force worked most accurately in battle. Combined operations and communication between the enemy's air and ground forces were very good. One could feel that the German pilots were familiar with the tactics of their own ground forces and ours.

One would very often see something like this: when German infantry had to take cover from our artillery or rifle and machine-gun fire, in a few minutes German aircraft would fly up, usually assault planes. Flying in a closed circle they would attack our military formations and artillery positions.

In modern warfare victory is impossible

Below: Smiling crewmen of a German panzer regiment take a break from their headlong pursuit of the Red Army in the early stages of Operation Barbarossa.

without combined action by all types of forces and without good administration. The Germans had this kind of polished, co-ordinated action. In battle the different arms of their forces never hurried, did not push ahead alone, but fought with the whole mass of men and technical backing. A few minutes before a general attack, their aircraft would fly in, bomb and strafe the object under attack, pinning the defending troops to the ground, and then infantry and tanks with supporting artillery and mortar fire would cut into our military formations almost with impunity.

These were the first deductions I came to about the enemy's tactics. I came to them not as a casual observer, and not so that I could talk about them afterwards. No, far from it. I had to know how the Nazi generals organized for battle, see the enemy's strong points, detect the weak ones and find his Achilles' heel.

Now, therefore, many years afterwards, remembering my constant attempts to observe the enemy and discern his battle tactics I can see that I did not do this for nothing. To observe the enemy, to study his strong and weak points, to know his habits and customs, means to fight with one's eyes open, to take advantage of his mistakes and not expose one's own weak spots to dangerous attack.

Chuikov underlines the importance of the delaying actions fought before Stalingrad.

In these battles we worked out our own special methods and our own tactics.

The enemy usually attacked between 10-12 noon. He would have to spend two to three hours crossing the Aksay and approaching our forward defences, which were in fact reinforced outposts. The infantry attack would be sup- ported by artillery and two or three formations of aeroplanes, nine in each.

Our outposts, opening fire with support from our artillery would slowly retreat towards the main defence positions. In such a situation the enemy could not select the moment to attack, and had to spend a further two or three hours in

Above: Despite the capture of large amounts of military transport and equipment after the fall of France, many German divisions were far from fully mechanized by the summer of 1941.

Far left: A German medium mortar is deployed to deal with a Russian defensive position.

Left: The crew of a T-34 surrenders to the German Army. The T-34 was perhaps the most effective and innovatory medium tank of the war.

reaching our main positions. To break through our main positions he had to stop, bring up men and guns, and organize communications and administration. By nightfall, therefore, the attackers had not succeeded in breaking through our defences, and they did not like, and possibly were unable, to fight by night. We would then counter-attack either in the evening or at dawn, when the enemy's planes were on the ground. Our artillery and mortars would go into action and our units would counter-attack swiftly and strongly at the enemy's weakest point and throw him back to where he started from.

The pattern was repeated several times.

Under orders from Hitler to take Stalingrad by 25 August, the German hordes, regardless of losses, tore through towards the Volga. 23 August 1942 proved to be a tragic day for the city, when, with several infantry divisions and one panzer division, and at the cost of enormous losses, the enemy managed to break through the 62nd Army's defences between Vertyachi and Peskovatka. The enemy's forward units, supported by a hundred tanks, reached the Volga north of the village of Rynok. Along a corridor five miles wide the Germans poured several infantry, motorized and panzer divisions.

An extremely dangerous situation had arisen. The slightest confusion, the slightest sign of panic, on our side, would have been fatal. This is what the Germans were banking on. With the deliberate intention of sowing panic, and, as a result of it, breaking through to the city, on 23 August they turned some 2,000 bombers on the town. Never before in the entire war had the enemy attacked in such strength from the air. The huge city, stretching for nearly 35 miles along the Volga, was en-

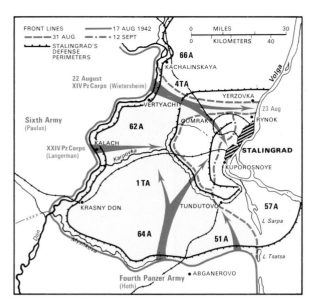

veloped in flames. Everything was blazing, collapsing. Death and disaster descended on thousands of families.

But the response to the enemy attacks was not panic or alarm. At the call of the Front Military Council and the Party organizations in the city, the soldiers and citizens replied by closing their ranks. The famous Barrikady (Barricades) and Krasny Oktyabr (Red October) tractor factories and the power stations became bastions of defence. The workers forged guns and fought for the factories alongside the soldiers. Grey-haired veterans of the defence of Tsaritsyn, foundry-men and tractor engineers, Volga boatmen and stevedores, railwaymen and shipbuilders, office workers and housewives, fathers and children – all became soldiers, and each and every one turned out to defend their city. Help soon came to them from military units belonging to Colonels Sarayev, Gorokhov and Andryusenko, and Lieutenant-Colonel Bolvinov.

Above left: The German drive on Stalingrad, showing the pincer movement of Hoth's Fourth Panzer Army and von Paulus' Sixth Army.

Above: Von Paulus (left) confers with one of his field commanders.

Left: Standing atop a Panzer III, a German infantryman lines up on a target in a burning Russian village.

Left: A German infantry
section advances through
the suburbs of Stalingrad;
a self-propelled gun
provides fire support.

The fighting grew more and more intense. Every step forward the Germans made was at the price of huge losses. The nearer they came to the city, the more intense became the fighting, the more fearlessly did the Soviet troops fight. During these days of fighting our defence was like a spring, which increases its resilience under pressure.

Chuikov had a narrow escape on 3 September.

I sent for my truck, and with Klimov, my aide-de-camp, and Kayum Kalikulin, the driver, I set off. But we had scarcely emerged from the gully when the enemy's aeroplanes again started peppering our command post with small bombs. We could see Ju 88s coming in for low-level attacks, dropping some ten or a dozen bombs each on the gully, and then going after individual vehicles. One Junkers came after us. We were saved, and I say this without embarrassment, by firmness and calculation.

Not taking my eyes off the Junkers, I shouted to the driver:

'Drive straight ahead and don't turn off!'

When I saw the first bomb leave the plane I ordered him to turn sharp right. The vehicle swung round 90 degrees at full speed. By the time the bombs hit the ground we were already over 100 yards away.

The Junkers dropped about a dozen bombs, but not one of us was hurt. Our vehicle's battery, however, had a hole in it and the electrolyte was running out; the engine would not start. All this happened about 350-550 yards from our command post.

5 September added to Chuikov's tactical experiences.

When we came out of the dug-out we saw German tanks attacking the Verkhnyaya Yelshanka cattle-yards from the direction of Voroponovo. Some twenty-five tanks, followed by infantry, were engaged in the attack. They were met with fire from our tanks, which had been well hidden and camouflaged in and to the south of the village of Verkhnyaya Yelshanka.

The first salvo sent seven German tanks up in flames, and the rest promptly turned back and raced off at full speed.

'Bravo our tanks – that was a splendid ambush!' I thought, and decided to go down and see the crews. When I got there I unexpectedly met the commander of the unit, Colonel Lebedev, with whom I had served in Kisselevichi in 1937. I had been commander of a mechanized brigade, and Lebedev of a single battalion.

Our meeting was brief, and the last – Lebedev, not leaving his tanks, was killed at the approaches to the city.

The month and a half of fighting which had begun at the other side of the Don on 23 July had taught me a great deal. During this time I had studied the enemy well enough to be able to predict his operational plans.

Pincers driven in depth towards a single point – that was the enemy's main tactic. With superiority in the air power and tanks, the enemy was able to penetrate our defences relatively easily, drive in his pincers, and make our units retreat when they seemed to be on the point of being surrounded. No sooner would a stubborn defence or counter-attack stop or eliminate one of the pincers, than another one would appear and try to find a foothold elsewhere in the ruins of the city.

The enemy stuck to the same pattern in his tactics. His infantry went into an attack wholeheartedly only when tanks had already reached the target. The tanks, however, normally went into an attack only when the *Luftwaffe* was already over the heads of our troops. One had only to break this sequence for an enemy attack to stop and his units to turn back.

The enemy could not sustain our sudden

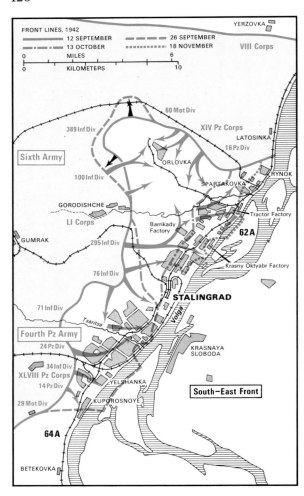

attacks, particularly by artillery and mortar fire. We had only to organize a good artillery bombardment on an enemy concentration and the Germans would scatter in panic.

The Germans could not stand close fighting; they opened up with their automatic weapons from well over half a mile away, when their bullets could not cover half the distance. They fired simply to keep up their morale. They could not bear us to come close to them when we counter-attacked, some threw themselves to the ground, and often retreated before our troops reached their lines.

Their communications between infantry, tanks and aeroplanes were good, especially through the use of rockets. They met their aeroplanes with dozens, hundreds of rockets, pin-pointing their positions. Our troops and commanders worked out this signalling system and began to make use of it, frequently leading the enemy to make mistakes.

Analysing the enemy's tactical and operational methods, I tried to find counter-measures and counter-methods. I thought a great deal, in particular, about how to overcome or reduce the importance of German superiority in the air, and its effect on the morale of our troops. I remembered battles against the White Guards and White Poles in the Civil War, when we had to attack under artillery and machine-gun fire, without any artillery support of our own. We used to run up close to the enemy, and his artillery would be unable to take fresh aim and fire on rapidly approaching targets. A short, sharp attack would decide a battle.

I came to the conclusion that the best method of fighting the Germans would be close battle, applied night and day in different forms. We should get as close to the enemy as possible, so that his air force could not bomb our forward units or trenches. Every German soldier must be made to feel that he was living under the muzzle of a Russian gun, always ready to treat him to a fatal dose of lead.

Those were the ideas which took shape in my hours of reflection about the fate of the city for which such fierce fighting was taking place. It seemed to me that it was precisely here, in the fighting for the city, that it was possible to force the enemy into close fighting and deprive him of his trump card – his air force.

On 11 September 1942, I was summoned to Stalingrad and South-Western Fronts Military Council (the one Military Council was covering both fronts), to see Comrades Khrushchev and Yeremenko. I had known Nikita Sergeyevich Khrushchev as Secretary of the Moscow Committee of the Communist Party, as Secretary of the Central Committee of the Communist Party of the Ukraine and as Member of the Front Military Council; I knew Andrey Ivanovich Yeremenko . . . from the days when we had served in the Belorussian military district.

Above: The crew of a 50mm anti-tank gun prepares to fire on a Russian strongpoint from their exposed position in the middle of a Stalingrad street.

Above left: The shrinking perimeter of Stalingrad, with the main thrusts of the Sixth Army toward the River Volga, September-November 1942.

Harrowing scenes met Chuikov as he waited to cross the Volga

Waiting for a ferry I go into some of the dressing-stations. The faces of the wounded are anxious, strained. In their eyes I read the same questions: 'How are things in the city? Are our troops retreating or not? Will transport come soon?'

At these dressing-stations I see many things wrong – the wounded are not being fed, they are lying in the open, they are asking for water. Their blood-soaked and dust-covered bandages look like a gaudy reproduction. I approach the medical staff and keep asking the same question: 'Why?' I know beforehand, however, that I will not hear anything in reply that I do not already know. 'We haven't slept for several days; in the daytime we are bombed, and at night so many wounded arrive that we don't know how to cope!' I ask them to hurry. They say they will and then go on working as slowly as before.

I grow more and more agitated, but I realize that the doctors, nurses and orderlies can do no more than they are doing. They are on their feet the whole time, without sleep, are probably hungry and so exhausted that they are incapable of working any faster. They are worn out.

Near one of the crossings there is a hospital. I go into the operating theatre. They are operating on a soldier who has been wounded in the buttock by splinters from a mine. The faces of the surgeon and the nurses are whiter than their gowns. I can see that everyone is exhausted from work and lack of sleep. The wounded man is groaning. Near the table is a basin with blood-stained gauze. The surgeon glances at me and goes on with his work. I watch the operation through to the end and then ask him:

'Why did you cut away nearly the whole buttock?'

'If I leave any flesh,' he replies, 'the man will die of gas gangrene. He won't come back from the dead. . .'

At night I cross the Volga.

I look round at the west bank and see it in flames. The glow lights up the road. There is no need to switch headlights on. Bends in the road frequently bring me back almost to the Volga. German shells frequently fly over the city, over the river, and explode on the left bank. The Germans are systematically bombarding the roads leading to the city from the east. Anyone without experience of war would think that in the blazing city there is no longer anywhere left to live, that everything has been destroyed and burnt out. But I know that on the other side of the river a battle is being fought, a titanic struggle is taking place.

I had a premonition that it would not be long before I was in that flame-covered city. Without asking, I could see from their eyes that my aide, G. I. Klimov, the driver, Kayum Kalimulin,

Above: Closing in on the central area of Stalingrad. Thick mud, made worse by heavy artillery and air attacks, slowed the German advance toward the city center.

Left: By the end of September units of the Sixth Army had fought their way into the center of Stalingrad, but in the city's industrial area in the north, the Red Army held a series of heavily defended factories. Seen here is the façade of the tractor factory close to the banks of the Volga.

and the orderly, Revold Sidorin, were thinking the same.

That night Chuikov reached Front HQ which was at the blitzed village of Yamy.

Front HQ was underground, in dug-outs, well-camouflaged from the air with bushes.

That night I slept well and peacefully, though at the other side of the Volga, five to six miles away, a battle was raging. It was a month and a half since I had slept so 'far' from the battlefield.

I arrived at Front HQ at exactly 10 a.m. on 12 September, and was received immediately by A. I. Yeremenko and N. S. Khrushchev.

The conversation was brief, I had been appointed Commander of the 62nd Army. Nikita Khrushchev added some more brief but useful comments.

The basic theme was that the Germans had decided to take the city at any cost. We should not and could not surrender it to them, we could not retreat any further, there was nowhere to retreat to. The 62nd Army's Commander, General Lopatin, did not believe that his Army could hold the city. Instead of fighting to the death, instead of dying in the attempt to keep the enemy from the Volga, he had been withdrawing units. He had therefore been relieved of his post, and the Army had been temporarily put under the command of the Chief of Staff, General N. I. Krylov. The Front Military Council, with the agreement of GHQ, had proposed that I should take over command of the Army.

He underlined, in saying this, that he knew of the successful operations of the Southern Group in soundly beating the enemy on the River Aksay, and so protecting our troop movements in the danger area.

I took this as a compliment, a compliment which also meant obligations for me.

Left: A section of battle-weary German infantry awaits the order to launch another attack on the ruins of the Barrikady Factory, September-October 1942.

Finally, Nikita Khrushchev asked me:
'Comrade Chuikov, how do you interpret your task?'

I had not expected to have to answer such a question, but I did not have to think for long – everything was clear.

'We cannot surrender the city to the enemy,' I replied, 'because it is extremely valuable to us, to the whole Soviet people. The loss of it would undermine the nation's morale. All possible measures will be taken to prevent the city from falling. I don't ask for anything now, but I would ask the Military Council not to refuse me help when I ask for it, and I swear I shall stand firm. We will defend the city or die in the attempt.'

They looked at me and said I had understood my task correctly.

Left: A T-34 fitted with a short-barreled 76mm gun lies abandoned in a gully – a victim of German fire.

Mamayev Kurgan

On the evening of 12 Sepember we arrive in our truck at Krasnaya Sloboda and make for the ferry. One T-34 tank has already been loaded on to the ferry and a second is being loaded. They will not allow my truck on. I present my documents as Commander of the 62nd Army and drive on to the boat.

The deputy commander of a tank formation introduces himself. I ask him how things are going.

'Yesterday evening,' he answers, 'we had about forty tanks, with only half of them or so in working order – the remainder are out of action but are being used as stationary firing positions. I am now taking up two more tanks, but how many have been put out of action and burnt out today I don't know.

Our ferry skirts round the sandy spit of land jutting out north of Golodny Island and heads for the central landing-stage. Shells occasionally burst on the water. They are firing aimlessly. It is not dangerous. We come in close to the bank. From a distance we can see that as our ferry approaches, the landing-stage fills with people. They are bringing the wounded out of trenches, craters and dug-outs, and people are crowding round with bundles and cases. Until the ferry approached they have been taking cover in trenches, shell holes and bomb craters.

All these people have stern faces, black with dust and streaked with tears. Children, racked with thirst and hunger, no longer cry, but merely whimper, trailing their little hands in the water . . . One's heart contracts and a lump comes into one's throat.

Our vehicle quickly drives off the ferry and we head for the 62nd Army's command post; they have told me at Front HQ that it is in the valley of the River Tsaritsa, not far from its mouth.

The streets of the city are dead. There is not a single green twig left on the trees: everything has perished in the flames. All that is left of the wooden houses is a pile of ashes and stove chimneys sticking up out of them. The many stone houses are burnt out, their windows and doors missing and roofs caved in. Now and then a building that is still standing collapses. People are rummaging about in the ruins, pulling out bundles, samovars and crockery, and carrying everything to the landing-stage.

We follow the railway line along the bank of the Volga to the mouth of the Tsaritsa, then along the valley as far as Astrakhanski Bridge but cannot find the command post anywhere. It is growing dark. No one I ask has any idea where the Army command post is.

We pass through barricades put up in the streets and are amazed at them. Who could have made such 'fortifications'? Not only will they not hold back enemy tanks – the bumper of a lorry will knock them down.

Near the station we meet an officer. He turns out to be the Commissar of a sapper unit. We are delighted to find that he knows where the Army command post is. He gets into the truck and guides us to the foot of Mamayev Kurgan.

We leave the truck and go up the hill on foot. In the darkness I clutch at bushes, scratch myself on all kinds of thorns. Finally I hear the long-awaited shout of a sentry:

'Halt! Who goes there?'

I have arrived at the command post. I go along a gully, striding and jumping over trenches and entrances to dug-outs. At the end of it all I find myself in the dug-out of the Army Chief of Staff, General N. I. Krylov, who has been Acting Commander. He is a thick-set, stocky man with a determined face.

Krylov's dug-out, strictly speaking, is not a dug-out at all, but a broad trench with a bench made of packed earth along one side, a bed made of earth on the other, and a table made of earth at the end of the bed. The roof is made of brushwood, with bits of straw sticking through it, and on top of the straw a layer of soil about 12-15 inches thick. Shells and mortar bombs are exploding nearby. The explosions make the dug-out shake and soil runs down through the ceiling on to the spread-out maps and on to the heads of the people inside.

Below: Two German officers attempt to gather information from Russian refugees who have dug shelters into the banks of the Volga.

There are two people in the dug-out – General Krylov, with a telephone in his hand, and the telephonist on duty, Elena Bakarevich, a blue-eyed girl of about eighteen. Krylov is having strong words with someone or other. His voice is hard, loud, angry. The telephonist is sitting near the entrance with headphones on, answering someone:

'He is speaking on the other telephone. . .'

I take out my papers and put them in front of Krylov. Continuing to tell somebody off, he glances at the papers, then finishes the conversation, and we introduce ourselves. In the poor light of a paraffin lamp I see a vigorous, stern and at the same time friendly face.

'You see, Comrade Commander,' he says, 'without my permission the commander of an armoured formation has transferred his command post from Hill 107.5 right to the bank of the Volga. In other words, the formation's command post is now behind us. It's disgraceful. . .'

I agree with him that it is disgraceful and sit down at the table. The telephone rings continually. Elena Bakarevich hands the telephone to Krylov. He is giving instructions for the following day. I listen, trying to understand the meaning of the conversation: I have decided not to interfere. I listen to Krylov and at the same time study his working map, the marks and arrows on it, trying to feel my way into the events taking place. I realize that he has no time to give me a report on the situation in peace and quiet. I have to trust Krylov; I do not disturb his operations or alter his plans for tomorrow, because in any case, necessary or not, there is nothing I am capable of changing.

Chuikov soon had a tight grip on his command and began to devise tactics dictated by his ever-increasing experience.

The enemy had firm mastery in the air. This dispirited our troops more than anything, and we feverishly thought about how to take this trump card out of the enemy's hand. But how, by what tactical method? The question was not easy if one remembers that the city's anti-aircraft defences had already been substantially weakened. Part of the anti-aircraft artillery had been destroyed by the enemy, and what remained of it had been moved to the left bank of the Volga, from where it could cover the river and a narrow strip along the right bank. From dawn to dusk, therefore, German planes were over the city, over our military units and over the Volga.

Watching the *Luftwaffe* in action, we noticed that accurate bombing was not a distinguishing feature of the German airmen: they bombed our forward positions only where there was a broad expanse of no man's land between our forward positions and those of the enemy. It occurred to us, therefore, that we should

reduce the no man's land as much as possible – to the throw of a grenade.

But above all it was necessary to raise the fighting spirit of the Army. And it was essential to achieve this as rapidly as possible. Losses in battle, retreats, the shortage of ammunition and provisions, difficulties in replenishing men and material – all these lowered the morale of our troops. Many of them had begun to want to get across the Volga as quickly as possible, and get away from this hell.

We had decided, above all, to defend the ferries from the enemy's artillery fire, to achieve which we would put up a stiff defence on the right and left flanks, and attack the centre to

Above: Firing over open sights, a German 105mm field gun lends support to an attack on one of Stalingrad's factories.

Left: Showing signs of battle strain, a lone infantryman moves through the desolation of Stalingrad.

occupy Razgulyayevka Station and the railway from it to the southwest as far as the sharp bend near Gumrak. This would make it possible to straighten out the front in the centre and, using the railway embankment as an anti-tank obstacle, to go ahead afterwards and occupy Gorodishche and Aleksandrovka. A tank formation, reinforced with infantry, was set aside for this purpose; it would have the support of the major part of the Army's artillery. The regrouping would take place on 13 September, and the attack the day after.

We were awakened early in the morning by heavy enemy artillery fire and bombing.

At 6.30 a.m. the Germans attacked with an infantry division and forty to fifty tanks from the vicinity of Razgulyayevka. The attack was aimed through Aviagorodok towards Central Station and Mamayev Kurgan.

On both flanks of our Army the enemy confined himself to holding actions, from the north attacking an infantry brigade with one of his battalions, aiming towards Orlovka, and on the left flank throwing individual battalions against the positions held by our composite regiment.

In the centre and on the left flank the battle went on all day. The enemy brought up fresh reserves and intensified the attack. His artillery and mortars pounded our units. His planes flew non-stop over the battlefield.

From Mamayev Kurgan both the ground and air fighting were clearly visible. We saw about a dozen planes – our own and the enemy's – burst into flames and crash to the ground. In spite of stubborn resistance by Soviet forces on the ground and in the air, the enemy's numerical superiority gave him the upper hand. Our command post, right at the top of Mamayev Kurgan, was showered with artillery shells and mortar bombs. I was working with Krylov in the same dug-out and from time to time we went out together to the stereoscopic telescope to observe the battle. A number of dug-outs were destroyed, and there were losses among the Army HQ staff.

Our telephone wires were constantly being broken, and radio communication worked with long and frequent interruptions. We threw all our signallers into the job of repairing communications. Even the telephonists on duty repeatedly had to abandon the telephones and climb out to find and repair damage to the lines. On 13 September I managed to speak to the Front Commander by telephone only once. I briefly reported on the situation to him and asked him to let me have two or three fresh divisions in the coming days – we had nothing to beat off the enemy's attacks with.

Despite all the efforts of our signallers, by 4 p.m. we had almost completely lost contact with the troops.

The situation was now somewhat disturbing. Although the enemy battalion which had attacked from the north towards Orlovka had

been wiped out by our infantry brigade, at the centre of the Army's positions our units had suffered losses and had been forced to withdraw eastward, to the western edge of a wood, west of the Barrikady and Krasny Oktyabr workers' settlements. The Germans had taken Hill 126.3, Aviagorodok and the hospital. On the left flank our composite regiment had abandoned the machine and tractor station east of Sadovaya Station. On the remaining sectors individual attacks had been beaten off and sixteen enemy tanks had been burnt out.

What happened afterwards we discovered only by messengers and through Army HQ signals officers. All the enemy's attacks in the latter part of the day were beaten off.

Before darkness fell I had to decide whether to carry out the plan of active defence we had drawn up the previous day, or, in view of the new enemy attack, to take more decisive action. There could be no delay, as we could only carry out the regrouping of our forces under cover of darkness – it would have been impossible in daylight because of the enemy's air raids.

We decided to counter-attack. In order to forestall the enemy, the counter-attack was scheduled to start early on the morning of 14 September. We knew that the Army's potential was very restricted, and that we could not allocate large forces to the counter-attack, but we were sure that the enemy knew this and that the last thing he was expecting was active operations on our part. We remembered Suvorov's

Above: A posed shot of three Russian soldiers amid the ruins of Stalingrad. They are armed with PPsh 7.62mm sub-machine guns and a Degtyarev light machine-gun.

dictum – 'to surprise is to conquer'. We were not counting on any rapid victory, but on surprising the enemy and upsetting his plans. It was important for our attack to be sudden, however partial and temporary a measure it might be, so as to take the initiative out of his hands.

The order to counter-attack was communicated to the troops at 10.30 p.m. It laid down precise objectives for every unit.

At 3 a.m. our artillery preparation began, then at 3.30 our counter-attack. I telephoned the Front Commander and reported to him that our counter-attack had started and asked him to cover our operations from the air at sunrise. He promised to do this and gave me the glad news that the 13th Guards Infantry Division was being attached to us from GHQ Reserve; the division would start to assemble at the Volga crossings towards evening that day, in the vicinity of Krasnaya Sloboda.

I immediately sent Colonel Tupichev, who was in command of army engineering, with a group of Army HQ staff officers to Krasnaya Sloboda to meet the Guards Division, and Krylov and I again began to get into touch with our unit and to find out what the position was.

We found that at the centre of the Army's sector our counter-attack had at the beginning met with some success, but as soon as day broke the enemy brought the *Luftwaffe* into action; groups of fifty to sixty aircraft flew in bombing and machine-gunning our counter-attack units, pinning them to the ground. The counter-attack petered out. At noon the enemy threw large infantry and tank formations into the battle and began to press our units back. Their attack was directed towards Central Station.

This was an exceptionally strong attack. In spite of enormous losses, the enemy broke through. Lorry-loads of infantry and tanks tore through into the city. The Germans obviously

thought that the fate of the city had been settled, and they all rushed to reach the Volga and the centre of the city as rapidly as possible, and to grab some souvenirs for themselves. Our soldiers, snipers, anti-tank and artillery men, hiding in and behind houses, in cellars and blockhouses, saw drunken Germans jumping down from their lorries, playing mouth-organs, shouting like mad and dancing on the damaged pavements.

Enemy troops perished in their hundreds, but fresh waves of reserves flooded into the streets. Enemy tommy-gunners infiltrated into the city east of the railway towards the station, and occupied the 'specialists' houses'. Fighting was going on half a mile from our command post. There was a danger that the enemy would occupy the station, cut through the Army and reach the central landing-stage before the 13th Guards Infantry Division arrived.

Fierce fighting was also taking place on the

Above: German infantry move through the twisted wreckage littering the floor of the Tractor factory, October 1942.

Left: Scenes of devastation on the Sixth Army front. As fall turned to winter, von Paulus' men began to suffer the effects of the severe Russian weather.

left flank, around Minina suburb. Our right flank was also giving the enemy no rest. The situation was growing more difficult with every hour.

I had a small reserve still intact – a single heavy armoured brigade consisting of nineteen tanks. It was on the Army's left flank, on the southern outskirts of the city. I ordered one battalion of this brigade's tanks to be sent immediately to the command post. It arrived two hours later, with nine tanks. General Krylov had already formed two groups consisting of staff officers and a guard company. The first of these groups, reinforced with six tanks, was put under the command of Communist I. Zalyuzik, who was in charge of the Army's operations section. It was given the task of blocking the streets leading from the railway station to the landing-stage. The second group with three tanks, under Lieutenant-Colonel Weinrub, was sent to the specialists' houses, from which the Volga and the landing-stage were under fire from the enemy's heavy machine-guns.

Both groups contained officers from Army HQ and the political section, almost all of them Communists. And they stopped the Germans from breaking through to the landing-stage, providing cover for the first ferries bringing across the 13th Guards Division.

At 2 p.m. the Commander of the 13th Guards Infantry Division, Major-General Alexander Ilyich Rodimtsev, Hero of the Soviet Union, arrived, covered in dust and mud. In getting from the Volga to our command post he had several times had to take cover in bomb craters and hide in ruins from enemy dive-bombers.

Major-General Rodimtsev reported to me that the division was pretty well up to strength, with about 10,000 men. But it was badly in need of weapons and ammunition. More than a thousand of his soldiers had no rifles. The Front Military Council had instructed the Front Deputy-Commander, Lieutenant-General Golikov, to see to it that the weapons the Division needed were delivered to the Krasnaya Sloboda area by the evening of 14 September. There was no guarantee, however, that they would arrive in time. I immediately ordered my deputy in charge of the Army's rear, General Lobov, who was on the left bank of the Volga, to collect guns among the Army's rear units and hand them over to the guardsmen.

General Rodimtsev already knew the position at the front. The Army Chief of Staff, Krylov, knew how to put people quickly in the picture, and rapidly showed General Rodimtsev how things stood. He was given the task of ferrying the division across to the right bank of the Volga during that night. The division's artillery, except for the anti-tank artillery, took up firing positions on the left bank, so as to support the operations of the infantry units from there. The anti-tank guns and mortars were ferried across to the city.

Left: Stukas prepare to swoop on a Russian defensive position in Stalingrad. Despite enjoying almost total air superiority, the *Luftwaffe* was unable to break the back of the Red Army's resistance.

The division went straight into battle. Two of its infantry regiments were to clear the centre of the city, the specialists' houses and the railway station of German troops; a third regiment was to occupy and defend Mamayev Kurgan. One infantry battalion would be kept in reserve at the Army HQ command post.

The division's sector stretched from Mamayev Kurgan and the loop of the railway line on the right, to the Tsaritsa on the left.

We proposed to Rodimtsev that he should set up his command post on the bank of the Volga, near the landing-stage, where there were dugouts, trenches and communications already in existence.

At the end of the conversation I asked him how he felt about it.

He replied: 'I am a Communist. I have no intention of abandoning the city.'

I added: 'As soon as the division's units have taken up position, all other troops on your sector will come under your command.'

After a moment's reflection, Rodimtsev said that he would find it embarrassing to be in a command post to the rear of the Army's command post. I reassured him, telling him that as soon as the division had carried out the task allotted to it, he had permission to move his command post forward. I underlined that we could not bank on the enemy's remaining passive. The enemy had decided to annihilate us and take the city at any price. We could therefore not merely remain on the defensive, but should exploit every favourable opportunity for a counter-attack, impose our will on the enemy and upset his plans with our active operations.

'I understand,' was Rodimtsev's brief answer, and we parted.

Left: A pall of thick black smoke rises from a devastated housing block, the victim of a German bombing attack.

It was about 4 p.m. There were nearly five hours to go before dusk. Could we, with the units we had available, splintered and broken as they were, hold out for another ten to twelve hours in the central area? This was worrying me more than anything else. Would our troops be able to carry out the seemingly superhuman tasks facing them? If they could not carry them out, then the newly arrived 13th Guards Infantry Division would watch the end of the tragedy as spectators on the left bank.

News then came in that the composite regiment had lost many of its officers and was without leaders. The regiment's commander had been missing since morning. If he had been killed, then all honour to his memory. But we feared the worst – had he abandoned the regiment? We had no reserves. Our last reserve, the HQ guard and the HQ staff, were out fighting. Through the roof of the dug-out we could hear the drone of the Luftwaffe's engines and the explosion of bombs.

In my search for reserves of one kind or another, I called in Divisional Commander Colonel Sarayev. He had been appointed commander of the garrison, and his division was occupying centres of resistance and strong-points in the city. Colonel Sarayev, in Krylov's words, considered himself indispensable and did not particularly like carrying out the Army's orders.

When he arrived, he reported in detail on the division's situation, on the defensive positions occupied by his troops, and on the position in the city and the workers' settlements.

It became clear from his report that the defence structure consisted for the most part of small blockhouses, 25-30 per cent of them com-

pleted, but of course not strong enough. Some of the defensive positions, in particular the barricades, I had seen myself: they were really no help at all in the fight against the enemy.

I asked Colonel Sarayev whether he understood that his division had been incorporated into the 62nd Army, and that he had to accept the authority of the Army Military Council without demur. I asked him whether there was any need for me to telephone the Front Military Council to clarify the position, which was in fact already clear? Sarayev replied that he was a soldier of the 62nd Army.

While talking to him I realized clearly that I could not count on any of his units as a reserve with which to ward off the enemy's attacks: they could not be taken away from their strong-

Below: Two German infantrymen wend their way through the shattered remains of a Soviet factory. Its stubborn defense blunted the attacks toward the Volga by the Sixth Army.

points. But Sarayev had at his disposal a number of formations of armed factory and local guards. These units, consisting of city militia, firemen and workers, totalled some 1,500 men. They were in need of weapons.

I ordered Sarayev to pick out some solid buildings, particularly in the centre of the city, place fifty to one hundred men in each one, under a Communist commander, to fortify these strong-points and hold out in them to the bitter end. Remembering that the division could obtain weapons and stores through the Army's supplies section, I proposed that Sarayev should keep in constant contact with my command post.

On my map of the city he there and then marked some particularly important strong-points. I agreed with his proposals.

Krylov listened to my conversation with Sarayev, and when it was over he took him aside to organize regular communication and administration.

Communication with the Army's units was frequently interrupted, and Gurov and I left the bunker a number of times, by the Pushkin Street exit, to find out what was happening, by listening to the sound of the fighting going on 400-500 yards away.

Historians maintain that in great battles outstanding generals would often have won a decisive victory if they had only had another battalion. During these days of fighting, it seems to me, Paulus had more than enough battalions with which to split the 62nd Army and reach the Volga. But the German efforts were frustrated by the courage of our troops.

Before dusk the commander of the armoured brigade, Major S. N. Khopko, came to see me and reported that his last solitary tank had been put out of action at the railway crossing near the station. He asked me what he should do.

The tank, I discovered, had been put out of action, but was still capable of firing. The brigade, in addition, had about a hundred men, armed with tommy-guns and pistols.

'Go to the tank,' I instructed him, 'collect all your men and hold the crossing until units of the 13th Guards Division arrive. If not . . .'

He understood and ran to carry out the order. As we later discovered, Khopko carried out his task with honour.

Dusk fell; the battle began to subside. Fewer German aeroplanes appeared overhead. I spent a lot of time at the telephone, finding out where the 13th Division's units were and what they were doing, and what means of ferrying them across were being prepared. Then, together with the HQ staff, I set about drawing some conclusions from the day's fighting.

The sum result was depressing. The enemy had advanced right up to Mamayev Kurgan and the railway line, and had crossed the city as far as the Central Railway Station, which was still in our hands. German machine-gunners had occupied many buildings in the centre of the city, after breaking through our depleted units.

Of our units in the Army's centre there was almost nothing left. The Army's observation post on Mamayev Kurgan had been destroyed by bombing and artillery fire.

It was reported from the left flank that although the enemy's attacks had been beaten off, everything went to show that the German troops were massing, carrying out reconnaissance and preparing for a fresh assault.

The Army HQ staff did not close their eyes the whole of that night: some of them were helping to reinforce the units in the front line; others were fighting at the specialists' houses and the station, helping to ensure that Rodimtsev's men could cross the river in safety; yet others were at the central landing-stage, meeting the battalions as they were ferried across and leading them up to the front line.

During the night only the 34th and 39th Regiments and one battalion of the 42nd Regiment were ferried across. Dawn and the appearance of enemy aircraft prevented any further crossings.

Above left: A machine-gun team, equipped with a bipod-mounted MG34, defends a vital intersection in the center of Stalingrad.

Above: A Soviet field gun in action during the winter fighting around Stalingrad's factory district.

The regiments that had arrived occupied a sector in the centre of the city from Krutoy Gully to the station; the 1st Battalion of the 42nd Regiment was sent to the station. Mamayev Kurgan was being defended by a battalion of Sarayev's division. To the left, that is to the southwest, of the station, the remnants of the armoured brigade, the composite regiment and Batrakov's 42nd Infantry Brigade were defending. On the remaining sectors there was no change.

On the morning of 15 September the enemy began to attack in two places: at the Army's centre, German 295th, 76th and 71st Infantry Division units supported by tanks attacked the station and Mamayev Kurgan; on the left flank, in the suburbs of Minina and Kuporosnoye, units of the 24th and 14th Panzer and 94th Infantry Division were attacking. On the right flank things were relatively quiet. The enemy attack was preceded by a colossal air raid, after which the enemy's aeroplanes circled over the heads of our units.

The battle immediately became extremely difficult for us. Rodimtsev's units, having arrived during the night, had not been able to get their bearings nor to consolidate their positions, and were attacked straightaway by superior enemy forces. The *Luftwaffe* literally hammered anything they saw in the streets into the ground.

Particularly fierce fighting went on at the station and in Minina suburb. The station changed hands four times during the day, and was ours at nightfall. The specialists' houses, under attack from the 34th Regiment of Rodimtsev's division plus tanks of the heavy armoured brigade, remained in German hands. Colonel Batrakov's infantry brigade, together with units of Sarayev's division, having suffered heavy losses, was pressed back to the forestry station. Dubyanski's Guards Infantry Division plus a number of other small units, also having suffered heavy losses, withdrew to the western outskirts of the city, south of the River Tsaritsa.

Towards evening on 15 September it was difficult to say whose hands Mamayev Kurgan was in – contradictory information was coming in. Enemy machine-gunners had infiltrated along the Tsaritsa towards the railway bridge and were firing at our command post. The Army HQ guard again went into action. Wounded began to be brought in to the command post. In addition, in spite of our guard and check-points at our entrances, lots of people flooded into the corridors of our bunker at nightfall to shelter from the incessant bombing and machine-gunning. Finally, officers and men from signals units and the guard battalion, drivers and others came in on 'immediate and urgent business' and stayed. But as the bunker had no ventilation, the oppressive heat and closeness of the atmosphere, particularly at night-time, made

those of us who were working at the command post faint. Our bodies were covered with cold sweat and our ears rang. We took it in turns to go out for some fresh air. South of the River Tsaritsa parts of the city were still ablaze. It was as bright as day. German machine-gun bullets whistled over our heads and round our feet. But nothing would keep us inside the oppressive underground bunker.

That night we were all concerned about the fate of Mamayev Kurgan. If the enemy took it he could command the whole city and the Volga.

I ordered Yelin's 42nd Regiment, which was still at the other side of the Volga, to be ferried across during that night at all costs, and to be sent to Mamayev Kurgan, so that it could take up defence positions there by dawn and hold the summit at any price.

To administer the whole Army from the bunker was becoming very difficult, so I ordered General Pozharski, with a group of officers from the operations section and artillery staff at HQ to organize an auxiliary admin-

Above: A Red Army sniper dressed in winter camouflage searches the horizon for a target. His weapon is a Mosin-Nagant Model 1891/30 rifle.

Below: Soviet cavalry, part of the Red Army's counter-attack against the Sixth Army, trot past one of the *Luftwaffe*'s Focke-Wulf 189 reconnaissance aircraft.

istration post on the bank of the Volga, near the landing-stage, opposite the south bank of Zaitsevski Island. This auxiliary administration post, under Pozharski, was an intermediary between the Army HQ and the units on the right flank. In the fighting on 15 September the enemy lost over two thousand men in killed alone. There are always three to four times as many men wounded as killed. During the fighting on 14-15 September the enemy had lost a total of eight to ten thousand men and fifty-four tanks. Our units had also suffered heavy losses in men and material, and had fallen back. When I say 'suffered heavy losses and had fallen back' I do not mean that they did so under orders, in an organized way, from one line of defence to another. It means that our soldiers (even small units) crawled out from under German tanks, more often than not wounded, to another position, where they were received, incorporated into another unit, provided with equipment, usually ammunition, and then they went back into battle.

The Germans quickly realized that they were not going to be able to rush in and take the city, that they had bitten off more than they could easily chew. They later began to act more circumspectly: they prepared their attacks carefully and went into battle without mouth-organs, and without singing and dancing. . . They were going to certain death.

'The land of the Volga has become slippery with blood, and the Germans have found it a slippery slope to death,' said our soldiers defending the city.

Our officers and men all knew that there was nowhere to retreat to, that there could be no retreat. The most important thing was that they knew that the enemy could be defeated, that he was not bullet-proof. Our anti-tank men were not afraid to let the German tanks come up to within 50-100 yards, so as not to miss them.

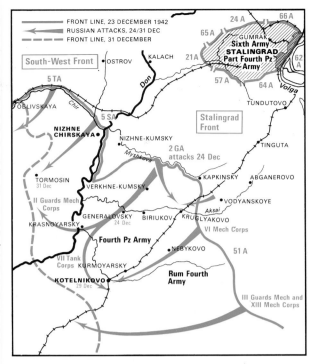

Left: The Soviet counter-attack against the German forces attempting to reach the beleaguered Sixth Army in Stalingrad.

Below: Soviet gunners cover an advance on a recently abandoned village.

On 16 and 17 September the fighting grew more and more fierce. Throwing in fresh reserves, the enemy kept up a non-stop attack in the centre against the units of the 13th Guards Division and Batrakov's infantry brigade. Particularly fierce fighting was going on near Mamayev Kurgan and the station.

On the morning of 16 September Yelin's 42nd Regiment took Mamayev Kurgan. Close engagements, or rather skirmishes to the death, began, and continued on Mamayev Kurgan until the end of January 1943.

The enemy also realized that mastery of Mamayev Kurgan would enable him to dominate the city, the workers' settlements and the Volga. To achieve this aim, he spared neither men nor material. We decided that we would hold on to Mamayev Kurgan whatever happened. Many of the enemy's panzer and infantry divisions were destroyed here, and our less-than-a-division withstood the fiercest battles, battles to the death, unparalleled in history in their stubbornness and ferocity.

In these conditions it was hand-to-hand fighting with bayonet and grenade that was most important and effective, and the real means of waging battle.

Mamayev Kurgan, even in the period of heaviest snow, remained black: the snow rapidly melted under artillery fire.

The fighting for the specialists' houses would die down, then flare up again with renewed vigour. As soon as our attacks or fire slackened off, the enemy would start firing on the central Volga landing-stage. This meant that we had to keep up the attack the whole time, in order to pin down the enemy troops who had occupied and consolidated their positions in the specialists' houses.

Near the station the fighting was going on with changing fortunes. The station and neighbouring buildings would change hands four or five times a day. Every attack would cost both

sides tens or hundreds of lives. The men's strength began to ebb, the units grew depleted. The enemy, like us, had to bring up reserves.

The firm resistance of our troops in the centre of the city upset Paulus's plans and calculations. Finally he brought up the whole of the 2nd Shock Group from the area of Voroponovo, Peschanka and Sadovaya and threw it into the battle.

Two panzer, one motorized and one infantry division launched a determined attack on the Army's left. The attack was not unexpected, but we had no forces with which to repulse it. But although the enemy was at least twelve to fifteen times as strong as we were, he paid dearly for every step forward.

In military history the height of tenacity in battle is considered to be those occasions when an object of attack – a town or village – changes hands a number of times. This was precisely our situation. On the southern outskirts of the city is an enormous building – the grain elevator. From 17-20 September fighting went on there day and night. Not only the elevator as a whole, but individual storeys and storehouses changed hands repeatedly. Colonel Dubyanski, Guards Infantry Division Commander, reported to me by telephone: 'The situation has changed. Before, we occupied the upper part of the elevator and the Germans the lower part. Now we have driven them out of the lower part, but German troops have penetrated upstairs and fighting is now going on in the upper part.'

There were dozens, hundreds of places defended as stubbornly as this in the city; inside them fighting went on 'with varying fortunes' for weeks on end for every room, every stair.

On the morning of 16 September I reported to the Front Military Council that we had no further reserves while the enemy was throwing fresh ones into the battle all the time; another few days of such bloody fighting and the Army would disintegrate, would be bled to death. I

Left: Russian infantry storm through a *Luftwaffe* airfield on the outskirts of the city of Stalingrad. The Soviet attack which began in late December quickly smashed through the low-grade divisions that held the flanks of the Sixth Army.

asked for the Army to be immediately reinforced by two or three fresh divisions.

The Front Commander obviously knew the position in the city clearly. On the evening of 16 September he placed one brigade of marine infantry and one armoured brigade at the Army's disposal. The marine infantry brigade was pretty well up to strength, and the men, from the North Sea fleet, were exceptional. It was given the job of defending a position along the railway line, between the River Tsaritsa to the north and the triangle described by the railways to the south.

The armoured brigade contained only light tanks with 45-mm guns. Its defence line formed an arc in the vicinity of the loop of the railway a third of a mile east of Mamayev Kurgan; it had to prevent the enemy from getting through to the Volga.

The fighting in the southern outskirts of the city round the grain elevator deserves special mention, because of the tenacity shown there by our men.

Here Chuikov inserts a letter from a former marine describing the fighting in this area, which, interesting though it is, has been omitted since it was not drawn from the General's personal experience.

By 18 September General Rodimtsev's 13th Division was exhausted.

They had gone into battle immediately upon being ferried across the Volga, and had borne the main brunt of the German attack, aimed at taking the city quickly. The guardsmen had inflicted heavy losses on the enemy. It was true that they had had to relinquish some sections of Stalingrad to the enemy. But this had been neither a withdrawal nor a retreat. No one was prepared to retreat. The guardsmen fought to the death; the only ones who were left were the seriously wounded, who crawled away one by one. The stories told by the wounded made it clear that the German forces which had seized the station were suffering heavy losses. When they were cut off from the division, the guardsmen singly or in groups of two or three, consolidated positions in pill-boxes, in the basements of station buildings, behind station platforms and under railway carriages, from where they would continue, alone, to carry out the job they had been given – to attack the enemy from the rear and flanks and destroy him night and day. In this way they forced the enemy into street fighting, which compelled the German officers to keep their companies and battalions on the alert right round the clock, to throw in more and more troops in different places, in order to surround and overcome the 'one-man fortresses' created by Soviet soldiers who had decided to fight to the last breath. Now I began to think more clearly about something which had been in my mind since my first days at the

front: how to answer the enemy's well-thought-out but stereotyped tactics?

What was needed was for us to act so that every house in which we had even one soldier became a fortress against the enemy. All would be well if every soldier fighting in a basement or under the stairs, knowing the general task facing the army, stood his ground alone and accomplished that task on his own. In street fighting a soldier is on occasion his own general. He needed to be given correct guidance and, so to speak, the trust of the generals.

You cannot be a commander if you do not believe in the soldier's abilities. During the fighting for the station, after consultations with the Member of the Military Council, K.A. Gurov, and the Chief of Staff, N. I. Krylov, we decided to change our tactics. We were going to break down the formations that existed in the

Above: Mounting a 76-mm gun and protected by thick armor, the Red Army's heavy KV1 was able to defeat any of the Wehrmacht's tanks in battle.

Below: The crew of a Soviet anti-tank gun suffer the attentions of German counter-battery fire.

Army: alongside platoons and sections in our companies and battalions appeared new tactical units – small storm groups.

City fighting is a special kind of fighting. Things are settled here not by strength, but by skill, resourcefulness and swiftness. The buildings in a city are like break-waters. They break up the advancing enemy formations and made their forces go along the streets. We therefore held on firmly to strong buildings, and established small garrisons in them, capable of all-round fire if they were encircled. Particularly stout buildings enabled us to create strong defensive positions, from which our men could mow down advancing Germans with machine-guns and tommy-guns.

In our counter-attacks we abandoned attacks by entire units and even sections of units. Towards the end of September storm groups appeared in all regiments; these were small but strong groups, as wily as a snake and irrepressible in action. When the Germans occupied an objective, it was quickly subjected to attack by storm groups. The Germans rarely stood up against an attack by bullet and grenade, backed up by bayonet and dagger. Fighting went on for buildings and in buildings – for a cellar, for a room, for every corner in a corridor. Streets and squares were empty.

Our commanders and men learned to crawl right up to enemy positions during enemy bombardments and bombing, and by doing so avoid being killed. German airmen and artillery men would not risk attacking our units, for fear of hitting their own troops. We deliberately fought as close as possible.

The Germans did not like, or rather were no good at, close fighting. Their morale would not stand it; they did not have the spirit to look an armed Soviet soldier in the eyes. You could locate an enemy soldier in a forward post from a long way off, especially by night: he would constantly, every five to ten minutes, give a burst on his tommy-gun, obviously to boost his morale. Our soldiers could easily find such 'warriors', creep up and polish them off with bullet or bayonet.

The troops defending the city learned to allow German tanks to come right on top of them – under the guns of our anti-tank artillery and anti-tank riflemen; in this way they invariably cut off the infantry from the tanks and destroyed the enemy's organized battle formation. The infantry and the tanks which had broken through were destroyed separately: the tanks were unable to do very much without infantry and, without achieving anything, they would turn back after suffering big losses.

Night and night-fighting were natural elements to us. The enemy could not fight at night, but we had learned to do so out of bitter necessity: by day the enemy's planes hung over our troops, preventing them from raising their heads. At night we need have no fear of the *Luftwaffe*. More often than not in the daytime we were on the defensive and beat off German attacks, which very rarely took place without tank and air support. The storm groups literally clung to buildings and to the earth, waiting for the enemy to come up within grenade-throwing distance.

We used ever possible means of killing the enemy. For example, we knew that not all Germans were on the look-out; the majority of them were resting behind shelter. In order to bring them out from behind their shelter, at night-time our Russian 'Hurrah!' rang out and our grenades exploded. The Germans would rush in alarm to their windows and loopholes to beat off an attack. And at that moment our artillery and machine-guns would open up at them.

Particularly effective were the salvos from our 'katyushi' rocket-launchers into concentrations of infantry and tanks which we detected before enemy attacks were due to begin. I shall never forget the 'katyushi' regiment under Colonel Yerokhin. This regiment spent practi-

Below left: The end of the Sixth Army. Miserable prisoners trudge into captivity – over 90,000 men surrendered when the battle for Stalingrad ended in late January 1943.

Below: A Soviet officer examines captured 12-cm heavy mortars, part of the vast haul of weapons that fell into Soviet hands when the battle for Stalingrad ended.

cally the whole time under the steep bank of the Volga, clinging to the very precipice. Before they opened fire, the lorries carring the rocket-launchers would reverse about ten yards from the precipice, leaving the wheels in the air. From here they would fire bursts of rockets. Their salvos claimed hundreds of German victims.

It would be impossible to enumerate all the new methods our troops worked out: in the most bitter days of fighting on the Volga we grew, learned, matured – everyone, from the private soldier to the commander.

Later, towards the end of the battle, from diaries taken from German dead and prisoners we learned how hard our new methods of battle had hit the Nazis. They never knew where, how and with what we were going to strike on any given day. We shattered their nerves so thoroughly at night-time that they went into battle in the morning exhausted from lack of sleep.

As soon as we knew that the enemy was levelling an attack against sectors where we had been inactive the previous evening, or where our units were weak, we would hurriedly re-inforce our troops there, organize a barrage of fire and lay minefields.

Our reconnaissance in Stalingrad worked well. We knew about the enemy's weak points and his concentration areas, and we did not miss a favourable opportunity for making an effective attack.

At the end of a day or of a whole battle we would make an attack, though not always a strong one. But for a weakened enemy even a weak attack was frightening. We kept the enemy in an almost permanent state of strain and fear of an unexpected attack.

I have related all this so that the reader can see clearly what activities the Army HQ staff and Army political workers were engaged in among the units, in the forefront of battle; what our units were doing and how they were preparing to beat off new attacks by the enemy on Stalingrad's factories and workers' settlements. These were the days when our troops defending the city, foreseeing the bitter battle which will be described below, used to say:

'For us, there is no land across the Volga! . . .'

Dark days still lay ahead for the defenders of Stalingrad before the coming of winter, Russia's most trusty ally, turned the tables on von Paulus. But later Chuikov's stand, based on the staunch defence of Rodimtsev's Guards division, showed that the German offensive had lost its momentum. The worst was over, but it was not until 26 January that the city was finally relieved.

On 25 January we sensed that our armies were approaching from the west, and on reaching the western outskirts of the settlements, the 62nd

Army discontinued its advance. Gorishny's, Sokolov's, Lyudnikov's, Guriev's and Rodimtsev's divisions turned northward to wipe out the Germans' northern group in the region of the factories and workers' settlements. Batyuk's division turned southward against the enemy's southern group. 26 January dawned – the day of the long-awaited link-up between troops of the 62nd Army and units of Batov's and Christyakov's armies, advancing from the west.

This was how the meeting took place.

At dawn it was reported from an observation point that the Germans were rushing about in panic, the roar of engines could be heard, men in Red Army uniforms appeared. . . Heavy tanks could be seen coming down a hillside. On the tanks were inscriptions: *Chelyabinsk Collective Farmer, Urals Metal-Worker. . .*

Guardsmen of Rodimtsev's division ran forward with a red flag.

This joyous, moving encounter took place at 9.20 a.m. near the Krasny Oktyabr settlement. Captain A. F. Gushchin handed representatives of the units of Batov's army the banner, on the red cloth of which was written: 'A token of our meeting on 26.1.1943'.

The eyes of the hardened soldiers who met were filled with tears of joy.

Guards Captain P. Usenko told General Rodimtsev, who had now arrived, that he had accepted the banner from his renowned guardsmen.

'Tell your commander,' said General Rodimtsev, 'that this is a happy day for us: after

Above: The long retreat begins. Although the German Army enjoyed local victories on the Eastern Front after the defeat at Stalingrad, it was the Red Army that held the strategic initiative for the remainder of the war.

five months of heavy and stubborn fighting we have finally met!'

Heavy tanks came up, and the crews, leaning out of the turrets, waved their hands in greeting. The powerful machines rolled on, towards the factories.

Soon other units of the 62nd Army met up with representatives of Batov's, Christyakov's and Shumilov's armies.

Courageous men, who had lived through many bitter battles, and had passed through the crucible of great ordeals, wept, and did not hide their tears.

The enemy continued to resist, but every day more and more of his soldiers and officers surrendered. A few Soviet soldiers would on occasion round up hundreds of German prisoners.

On 31 January, soldiers of the 64th Army took prisoner the Commander of the 6th Army, Field-Marshal von Paulus, and the whole of his HQ. On that day the Germans' southern group abandoned its resistance. The fighting in the centre of the city was over. On the evening of the same day troops of the 62nd Army took prisoner the HQ staff of the 295th Infantry Division, led by its Commander, Major-General Korfes, and also the 4th Army Corps Commander who was with them, Lieutenant-General Pfeffer, the Commander of the 51st Corps – Lieutenant-General von Seydlitz-Kurzbach, the Chief of Staff of the 295th Division – Colonel Dissel, and a number of senior staff officers.

The German generals were made prisoner by three soldiers of the 62nd Army, under an eighteen-year-old Komsomol organizer of a signals regiment, Mikhail Porter, who had been in the fighting at Odessa, Sevastopol and Kerch, before coming to the Volga.

On the evening of 31 January, Gurov, Krylov and I talked in my dug-out, now spacious and light, with the captured German generals. Seeing that they were hungry and nervous and anxious about their fate, I ordered tea to be brought in and invited them to have a snack. They were all dressed in parade uniform and were wearing their medals. General Otto Korfes, picking up a glass of tea and a sandwich, asked:

'What's this, propaganda?'

I answered: 'If the general thinks that the tea and the sandwiches contain propaganda, we certainly won't insist that he accept our propagandist food. . .'

My reply made the prisoners somewhat brighter, and our conversation lasted for about an hour. General Korfes spoke more than any of the others. General Pfeffer and Seydlitz kept silent, saying they did not understand political affairs.

In the discussion General Korfes developed the idea that the position of Germany at that time had much in common with that at the time of Frederick the Great and Bismarck. Considering Hitler's mental stature and deeds to be no less than those of Frederick and Bismarck, Korfes obviously meant that if the latter had had their setbacks and nonetheless emerged to greatness, then Hitler's defeat on the Volga did not mean the end of Hitlerism. Germany, under Hitler's leadership, would survive this defeat and would in the end be victorious. Generals Pfeffer and Seydlitz sat, from time to time uttered the words 'jawohl' or 'nein', and wept copiously.

Finally, Lieutenant-General von Seydlitz-Kurzbach asked:

'What will happen to us?'

I told him the conditions of captivity, adding that they could if they wished wear their decorations and regalia, but could not carry weapons.

Left: Field Marshal Friedrich von Paulus (1890-1957) surrenders to the Soviet Sixty-second Army under the command of General Vasili Chuikov.

'What kind of weapons?' said Pfeffer, looking interested and seemingly not to understand. He glanced at Seydlitz.

'Captured generals are not allowed to carry any kind of weapons,' I repeated.

Seydlitz then took a penknife out of his pocket and handed it across to me. Of course, I returned it to him, saying that we did not consider such 'weapons' to be dangerous.

After our conversation with the captured generals, we sent them off to Front HQ, expressing the hope that they would soon get to know the real situation in the Soviet Union, so as to shake off their mistaken notions and the poison of Nazism.

Above: The litter of a defeated army covers a winter landscape – vehicles include half-tracks and Panzer IV tanks. German losses at Stalingrad included 60,000 transports, 1,500 tanks and 6,000 guns of all calibers.

Left: The defense of Stalingrad also cost the Red Army dear – here are just a handful of the Soviet troops who fell into German hands during the battle.

Atlantic Convoy

by Sir Peter Gretton

No battle of the Second World War was more vital to Britain than the Battle of the Atlantic. Submarine warfare had brought her perilously near to defeat in 1917. Once again U-boats were to prove one of Germany's most effective weapons, but fortunately not from the very beginning of the war. Strange though it seems, the Germans began the war with only 56 submarines – rather less than the British themselves had in commission. During the early months of the war the Germans lost 31 U-boats, which were not replaced, so that by the end of 1940 Hitler only had 25 left! The British for their part, instead of employing the maximum number of vessels in the escort role, wasted a great deal of energy in hunting for submarines in the open ocean.

In the spring of 1941 the U-boats became active once more, sinking 41 ships in March. By midsummer escorts were becoming stronger, and were developing the strategy of 'support groups'. But by September the U-boat strength had risen to 150 and sinkings were very serious, but during the last three months of the year Allied casualties fell, thanks to American co-operation, the departure of U-boats to the Mediterranean, and the increasing efficiency of Coastal Command.

The entry of Japan into the war compelled the Americans to send many of their best ships to the Pacific, and in the first six months of 1942 Dönitz's submarines took a terrible toll against unescorted ships on the eastern seaboard of the United States. During this period U-boats sank 585 merchantmen, more than 3,000,000 tons of shipping. By the autumn of the year the Allied navies had gained the upper hand and losses began to diminish, until in May 1943 it cost the Germans 41 U-boats to sink 50 merchantmen. Still the Germans were producing 40 submarines a month, but Dönitz, seeking for soft spots, was keeping clear of the North Atlantic, where that June not a single convoy was attacked. In September the Germans sent 28 U-boats into the North Atlantic, but they only succeeded in sinking nine of the 2,468 merchantmen which attempted the Atlantic crossing during the next two months.

The early months of 1944 were a grim period for the Germans. The sinking of three merchantmen (January-March) cost them 29 U-boats. By the end of the year a stalemate had developed. The U-boats were equipped with the *schnorkel* and had become very difficult to sink, but were themselves unable to make many successful attacks. The advance of the Russians along the Baltic coast compelled the Germans to remove their remaining U-boats to Norway, where they carried out their training in Oslo-fjord. German U-boat strength reached its peak, 463 boats, in March 1945. Altogether, from first to last, they had 1,162 U-boats, of which 785 were destroyed; 500 of them by British ships and planes. They had sunk 2,828 Allied and neutral merchantmen (14,687,231 tons). They had sunk 145 warships, most of which were British. Throughout the war the Merchant Navy lost 30,248 men, and the Royal Navy had 51,578 killed and missing. The majority of these men lost their lives in the war against the U-boats. The survival of their country depended quite literally on their victory. In this chapter, one of the men who turned the tide describes one of his most dangerous convoys and evokes the desperate nature of that long struggle.   EDITOR

These pages: An Allied convoy comprising heavily laden merchant ships plows through a calm sea *en route* for Britain.

Chronology

1939

19-31 Aug.	30 German U-boats sail for their war stations.
21-24 Aug.	The pocket-battleships *Graf Spee* and *Deutschland* sail for the Atlantic.
3 Sept.	U-30 sinks the liner *Athenia*.
5 Sept.	President Roosevelt orders the organization of the Neutrality Patrol.

1940

12 March	British ships to be 'degaussed' against magnetic mines.
May	British occupy Iceland.
17 Aug.	Hitler declares a total blockade of Britain.
2 Sept.	USA transfers 50 destroyers to Britain.

1941

23 Jan.	*Scharnhorst* and *Gneisenau* leave Kiel.
9 May	Capture of U-110.
24 May	Sinking of HMS *Hood*.
27 May	*Bismarck* sunk.
22 June	Invasion of Russia.
7 July	US forces land in Iceland.
12 Aug.	Churchill and Roosevelt draw up the Atlantic Charter.
27 Aug.	Capture of U-570.
4 Sept.	US destroyer *Greer* attacked by a U-boat.
17 Oct.	US destroyer *Kearny* torpedoed.
7 Dec.	Pearl Harbor.

1942

mid-Jan.	*Tirpitz* at Trondheim.
11-13 Feb.	*Scharnhorst* and *Gneisenau* dash up the English Channel.
18 March	The St Nazaire Raid.
8 Nov.	Operation Torch.
Nov.	Admiral Sir Max Horton takes over command of the Western Approaches.

1943

30 Jan.	Dönitz appointed C.-in-C. of the German Navy.
Jan.-May	Unsuccessful bombing offensive against U-boat building yards and bases.
Feb.	Heavy sinkings of merchantmen in the Atlantic.
May	41 U-boats sunk.
22 May	Dönitz withdraws his U-boats from the North Atlantic.
Oct.	Agreement with Portugal. Allied bases established in the Azores.
26 Dec.	Battle of North Cape. *Scharnhorst* sunk.

1944

3 April	*Tirpitz* bombed in Altenfiord.
6 June	Operation Overlord.
12 Nov.	*Tirpitz* sunk by RAF Lancasters.

1945

7 May	The Admiralty orders all attacks to cease.

A Long Fight

'What would the Naval Staff College appreciation have been in, say, 1934 of a situation in which a convoy of forty ships with a best speed of seven knots was preparing to sail westwards in ballast in bad weather, with an escort consisting of two destroyers, one frigate, and four corvettes which were slower than the opposing U-boats? – In which air cover for the convoy was scanty generally and non-existent in the mid-Ocean gap, and in which no less than sixty U-boats were deployed in the Atlantic, poised to attack the convoy at one stage or another of its passage? A situation, also, in which the enemy were able to break our cyphers and thus establish the position of most convoys in the Atlantic? I think the staff solution would have been "annihilation".'

We had just over a week in Londonderry after convoy HX231, which had brought us our first taste of pack attack. There were many commitments and time passed all too quickly. I found my own ship, the *Duncan*, waiting for me, and there was much to do to take her over from the temporary Captain and to get to know her and her company. The officers and men were all new to me and most of them had never seen a convoy before, for the ship had been recommissioned after a long refit and had just worked up at Tobermory on the west coast of Scotland.

She was a Flotilla Leader of the 'D' class which had been built in Portsmouth dockyard in the early 1930s. She was well equipped with weapons and detecting instruments and also had the new 'hedgehog', together with a monstrously big depth-charge which was discharged from a torpedo tube. She had kept a couple of guns for use against U-boats and a couple of torpedoes in case a surface warship was encountered. She had all the latest ASDIC, radio, radar and H/F D/F sets.

But being designed for short sharp dashes out to sea with the fleet, her endurance was too short for convoy work, which was a source of endless worry.

The *Duncan* had spent a couple of weeks at Tobermory, where Admiral Sir Gilbert Stephenson had given her the thorough training which he had perfected during the years. Before sailing, it was necessary to see that everyone knew exactly what was expected of him and to ensure that the group ideas were clearly understood.

I had also to crawl about to see for myself her condition, a tiring and dirty proceeding which took all one day.

The reports and track charts of our last convoy battle had to be finished, and the problems which had arisen had to be worked out on the tactical table and discussed by all concerned, and I had to address a large audience of naval and air force officers on the last operation. It was particularly important to meet the aircrews who had flown so far to escort us, because although they had done great work, there were still a number of details to be put right. This is the only method which works. The correct official procedure of writing a report only stirred up a host of acrimonious minutes in headquarters and, in any case, never reached the men concerned in time to be of any value.

There were changes in the group. The *Loosestrife* had a new Captain and the *Sunflower*, also with a new Captain, had returned from refit, relieving the *Alisma* which was well overdue for a rest. So much time was taken up in talks with the newcomers in which we discussed every possible contingency. Another day was taken up by a flight to Derby House, Liverpool, to

Above: Commander Peter Gretton won the DSO and two bars for his work in the Battle of the Atlantic.

Below: A German U-boat leaves the protection of its concrete pen for a cruise in the North Atlantic. The defeat of France allowed U-boats to spend a greater period on patrol and avoid the dangers of traveling through the Icelandic gap and the English Channel.

Vice-Admiral Sir Peter Gretton
KCB, DSO, OBE, DSC
(1912-)

The son of a major, Admiral Gretton was educated at the Royal Naval College, Dartmouth. Promoted Commander in 1942, during the Second World War he won the DSO and two bars.

From April 1958-60, he was Senior Naval Member of Directing Staff of the Imperial Defence College, and from 1960-1 he was Flag Officer, Sea Training. He was promoted Vice-Admiral in 1961 and from 1962-3 he was Deputy Chief of Naval Staff and Fifth Sea Lord.

give Sir Max Horton a first-hand account of convoy HX231 and to get the latest news of the Battle of the Atlantic. Time was pressing, and to cap it all I was in the throes of 'urgent personal affairs' which required careful organization.

Summer had not yet arrived. Weather damage was frequent and it was still a difficult task to produce a complete group at sea on the right day. Skilled labour was short, and all our technical devices were getting increasingly more complex. The last few days before meeting a convoy were often more tiring than the passage which followed!

During the winter, too, the *Philante* group training scheme had become fully developed, and very good it was. The yacht *Philante*, now the Norwegian Royal Yacht, was stationed at Larne at the mouth of the Belfast Lough, which was centrally placed for escort groups from Londonderry, Liverpool and Greenock, for submarines from Rothesay in the Clyde, and for aircraft from the Northern Irish bases, both Royal Air Force and Fleet Air Arm. With the *Philante* representing a convoy and the Rothesay training submarines acting as U-boats, complete escort groups and squadrons of aircraft were exercised together before convoy passages under realistic conditions, followed by careful analysis and discussion. Groups were welded together into teams, aircraft were able to carry out in practice the tactics in which they had been trained, and the results were excellent. It was a pity that it was not possible to start the scheme much earlier, for the Joint Air Force Anti-Submarine School at Maydown in Northern Ireland had also only just started work, and the combination provided excellent training.

This time we succeeded in getting out to the Londonderry exercise area with a complete group. We had one more ship than the last convoy – the *Duncan* – and we were confident that we would do better. We tried hard not to waste time during these exercise periods which were always too short and which were usually interfered with by the weather. The venerable submarines with which we exercised, last war models which had been condemned years before, were not always reliable and life was often frustrating.

In the main, however, eveything went rather better than usual. The weather was good, the submarines kept going, and targets were in the right position at the right time, the aircraft were punctual and were equipped with radio sets which worked.

I had been horrified by the apparent difficulty of hitting a submarine at night at close range, for only the Oerlikon gun had been any good against the U-boat which nearly scraped the paint off the *Tay*'s bows – so I designed an exercise to represent realistic conditions. The Oerlikon gun was 20 mm and was only effective

against personnel. In exercise 'Pointblank' one ship towed at her best speed a splash target representing a U-boat's conning tower. The firing ship headed straight for her on opposite courses at full speed. At the last moment she steered so as to pass less than 100 yards clear and on getting abeam fired at the splash target with every gun on board. We also tried throwing a live depth-charge at it, but the result was so dangerous that a special exercise charge had to be used instead.

For the towing ship, this exercise was alarm-

Above: The officers and men of the U-99 pose for the camera after a successful mission. Under Otto Kretschmer (front row, second from right), the submarine was one of the most successful hunters of the early war period. Kretschmer, however, fell into British hands after an encounter with several escorts on 27 March 1941.

Left: Two lookouts dressed in oilskins to combat the worst of the Atlantic weather scan the horizon in search of a suitable target.

ing enough by day; by night it was suicidal. Usually some enthusiast would open fire too soon, and always at least one gun's crew, intoxicated with excitement and deafened by noise, would fail to see or hear the cease-fire signal and would continue to direct a stream of lead at the unfortunate towing ship. But we escaped damage and found the exercise of great value in teaching the guns' crews to shoot quick and straight.

Before sailing we had a final meeting in the anchorage at Moville at which the exercises were analysed and the last points of policy discussed. A couple of trawlers were joining the group temporarily as rescue ships, and they, fitted with ASDIC, were a useful addition to the escort – which now would consist of two destroyers, one frigate, four corvettes and two trawlers.

There was the escort tanker to be visited, too. This ship, the *British Lady*, was fitted with buoyant rubber hose which she streamed astern and which we picked up and secured at our forecastle. Oil could be pumped through the hose at a reasonable rate, and once secured the operation did not take very long, perhaps two hours for a normal refuel. But picking up the gear was not easy, especially in bad weather, and station-keeping astern of the tanker was a difficult task. The *British Lady* and the *Duncan* had not refuelled at sea together, so on the way to meet the convoy we exercised the operation. It was as well that we did for many mistakes were made and much of the gear had to be adjusted. The *British Lady*, an old friend from the days of the Norwegian campaign, did us splendidly through the passage – though she had not been given enough fuel and we sucked

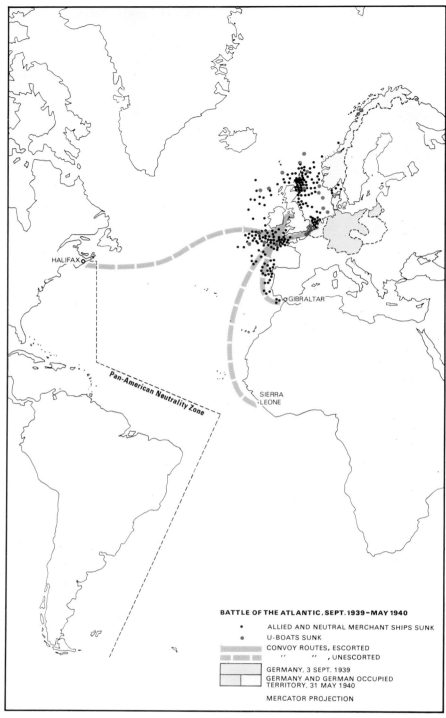

BATTLE OF THE ATLANTIC, SEPT. 1939 – MAY 1940

- •   ALLIED AND NEUTRAL MERCHANT SHIPS SUNK
- •   U-BOATS SUNK

   CONVOY ROUTES, ESCORTED
   "   "   , UNESCORTED

   GERMANY, 3 SEPT. 1939
   GERMANY AND GERMAN OCCUPIED TERRITORY, 31 MAY 1940

MERCATOR PROJECTION

her dry before the end. There was another escort oiler with the convoy, the *Argon*, but unfortunately she was fitted for oiling alongside and not astern and, worse still, she had canvas hose only instead of rubber. It was only possible to use her in a flat calm which we never experienced, and the one attempt to fuel from her nearly ended in disaster. Consequently we were not able to get at her precious cargo of oil, which was to have serious results.

By two o'clock in the afternoon of 22 April 1943, we had found the convoy off Oversay, transferred documents to Commodore J. K. Brook, RNR, and discussed plans over the loud hailer. We had joined the various parts of the convoy together and we had settled down in our stations. The convoy was a slow one with a

Above: The Battle of the Atlantic from June 1940 to March 1941. The successes of the submarine offensive are clearly visible.

Left: The crew of a Focke-Wulf Condor long-range maritime aircraft patrol the Atlantic. Often used to report convoy sightings to U-boats, Condors were also highly successful in the more aggressive role of maritime raiders.

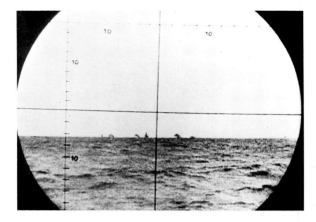

reputed speed of seven and a half knots (which it never reached) and consisted of thirty-nine ships. I spent the first four days, which were uneventful, steaming in the middle of the convoy in order to save fuel, for the *Duncan* had a bad reputation for oil consumption. Our chief concern was the weather, which held us up badly and threatened to make the passage a long one.

The ships, being light in the water, found great difficulty in station-keeping and the escorts were kept busy chasing them back into position. One night we could see no less than eight sets of 'two red lights vertical' from ships out of control due to the weather. On 26 April the inevitable happened and two ships collided with each other. One was sent off to Iceland unescorted and the other was able to remain in the convoy. It was not a pleasant prospect for a damaged ship to sail off alone, but no one could be spared to go off with her. I now know that she arrived safely.

That day the *Vidette* joined with three ships from Iceland. I was getting alarmed about my fuel and asked our headquarters at Liverpool to arrange for me to nip into Greenland to top up if the weather continued to prevent me from fuelling at sea. Luckily on the 27th the weather improved and both the *Duncan* and the *Vidette* were able to top right up. It was a great relief for Greenland is in the ice pack at that time of year and it would have been a difficult journey. We also got some good air cover from Hudsons based in Iceland. About this time, 27 April, we heard that an east-bound convoy to the south of us was being attacked, the visibility dropped and our hopes ran high that we should miss the U-boats whom we thought would concentrate on a laden convoy homeward bound.

But at noon on 28 April we heard a submarine transmitting apparently quite close, dead ahead of the convoy. Visibility was only three miles, and I went out at full speed in the *Duncan* to see if we could find anything – we had no success. But it was certain by then that the U-boat must have sighted or heard us on her hydrophones, and it was clear that we were in for a heavy attack – again that horrible sinking feeling appeared.

I now know that U-650 sighted us in the

morning and shadowed all day. In his report he complained that the zig-zagging of the escorts made shadowing difficult, but he also said that he got within 2,000 yards of one destroyer ahead of the convoy 'which must have been asleep'! This must have been the *Vidette* and he was lucky, for it was most unusual for her to miss anything. Fourteen other U-boats were ordered to close on the convoy and attack its vessels that night.

The weather was so bad that no flying from Iceland was possible and so we could do little to prevent the pack assembling at its leisure. A couple of hours before dark we sighted a submarine on the port bow. The *Duncan* was able to get quite close before it dived, but the high seas made an accurate attack difficult and I fear that little damage was caused. It was clear by then that the pack was going to leave the other convoy and concentrate on us. The night promised to be a busy one.

Placing the field was simpler than usual. The wind and sea were strong, making attack from abaft the port beam probable. Owing to the weather, an alteration of course was out of the question, for ships were finding station-keeping very difficult, so the *Tay* was left to deal with our U-boat, and we rejoined at high speed. I put the *Duncan* on the port quarter with other

Above left: Two convoys, HX229 and SC122, as seen through the periscope of U-632, 15 March 1943. The increasing success of the convoy system forced German submarines to abandon surface attacks.

Above: Allied merchantmen take advantage of a calm sea in the North Atlantic to make the passage of the dangerous mid-Atlantic gap.

escorts ahead, on the port bow, on the port beam and astern, leaving the starboard side completely unprotected.

We were back in station before dark, the *Tay* shortly after that, and the stage was set for the night's performance in weather which had just started to improve. There was little delay before the *Sunflower* raised the curtain with her report of detecting a U-boat coming in to attack, from the port bow. She attacked it with gunfire, forced it down and then dropped depth-charges. By then it could no longer fire at the convoy, so the *Sunflower* returned to her station, for the enemy liked to lure away escorts leaving a gap for more attacks.

About eleven o'clock, a half-hour later, the *Duncan* detected a U-boat on radar and went straight for it, catching it unawares and getting in close before it dived. At the time, I had hoped that it might have been sunk by our pattern which had been very close, but there was no time to investigate. There were better things to do. As we turned to regain station, yet another U-boat was detected by radar also coming in down wind to attack. We turned towards it and this time the sea was directly ahead and although the wind had dropped the swell was still heavy. The speed increased, the ship moved into the waves, sending spray over the mast and drenching the guns' crews and everyone on the bridge. There was no question of surprising it, therefore, because it could see us coming for over a mile, and the U-boat dived quickly, making our depth-charge attack of doubtful accuracy.

The depth-charge crews on the quarter deck were having a very difficult time. The ship was pitching and rolling badly; the seas were washing down the quarter deck, soaking the men there, while the heavy and cumbersome depth-charges were difficult to reload. We were able to keep them aware of what was going on by a running commentary on the loud hailer. There is nothing worse than working on blindly, literally in the dark as to what is happening. The crews made no mistakes, however, and were quick reloading.

After this attack we found no sign of the U-boat so we turned again to rejoin the convoy, dropping another pattern in the area as we passed to discourage any idea of a premature surfacing. Once again, soon after starting back, there was a shout from the radar office 'Submarine green three zero', and again we were able to close down sea from astern to the submarine and get very near before it dived, it was a difficult moment. I could not decide whether we were going to hit or not. Ramming is a splendid method of sinking submarines, especially with the sharp bow of destroyers, but the rammer is left in a shaky state of health. The nearest harbour was nearly 1,000 miles away and the convoy still had many days before it was safe from further attack. The escort could not afford

the loss of its best ship, and I therefore preferred to refuse the chance – a decision which required more moral than physical courage to execute. Fortunately, however, the U-boat helped me to decide and got down quick, and I dropped an accurate pattern over the swirl of the conning tower. I had great hopes of that attack, although they were not shared by the Admiralty Assessment Committee.

For the third time we turned to rejoin. For the third time we dropped another discouraging charge *en passant*, and then to our amazement yet another U-boat was picked up on its way to the convoy. Like the second one it was up to windward, so the sheets of spray soon showed us up. It dived quickly and again our attack was a poor one.

After this last attack we succeeded in getting back to our correct station without interference and there was a temporary lull in the operation. There had been no opportunity to look at the ship's track during the attacks, but a quick glance now showed that there must have been four separate submarines involved. Apparently they had approached the convoy in line ahead in the hope that the leading boat would attract attention, leaving a free passage for the rest.

We were extremely pleased with the result. In less than an hour we had driven off four boats and we hoped that we had at least damaged two of them. It had been a very testing baptism of fire for the ship's company who had behaved splendidly, as I had the pleasure of telling them over the loud hailer.

Below: A destroyer escort keeps careful watch over its charges. Better co-ordination between the Royal and US Navies gradually forced the *Kriegsmarine* to search for less well-defended areas of maritime trade, particularly the eastern seaboard of the United States and the waters of the Caribbean.

The history shows that one of the U-boats which attacked us that night was badly damaged but got home and gave a good account of the proceedings. Another one, U-528, after being damaged in the battle, was sunk by an aircraft in the Bay of Biscay during its passage back to base. So we did not do too badly for a ship which had only just been commissioned and was on its first operation.

Shortly after we had rejoined, the *Snowflake* piped up and reported a torpedo passing ahead of her. The submarine was sighted a moment later and at once attacked. Unfortunately there was, for the *Snowflake*, an unusual slip in the drill, and owing to a phonetic error the order 'Hard a port' was not obeyed until too late. The U-boat got clean away, but the convoy was not attacked. While the *Snowflake* was thus engaged, we took her position on the screen, but there was only one more attempt that night, from astern, which was beaten off without difficulty by the *Tay*.

At dawn on 29 April, the *Tay* was sent back to sweep astern in case there were any damaged U-boats on the surface and to discourage shadowers. The convoy, still unscathed, was in good order and the weather was now better. After seeing that all escorts were in their day stations, I exchanged congratulatory signals with the Commodore and went below for a sleep. About five minutes after leaving the bridge, the alarm bell rang and I dashed back. 'Ship torpedoed astern,' the Officer of the Watch reported, and we could see that one ship had hauled out of the line to avoid her next ahead. The group at once carried out the routine search plan for the U-boat responsible. It was, as usual, extremely difficult to determine from which side the torpedo had been fired. One ship said one side, and another the opposite, while the victim signalled that she did not know. But the sight of the explosion in the water well outside the convoy was a great help, for another of the same salvo of torpedoes had exploded at the end of its run after passing through several columns without hitting another ship. I now think that the submarine must have fired from between the columns very close to her target.

After a short time the *Northern Gem*, one of the rescue trawlers, detected what must have been the U-boat responsible, but it was not possible to spare any ships for a prolonged hunt. After half an hour the torpedoed ship, an ancient American freighter which had maintained station without trouble, suddenly stopped and abandoned ship. The bulkheads had cracked and the engine room had flooded. The *Northern Gem* was left to pick up the crew, the *Tay* was ordered to screen her, and the rest of us hurried back to station before the next attack. The *Northern Gem* rejoined some hours later with all the survivors except one who had been killed by the explosion. The Skipper was a

Left: A British sailor watches the skies for German maritime reconnaissance aircraft; the quadruple-mounted pom-poms would be used against any sighting.

Below: The sleek lines of a U-boat are revealed as this craft cuts through the North Atlantic at dusk.

North Sea fisherman who knew more about minesweeping than convoy work, and when I asked him some pertinent questions I found that the charts which showed the route of the convoy had been left on board the wreck, which had not been sunk. So the *Tay* had to go back to make sure that the wreck had sunk or to collect the charts. As it happened, she found no trace of the ship, but she detected a submarine on the way back and spent some hours attacking it. The U-boat was tough and she did not succeed in making a kill, but the sweep astern had been well worth while.

There was no more excitement that day, 29 April, although we received the welcome news that the destroyer *Oribi* was joining us from Iceland and that another group of four Home Fleet destroyers had sailed to support us from Newfoundland. But they were a very long way off and it was clear from the radio traffic that at least three or four U-boats were still in touch.

I then considered topping up with fuel, but the weather had got worse again and it seemed too risky. This weather was astonishing for even the North Atlantic. It was uniformly bad throughout the passage, with short spells with no wind but with big swells, sandwiched in between the gales. Again the weather prevented any air cover being provided.

The night was reasonably quiet. One rather half-hearted attack was driven off by the escorts on the windward side, but prospects were gloomy because there was a long way to go to Newfoundland, the weather forecast was shocking, and the convoy seemed to get slower and slower.

There was another brief spell of calm next morning, 30 April, when the *Oribi*, which had joined during the night, was able to fuel. Unfortunately she was new to the game, the weather got worse during the operation, and she made such a mess of the oiler's gear that no one else could fuel that day. This was to bring serious consequences to my *Duncan*.

The *Tay* rejoined at dawn and the day was quiet. By the evening another full gale was blowing from ahead and speed was further reduced. Flying was dangerous, and the only aircraft which took off had soon to return to its base, so that we had no help to deal with the pack, who were holding on tight, waiting for better weather in which to attack. Nothing was seen of them that day, but during the night (30 April/1 May) an attempt to get through the screen was detected by H/F D/F and prevented by the combined efforts of the *Snowflake* and the *Sunflower*.

We tried to establish the rough position of the transmitting U-boat by cross bearings, we plotted it on the chart, and then when we later arrived near the position we dropped one or two depth-charges in order to discourage it if it was still close. The weather was much too rough to send ships out on a bearing as we normally did,

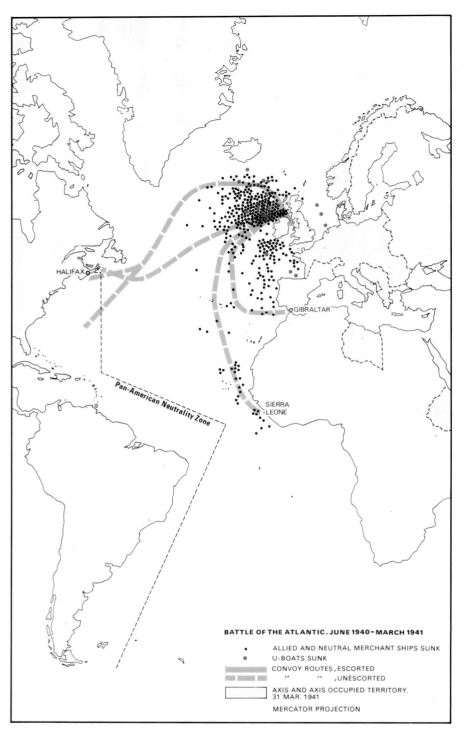

BATTLE OF THE ATLANTIC, JUNE 1940–MARCH 1941

· ALLIED AND NEUTRAL MERCHANT SHIPS SUNK

● U-BOATS SUNK

▬▬▬ CONVOY ROUTES, ESCORTED

▬ ▬ ▬ " " ,UNESCORTED

☐ AXIS AND AXIS OCCUPIED TERRITORY, 31 MAR. 1941

MERCATOR PROJECTION

and detection by ASDIC in that sea was also impossible.

I remember one worrying incident during that night. We were dropping depth-charges in support of the two corvettes, an operation which was highly hazardous in that weather. We could only manage eight knots and it was necessary to set the depth-charges to explode deep, for at a low speed a shallow charge does much damage to one's own ship, because the explosion is too close to the stern. One of our charges went at about 50 feet, lifting the stern out of the water and causing leaks in the tiller flat. More serious still, the wardroom gin glasses were smashed – but the ship's rum and the wardroom wine had been carefully packed and avoided damage! The next morning I had

Above: The early stages of the Battle of the Atlantic, with the cluster of U-boat attacks in Britain's coastal waters clearly evident.

to investigate the premature depth-charge firing. The man responsible was a respected and reliable elderly able-seaman of the best type who helped to provide the backbone of a ship in those days of dilution. He denied setting it wrongly, and there seemed no point in arguing in those circumstances and we had no further trouble with our settings that commission.

The gale grew steadily worse all day, 1 May, until the wind was blowing like the bells of hell. The convoy was almost stationary and ships were heaving to as best they could, gradually spreading over the ocean as they drifted about mostly out of control. Two ships had to turn and run before the wind and we never saw them again, although I believe they reached Iceland safely.

The *Duncan* was hove to first with the wind on one bow and then on the other, and we could do little except make sure of keeping reasonably close to the Commodore's ship. It was most frustrating to see the convoy melting away before our eyes, but we could do nothing about it for at that time I did not understand how it was possible to heave to a convoy without very much difficulty.

At noon on this day, 1 May, one of our old friends from 120 (Liberator) Squadron turned up from Iceland, a magnificent effort in shocking weather. But the U-boats were all sitting comfortably below the waves, waiting for the gale to stop, and he could do no more than confirm our worst fears about the convoy and give us the unwelcome news that there were icebergs 30 miles ahead of us. He added for good

measure that if we continued on our present heading for 50 miles, we would be well inside the Greenland ice pack.

There was little to do except to pray that an improvement in the weather next day would allow us to alter course in time. In that 24 hours the convoy made about 20 miles' progress; at times we seemed to be moving backwards.

To add to my worries, the Chief came on the bridge to report that the foremost tanks were leaking oil into the boiler room and that he had now to close down the forward boiler, which meant that we would have to rely on the after boiler room alone. I went down to have a look

Above: An escort sails close to its charges. In the first stages of the Battle of the Atlantic, such vessels were in short supply. Those that were available were often too old to be fully effective.

Left: A convoy gets under way. Barrage balloons provided little protection from enemy aircraft flown by a determined crew.

Left: A blazing oil tanker settles in the water after a direct hit from a torpedo.

around and found the situation worse than I would have thought possible. A highly combustible mixture of air and fuel vapour filled the boiler room, several feet of oil and water were swishing from side to side of the bilges, and the unfortunate men on watch were sliding about on the slippery deck plates. It was a bitter thought that we had just come out of a long refit, and we commented most unfavourably on the managers and men of the firm which we had just left.

During the afternoon a Mitchell bomber, apparently from Greenland, passed several times over the convoy. He belonged to the US Army Air Force and apparently knew no known language, nor could he understand signals flashed, made by voice or key, so he seemed of little use to us.

However, this aircraft had forgotten to switch off its navigation lights, which were merrily flashing and giving away its position for miles. I was worried, but the mistake had the unlikely outcome of making U-380 think there was a new secret weapon in production, and he reported to Dönitz accordingly. So the aircraft was of more use to us than we thought!

It is now clear that Dönitz called off all the boats of Group Star that evening as he did not reckon it was worth while continuing the battle; but of course one could not guess this at the time. I think that the weather, the aircraft, and, I hope, the performance of the escorts all persuaded him that ONS5 should be left alone.

After a worrying night there were signs of improvement in the weather in the small hours, and by dawn of 2 May the sea was going down rapidly. The group at once set about collecting the convoy. Some of the ships were over 30 miles from the Commodore and the process was lengthy; but again a Liberator arrived from Iceland, flying over 1,000 miles to reach us, and proving invaluable in rounding up ships. We blessed our forethought in sticking close to the Commodore's ship, for we were now able to form a nucleus on which the rest of the ships formed. The great question was whether we should be able to get them all together in time to dodge the ice pack which was in sight on the starboard hand. We just managed it, though many small growlers and isolated floes passed down the columns and the *Duncan*'s attempt to oil met with failure owing to the continual twisting and turning of the tanker as she avoided the ice.

By the time we were clear of the ice pack the wind had got up again and fuelling remained impossible. However, the situation, if still gloomy, was better, because we had collected most of the convoy – except for one or two odd ships and a group of five who were being chased along by the *Pink* some distance astern.

Below: A Liberator prepares for a sortie over the North Atlantic. Capable of flying for many hours and armed with an array of sophisticated electronics and weapons, these aircraft, part of the RAF's Coastal Command, played a key role in the defeat of the U-boat menace.

That afternoon the support group, consisting of four destroyers of the Home Fleet with Captain D 3rd Flotilla, in charge in the *Offa*, joined. Captain D had been in Liverpool when I had been in the *Wolverine* and I knew him well. It might have been embarrassing to give instructions to a vastly senior officer, but I made 'requests' and he complied with them in the most friendly way, and these unusual but necessary command arrangements worked quite admirably throughout the operation.

During the early part of the evening the support group split up into two parts and swept slowly out on each bow of the convoy. At midnight they were moved to a line-abreast formation, two miles apart and seven miles ahead of the convoy. At daylight two ships of the support group covered each side of the convoy at visibility distance, while the *Duncan* looked out ahead and the *Offa* swept astern – all with the object of forcing down any shadowers. But nothing was seen.

So there was a quiet night, except for the wind which continued to blow very hard indeed. The convoy crawled on into heavy seas and in the *Duncan* we were rapidly reaching the point when we had only enough fuel left to make Newfoundland at economical speed. I had to decide whether to leave the convoy or to continue and to hope for an improvement in the weather. On the one hand, the enemy was still in touch, and I did not want to leave my group at such a time. On the other hand, the weather forecast was very bad indeed and I did not like the idea of running out of fuel altogether and having to be towed, possibly at a very inconvenient phase of the operation.

After much heart-searching, I decided that the *Duncan* had to go. The weather would not allow boat work, nor transfer by a jackstay, so I had to go with her. Command was therefore handed over to Lieutenant-Commander R. E. Sherwood, RNR, in the *Tay* and we left at the best speed the weather would allow. After two days the wind shifted in our favour, we met an unexpected favourable current, and we managed to make St John's with four per cent fuel remaining. We were most depressed because we felt we left the group in the lurch and were thoroughly ashamed of ourselves, though there was really no one to blame except the staff who had decided the endurance of such destroyers.

The story of what happened after we left on the morning of 4 May is probably the most stirring of convoy history. That afternoon three destroyers of the support group had to follow our example owing to fuel shortage, leaving the escort painfully weak. By cracking our cyphers Dönitz's radio intelligence service had established the position of convoy SC128, which was eastbound in the general area of ONS5. By some chance of fate all the U-boats which were directed on to SC128 missed it, but ONS5 was again sighted by the middle man of a big group,

Left: The death plunge of a British freighter.

and soon no less than thirty boats found themselves unexpectedly in a most favourable position for attack. On 5 May the weather moderated somewhat and the enemy attacked with much success. That night and again next day, 6 May, more attacks followed with further successes, despite a tough defence, and altogether eleven ships were sunk.

Below: The lookout on a U-boat watches the destruction of a merchantman; the vessel was probably despatched by the submarine's deck-mounted gun, rather than a torpedo.

There were no aircraft available which could reach the convoy, and by dusk the position seemed desperate, for there were only five of the close escort and two destroyers of the support group, the *Offa* and *Oribi*, remaining with the convoy. All ships were worn out after many days of bad weather and a running fight which had already lasted more than a week. There were over thirty U-boats in firm contact and the first support group, which had been sailing from Newfoundland to help, could not arrive till the next morning. All escorts were short of fuel and some of depth-charges as well. In the words of Captain D, 'The convoy seemed doomed to certain annihilation.'

Professor Samuel Eliot Morison, the official US naval historian, says in his account of the battle that Dönitz realized that it was essential to attack in force that night, for the convoy would soon be under the protection of the air 'umbrella' from Newfoundland. So he exhorted his U-boats to make this final attack 'with the utmost effort', and he even ordered them to remain on the surface when attacked by aircraft and fight it out with the gun, in order to avoid losing touch with the convoy.

By the intervention of providence the convoy entered fog at dusk, and by a combination of skill, luck, initiative and sheer guts, the pack was heavily defeated. The enemy made twenty-four attacks that night, all were driven off, and not one more ship was sunk. The U-boat casualties were very heavy and four were sunk and three more heavily damaged during the course of the night. Two of these were surprised on the surface in the fog and were rammed, and two others were sunk by depth-charges or 'hedgehog' attacks. In his report, the captain of *Tay* remarks, 'All ships showed dash and initiative. No ship required to be told what to do and signals were distinguished both by their brevity and their wit.'

All this time the *Pink* with her five ships was trundling steadily along astern. She had her troubles, but she got four of her charges into harbour and succeeded in sinking U-192.

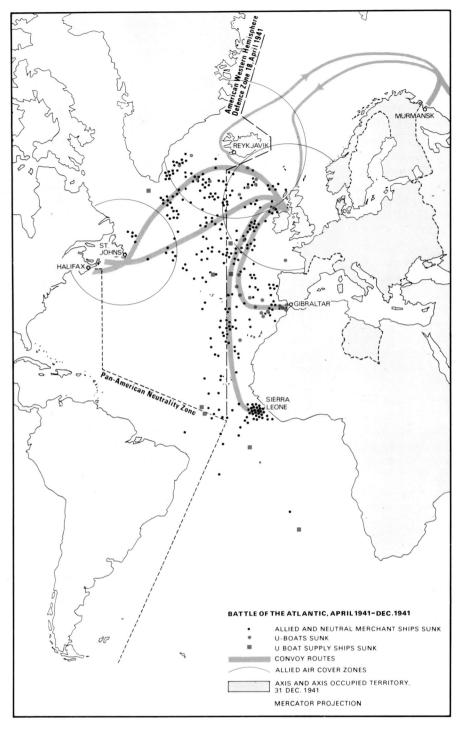

BATTLE OF THE ATLANTIC, APRIL 1941–DEC. 1941

- ALLIED AND NEUTRAL MERCHANT SHIPS SUNK
- U-BOATS SUNK
- U BOAT SUPPLY SHIPS SUNK
- CONVOY ROUTES
- ALLIED AIR COVER ZONES
- AXIS AND AXIS OCCUPIED TERRITORY, 31 DEC. 1941

MERCATOR PROJECTION

Next morning, 6 May, the 1st Escort Group on its way to the convoy came upon some unsuspecting submarines and shook them severely, sinking one; and a Canso flying-boat of the Royal Canadian Air Force also did some useful work and destroyed one.

At 9.15 a.m., 6 May, Dönitz called off both packs and ordered all boats to proceed to the eastward for replenishment. The convoy was still together and the longest and fiercest convoy action of the war had ended with a clear-cut victory. The passage from 'Oversay' to 'Westomp' took sixteen days, and the enemy had been in contact for ten of them.

In addition to the five submarines sunk by surface ships, two others collided, both U-boats being lost, so that for the thirteen merchant ships which the enemy had sunk, he had lost seven U-boats, with several others badly damaged, while the RCAF got another. German records recognize this battle as the turning point of the Atlantic war, and while I am very proud that ships of my group should take such a prominent part, I shall never cease to regret that I did not risk the weather and stay with them until the end.

This decision has haunted me ever since. It was entirely correct and based on common sense. I had been in the *Tay* with Sherwood during the last battle and I knew that he could compete. My own ship was new to me, just out of refit, leaking badly, and I did not trust the fuel-consumption figures.

It is now clear that Dönitz had no intention of continuing the attack – though I did not know it at the time – and this is some balm to my wounded vanity. Yet the weather did improve and I would probably have been able to fuel. As we have seen, Dönitz attacked 'by mistake' and I had missed the 'golden moment' which comes but once in a lifetime. And of course if I had had any idea that the U-boats were piling up ahead as they were, I would have stayed with the convoy and risked needing a tow to base.

Discussions after the war with the Germans were most interesting. They showed that no less than sixty U-boats were directed on to the convoy. Sixteen of Group Star sighted us on 28 April and four claimed to have fired torpedoes, though only one ship was sunk. As has been mentioned, two boats were damaged and had to return to harbour, U-386 and U-528, the latter of which was sunk by aircraft in the bay, so the attacks of the *Duncan* had at least done some good. On 3 May, Group Specht, consisting of seventeen U-boats, sighted us, six claiming to have fired torpedoes during the subsequent three days. No less than three of this group were sunk and one was damaged. On the 4th a large group, Ansel, containing some of the Star Group, with twenty-four in all made firm contact, but only one even claimed to have fired torpedoes and three were sunk. The last group to get into touch, the Drossel Group of sixteen

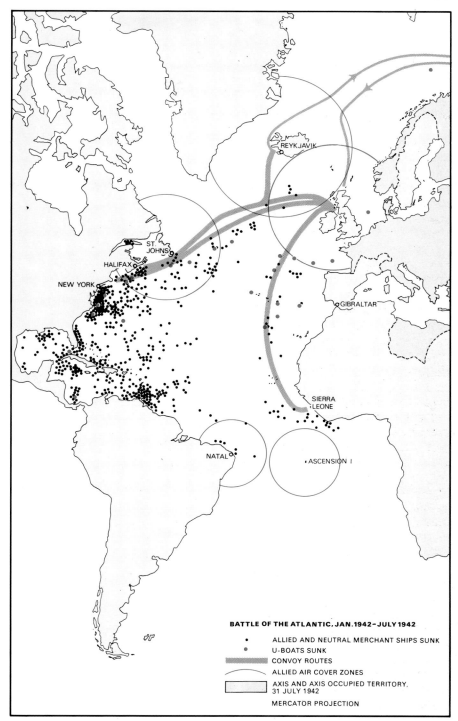

BATTLE OF THE ATLANTIC, JAN.1942–JULY 1942

· ALLIED AND NEUTRAL MERCHANT SHIPS SUNK

• U-BOATS SUNK

▬ CONVOY ROUTES

◠ ALLIED AIR COVER ZONES

▢ AXIS AND AXIS OCCUPIED TERRITORY, 31 JULY 1942

MERCATOR PROJECTION

boats, did not fare very well either. No boat claimed to have fired torpedoes, and two were sunk in a collision on 3 May.

In his review of Admiral Dönitz's memoirs in *The Sunday Times*, Captain Roskill writes, 'The seven-day battle fought against thirty U-boats is marked only by latitude and longitude and has no name by which it will be remembered; but it was, in its own way, as decisive as Quiberon Bay or the Nile.' Professor Morison made the total fifty-one and I reckon that fifty-one or sixty U-boats were engaged against us at one time or another, but this is a carping complaint to make about a generous and stirring tribute for which my group is both proud and grateful. Without doubt this convoy altered the course of the Battle of the Atlantic.

Above left and above: Two key stages in the Battle of the Atlantic, highlighting the switch in U-boat attacks between the periods.

Far left: An Allied convoy waits for its escorts off the coast of Iceland, June 1942.

Left: Caught on the surface in daylight, the U-858 receives the full force of an attack from a Coastal Command aircraft.

Monte Cassino

by Frido von Senger und Etterlin

In the autumn of 1943 the Germans in Italy established themselves on the Gustav Line – which, according to Norman Hillson, took its name from a well-known cab-driver on the Unter den Linden. The great fortified hill of Cassino, crowned by its Benedictine monastery, was the key point. Here, during the winter and early spring of 1944 the Germans made a skilful and determined defence, guarding the approaches to Rome.

At times the conditions under which men fought recalled the First World War. General Alexander attempted to turn the German line by a landing at Anzio, but unfortunately Major-General Lucas proved as unenterprising as General Stopford had been at Suvla Bay in 1915. He was content to consolidate his beach-head where he permitted Kesselring to seal him off. At long last the Allied Army, American, British, French and Polish, battered its way through and entered Rome two days before the Normandy landings.

The monument on Point 593, which commemorates the sacrifice of the Poles in this bitter struggle recalls at once their heroism and their ideals.

We Polish soldiers
For our freedom and yours
Have given our souls to God
Our bodies to the soil of Italy
And our hearts to Poland

The Italian Army played no part in the battle of Cassino. All the men who fell there were fighting a long way from home.

General von Senger gives a detailed account of every stage of the fighting. This is summarized in the Chronology. The extracts given here are taken mainly from his illuminating comments on the operation at Cassino. EDITOR

These pages: German paratroopers, captured during an attack on Monte Cassino by men of the New Zealand Division, are escorted to the rear. Plumes of smoke from incoming German artillery fire can be seen in the background.

Chronology

1943
12 May	The end in Africa.
10 July	Allies land in Sicily.
17 Aug.	Capture of Messina.
3 Sept.	Invasion of Italy.
8 Sept.	Italy surrenders.
9 Sept.	Allied landing at Salerno.
10 Sept.	German occupation of Rome.
1 Oct.	Americans capture Naples.
8 Oct.	Von Senger takes over command of XIV Panzer Corps.
October	Germans fall back to the Garigliano.

1944
18 Jan.	First Battle of Cassino begins.
23 Jan.	Landing at Anzio.
29 Jan.-	
14 Feb.	First offensive at Cassino.
15 Feb.	Allied bombing destroys the Abbey.
15 Feb.-	
23 March	Allies again attack Cassino.
15 March	Second Battle of Cassino.
11 May	Flanking attack on Cassino.
17 May	Fall of Cassino.
18 May	Poles take Monastery Hill.
4 June	Fall of Rome.

The First Battle of Cassino

The big attack on the Gustav Line started on 18 January. According to the Allied plan this was to mark the end of the slow and laborious advance since crossing the Volturno. Once they had reached the Liri valley they could use their armour, and the gateway to Rome would be wide open.

The large-scale attack, employing material resources of unknown extent, resolved itself into three phases of separate thrusts against XIV Panzer Corps along its whole front, and an outflanking operation from seaward. It now transpires from American sources, especially from Mark Clark's *Calculated Risk*, that the attack on 5th Mountain Division was actually the first part of an overall Allied plan to outflank Cassino in the north. But we still counted this attack as one of the battles on the immediate front, because it had come to a halt before reaching the main battle line.

Yet the attacks were all parts of one plan. The thrust by the British X Corps against 94th Infantry Division had special significance, for if it had led to a break-through, the entire German front would have been rolled up from the south. Compared with this, the subsequent attacks in the centre by the US 36th Division against 15th Panzer Grenadier Division, and north of this, the attack by the US 34th Division and the French Corps against the H. & D. Division would have been of secondary importance. As so often happened, the attack on 94th Infantry Division came as a surprise. The enemy overran the battle outposts through a tactical landing in the rear. Thereupon his first onslaught captured the division's lengthy fortified position on the slope and overran it, as had been done before in the Bernhard Line. Thereafter he took possession of the moderately elevated terrain lying behind this position in the floor of the valley, whence he was able to overlook the Aussente valley, where our artillery was stationed. From numerous inspections of the troops and from a visit as late as 17 January to the region of S Maria Infante I was well aware of the weakness of the position and of the unfavourable terrain. I also envisaged the possibility that once 94th Infantry Division had been thrown out of its position, it would be split in two, since the massif of the Monte Patrella in its rear, though not actually blocking its supplies, would greatly impede them. The division possessed no mountain artillery, so its artillery had to take up positions along the coast, where it also served as coastal defence, or in the Aussente valley. The infantry, which always tends to fall back to its own artillery positions, thus had the choice of two alternative directions, both eccentric. The divisional commander, General Steinmetz, was a competent officer, thoroughly grounded in the General Staff, who saw things as they really were. He had a basically insoluble task, for the defence of so wide a sea and land front was beyond the capacity of an infantry division. If he had possessed tanks, these could at least have blocked the narrow part of the Via Appia and of the Aussente valley. Visiting him again on 18 January at his battle HQ, I had to share his pessimistic outlook. While still with him I therefore made a

---

General Frido von Senger und Etterlin
(1891-)

A Catholic from Baden, von Senger was a Rhodes scholar at St John's College, Oxford, just before the First World War. He fought as an infantry officer on the Western Front, but when he joined the Reichswehr he transferred to the cavalry, and in 1939 was commanding one of the few regiments which were still horsed. In 1940 he led a motorized brigade, and thereafter spent two years as chief German liaison officer with the Franco-Italian Armistice Commission. Promoted to command 17th Panzer Division he took part in the attempt to relieve von Paulus at Stalingrad.

In June 1943, he was posted to Sicily, as chief German liaison officer with the Italian Army. He distinguished himself so greatly that, though he was no Nazi, he was next sent to extricate the German troops from Sardinia and Corsica. In October he was given command of 14th Panzer Corps in Italy. During the next six months he fought a skilful delaying action and commanded the German defenders of Cassino.

He continued in Italy until the end of the war, when he was taken prisoner, and spent some time in a P.O.W. camp at Bridgend.

An impartial writer and a skilled tactician, von Senger has written one of the most revealing and interesting books by a German commander of the Second World War.

Below: US troops come ashore at Anzio. Little German opposition was encountered, allowing the Allies to build up their strength in the beachhead, but elements of the German Tenth Army were quickly rushed to the scene to contain the landing force.

direct telephone call to Kesselring. It had become the regular practice to subordinate all reserves to the Army Group, and I knew that two divisions were available behind the right wing of the corps, where they naturally also formed an operational reserve in the event of a further landing. As I knew that Kesselring would decide on a delaying defence, I asked for the allocation to me of these two divisions as a prerequisite for a success that I felt I could guarantee with some assurance. Had I been in Kesselring's position, I would probably not have released the divisions, but he was determined that a stand should be made. Being firmly convinced of the value of so-called built-up positions, he looked to the Gustav Line for the eventual stabilization of the Italian front. And so he played his trump card: the two Panzer Grenadier Divisions stationed south of Rome as Army Group reserves, the 29th and the 90th, were allocated to the corps.

I was pretty confident of achieving a tactical success by throwing in these divisions. The counter-attack struck the enemy at the moment when, from long experience, the impetus of his attack was bound to slacken and there could be no resumption until he had regrouped and re-inforced his troops and drawn up a new plan of attack. If in this process he is disturbed by the defender's counter-attacks and has himself to resort to defence, his morale will suffer, and the defender has then virtually won the game, even if he has not in fact recaptured the main battle line as the German operational doctrine expects him to do.

On 22 January the enemy landed at Nettuno (the Anzio bridgehead). The 29th Panzer Grenadier Division had to be rapidly taken out of line in order to take part in the Nettuno fighting. The 90th Panzer Grenadier Division

Left: General Eisenhower, Commander-in-Chief of the Allied forces in Europe, leaves a conference accompanied by Lieutenant-General Mark Clark, commander of the US Fifth Army. Major-General Lucas (with pipe) led the US VI Corps during the first stages of Operation Shingle, the landings at Anzio on 22 January 1944. He was subsequently replaced by Major-General Lucian Truscott.

became the new Army Group reserve behind the Cassino front, but was still under my orders. In view of the Nettuno landings, Kesselring may later have considered it a mistake to allow the two divisions to reinforce the front of 94th Infantry Division. Yet one may also regard this assignment of the reserves as a fortunate example of dual employment. Their absence from the scene of the landing had no adverse consequences, for while the actual landing could not be prevented, the enemy was robbed of success since he was unable to issue from the bridgehead into the interior. The 29th Panzer Grenadier Division thus joined the 14th Army, assembled at Nettuno, in sufficient time to prevent a break-through, but not soon enough to throw the enemy back into the sea. This division's task with XIV Panzer Corps had been accomplished to the extent that the offensive by the British X Corps failed. It is true that the division's withdrawal from the front caused some friction, for the Army Group, for whom things could not go quickly enough, was most insistent. Yet the division was able to claim

Below: German paratroopers head for Anzio; their transport comprises armored cars and motorcycle combinations.

several victories in rapid succession when used as an operational reserve.

After the Nettuno landing I could no longer rely on being supplied with Army Group reserves to the same extent as before. In all responsible quarters this situation naturally provoked the question whether the Cassino front could really be held in the event of a major attack, or whether it would be better to withdraw the front so far that it would run behind the Anzio bridgehead, thus allowing the two German armies to unite and economize their forces. Kesselring, who now visited my battle HQ as he had frequently done in the past, emphasized that he was against withdrawing the front, 'because the present line is shorter and therefore more economical, than a line running directly in front of the gates of Rome straight across Italy'. Yet the field marshal's appreciation of the situation presupposed that a big attack on the Nettuno bridgehead would clear it of the enemy – an assumption in keeping with his known optimism. An offensive plan of this nature against the bridgehead meant that we would have to give up the idea of operational reserves for use in northern Italy in the event of further landings, and XIV Panzer Corps would have to rely mainly on its own resources for the defence of its own front. I had to create reserves without denuding those sectors of the front that were under attack.

During the first week the front to the north of Cassino became deeply indented through the continuous attacks, and finally the enemy captured the hills to the northwest of the place. This enabled him to overlook the Via Casilina, the only road communication with Cassino. He threatened the village of Terelle, from which place he could pass north of Monte Cairo and within one hour's marching time reach Roccasecca, where my corps HQ was located.

Meanwhile the divisions engaged in the main battle area were losing fighting strength at a daily rate of one or two battalions, and it would be only a matter of time before they were annihilated. As the individual battalions were weak, the divisions' figures of losses remained small in relation to its total victualling strength. Thus, a single division which within one week had lost the infantry strength of six weak battalions can be considered as used up, although its victualling strength has only dropped from 12,000 to 11,000 men. The attempts that were made by some command centres to maintain the infantry strength of a division by filling up from other parts of the division invariably failed. A modern division is too complicated to undergo organizational changes on the battlefield. The so-called 'emergency units' that were formed at short notice from the artillery, from other battle groups or from supply and communications units were unaccustomed to infantry fighting

and were usually 'eaten up' much sooner than the regular infantry.

Consequently, at the moment when the enemy's penetration had given him an unimpeded view of the Via Casilina, I mustered all the weight of my authority to request that the battle at Cassino should be broken off, and that

Above: The initial Allied attacks against the Gustav Line in early 1944 floundered on the slopes of Monte Cassino.

we should occupy a quite new line – the so-called C Line, situated much farther back and behind the Nettuno bridgehead – instead of exposing the mass of the German forces in Italy to inevitable defeat south of the bridgehead. My request was not approved. However, the fortune of war now turned in our favour to the extent that the enemy too was declining in strength. He, too, seemed to have no further reserves.

When I look at the Allied plan for a breakthrough from the point of view of the defender who was not overthrown, I cannot refrain from criticism. According to the original plan, which was tactically well thought out, there was to be an attack against the right wing of my corps, followed by a number of blows against the Cassino front. But after the first attack had failed, the original plan was followed too rigidly. This gave me the chance to draw reserves from the sectors where the attacks had failed, to constantly change the boundaries of the divisions, and to parry the blows one by one.

Nor did I understand why the enemy attempted to break through at so many points of the front. It seemed to me that in so doing he was dissipating his forces. The British X Corps attacked the German right wing with three divisions side by side, and had no reserves with which to feed the attack. Linking up with this operation both in time and in area came the attack by the US II Corps. First the US 36th Division attacked alone to the south of Cassino, then the US 34th Division to the north of the town, and here there was a simultaneous and continuous attack by the French expeditionary Corps under General Juin.

After the war I had the opportunity of meeting the erstwhile commander of the British X Corps, General McCreery, in England, as well as General Keyes, former commander of the US II Corps, in Washington. Through my discussions with them I obtained a more precise picture of the planning of those days, but I still have cause to be critical of it.

After the British X Corps' attack had been brought to a standstill, there was no point in the Allies continuing with their original concept of rolling up the German front from the south by means of a thrust into the Liri valley. The subsequent attacks by the other Allied corps in the centre and in the north had now lost their original purpose and achieved only tactical results.

One must in truth concede to the commander of the US 5th Army that it was the attack by the British X Corps that made it possible to land at Anzio. The British Corps had drawn our reserves from their dispositions in depth towards itself, so that when the landing occurred we lacked the forces that should have attacked in the first phase and might even have annihilated the landing force. In later Allied operations this bridgehead provided a spring-

board for a second attack at the time of the break-through in May 1944 when the bridge-head was still in the rear of our main front.

Yet even on the Allied side the First Battle of Cassino was marked by excessive casualties. But the Allies drew the right conclusions from their setbacks. In May they formed a centre of pressure *south* of Cassino by launching a simultaneous offensive by three Army corps, leaving the northern front unmolested and under the threat of being outflanked.

In the first Cassino battle the centre of pressure had lain *north* of the town. After the New Zealand Corps had been brought up, this area contained six of the nine divisions that the US 5th Army launched into the attack. According to the German operational doctrine at least three of these six divisions should have stood behind the Allied right wing, ready to force a break-through into the mountains. Even in the fighting at the Gustav position I feared a possible thrust by the French Corps into the Atina basin. This anxiety recurred during the first

Above: German shells send up plumes of water around several DUKWs as they come ashore with supplies at Anzio.

Below: A waterproofed Sherman tank lands at Anzio. The battle for the beach-head degenerated into a desperate slogging match reminiscent of the trench fighting in the First World War.

Cassino battle. But even if the Allied commander did not wish to run the risks of mountain warfare to achieve so ambitious an objective, the six divisions could have been sent into action at the centre of pressure, which was also the weakest German position on the front, and could have forced their way downwards either from Terelle to Roccasecca or from south of Terelle towards Piedimonte. For the attacker differs from the defender in that he is able to thin out or even entirely denude those parts of the line that lie outside the zone of the offensive operations.

Change of Surroundings

After the first battle of Cassino I reflected on the part I had played in this event. In modern war a commander in the field, with his complete system of communications, is so much the executive agent for directives already received that he cannot claim the mantle of fame. For my corps the battlefield ranged from the Tyrrhenian Sea to the hills of the Abruzzi. The entire mainland front was shared by two Army Corps, of which mine was the right-hand one. I knew this whole field of battle better than anyone else, for even the divisional commanders could overlook only a limited sector of the front, and then only while the division was in its front-line positions. I, on the other hand, had ranged over the entire sector of my corps, seeing all the focal points on the 80 kilometre-long front, as far for-

ward as the battalion battle HQs. I had climbed every single hill that offered a long view, and this gave me a complete picture of the fissured mountain terrain. I could thus appreciate fluctuations in the situation from changes in artillery fire and air activity.

For three months I was accommodated in a decrepit old *palazzo* at Roccasecca. As usual I had made my room as homely as possible with some fine old pictures and cretonne-covered furniture. An adjoining house contained a library that was not very extensive but included books in every language which is unusual in Italy. I found the reason when on one of my occasional walks I encountered an old lady. Her dessicated face, her solid shoes and walking-stick proclaimed her to be of Anglo-Saxon stock. American by birth, she had been educated in Germany and France and had married an Italian. When visiting the front I enjoyed climbing the hills; this gave me the necessary exercise and benefited me physically. I loved spending whole days in the open with the wind whistling in my ears, when I could see something of the fighting and look my men in the face. In the evening I would relax for an hour over a good book or radio concert. Having to stay up late into the night during the big battle, we often sat with a bottle of wine by the fireplace in the large cosy hall, which at other times served as a reception-room or cinema or dining hall for big functions.

The town of Gaeta was nothing but a heap of

Above: The town of Cisterna saw some of the toughest fighting along the Anzio perimeter. Here, an Allied supply column heads for Rome during the breakout.

Below: General Heinrich von Vietinghoff commanded the German Tenth Army during the battles along the Gustav Line.

rubble. But the drives to the coastal fortifications were a pleasant relief, for here was no fighting and the roads, relatively unmolested by enemy fighters, led to the sea, to the oranges and lemons.

Minturno was a frequent centre of attacks. It was always oppressive to pass the Ausonia defile, for operationally it was a source of anxiety. Farther back lay Esperia, which during the winter still accommodated a divisional staff, but by May had become the centre of bitter fighting. Towards the north the scenery changed as one approached the famous Liri valley. The precincts of Pontecorvo were under almost continuous fire. I cannot recall a single drive to this place when I was not aware of smouldering shell craters all around me. Aquino, the birthplace of St Thomas Aquinas, was soon in ruins. The castle where he was born lay outside the town and close above my corps battle HQ.

During the winter until January Cassino could be negotiated without difficulty. I had to drive through the town on my visits of inspection to the concentration of divisions at Mignano, and to all the intermediate country of the Bernhard Line.

One of the most unpleasant passes was on the road from Elia to Aqua Fondata. It may be a coincidence that I never drove along it without running into heavy artillery fire at the latter place. On returning from these journeys my Chief of Staff used to make a reproachful inspection of the little Volkswagen, usually spattered with shell-splinters.

By passing through the Atina basin I reached the more northerly battle area. I liked to come to this place. The basin lies like a circular plate in the middle of the Abruzzi, and in the spring these high hills still sparkled in the snow.

During the First Battle of Cassino I found it necessary to move my battle HQ from Roccasecca. At Castel Massimo we were in a more

secluded and quiet position, but the drives became longer, and instead of reaching a regiment or a battalion in an afternoon, it now took the whole day to visit it. Castel Massimo too was rich in history. In earlier wars it had been the headquarters of Murat and of Garibaldi. I deliberately chose to move to this place immediately after one successful battle, thus obviating the risk, in the event of a setback at the front, of having to be the first to withdraw – a situation that can be harmful to the morale of the troops. For me the position was materially improved by a change of Chief of Staff. My new COS, Colonel Schmidt von Altenstadt, also saw eye to eye with me on political questions. After the move the two of us formed a smaller household away from the big officers' mess, and this we shared with the GSO1, the adjutant and one of my assistant adjutants. Being thus among ourselves, we could talk openly, which had never been possible in the past. My COS was a friend of Count Stauffenberg, having got to know him while they were working together in Berlin. He told me of their combined efforts to persuade the individual C.-in-C.s of Army

Above: Artillery of the US Fifth Army opens fire on the Gustav Line, March 1944. The mountainous terrain conferred an enormous advantage on the defending forces.

Left: A mixed force of B-17s, B-25s and B-26s unloads its bombs on the abbey of Monte Cassino, 15 February 1944. The operation remains controversial as the Germans only occupied the position after the raid. Its ruins made a superb defensive redoubt.

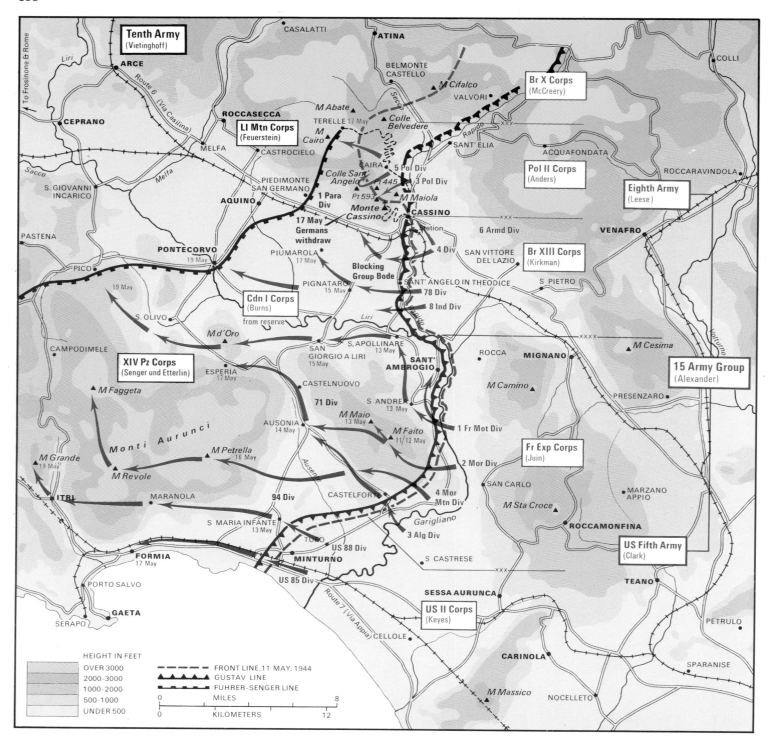

Tenth Army
(Vietinghoff)

Br X Corps
(McCreery)

LI Mtn Corps
(Feuerstein)

Pol II Corps
(Anders)

Eighth Army
(Leese)

Br XIII Corps
(Kirkman)

Cdn I Corps
(Burns)
from reserve

XIV Pz Corps
(Senger und Etterlin)

15 Army Group
(Alexander)

Fr Exp Corps
(Juin)

US Fifth Army
(Clark)

US II Corps
(Keyes)

17 May
Germans
withdraw

Blocking
Group Bode

5 Pol Div
3 Pol Div
1 Para Div
4 Div
78 Div
8 Ind Div
6 Armd Div
71 Div
1 Fr Mot Div
2 Mor Div
4 Mor Mtn Div
94 Div
3 Alg Div
US 88 Div
US 85 Div

HEIGHT IN FEET
OVER 3000
2000-3000
1000-2000
500-1000
UNDER 500

FRONT LINE, 11 MAY, 1944
GUSTAV LINE
FUHRER-SENGER LINE

MILES
0   8
KILOMETERS
0   12

Groups to opt for the overthrow of Hitler. My GSO1 was a son of General Oster, whom we knew to be at the head of the resistance movement and who had many irons in the fire. These young officers were not afraid to criticize Hitler and National Socialism, and consequently a more trustful relationship developed between us than with the previous staff. In the operational control of the corps there was also less friction. We always managed to agree quickly on the current situation and on the decisions that had to be made. Those generals and officers of the General Staff who were followers of Hitler took the setbacks in a very personal way. In their blind optimism they readily ascribed failures to this or that third party, who

in their opinion was prejudicing the leadership of Hitler, the man of genius. We, on the other hand, saw clearly that from every point of view the war was lost, that wars cannot be decided with uncompleted secret weapons, that it was immaterial whether the fight was continued on this or that battle line, and that it was now only a question of ending hostilities and getting rid of the regime. True that at this period opinion varied among us as to how this was to be achieved – not that we became heated in our discussions. My younger friends were more confident of results than I, who was very doubtful of the chances of forcibly overthrowing Hitler and ending the war. Opposition to the prevailing instruments of state authority was

Above: The third Allied attack on Cassino met with success. After heavy fighting, the Germans were forced back to the Führer-Senger Line.

too weak, and there were too few opportunities for co-ordinating the individual currents of resistance. The overthrow could not be prepared in detail if so few people were in the know, but if the number were increased, the essential secrecy of the plot would be compromised. Moreover, it had to be admitted that the mass of the people, and even the generals, property owners, industrialists and the universities were in favour of Hitler. My young friends failed to realize something of which I myself was convinced, namely that the Russians, having at this stage made immeasurably greater contributions to the defeat of Hitler, would claim the lion's share of the spoils by occupying the country and establishing spheres of influence.

I felt it as a personal tragedy that the defensive success of my own Army Corps at Cassino would reduce the Allies' chances of asserting themselves at least as much as the Russians. I felt that the Allies must at all costs establish a second front by a landing in Europe. That alone would prove that the collapse of Germany and the Russian invasion were imminent.

Sometimes my friends would discuss the oppression of the Jews. Although we had no precise information, it was common talk that evil things were afoot. We felt ashamed at these developments, at this discrimination against a small but intellectually gifted minority of the population. This in itself was sufficient to brand the responsible authorities as sadists and perverts.

After the situation conferences the C.-in-C. of the 10th Army, Colonel-General von Vietinghoff, was a frequent guest at my battle HQ. I found him and his COS, General Wenzel, to be in harmony not only with my views, but also with those of my operational staff. All of us had a similar attitude towards the political leaders and consequently towards the problems of high command.

Destruction of the Abbey of Monte Cassino

On 15 February 1944, at the end of what we called the first battle of Cassino, the abbey was destroyed from the air. We could not see any military reason for choosing this moment for its destruction for although a few single attacks were to follow, the main battle had already petered out.

Before I took over the command, XIV Panzer Corps under my predecessor had already developed friendly relations with the monastery in the summer of 1943, as it was then stationed at Cassino before being moved to Sicily. On my return journey from Sicily I had paid a visit in the monastery to the abbot and Bishop of the Cassino Diocese. I had again been up there for Christmas Mass in 1943, in order to

Left: Smiling GIs move along a dusty Italian road, heading for the German lines along the River Garigliano.

confirm that no German soldiers were visiting the place once the fighting had broken out in the general area. Kesselring had always tried to find ways and means of protecting valuable works of art and places of worship from the ravages of war, and had accordingly issued the order to 'neutralize' the monastery. Now he also looked to me to ensure that if I were forced to retreat, no harm should befall the ancient bishoprics at Veroli, Alatri and Anagni.

I was only too pleased to agree that the principal abbey should be spared from military operations. Nobody would want to sponsor the destruction of a cultural monument of this kind merely to gain a tactical advantage. But even under normal conditions Monte Cassino would

Below: US troops march past an abandoned Tiger tank, possibly a victim of an Allied ground-attack aircraft.

never have been occupied by artillery spotters. True, it commanded a view of the entire district, the town and the Via Casilina. But on our side it was considered tactical opinion that so conspicuous a landmark would be quite unsuitable as an observation post since we could expect it to be put out of action by heavy fire very soon after the big battle had started. It was the German practice to place the artillery observers half way up the hills in a concealed position with a camouflaged background.

The bombing had the opposite effect to what was intended. Now we would occupy the abbey without scruple, especially as ruins are better for defence than intact buildings. In time of war one must be prepared to demolish buildings which are required for defence. Now the Germans had a mighty, commanding strongpoint, which paid for itself in all the subsequent fighting along the front.

Ever since the Abbey was bombed there had been argument over who was to blame. In this matter it is perhaps best to quote the other side. In 1951 General Mark Clark, the responsible C.-in-C., wrote:

'I say that the bombing of the Abbey . . . was a mistake, and I say it with full knowledge of the controversy that has raged round this episode. . . Not only was the bombing an unnecessary psychological mistake in the field of propaganda, but it was a tactical military mistake of the first magnitude. It only made our job more difficult, more costly in terms of men, machines and time.'

This passage from Clark's *Calculated Risk* was quoted by Fred Majdalany in his own book *Cassino, Portrait of a Battle*, and he added: 'So the bombing expended its fury in a vacuum, tragically and wastefully. It achieved nothing, it helped nobody.'

Much as I respect Majdalany's objective account, I cannot approve his condemnation of Mark Clark. He bases his judgement on the fact that while Clark himself gave the order for the bombing, he later denied responsibility for it. Majdalany details the motives for the bombing, and these agree with the official war history of the New Zealand Government (Wellington, New Zealand, 1957).

With the decision to move the New Zealand Division and the 4th Indian Division from the eastern side of the peninsula into the major battle in the west, a political factor entered into the military considerations.

The New Zealand Division belonged to the Commonwealth. During the First World War its commander, General Freyberg, had commanded New Zealand contingents with distinction. Like all leaders of small contingents in a coalition war, he was responsible to his government for the fate of his division. The Allied High Command up graded his divisional staff to the status of a corps command over two divisions, the New Zealand and the 4th Indian Divisions, which were to force a decision at Cassino. Where the Americans, the British and the French had failed, the New Zealanders were to do the job. The objective, which was to be captured in an outflanking operation, was the dominating hill on which the monastery stood, as they saw it, intact, hostile and threatening. In extenuation it can certainly be said that the ordinary soldiers refused to believe that the place did not contain Germans, or that German observers would not be sent there very soon.

In the course of the attack the New Zealanders suffered heavy losses. Were they to run the risk of still heavier losses in order to avoid destroying the abbey? Were the people of New Zealand to be asked to pay for the preservation of the monastery with the lives of their own sons? These questions show the dilemma confronting not only the British commander, General Sir Harold Alexander, and the British government itself, but also the 'accused', General Mark Clark. Germans and Italians alike were convinced that the bombing of the abbey could not have been ordered without the prior approval of the British government, and

Above: Major-General Bernard Freyberg, VC (1889-1963), led the New Zealand Division throughout the war. He fought at Gallipoli and won his VC on the Western Front during the First World War.

Below: A New Zealand six-pounder in action against German positions on Monastery Hill.

that once the decision had been made, even the commander of the US 5th Army could not disregard it. This kind of interdependence is an inevitable feature of any coalition war. Strangely enough the New Zealand Corps waited for two days after the bombing before making serious and costly efforts to force a break-through by means of a pincer movement from Hill 593, northwest of the abbey. Despite three further days of intense effort and sacrifice there was no result. The exact time of the bombing had not been decided, but the situation in the Anzio bridgehead made it necessary to ante-date it by twenty-four hours, a fact that was unknown to the troops! But even without this error the result could not have been different. On all the hills to the northwest of the abbey that came under attack the grenadiers of 90th Panzer Grenadier Division had built powerful strong-points in the cliffs, against which all attacks by the brave 4th Indian Division failed. In Cassino itself the Allies captured the station, but it was recaptured by German tanks on 18 February. The tanks had taken advantage of the smoke from the enemy's artillery to force their way into the station in a surprise attack. The impressions left by these events were not the same on both sides. In our war histories we do not regard the bombing as a special 'second battle for Cassino'. In general we still had the same troops in the battle. The newly arrived battalions of the 1st Parachute Rifle Division were allocated to the local commander, General Baade. The ordinary soldier on those parts of the front that were not under attack witnessed the destruction and looked upon it more as a devastating gesture of disillusionment over previous failures than as a serious military operation.

It is idle to criticize the enemy's tactical failure in the fighting between 15 and 18 February. It goes without saying that there were military failures on the side of the Allies. It has already been said that the 4th Indian Division was unaware of the decision to advance the time for bombing the abbey. But there was no need for the infantry attack and the bombing to be so close together. In any case the first objectives were the hills to the west of the abbey. The opposite argument is also valid, namely that tactically it would have been wiser if the Allies had not launched their infantry attack at the moment of increased watchfulness after the bombing. But as one who was brought up in the German school of tactics I cannot refrain from making another criticism. What we described as the 'slackening of the battle' after the bombing was in reality a quite serious Allied effort to break the monastery hill out of the German front by means of a smaller pincer attack. The plan was so similar to the first one (which was a combined attack by the US 36th Division across the Rapido at S Angelo, followed immediately by an attack by the US 34th Division

Left: General von Vietinghoff (left) confers with the commander of the German forces defending Monte Cassino, General Frido von Senger und Etterlin (second from left).

north of Cassino) that it could not hold any surprise. There was nothing new in it. I knew the terrain round Albaneta Farm, Hill 593 and Hill 444 from the day that I proceeded on foot to visit a battalion of 90th Panzer Grenadier Division, when the trail of blood from the wounded that had been brought back marked for me the way up the track. These were all defensive positions in excellent condition, and they were being improved every day. According to German ideas, anyone wishing to continue the attack in the same direction from the terrain won in the earlier assault would have had to assemble a much more powerful mass as an attacking force. To achieve this, the attacker could have ruthlessly denuded his secondary fronts, a measure that I too was constantly compelled to adopt for my defensive operations. I feared an attack from the hills down to the Via Casilina, which would have severed my supply line to Cassino. But what I feared even more was an attack by Juin's corps with its superb Moroccan and Algerian divisions. I anticipated

Below: Members of the New Zealand Division tackle a German strongpoint in Cassino town. Despite their heroic efforts, their attacks between 15 and 18 February were repulsed with heavy losses.

a wide-sweeping operational thrust into the Atina basin against our thin lines, behind which we had no collecting positions. I have already described the implications of that danger. The enemy could indeed have avoided the costly battle for Cassino.

The Second Battle of Cassino

The second battle of Cassino, which started on 15 March 1944, will go down in history as one of the most perplexing operations of war. To understand this battle as clearly as possible it is essential to study the sources on both sides, and even then one is left with a puzzle, for the commanding generals on each side had widely differing impressions of it.

When the battle started I was on my way to the front in the region of Piedimonte and ran into the fringes of the monstrous carpet-bombing. All that happened to me was that occasionally the blast from the falling bombs would hurl me a few yards forwards or backwards before I could reach some hole in the ground. I knew the effect of these aerial bombs from my time in Sicily.

Two days after the Allies had laid this great carpet of bombs in such a minute area, I was already convinced that their effort had failed. But their leaders, or at any rate the commander of the New Zealand Corps on this small sector, thought otherwise. From the Tyrrhenian coast to the 2,000 metres high watershed of the Abruzzi the battles were part of a general plan, as already explained. The second battle of Cassino developed out of the first battle in accordance with operational laws. It was the natural consequence of the failure implicit in the destruction of the abbey without any compensating tactical advantage. The responsible Allied leaders therefore decided on a much more extensive bombing than that of 15 February, but this time it was to be directed against the German troops in the plain, and the result immediately exploited. And so it came to the bombing of the town of Cassino on 15 March.

The plan of battle was decided on immediately after the failure of the last attacks in the first battle of Cassino. At that time it had the additional purpose of tying down German forces at Cassino in order to relieve the pressure on the Allied bridgehead at Nettuno through the counter-attacks by the German 14th Army (Mackensen). But the start of the attack at Cassino was repeatedly postponed by bad weather, so that this additional purpose was no longer relevant. The counter-attack by the German 14th Army was finally abandoned on 4 March.

After Juin's attacks against the left wing of XIV Panzer Corps in November 1943 and McCreery's against the right wing in January 1944 the Allied attacks had concentrated more

and more on the centre of the corps' long front, until in the end the sole objective was the town of Cassino. This was not an arbitrary choice. A break-through into the Liri valley would allow the deployment of major armed forces. Cassino was the key point on the road to Rome, and it offered the quickest link with Valmontone, where General Alexander hoped, after the break-through, to seal the fate of von Vietinghoff's 10th Army.

This Allied tactical evaluation of geography could hardly be expected to produce an operational surprise. Instead the Allies attempted a tactical surprise to the extent that after all their setbacks they again went for Cassino without regrouping their forces. In the official New Zealand history of the Second World War, A. C. Philipps has this to say about it:

Above: German prisoners are escorted to the rear, crossing a landscape shattered by heavy artillery fire and bombing. The abbey is visible in the distance.

Below: The ruins of Cassino town, overshadowed by the steep slopes of Monte Cassino.

'From the military standpoint no competent soldier would in March 1944 have selected Cassino as the objective of an attack. He would have rejected the idea of assaulting the strongest fortress in Europe in midwinter, using a single corps without the aid of diversionary operations.'

It is hardly to be wondered at that not only the decision to launch the attack but also its further prosecution brought surprises to both sides. A layman without any local knowledge could not be expected to make sense of even the initial direction of the attack. In an Allied offensive starting from the southern extremity of Italy one inevitably thinks in terms of a south to north movement. In actual fact the attack was made from north to south.

It is necessary to bear in mind that the peninsula runs diagonally in a southeast direction. At Cassino the front ran almost north and south, and the enemy had on many previous occasions attacked due westwards. But now he adopted a special plan, whereby instead of penetrating into the town along the plain from east to west, he would start from the places into which he had broken during the first battle of Cassino, which lay north of the town, and thence push southwards into the town. By this means Freyberg wanted to seize the slope of the monastery hill in order from there to cover his forces against the flanking strong-point of the ruined abbey. Together with the main central thrust, a pincer movement would be made by means of attacks from the hill position west of the monastery towards the south, and from the southern edge of the town westwards towards the Via Casilina.

For this purpose a very careful plan was elaborated, which in the German opinion went into far too much detail. The crux of the plan was to destroy the town and its garrison by using all available bombers, including the strategic bomber force. Consequently on the morning of 15 March something over 1,000 tons of bombs were dropped on Cassino from 300 heavy and 200 medium bombers. Perhaps this no longer impresses people living in the atomic age, but its effect then was staggering.

The strategic bombers had not been trained to the method whereby a target is bombed until it is ready to be assaulted by ground forces. While they were still approaching the target, things went wrong. Some released their bombs prematurely, killing several hundred civilians at Venafro, which they mistook for Cassino. This also caused some casualties among the French Corps. Bombs released too late fell on Piedimonte and Castrocielo. The Allied commanders had assembled at the New Zealand Corps HQ at Cervaro, whence they could overlook the battlefield. The New Zealand historian Philipps, already quoted, has this to say: 'In the relative security of the hills round Cervaro the picnic atmosphere was both inappropriate and unavoidable.' Yet from the Allied viewpoint it

Left: General Sir Harold Alexander (1891-1969) succeeded Eisenhower as Supreme Allied Commander in the Mediterranean and later accepted the unconditional surrender of the German forces in Italy, 29 April 1945. He was in charge of 15th Army Group during the Cassino battles.

was perhaps not so 'inappropriate'. Their assault infantry had been moved well away from the danger zone. In view of the destructive capacity of these huge bomb-loads there seemed no urgency for the ground attack. Consequently the assault battalions had a co-ordinated timetable that reduced the rate of attack to a minimum, allowing for various alternative situations. A German plan would have been wary of this kind of co-ordination, which was bound to put too much of a brake on the development of the first attack, thereby missing the opportunity of sending up reserves. Nor did the Allies conform to the orthodox doctrine of street-fighting, whereby enemy strong-points

Below: A Polish Bren-gunner takes cover among the ruins of Cassino. Led by General Wladyslaw Anders, the Polish II Corps carried out the final, successful assault on Cassino, taking the abbey on 17-18 May 1944.

are isolated and by-passed, their destruction being assigned to subsequent waves.

The bombing was an erroneous concept inasmuch as it failed to destroy all life in Cassino. The bombing of the abbey had already shown that the many arched cellars provided secure shelters because aircraft bombs are not designed to penetrate deep into the ground.

At Cassino the bombing was not directed against frightened refugees but against the Wehrmacht's toughest fighting men. The 1st Parachute Rifle Division had slowly relieved 90th Panzer Grenadier Division, thus allowing the new troops gradually to familiarize themselves with the terrain. Their commander, General Heidrich, had taken over on 26 February.

This step-by-step handing-over was a minor tactical expedient. But what exceeded all expectations was the fighting spirit of the troops. The soldiers crawled out of the shattered cellars and bunkers to confront the enemy with the toughest resistance. Words can hardly do them justice. We had all reckoned that those who had survived the hours of bombing and the casualties would be physically and morally shaken, but this was not so.

In all armies the paratroops are an élite of fighting men. To begin with, the parachute jump calls for self-control and the more numerous the jumps, the greater the demand on self-control. Contact with the ground still resembles a free jump from a height of several metres, the parachutes are smaller than the normal life-saving ones. Their size is limited by the need to keep the units close together while still

airborne. However, the units usually land without any co-ordination, which they then have to establish on the battlefield, despite the lack of any communications with the rear. This tradition proved its value at Cassino. It was no longer a question of permanently occupying the town. The fighting was done from fortuitous new strong-points which usually had no contact on the flanks or towards the rear, and were ignorant of what was happening elsewhere on the narrow front.

The individual nests of resistance had not become isolated through the bombing alone. Such isolation is typical of all fighting in towns. At first the fighting in Cassino fluctuated, then the New Zealand Division slowly forced its way south deeper into the town, and

Above: Battle-weary German paratroopers wait for evacuation from Cassino in the lee of a Sherman tank.

Left: B-25 Mitchell medium bombers of the US 12th Air Force drop their bombs on Monte Cassino.

was able to hold parts of it. But between these parts were strong-points that the Germans had not given up or had recaptured in counter-attacks. The fighting was at such close quarters that one floor of a building might be held by the defender while the next was occupied by the attackers. If the latter wished to use their artillery to soften up the building before storming it, they would first have to evacuate this floor!

The town area of Cassino came under Para-troop Regiment 3, Colonel Heilmann. When the bombing started, the divisional commander, General Heidrich, happened to be at Heilmann's command post, two-and-a-half kilometres south of Monte Cassino. Heilmann stayed there during the entire battle, and this was right, for it was the centre of resistance. In order to meet both these commanders at that place I had to cover much ground on foot from Aquino through a seemingly unoccupied terrain. I crossed a large field full of craters which had been ploughed up more and more by heavy-calibre shells although it seemed to be unoccupied. No tree escaped damage, no piece of ground remained green. On my lonely walk the only accompaniment was the jarring explosion of shells, the whistling of splinters, the smell of freshly thrown-up earth, and the well-known mixture of smells from glowing iron and burnt powder. Yet distributed round this terrain were hidden batteries, whose men rushed from cover to man their guns for sudden bombardments, then disappeared again with equal speed. What I saw and felt took me back across twenty-eight years, when I experienced the same loneliness crossing the battlefield of the

Somme. Hitler was right when he later told me that here was the only battlefield of this war that resembled those of the first.

It was never possible to obtain a clear picture of the course of the battle from the command post of Regiment 3. The paratroops were in the habit of not reporting the smaller losses of ground, because they hoped soon to recover it. Often reports from the corps artillery, which I had allocated in good measure to this division, were more accurate.

I gave the division plenty of freedom to fight the battle in its own way. Exhortations of the kind that one addresses to other troops to shake them up would have been out of place here. I also said nothing when we lost the railway station due to a tank attack from the east, and when our counter-attack failed to recapture it. It was more important to preserve our irreplaceable forces than to hold on to this or that part of the town.

Above: The evacuation of the *abbé* from Cassino. Due to a misinterpretation of German signal traffic, the Allies believed that a German detachment was being stationed in the monastery. The decision to bomb the position was taken in the light of this intelligence-gathering error.

Below: Bombs explode in Cassino town. Castle Hill can be seen on the right.

To the west of the New Zealand Division, the 4th Indian Division also attacked in a general southerly direction on the monastery hill. Anyone who has climbed this hill with its gradient of 500 metres up for every 1,000 metres horizontally will know the difficulties of attacking across a slope of this kind. And the strongpoint in the ruins of the monastery was still on the flank of the enemy's thrust. The slope of the hill was, however, so cut up that this gave the outstanding Indian troops the possibility of pressing on, with the result that Castle Hill (Hill 193) north of the Continental Hotel was soon lost. In the end the Gurkhas thrust forward as far as the well-known Hangman's Hill (Hill 434) which is 350 metres south of the Abbey, and here they formed an isolated strong-point. This was the western arm of the pincer which was intended to unite with the other pincer movement that had developed from the Cassino railway station. In this way the Via Casilina would have been cut off and the town of Cassino surrounded.

But this did not happen. The fighting on the hill continued for a week without any decisive result, until a balance of forces was achieved, and so we maintained our position in Cassino. Here as elsewhere the onslaught had failed due to the steadfastness and desperate courage of the paratroops. It will not detract from their fame if I fill in the picture with one or two lucky incidents of the kind that in war always seem to assist the brave.

Although the bombs falling on the town had extinguished many lives and destroyed many defensive works, they also eased the burden of the defenders. The Allied infantry attacks showed clearly that they had been wrong in thinking that their tanks could operate in the town. The bombs had produced an area of craters so extensive that the tanks could only force their way along narrow lanes after the pioneers had laboriously cleared the obstructions. The craters were filled with the rubble of the houses, so that they could not even be negotiated by climbing over them. We were also aided on the very first night by the rain showers which turned the rubble into sticky sludge. Consequently in the first assault the infantry lacked support from any forward rushing tanks. The German infantry in Cassino and the few tanks knew their job because they had long been on the defensive. The tanks, operating singly, were held back under cover until at very close range they engaged the enemy's tanks, then immediately disappeared into fresh cover. That the Continental Hotel was held is attributable to one tank, which had been built into the entrance hall.

The enemy's artillery had difficulty in laying a creeping barrage in front of the infantry, which was advancing too slowly. The mass of this artillery was located in the valley east of Cassino, not north of the town, whence the

Left: A pair of German paratroopers take up position in the ruins of Monte Cassino.

infantry had started out. More than one critic of our opponent at that time maintains that he did not suffer too much from the German artillery fire. But this is a characteristic of all street- and town-fighting. We, however, were in no doubt that our artillery, consisting of many batteries concentrated in the corps unit and centrally directed, made a substantial contribution to the success of the defence.

In my opinion the smoke-making battery under Lt.-Colonel Andrae was a highly effective weapon. Thanks to its well-directed searching fire, its demoralizing effect stifled the enemy's initial effort to assemble his tanks and infantry, and helped our own infantry in many an apparently hopeless situation.

From sources provided by our opponent we now know that his own tactical mistakes made our task less difficult. These were mistakes

Below: The monastery after the Allied bombing raid. Steep slopes, caves and vast amounts of rubble made the hill an excellent defensive position.

which in another context we had learned to avoid as a result of experiences at Stalingrad. The slow tempo of the first infantry attack was in line with the reluctance to throw in reserves at the very places where the attack needed backing. During the first two days the enemy had no battalion staff in the town. This went against our principles. With us, if the situation demanded it, the battalion commander would normally be seen in the front line, sometimes even rushing out of his bunker armed with a hand-grenade, like any patrol leader. Thus he could be expected to send back tactically relevant situation reports and to make his own decisions. In the end the strength of our battalions at the climax of the battle was never more than about a hundred men, of whom a proportion were tied to anti-tank guns and mortars.

As was always the case in this type of close-in fighting, the physical proximity of the opponents induced a comradeship between the front-line soldiers which showed itself particularly in the imperative need to remove the wounded. Frequently a local armistice was arranged to allow both sides to rescue their wounded. I myself had often seen this in mountain warfare. Sometimes the paratroops on the hills would allow wounded to pass unmolested without any prior agreement. In places where there was no alternative the wounded were rescued in broad daylight under the shield of the Red Cross. The negotiators usually imposed a limit on the time allowed for rescue. When at the end of the battle the enemy had to evacuate the salient formed by Hangman's Hill, he left his wounded behind, as the last of his occupying forces would not otherwise have been able to fight their way back through the German lines. But the lightly wounded got moving and, giving each other mutual support, passed through the lines. The local German commander had intimated his approval for this procedure. To quote Fred Majdalany:

'The medical orderlies of both sides fell into the habit of wandering, almost at will, in a mute kinship that in its spontaneous charity was perhaps the most ironic witness of all to the folly of battle that made it necessary.'

I associate myself with these sentiments of my young friend, and I bow to those New Zealanders, Indians and Germans who in the midst of hellish, death-dealing battle saved others at the risk of their own lives.

On 19 March, only four days after the bombing and the start of the attack, General Freyberg had to consider sending into action at Cassino the reserves that had been intended for the pursuit following a break-through.

The next day Churchill asked General Alexander to explain why he was attacking on the Cassino front on a width of only two or three miles, which had already used up five or six divisions against the German pincer defence, and why he had attempted no flanking move-

Above: A British medical squad moves into Cassino town to search for casualties. Both sides observed the truce flag.

ment. Alexander was at pains to explain the peculiarities of the battlefield to the Prime Minister.

But on the same day Alexander summoned the Army Commanders and General Freyberg to discover whether a continuation of the attack would be likely to lead within the next few days to the capture of the Abbey, or whether the offensive should be broken off while holding on to important points with a view to later operations. The council of war decided in favour of breaking off the attack. In Cassino, Castle Hill and the northwest sector of the town were held on to, as were the botanical garden in the centre and the railway station with the adjoining hill. The salient strong-point on Hangman's Hill, immediately southeast of the Abbey (Hill 435), was evacuated under great difficulties.

Below: A glum-looking Hitler underlines the success of the Polish capture of Monte Cassino. Its fall opened the road to Rome, which fell in June 1944.

Imphal

by Viscount Slim of Yarralumla

When the Japanese overran Burma they do not seem to have intended to push on into India. The first Chindit expedition demonstrated, however, that the River Chindwin was not a secure frontier, and on 15 March 1944 they took the offensive. It was their aim to get into the valley of the Brahmaputra and overrun the airfields from which the Allies were supplying China. This would have meant that the Chinese, starved of supplies, might not have been able to carry on the struggle, which tied up approximately a third of the Japanese Army throughout the war. It is unlikely that had the Japanese succeeded they would have invaded eastern India.

In the battle that followed the Japanese suffered the worst defeat in their military history. Five divisions were destroyed. Not less than 53,000 men and 250 guns were lost. The Fourteenth Army suffered 16,700 casualties, but did not lose a single gun.

Generals are not noted for pointing out their own mistakes. Field-Marshal Slim discusses his with refreshing candour, but he made so few that he can afford to.   EDITOR

These pages: Sherman tanks of an Indian armored unit move down the main road through Pegu, a vital point on the road to Rangoon. The swift advance on the city owed much to the victories at Kohima and Imphal which broke the back of the Japanese Fifteenth Army in Burma.

Chronology

1941
7 Dec.   Japanese attack Pearl Harbor.

1942
15 Jan.   The Japanese invade Burma.
15 Feb.   Surrender of Singapore.
9 March   Fall of Rangoon.
29 April   The Japanese cut the Burma Road.
1 May   Evacuation of Mandalay.
4 May   Loss of Akyab.
Dec.   Unsuccessful British offensive in the Arakan.

1943
Feb.-May   First Chindit expedition.
Aug.   South-East Asia Command (SEAC) set up.

1944
3 Feb.-May   Japanese offensive in the Arakan.
5 March   Second Chindit expedition begins.
15 March   Japanese offensive in Assam.
24 March   Death of Wingate.
7 April   Siege of Kohima.
7 June   Japanese retreat from Imphal and Kohima.

1945
3 Jan.   Re-occupation of Akyab.
20 March   Mandalay retaken.
3 May   Recapture of Rangoon.
6 Aug.   Atomic bomb dropped on Hiroshima.
14 Aug.   Surrender of Japan.

The opening moves in the Imphal-Kohima battle took place in the first days of March 1944. Then the 17th Division about Tiddim was at the top of its form. Cowan, who still commanded it, and his men, far from being depressed by the set-backs they had sustained, were thirsting for revenge. He had benefited from experience and was no longer trying to capture the Japanese positions by attacks along the knife-edge ridges of the Chin Hills. In the constant patrol fights, ambushes, and raids that his Gurkhas and the Japanese carried on against one another, the 17th Division was now having very much the better of the exchanges. Cowan was skilfully using the freedom of movement this gave him to begin the systematic isolation and piecemeal reduction of the enemy positions. He had already captured some of the most important of the lost ground, and the whole of it seemed relentlessly falling within his grasp, when the conditions of his local war changed suddenly and completely.

The Japanese offensive began on 6 March 1944. On that day troops of 214 Regiment of the enemy 33rd Division began a series of attacks on our detachment covering the Manipur River bridge near Tonzang, 20 miles north of Tiddim. Cowan sent a battalion to reinforce our men. The assaults grew in strength, until it was evident the whole 214 Regiment, the equivalent of one of our brigades, was flinging itself against our Tonzang positions. Our defences held stoutly, but were in danger of being overwhelmed. Cowan, therefore, on the 13th, dispatched his 63 Brigade to make sure of this vital position in his rear.

Meanwhile, on 8 March, another Japanese column, 215 Regiment, crossed the Manipur River from east to west, several miles south of our positions about Tiddim, and moved north by tracks through the hills. Its move was reported, but it was difficult to judge its strength, and neither patrol nor air reconnaissance could keep touch with it in the thick jungle. On the 13th came ominous news. The engineer officer commanding at Milestone 109, nearly 60 miles north of Tiddim, reported that a Japanese force was in the hills a few miles to the west of his camp. In that camp, except for a few Indian Sappers and Miners, were only administrative units of no fighting value, including some 5,000 unarmed labour who had halted there on their way to Imphal. Part of a Jat Indian machine-gun battalion, the only fighting troops within reach, was hurriedly diverted to the camp, which, scattered and low-lying, was most difficult to defend. These rather alarming events had been reported to Scoones, and at 2040 hours on 13 March he telephoned Cowan ordering him to withdraw his division to the Imphal plain. At 2200 hours Cowan gave out warning orders for the withdrawal of his division the next day.

It was a long column that began to wind through the hills in the afternoon of the 14th. The whole division, including its headquarters, went on foot; transport was kept for stores, ammunition, supplies, and wounded. It took with it 2,500 vehicles, 3,500 animals, and a number of sick. The first day it covered 20 miles, blowing up bridges behind it and sowing mines and booby traps in the camps it had left. The

Below: Brigadier Orde Wingate (with stick) discusses plans for the second Chindit operation behind enemy lines in northern Burma. In the campaign several of Wingate's units were cut off and had to be resupplied by air. Their success clearly showed that British and Commonwealth troops could fight against both the jungle and the Japanese.

Field Marshal Viscount Slim, KG, GCB, GCMG, GCVO, GBE, DSO, MC
(1891-1970)

Served in the Royal Warwickshire Regiment at Gallipoli, where he was wounded, in France and in Mesopotamia, where he was wounded for a second time and won the Military Cross. After the Great War he transferred to the Indian Army and served in the Gurkha Rifles. Among other appointments he was an instructor at the Staff College, Camberley, and Commandant of the Senior Officers' School, India.

During the Second World War he fought in Eritrea, where he was wounded; commanded the 10th Indian Division in Syria, Persia and Iraq, winning the DSO; and then became commander, first of the Burma Corps, then of the Fourteenth Army, with whom he destroyed the Japanese Army in Burma.

He was Chief of the Imperial General Staff from 1948 to 1952, and Governor-General and Commander-in-Chief of Australia from 1953 to 1960. In 1964 he became Constable and Governor of Windsor Castle. His works include *Defeat into Victory*, from which this chapter is taken, and *Unofficial History*.

Japanese followed the tail of the column cautiously, with sound tactical sense, concentrating on cutting in ahead, and blocking the road at an advantageous point in front of the division.

This they did in two places. The first near Tonzang, where the 214 Regiment made a detour round our detachment while it was heavily engaged, and established itself astride the road on the Tuitum Saddle, two miles north. The second was at the unhappy Milestone 109 camp. As the Japanese 215 Regiment closed in, the small garrison there soon found itself in difficulties, hampered as it was by a mass of non-combatants. On 14 March the road to Imphal was cut, the 17th Division dealt promptly and effectively with the first block, that beyond Tonzang. On the 16th, Gurkhas with strong artillery support stormed up the Saddle, broke into the Japanese defences with bayonet and *kukri*, and, with surprisingly few casualties to themselves, chased the enemy off the Saddle. The Japanese would have been wiser to have held it in greater strength, but they were having their difficulties. The road was now open, but only to Milestone 109.

Nor was the Tiddim road the only sector from which danger threatened. By the beginning of March 1944, the Japanese 15th and 31st Divisions were poised along the east bank of the Chindwin, from Tanga in the south to Tamanthi in the north. Apart from patrols, no troops of these divisions crossed the river until on 14 March a small detachment attacked one of our 'V' Force observation posts, 12 miles west of Homalin, and was repulsed. On the night of 15/16 March, however, both divisions began to move in earnest. The 15th Division, to whom

had been entrusted the honour of taking Imphal, crossed in three columns about Thaungdut, with orders 'to advance through the hills like a ball of fire'. It was to follow the main axis Myothit-Sanghak-Litan and thence round the north of Imphal. Its task was first to isolate and then capture the town. Its columns moved light and fast. On 18 March, while one of them was pressing our 20th Division's flank near Myothit, others were approaching Ukhrul and contact was made with them about ten miles southeast of the village, some 50 miles from Imphal itself.

The 31st Japanese Division at the same time crossed the Chindwin in eight columns on a 40-mile front from Homalin to the north. Keeping on the right of their 15th Division, these columns began to push westward like the

probing fingers of an extended hand. It was difficult in such close country to discover either their strength or their objectives, but Scoones managed to make a fairly accurate estimate of both. As fighting developed it seemed that one main column, 58 Regimental Group, was to capture Ukhrul and then push for Kohima while another, 60 Regimental Group, turned west on Imphal. Other columns were to cut the main Kohima road north of Imphal, and still more to stream through the Somra Hills towards Jessami, southeast of Kohima. Then the hand was to close, the columns would converge, and, as the Japanese commander described it, they would 'at one fell swoop fall on Kohima and annihilate the British on that front'. Full of confidence in themselves and contempt for their enemy, the Japanese plunged forward.

In Imphal I was impressed by the steadiness of commanders and troops. Scoones, in control of the tactical battle on the whole Assam front, had been faced with a difficult and momentous decision. The fog of war had descended. He was deluged with reports and rumours of Japanese columns which seemed to flit in and out of the jungle, now here, now there; little was definite and nothing certain. Two things, however, were clear: first that the 17th Division was cut off, and second, that a strong threat to Imphal itself from the east was developing. Time was short. The commander of IV Corps had to make up his mind, there and then, whether he would hold his reserve, the 23rd Division, to meet the thrust at Imphal or send the bulk of it towards Tiddim to help out the 17th Division. Calmly he balanced the risks of each course. Rightly he decided to hold to our plan for the battle and to follow the course which would, if successful, more quickly concentrate his corps in the Imphal plain. He therefore sent, first one brigade, and then a second of the 23rd Division to fight down the road towards the 17th Division.

On how fine a margin the success or failure of these decisions depended can be seen from the history of the Japanese thrust at Imphal from the east. On 19 March part of the enemy 31st Division surged against the Indian Parachute Brigade and one battalion of the 23rd Division, dug in to cover Ukhrul. For two desperate days the fight went on, then the brigade was pushed back and Ukhrul fell to the enemy. The three battalions, now considerably weakened, stood again at Sangshak, nine miles to the south. There, from the 21st to the 25th, they resisted desperate night attacks, which were closely supported by the Japanese artillery while by day snipers and shelling took their toll. With the Japanese came the Jiffs, as we called members of the Indian National Army, who were employed not in direct attacks but in unavailing attempts to confuse and suborn our Indian troops. On the morning of 26 March the enemy

put in an all-out daylight assault. Our losses and theirs were heavy in hand-to-hand fighting. The main positions held, but unfortunately one of the two meagre water-supply points was lost. Throughout the action the RAF had kept up the closest support, and they now attempted, in spite of heavy fire from the ground, to deliver water, but the area held by our troops was so restricted that most of the drops were lost. Almost without water, it was impossible to hold on any longer, and, after dark on 26 March, what was left of the brigade was ordered to break out and make for Imphal. The ten days' delay and the heavy casualties this small force and the RAF who supported them had inflicted on the enemy were of inestimable value at this critical stage of the battle.

While this savage fighting was going on around Ukhrul and Sangshak, an equally severe action was developing at Litan on the Ukhrul road, about ten miles to the southwest. Here, small detachments from the Parachute Brigade, hurriedly reinforced by a newly landed battalion of the 5th Division, had dug in to block the road to the Japanese advance. Our positions were attacked by superior forces on the night of 24/25 March and in spite of several counter-attacks the battalion, having suffered heavily, lost its forward localities. Next day the Japanese attempted to cut the road to Imphal in its rear. But now, in the nick of time, the troops of the 5th Division flown from Arakan were coming into action, practically straight from their aircraft. 123 Brigade moved up the road, clearing it to six miles from Litan. The detachment at Litan was withdrawn on the 28th, and 9 Brigade of the 5th Division brought up. The Japanese advance from Ukhrul direct on Imphal now met strong resistance, was roughly handled, and, in a week of clashes and ambushes, was held.

Above: The crew of a mortar deploy their weapon against the Japanese during the second Chindit operation.

While the direct blow was thus parried, the Japanese thrust from Ukhrul against the Kohima-Imphal road broke through, and on 30 March the enemy blew up a bridge 30 miles north of Imphal and established strong road-blocks. Except for the Silchar track to the west, Imphal was thus cut off by land.

While all this was going on, the 23rd Indian Division, less one brigade left for the defence of Imphal, had begun its fight on the Tiddim road towards the 17th Division. Major-General Ouvry Roberts, who commanded the 23rd Division, was a good man for such a job. Years before, when I had taught him at the Staff College, he had been marked as likely to become not only a first-class staff officer but a successful commander. He had been my chief staff officer in the 10th Indian Division in Iraq in 1941. There he had done what I have always considered to be one of the best single-handed jobs any officer of his then rank had performed in the war. The Iraq Army was besieging the Royal Air Force base at Habbaniyeh, and, in spite of the gallantry of the pilots of the Flying School, in their obsolete machines, and of Assyrian Levies and airmen on the ground, it looked as if it might fall. At the most critical moment of the siege we flew in Roberts. By his energy, by the direction he imparted to the operations, and by the confidence he inspired, he transformed a somewhat bewildered defence into a successfully aggressive one. Had Habbaniyeh fallen, the results would have been disastrous to the whole Middle East. Now he had transferred those qualities to the command of a division.

The leading units of Roberts' 37th Brigade, with a few light tanks, moving rapidly, drove off a Japanese force which was besieging a small detachment of ours at Milestone 109 on the Tiddim road. Before our troops could push on to the relief of the camp at Milestone 109, the enemy, infiltrating through the jungle, had established a series of roadblocks behind them. They were thus forced to turn and clear the road towards Imphal while the second brigade of the 23rd Division fought south towards them. The situation on the Tiddim road was now for a time as it had once been on the Arakan coast – a Neapolitan ice of layers of our troops alternating with Japanese – but in both training and morale our men were much better fitted to deal with such a confused and harassing business than they had been in 1943.

Still, with relief thus delayed, the situation at Milestone 109 grew critical. Japanese pressure and shelling intensified and in such a restricted area, congested by non-combatants, effective defence became impossible. During the night of the 16/17 March, these non-combatants were skilfully led out by jungle paths through the enemy positions to join the 23rd Division. The handful of fighting troops held on for two more days and then they, too, broke out and escaped.

The Japanese swarming in found much in the way of stores and a number of abandoned vehicles. They at once began to build powerful defences to deny passage to the 17th Division approaching from the south.

Cowan, knowing that the camp at Milestone 109 had fallen, anticipated rightly that the road itself would be strongly held against him. He therefore sent infantry detachments along the ridges on each side of it, while his main force pressed on up the road. The right column, in a series of hard-fought small actions, cleared the enemy from the crest, and then, during 21 and 22 March, closely supported by the fighter-bombers of the RAF, 48 Brigade, in heavy fighting, broke through the desperately defended enemy position astride the road a mile south of the camp. The Japanese withdrawing were caught by our western flank detachment and again very roughly handled. To complete their discomfiture they were effectively bombed by the RAF in the area to which they

Below: Chinese troops, part of the force led by General Joseph Stilwell (1883-1946), move forward to attack the Japanese threatening the Burma Road, the vital link between China and the British forces in northern Burma.

had retired to lick their wounds. After another grim fight the camp was recaptured on the 25th. Much of its contents and most of the lost vehicles were recovered intact and brought out with the 17th Division.

While the head of the division was thus effectively dealing with the Japanese 215 Regiment, the rearguard on Tuitum Saddle was nightly beating off fierce attacks from a reinforced 214 Regiment with greatly increased artillery and tank support. A final all-out assault on the 24th, when several enemy tanks were knocked out, was repulsed with heavy loss. On the 26th, the Japanese block at Milestone 109 having been cleared, the rearguard withdrew from Tuitum across the Manipur River and blew up the bridge, while the division resumed its march. Japanese parties were still encountered, on and near the road, but they were easily brushed aside. On 20 March patrols of the 17th Division and 23rd Division met at Milestone 102. Several small fights were still required to clear the road to the north, but the back of the Japanese opposition had been broken, and they were not, at the moment, capable of another major effort to intercept the 17th Division. Leaving the two brigades of the 23rd Division to hold back the enemy, the 17th Division reached Imphal on 5 April.

During the later stages of its withdrawal, the division had been maintained by supply dropping from the air. The Japanese Air Force made only one major attempt to attack the long, retreating column and that without serious effect. The enemy's inactivity in the air at this critical time is a measure of what the 17th Division owed to 221 Group RAF. Had not our fighters maintained continuous cover and given quick support at call, the withdrawal, if it could have been carried out at all, would have been a much grimmer and more protracted affair, with serious consequences to the main battle around Imphal.

This action on the Tiddim road was, in itself, a considerable success. The 17th Division was now in the Imphal plain, intact with all its transport and wounded. It and the air forces supporting it had inflicted heavier losses on the Japanese than it had suffered. It had beaten them on every occasion in stand-up fights, and, as I saw for myself when I met the division just outside Imphal, its morale was correspondingly high. The 23rd Division had similarly shared in these successes and, in addition, took a slightly mischievous pride in the fact that it had had to come to the rescue of the redoubtable 17th. Yet, looked at from the overall picture of the battle, the fact that the 17th Division had been delayed, and still more that the bulk of Scoones' reserve had of necessity been drawn away at a critical time, might have had tragic military consequences.

The other forward division of IV Corps, Gracey's 20th, operating in the Tamu area and at

the head of the Kabas valley, had plenty of excitement in its withdrawal to the Imphal plain, but was never in so difficult a position as the 17th. By the beginning of March, patrols of the 20th Division had penetrated well down the Kabaw Valley and across the Chindwin. A brigade of the 23rd Division had been sent temporarily to the banks of the Chindwin, a few miles north of Sittang, where it was demonstrating to distract attention from the fly-in by the Chindits then in progress.

The Japanese assembled in the southern Kabaw Valley a force under Major-General Yamamoto the core of which was three battalions of infantry from the 33rd Division, later, in the north of the valley increased by two more battalions. Round this nucleus they grouped considerable bodies of their auxiliaries, the Burma Traitor Army and the Jiffs. To this somewhat heterogeneous party they entrusted a large part of their available medium artillery, most of their one tank regiment, and a great deal of their mechanical transport. Their reason for this was that the Sittang-Palel-Imphal road

Above: An aerial view of the Imphal-Tiddim road. During the battles around Imphal, elements of the Japanese 33rd Division attempt to infiltrate the lines of the British IV Corps; their attacks were blunted by the 17th Indian Division.

Above right: The Battle of Kohima (April-May 1944) saw some of the bloodiest fighting of the war in Burma.

Right: Japanese dead, caught in an ambush by Chinese troops, litter a Burmese road.

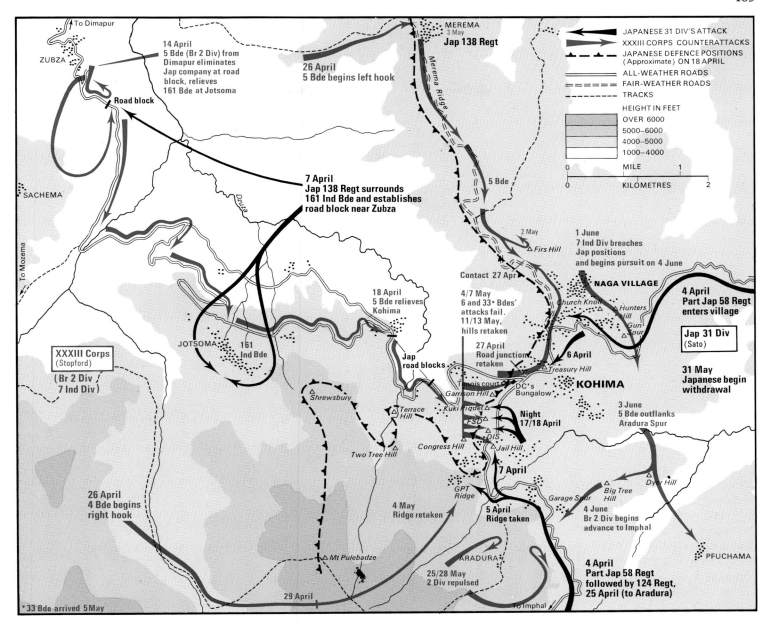

14 April
5 Bde (Br 2 Div) from Dimapur eliminates Jap company at road block, relieves 161 Bde at Jotsoma

ZUBZA

To Dimapur

Road block

SACHEMA

To Mozema

Druia

26 April
5 Bde begins left hook

MEREMA
3 May
Jap 138 Regt

Merema Ridge

5 Bde

2 May
△ Firs Hill

7 April
Jap 138 Regt surrounds 161 Ind Bde and establishes road block near Zubza

JAPANESE 31 DIV'S ATTACK
XXXIII CORPS COUNTERATTACKS
JAPANESE DEFENCE POSITIONS (Approximate) ON 18 APRIL
ALL-WEATHER ROADS
FAIR-WEATHER ROADS
TRACKS
HEIGHT IN FEET
OVER 6000
5000–6000
4000–5000
1000–4000

0   MILE   1
0   KILOMETRES   2

1 June
7 Ind Div breaches Jap positions and begins pursuit on 4 June

Contact 27 Apr

NAGA VILLAGE

Church Knoll
△ Hunters Hill
Gun Spur

4 April
Part Jap 58 Regt enters village

18 April
5 Bde relieves Kohima

4/7 May
6 and 33* Bdes' attacks fail. 11/13 May, hills retaken

27 April
Road junction retaken

6 April

Treasury Hill

KOHIMA

Jap 31 Div (Sato)

31 May
Japanese begin withdrawal

XXXIII Corps (Stopford)
(Br 2 Div)
(7 Ind Div)

JOTSOMA

161 Ind Bde

Jap road blocks

Tennis court
Garrison Hill
Kuki Piquet △
FSD
DIS
Congress Hill
△ Jail Hill

DC's Bungalow

Night 17/18 April

3 June
5 Bde outflanks Aradura Spur

△ Shrewsbury

△ Terrace Hill

△ Two Tree Hill

7 April

GPT Ridge

5 April
Ridge taken

Garage Spur

△ Big Tree Hill

△ Dyer Hill

4 June
Br 2 Div begins advance to Imphal

26 April
4 Bde begins right hook

4 May
Ridge retaken

25/28 May
2 Div repulsed

ARADURA

4 April
Part Jap 58 Regt followed by 124 Regt, 25 April (to Aradura)

PFUCHAMA

△ Mt Pulebadze

29 April

To Imphal

*33 Bde arrived 5 May

was not only the most direct, but by far the easiest way by which to bring heavy equipment into the Imphal plain.

On 12 March, the Japanese began to push up the Kabaw Valley in two columns covered by a wide, and to our men, confusing screen of Burmans and Jiffs, whom it was most difficult for our men to distinguish from the local inhabitants and our own troops. Nevertheless our patrols frequently penetrated this screen and inflicted casualties on the Japanese. On the 17th, after a severe three-day fight which momentarily halted the enemy, the forward troops on the 20th Division's southern sector fell back slowly under orders on Tamu, holding successive positions while the 'thinning out' process beind them continued. The Japanese made several minor attacks and one serious one, supported by medium tanks. All these were beaten off and the withdrawal continued at our own pace. Throughout, the Japanese showed their usual fanatical courage, on one occasion attempting to rush and destroy our guns with pole charges and magnetic mines.

Left: Japanese troops prepare to cross the Chindwin River. Three divisions of Lieutenant-General Mutaguchi's Fifteenth Army launched Operation U-GO against Imphal and Kohima. His aim was to pre-empt an Allied offensive by cutting the single railroad to Assam in northern India.

This party was lured into an ambush, set round evacuated gun pits, and wiped out. Three Japanese, all wounded, including an officer, were the only survivors. They were the 20th Division's first prisoners and of great value to our intelligence.

During 16 March, Japanese of the forces which had crossed the Chindwin a few miles north of Thaungdut began to threaten the division's flank. As pressure increased, the order to fall back to the defended locality of Moreh, two miles south of Tamu, was given. On the 20th, one of the few tank versus tank actions of the campaign took place, between a troop of the 3rd Dragoon Guards and Japanese medium and light tanks. The enemy armour was routed, with the loss of four tanks destroyed and one captured, which, to the great satisfaction of the Dragoons, they were able to bring back. After dark on 22 March the Japanese heavily attacked our Moreh positions, but were repulsed.

By now the threat of the main Japanese advance on Imphal from the east was growing more menacing, and Scoones was compelled to look for a reserve to replace the brigades of the 23rd Division that had gone to the rescue of the 17th. He could only find this by drawing on the now heavily pressed 20th Division, and to provide it he had to order Gracey to evacuate Moreh and come back to Shenam and Tengoupal, about nine miles from Palel. On 2 April, 32 Brigade was, therefore, withdrawn into Corps Reserve, leaving only two brigades to cover Palel and hold the southeastern approaches to the plain.

Within a week of the start of the Japanese offensive, while the 17th Division was still fighting its way out, it became clear that the situation in the Kohima area was likely to be even more dangerous than that at Imphal. Not only were enemy columns closing in on Kohima at much greater speed than I had expected, but they were obviously in much greater strength. Indeed it was soon evident that the bulk, if not the whole, of the Japanese 31st Division was driving from Kohima and Dimapur. I had been confident that the most the enemy could bring and maintain through such country would be one regimental group, the equivalent of a British brigade group. In that, I had badly underestimated the Japanese capacity for large-scale, long-range infiltration, and for their readiness to accept odds in a gamble on supply. This misappreciation was the second great mistake I made in the Imphal battle.

It was an error that was likely to cost us dear. We were not prepared for so heavy a thrust; Kohima with its rather scratch garrison and, what was worse, Dimapur with no garrison at all, were in deadly peril. The loss of Kohima we could endure, but that of Dimapur, our only base and railhead, would have been crippling to an almost fatal degree. It would have pushed into the far distance our hopes of relieving Imphal, laid bare to the enemy the Brahmaputra Valley with its string of airfields, cut off Stilwell's Ledo Chinese, and stopped all supply to China. As I contemplated the chain of disasters that I had invited, my heart sank. However, I have always believed that a motto for generals must be 'No regrets', or crying over spilt milk. The vital need was now to bring in reinforcements to ensure that Dimapur was held.

I had available for the purpose under my own command the 5th Indian Division, and 3 Special Service Brigade, composed of one army and one Royal Marine commando. Both these formations were in Arakan. Plans had already been made for the move of the 5th Division, either by road and rail or by air, to Assam. As time was short I ordered it to begin to fly at once. Here I found a serious difficulty. The need for speed had increased and was desperate, but Troop Carrier Command had only eight Dakota squadrons, four British and four American, which, with the demands already on them could not lift the division at anything like the rate I now demanded.

At this time large numbers of transport aircraft were employed on the Hump route, carrying supplies to China from India. If we lost the Imphal-Kohima battle the Hump route would be closed. It seemed obvious therefore that it would be madness not to divert some of the China list to the vital needs of Fourteenth Army. Unfortunately not even the Supreme Commander himself had the authority to do this – only the American Chiefs of Staff in far-off Washington could give the word. However, Baldwin and I seized the opportunity of a meeting with Admiral Mountbatten on 13 March to press hard for such a transfer. He saw the urgency at once, and, on his own responsibility, ordered thirty Dakotas, or their equivalent in other aircraft, to join Troop Carrier Command – a decision which earned my gratitude and played a major part in the result of the battle.

The fly-in of the 5th Indian Division began on 17 March. By the 20th its first brigade, 123, had deplaned in Imphal. On the 24th, Divisional Headquarters was complete and by the 27th the divisional troops and a second brigade, 9, were also in. Their transport was limited to mules and jeeps, but the officers and men, fresh from their Arakan triumphs, were in fine form. The third brigade, 161, I diverted to Manipur. I disliked breaking up a division, but the Japanese pressure on Kohima made the quick arrival of help imperative. I had warned Christison in Arakan to get the 7th Indian Division to Chittagong, ready to follow to Assam with all speed. 3 Special Service Brigade later, in early April, I sent by rail to Silchar to guard the Bishenpur-Silchar track, the western entrance to the Imphal plain, and from it to threaten the flank of any Japanese move round Imphal.

I asked General Giffard, who was, as always, a tower of strength in emergency, to let me have Wingate's 23 Long-Range Penetration Brigade, which was still in India. He agreed to rail it to Jorhat, where I could place it as a mobile force to cover the railway to Ledo, and, if necessary, use it against the flank of an attack on Dimapur. He also sent from India, as previously arranged, the new 25th Indian Division to replace the 5th Division in Arakan. This, being largely a sea move, did not increase the extreme

Left: Elephant-mounted troops cross the Chindwin, heading for the southeast sector of the British defensive perimeter around Imphal. The Japanese 33rd Division launched sustained attacks against hill-top positions defended by, first, the 20th Indian Division and, later, by the 23rd Indian Division. The fighting lasted from 5 April to 22 June.

pressure of traffic which now fell on the Bengal and Assam railway system or add to the air-transport problem. I asked General Giffard also to send to my aid 33 Corps Headquarters and the 2nd British Division from his reserve in India. He at once agreed. He and Auchinleck had already, before I asked, begun preparations for this move. There was still considerable anxiety as to whether, if we did receive these substantial reinforcements, we should be able to maintain them, especially in heavy fighting which would increase greatly demands for supplies and replacements of all kinds. The risk was there but I declared my willingness to accept it and my belief that it could be over-

Below: Japanese troops cross the remains of a railroad yard near the town of Katha during the attack on Imphal and Kohima.

come. My experience has always been that British administrative staffs, like British engineers, work to such safety margins that there is always quite a lot in hand. We continued to evacuate the non-combatants from Assam at the rate of thousands a week by air, road, and rail, so that without increasing the Imphal ration strength we could replace them by fighting men. Snelling, my Chief Administrative Officer, nobly supported me. We could, he declared, maintain the extra fighting formations, although if the Imphal road were cut, as he somewhat ruefully admitted, we should be hard put to it. On 18 March, General Giffard ordered the 2nd Division to move to Fourteenth Army. Its original destination was to have been Arakan, as a relief for the 7th Division, but this was changed, at my request, to Dimapur, as the situation there was becoming more threatening. I sent Fourteenth Army movement staff officers to work out details with their opposite numbers in India. Lieutenant-General Stopford, 33 Corps Commander, reported to me at my headquarters on the 23rd.

Even when these moves were in hand my anxiety was hardly lessened. They would take time – and time was so short. It was a race between the Japanese onrush and the arrival of our reinforcements. As I struggled hard to redress my errors and to speed by rail and air these reinforcements I knew that all depended on the steadfastness of the troops already meeting the first impetus of the attack. If they could hold until help arrived, all would be well; if not,

we were near disaster. Happily for the result of the battle – and for me – I was, like other generals before me, to be saved from the consequences of my mistake by the resourcefulness of my subordinate commanders and the stubborn valour of my troops.

Pushed out some 30 miles to the east, to cover the approaches to Kohima, was one battalion, the newly formed Assam Regiment, with detachments of the Assam Rifles, the local armed police. The main weight of the enemy advance fell on this battalion, in the first battle of its career. Fighting in its own country, it put up a magnificent resistance, held doggedly on to one position after another against overwhelming odds, and, in spite of heavy casualties, its companies although separated never lost cohesion. The delay the Assam Regiment imposed on the 31st Japanese Division at this stage was invaluable.

Behind this screen, desperate efforts were in hand to make Kohima ridge into a great roadblock to bar the way to Dimapur. Non-combatants and hospital patients had already been evacuated, and, under the energetic and determined leadership of Colonel Richards, commanding Kohima, the men in the convalescent depot, some five hundred of them, were issued with arms, organized into units, and allotted to the defences. Every man who could be scraped up from administrative units was roped in to fight. More trenches were dug, dressing stations prepared, defences manned, but it was a very miscellaneous garrison of about a

Above: Lieutenant-General Kotoku Sato, the commander of the Japanese 31st Division during the fighting around Kohima.

Left: Camouflaged British infantry prepare to advance through thick jungle.

thousand who stood-to as the covering troops were forced slowly back, and it was a grim prospect they faced as 15,000 ravening Japanese closed in on them.

I had flown to Dimapur, and with Imphal in grave danger of being cut off and with the battle there by no means going according to plan, I realized I could not expect Scoones properly to control what would be tactically a separate battle of Kohima. I therefore placed Major-General Ranking, who commanded the base and rear of Assam, known as 202 Line of Communication Area, in control of all operations in the Kohima-Dimapur-Jorhat theatre, until the arrival of 33 Corps. It was for him a sudden plunge from administrative duties in a peaceful area into the alarms and stresses of a savage battle against desperate odds. And it would be against odds. In front of Kohima, Ranking had the Assam Battalion; in Kohima, besides the convalescents, he had a raw battalion of our allies, the Nepalese Army, and a couple of independent companies of the Burma Regiment. The only fighting unit he had in hand was a battalion of the Burma Regiment. Not much, all told, with which to meet a full-strength Japanese division. I admired the way in which he and his subordinate commanders faced their peril. In Dimapur I had asked the brigadier commanding the base what his ration strength was. 'Forty-five thousand, near enough,' he replied. 'And how many soldiers can you scrape up out of that lot?' I inquired. He smiled wryly. 'I might get five hundred who know how to fire a rifle!' But, as at Kohima, everything that could be done to put the sprawling base into a state of defence was being done. As I walked around, inspecting bunkers and rifle pits, dug by non-combatant labour under the direction of storemen and clerks, and as I looked into the faces of the willing but untried garrison, I could only hope that I imparted more confidence than I felt.

During the last days of March, 161st Brigade of the 5th Indian Division completed its fly-in from Arakan. Never was a reinforcement more welcome. Reports now showed that the whole of the Japanese 31st Division was ten to 20 miles from Kohima and that our covering force could not hope to delay them seriously, still less hold them. Even if the Assam battalion managed to fall back reasonably intact, it was doubtful if Kohima could hold out. The immediate problem was whether to give up Kohima and concentrate on holding Dimapur or to reinforce Kohima with 161st Brigade as it arrived and try to hold the enemy on the ridge until the 2nd British Division came to the rescue.

Above: Covered by a Bren-gun team, British troops move through a jungle thicket on the Kohima front in a sweep against Japanese snipers.

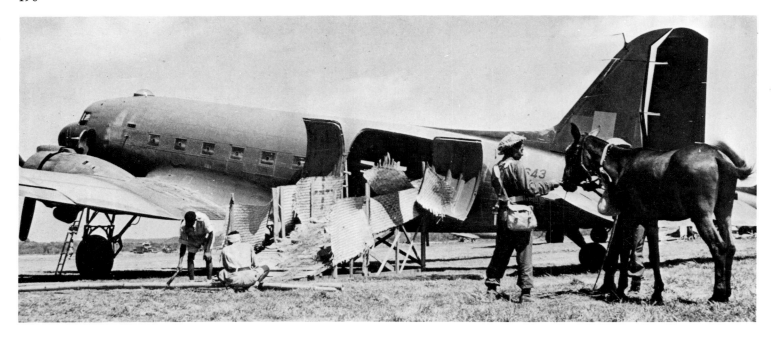

I discussed the situation with Ranking. Kohima Ridge was an infinitely preferable defensive position to Dimapur, which it covered. If we had not enough troops to hold Kohima, we certainly had not enough to hold Dimapur and, as long as we clung to the ridge, we had some chance of concentrating our reinforcements as they arrived, without too much hostile interference. We decided, therefore, to hold the Kohima Ridge, sending forward for the purpose 161st Brigade to meet the Japanese and stop them, temporarily at least, on or south of it.

Later when in one of the Dimapur offices I held a conference of commanders, it was not surprising that I saw some apprehensive faces turned towards me. I gave them three tasks:

1. To prepare Dimapur for defence and when attacked to hold it.
2. To reinforce Kohima and hold that to the last.
3. To make all preparations for the rapid reception and assembly of the large reinforcements that were on the way.

As always happens on these occasions, as soon as everybody was given a clear task into which he could throw himself, spirits rose and even I began to feel a little better. I took Warren, who commanded 161st Brigade, outside and walked him up and down the path while I gave him, without any attempt to minimize the hazardous task he was being set, a fuller view of the situation, and especially of the time factor. I told him I calculated that the enemy could reach Kohima by 3 April and, even if we held there, might by-pass our garrison and be attacking Dimapur by the 10th. I could not expect more than one brigade of the 2nd Division to have arrived by that time, or the whole division before the 20th. Actually the Transportation Services materially improved on these timings. Steady, unruffled, slow-speaking, Warren heard me out, asked a few questions, and went

off quietly to get on with his job. I hope I had as good an effect on him as he had on me.

After my talk with him, Warren took his brigade to Kohima on 29 March, and, such was his energy, that the next day one of his battalions was in action with the enemy, over 20 miles south, while the rest of the brigade was disposed to cover the withdrawal of the Assam Battalion. I had meanwhile left Dimapur and sent Ranking my written directive, in which I stressed that his main task was to safeguard Dimapur base. There were at this time reports and rumours of Japanese forces within striking distance of Dimapur, and he decided that the situation necessitated troops for the close defence of the base if he was to carry out this task. He, therefore, much to Warren's annoyance, ordered 161st Brigade back to the Nichugard Pass, eight miles southeast of Dimapur, to be in position there by the evening of 31 March. In taking this action Ranking was, I

Above: Loading a Dakota prior to a supply drop. With the main roads to both Imphal and Kohima blocked, the garrisons relied heavily on the war materials supplied by air transport.

Below: A painting of Kohima's Jail Hill after the battle. Japanese assaults captured the position on 17-18 April, but a British attack between 11 and 13 May retook the hill.

think, influenced understandably by the stress I had laid on his primary task – the defence of Dimapur base. The reports proved untrue, and the withdrawal of the brigade was an unfortunate mistake. Had it remained south of Kohima, Warren would almost certainly have at least delayed the Japanese advance on Kohima for several days. That would have put a very different aspect on the hard battle which followed.

Japanese pressure towards Kohima was mounting.

With the withdrawal of 161st Brigade, the covering troops were in grave difficulties as the enemy outflanked and enveloped them. The Assam Battalion, still fighting stubbornly and losing heavily, was split in two. Half of it, about two hundred strong, made its way into Kohima and joined the garrison; the rest evaded the encircling Japanese and, in good order but exhausted, reached the main Dimapur road behind 161st Brigade.

I have spent some uncomfortable hours at the beginnings of battles, but few more anxious than those of the Kohima battle. All the Japanese commander had to do was leave a detachment to mask Kohima, and, with the rest of his division, thrust violently on Dimapur. He could hardly fail to take it. Luckily, Major-General Sato, commander of the Japanese 31st Division, was, without exception, the most unenterprising of all the Japanese generals I encountered. He had been ordered to take Kohima and dig in. His bullet head was filled with one idea only – to take Kohima. It never struck him that he could inflict terrible damage on us without taking Kohima at all. Leaving a small force to contain it, and moving by tracks to the east of Warren's brigade at Nichugard, he could, by 5 April, have struck the railway with the bulk of his division. But he had no vision, so, as his troops came up, he flung them into attack after attack on the little town of Kohima. I have said I was saved from the gravest effects of my mistake in underestimating the enemy's capacity to penetrate to Kohima by the stubborn valour of my troops; but it needed the stupidity of the local enemy commander to make quite sure. Unfortunately, at the time, I did not know this was to be supplied, or I should have been saved much anxiety. Later, when it was evident, I once found some enthusiastic Royal Air Force officers planning an air strike on Sato's headquarters. They were astonished when I suggested they should abandon the project as I regarded their intended victim as one of my most helpful generals! But the time to indulge in such frivolities was not yet.

Lieutenant-General Montagu Stopford, commander of XXXIII Indian Corps, with some of his staff, had reached my headquarters at Comilla on 23 March. I knew him and had every confidence in him as a commander, but his corps headquarters had not previously operated and, indeed, had done little training. They would have to shake down and gain experience as they fought – never an easy thing to do. The success and speed with which they overcame their teething troubles were a measure of their ability and their commanders' leadership.

Above: Naga tribesmen make do with rough shelters during the fighting around Kohima.

I had at first considered Silchar as the location for XXXIII Corps Headquarters. It was central, had certain advantages in approach to Imphal and in communications; but the unexpected seriousness of the threat to Dimapur made it imperative to get not only the bulk of the reinforcements but Corps Headquarters also into that area. I also decided that Kohima at this stage must have priority over Imphal. Stopford himself urged this and I agreed with him. I gave Stopford as his objects:

1. To prevent Japanese penetration into the Brahmaputra or Surma Valleys or through the Lushai Hills.
2. To keep open the Dimapur-Kohima-Imphal road.
3. To move to the help of IV Corps and to co-operate with it in the destruction of all enemy west of the Chindwin.

These tasks were not changed throughout the battle, and remained the overall directive for XXXIII Corps. I gave him tactical freedom in the methods he chose to carry them out, and he, therefore, deserves the credit for accomplishing them.

On 3 April, Stopford arrived at Jorhat on the Assam railway, some 65 miles north-northeast of Dimapur, and established his headquarters there. Next day he took over control of operations from Ranking. In the ten days that had passed since Stopford had received his original orders the Kohima situation had developed, but not, alas, to our immediate advantage, and I decided that his immediate tasks had now become:

(i) To cover the concentration of his corps as far forward as practicable.

(ii) To secure the Dimapur base.

(iii) To reinforce and hold Kohima.

(iv) To protect, as far as possible without jeopardizing (i) to (iii), the Assam railway and the China route airfields in the Brahmaputra Valley.

The XXXIII Corps plan to achieve these various ends was:

(a) To concentrate the corps as it arrived northeast of Dimapur. This would avoid its becoming immediately involved in an enemy attack on the base and would place it advantageously to deliver a counterstroke. It would also automatically protect the railway to Ledo.

(b) To send forward the first brigade of the 2nd Division as soon as it arrived to hold the Nichugard Pass, eight miles southeast of Dimapur, thus covering the base against a direct Japanese advance.

(c) To reinforce Kohima with 161st Brigade of the 5th Indian Division at once.

(d) To use 23rd Brigade (Chindits), expected about 12 April, to strike south on Kohima and to the east of it, with the double object of checking Japanese infiltration towards the railway and of cutting the enemy line of communication to the Chindwin.

(e) To cover the western end of the Silchar-Bishenpur track with another Nepalese battalion which I had made available until the arrival of 3rd Special Service Brigade.

(f) To continue to use the newly formed Lushai Brigade to prevent an enemy advance into the Lushai Hills.

Wasting no time, on the evening of 4 April, Stopford ordered 161st Brigade to move again to Kohima. It left Nichugard the next day, and its leading unit, the 4th Battalion, the Royal West Kent Regiment, joined the garrison late the same day, just after the first Japanese night attack had overrun some of our positions. The rest of the brigade, warned of the congestion in Kohima, halted and dug in for the night. Early on the morning of the 6th, a company of Rajputs got into Kohima and one platoon of it brought out two hundred walking wounded and non-combatants. During the morning, however, the Japanese closed round the town, and the brigade was unable to gain the ridge. The road behind was soon afterwards cut by a strong enemy detachment, who established a block between the brigade and Dimapur. The situation at Kohima was thus: its garrison of about 3,000 men closely invested by superior forces, 161st Brigade cut off five miles to the north, a small detachment holding the important Nichugard defile southeast of Dimapur, and the base itself in no state to resist a serious attack. A decidedly unpleasant situation for all concerned, but there were not wanting more hopeful signs.

At the end of March, the 2nd British Division had been dispersed in training in Southern India. Such was the rapidity of its move, carried out by the Movement Staffs of GHQ India and of General Giffard's headquarters, that on 2 April its leading elements were arriving at Dimapur, two brigades and the Divisional

Headquarters were on the way by air, and one brigade by rail. A regiment of tanks and later 268th Indian Motorized Brigade were also thrown into action for good measure by General Auchinleck.

As I shuttled between Dimapur, Imphal and my headquarters at Comilla, I was beginning to see light. We had hard days ahead of us, but everywhere our troops, unperturbed by events, were steady and full of fight. We had lost nothing vital.

Above: A British armored column led by two Grant tanks moves down the Dimapur-Kohima road. On 14 April units from the 2nd Division's 5th Brigade broke through a Japanese roadblock and then pushed on to relieve the 161st Brigade.

Below: The ruins of Kohima.

Attrition

On the Assam front the first week of April had been an anxious one. Thanks to my mistakes the battle had not started well; at any time crisis might have slipped into disaster – and still might. We were in tactical difficulties everywhere. The Japanese were pressing hard on the rim of the Imphal plain; they still threatened the Dimapur base, while Kohima garrison was in dire peril; and they had cut the Kohima-Imphal road, which was certainly no part of *my* plan. Yet for their gains they had paid a higher price in dead and wounded, and, above all, in time, than they had calculated on in *their* plan. Now our air forces, tireless and bold, dominated the skies. Under their wings our reinforcements were flowing in more smoothly and rapidly than I had hoped. As I watched the little flags, representing divisions, cluster round Imphal and Kohima on my situation map, I heaved a sigh of relief. As the second week of April wore on, for all its alarms and fears I felt that our original pattern for the battle was reasserting itself.

In my visits to formations I tried to impart this feeling, and I found it shared by commanders and troops. By the beginning of April when the 5th Indian Division, less the brigade sent to Dimapur, had arrived, Scoones at Imphal would have the best part of four divisions, and under his steady leadership I was confident the tide would turn. It was on the Kohima side of the picture that I looked the more anxiously. Here it would take all Stopford's energy and optimism to right the battle. Not only were the defenders of Kohima in desperate case, but it was still open to the Japanese 31st Division to sidestep them and go for Dimapur. I therefore decided that the Kohima battle should have preference over that at Imphal for reinforcements, supplies, ammunition, indeed for anything XXXIII Corps required, and that even at the cost of skimping Scoones I must nourish Stopford. Luckily Sato continued to limit himself to frontal attacks on Kohima, first by day and then, as the toll exacted by the garrison and by the swift retaliation of our aircraft in daylight proved too high even for Japanese stomachs, by night. Throughout the day and in the intervals between these night attacks, the enemy artillery, mortars, and machine-guns hammered relentlessly at our positions on Garrison Hill. British and Japanese trenches were within yards of one another, every move brought a shot, rest was impossible. Sheer exhaustion rather than the enemy threatened to vanquish our men. Then came the worst blow of all. During the night of 5/6 April the Japanese gained possession of the water supply, and thirst was added to the horrors. The RAF, regardless of fire from the ground, swept over at tree-top level to drop motor-car inner tubes filled with water. By good fortune a small spring was found inside our lines, yet, even with this to supplement the air force contribution, the water ration dropped to less than a pint a man and a little more for the wounded. Gradually the area we held was squeezed until, from a rough square with sides of 1,000 yards, it became a meagre 500 by 500. Into this confined space the enemy rained down a pitiless artillery bombardment; against its haggard, thirsty garrison, they hurled ferocious attack after attack.

But help was at hand. By 11 April, headquarters and two brigades of the 2nd Division had reached Dimapur; the third was following close behind, and next day the Chindit 23rd Brigade arrived at Jorhat. We had thus drawn about level with the Japanese in numbers, and, as soon as the 7th Indian Division, now under

Below: The advance of the Kohima relief force continues. The first units to break through the encircling Japanese reached the garrison on 18 April.

orders from Arakan, could be got in we would be on the way to superiority.

Immediately it was available, Stopford sent the leading 5th Brigade of the 2nd Division up the road towards 161st Brigade, now held up short of Kohima. The first enemy road-block encountered was rushed, but the second, six miles farther on, repulsed an unsupported infantry attack. Next day the division artillery and some tanks arrived. A second attack broke through, but the Japanese counter-attacked. They were beaten off and the column pushed on. During the next few days several positions barring the road were taken in stiff fighting until, on 15 April, 5th Brigade and 161st Brigade joined hands. The next brigade (6th) of the 2nd Division was then brought up and freed 161st Brigade for its advance to relieve Kohima. On the 18th, the brigade with tank, artillery, and air support, launched an assault astride the main road and along the ridge on its right. Progress was at times slow, as the enemy reacted with fierce local counter-attacks, but Warren's men finally broke through and joined up with the hard-pressed garrison, clinging grimly to their smoking hill-top. A Punjabi battalion was the first to enter, and at once took over part of the perimeter from the exhausted defenders. Kohima was relieved.

After dark, the wounded were brought out under fire and carried to ambulances that had crept close up under such cover as could be found. Next day, the 19th, 161st Brigade continued its attack, but failed to take Kuki Piquet, though some advance was made. Throughout the day, the road back was kept open, and by it Kohima was restocked, so that many of the garrison got their first full meal since the siege began. On the 20th, 6th Brigade of the 2nd Division moved in under cover of artillery and relieved the rest of the original garrison. At six o'clock on that morning Colonel Richards handed over the command he had so gallantly held and collected his men. Three hours later they marched out, and, just below what had been the hospital, they found lorries waiting to take them from the dust, din and stench of death in which they had lived for eleven days.

They had endured much. Forced into an ever-contracting circle by the relentless assaults of vastly superior numbers, their casualties had been severe. There had been no evacuation for the wounded, and men were hit again and again as they lay in the casualty stations. Thirst was not the least of the trials of these devoted men. Sieges have been longer but few have been more intense, and in none have the defenders deserved greater honour than the garrison of Kohima.

Although the small force that had been cut off on Garrison Hill had now been relieved, most of Kohima Ridge itself remained in hostile hands. With their centre on the town, the

Above: A stoutly constructed Japanese strongpoint hidden beneath a canopy of foliage. Such defenses slowed the advance of the relief forces during the Imphal-Kohima campaign.

Japanese held an immensely strong position, some 7,000 yards long, astride the main Imphal-Dimapur road. The natural defensive strength of a succession of steep, wooded ridges had been improved by the Japanese genius for inter-supporting field works and concealment, until it was as formidable a position as a British army has ever faced. Its flanks, extending into high and most difficult country, were protected by inaccessibility. The enemy also had detachments dug in well forward on tracks which led through dense jungle to the main road and railway. There was thus the constant threat of infiltration and of movements against our rear. It was always a wonder to me why Sato did not attempt a bold strike of this kind. It would have been typically Japanese, and he had, even at this stage, enough troops for it if he cared to take some risk at Kohima itself.

Our own build-up was proceeding rapidly. The concentration of the 2nd British Division was practically complete – too complete as far as its transport was concerned, for its lorries, parked nose to tail, threatened to turn the two-way main road into a one-way track. An attack by twelve Oscars on a mass of this useless transport, jammed into a village, lent point to my exhortations to XXXIII Corps to get it out of the area. Luckily the RAF maintained such a degree of air superiority that we did not pay the heavy penalty that should have been exacted. Relieved of this excessive transport, the division found, like others in Burma, that it could move faster and more freely without it. The leading brigade (33rd) of the 7th Indian Division had arrived, also by air, from the Arakan fighting, and 23rd Chindit Brigade was already advancing in several columns southeast from the railway. One of these columns had its first serious and successful brush with the enemy on 16 April. On the 22nd it attacked a strongly held village but was repulsed. Within the next few days, in co-operation with a well-directed air strike, it again attacked and took the village.

Stopford, commanding XXXIII Corps, whose headquarters was established at Jorhat, was rightly urging the 2nd Division to advance, but the terrain and the type of warfare were new to British troops, while the unavoidable arrival of the division piecemeal made the task of Grover, the divisional commander, a difficult one.

His plan was for one brigade of the 2nd Division, supported by the bulk of the artillery, to keep up heavy pressure against the Japanese centre at Kohima while the two remaining brigades, one on each flank, carried out turning movements to seize high ground behind the Japanese front line. 161st Brigade was placed centrally as a General Reserve, and 33rd Brigade of the 7th Division was held back to cover Dimapur. The columns of 23rd Chindit Brigade were to continue their thrust southeast towards Jessami to cut the Japanese supply routes from the Chindwin. When the two flank brigades had reached their objectives it was intended to launch the main attack in the centre.

Starting on 21 April, the leading battalion of the left brigade (5th) crossed the valley by jungle tracks to the east of the main road and climbed 2,000 feet to a track running along the ridge due north from Kohima. Here it found a large Japanese position prepared for defence ↑ unoccupied. During the next few days, hampered by rain on the slippery ascent and dependent entirely on animal and porter transport, strange to British troops, the rest of the brigade joined them. On the 29th, an attack on further Japanese positions, this time occupied, failed; and the brigade was held up well short of its final objective.

Meanwhile the other flank brigade (4th) had scrambled up steep ridges towards the enemy left, meeting little opposition, but owing to rain and the difficulties of movement and supply it did not make progress as fast as had been initially expected.

The centre brigade (6th) was, on the night of the 22/23 April, heavily attacked on the shambles of Garrison Hill. In fierce hand-to-hand fighting the Japanese were beaten off, but for the next two days our men were under constant pressure and bombardment, much as the original garrison had been. On the 22nd, an attempt with infantry and tanks to relieve the pressure failed, as the tanks were held up by difficult ground. Then, on the night of the 27th, a more formidable assault – the first of a series of attacks and counter-attacks – was launched on the Deputy Commissioner's bungalow. This had once been a charming house in a delightful garden, but was now a heap of rubble in a devastation with one chimney only standing, black and twisted against the sky. This attack, after desperate fighting, succeeded in reaching and holding, not only the site of the

house but the bluff in the garden, which overlooked the Kohima crossroads and denied them to the enemy – a very valuable tactical success. On the night of the 29th/30th the Japanese made a final attempt, in an all-out counter-attack, to regain possession, but failed with heavy loss. Each side was left holding part of the garden, with the tennis court as a no man's land between them, and with hand grenades shuttling back and forth across the court in the place of tennis balls.

As neither flank brigade could make the progress hoped for and as the centre brigade was hard pressed opposite Kohima itself, the divisional plan was changed. The wider turning movements were abandoned, and it was decided to deliver a more concentrated attack on the Japanese position so that all three brigades could act in close tactical combination and in turn have the full support of the divisional and corps artillery.

Below: British troops repair the damage caused by a landslide during the approach to Imphal.

This set-back was disappointing, but the 2nd British Division was now complete, the 7th Indian was coming in well and would be followed by 268th Indian Motorized Brigade. I should soon have here the two-to-one superiority over the Japanese that was my aim at both Kohima and Imphal, but I was determined not to push Stopford, at this stage, beyond the pace he considered wise. He was the last commander to drag his feet, and his 2nd Division, the spearhead of his attack, while as brave as troops could be, was inexperienced; its very dash rendered it liable to heavy casualties unless its attacks were deliberately prepared with all possible support. So, although I continued to divert artillery, ammunition, petrol, and air strikes, badly needed on other fronts, to XXXIII Corps, I did not nag at them to hurry. The corps had to win its first battle; IV Corps, comparative veterans could wait.

There were not wanting at this time those who, crediting from a distance the alarmist reports that always circulate at such moments, urged me at all costs to break through and relieve Imphal. I had no intention of yielding to pressure; Imphal was in no danger of falling. It is not the easiest task of a superior commander to stand between such pressure and his subordinate commanders, but at times it is his duty. General Giffard, who understood the situation well, increased my debt to him by the firmness with which he did this now.

The battle of Kohima was a bloody one. The first full-scale assault by the 2nd Division under the new plan was so delayed by rain that it was not until 3 May that deployment was complete. The plan was for 4th Brigade on the right to capture GPT Ridge, advance to Jail Hill, and link up with 6th Brigade in the centre, which by then, having broken out from Garrison Hill, should have taken Kuki Piquet and FSD Ridge. 5th Brigade on the left was to occupy Naga village and dominate the Treasury area. The attack was to be supported by tanks and by all available guns, firing time-concentrations in support of each brigade in turn.

The attack began in the early morning of 4 May. 4th Brigade, delayed by undiscovered Japanese bunkers, reached GPT Ridge, but was unable to secure the whole of it, nor to approach Jail Hill. By nightfall on this part of the field the enemy positions and ours were inextricably mingled. 6th Brigade failed to take Kuki Piquet and, although its tanks reached

Above: Lieutenant-General Sir Geoffrey Scoones (1893-1975) led the British IV Corps in the epic defense of Imphal. After containing the Japanese attacks on the town, he launched his own forces in a counter-attack during late June.

Left: Its carriage smashed, a Japanese 75mm field gun litters the roadside. The retreat from Kohima and Imphal tore the heart out of the Fifteenth Army.

FSD Ridge, the infantry, subjected to devastating fire from other enemy positions, could not dig in or remain. A portion only of the ridge was held by nightfall and here again British and Japanese were mixed up together. 5th Brigade entered Naga village, but during the night of 4/5 May were counter-attacked heavily and pushed back to the western edge of the village, which they managed to hold. The Treasury area remained firmly in the enemy's hands.

During 5 May both sides were exhausted. The British could attempt no more local consolidation, and, luckily for us, the Japanese launched no counter-attacks. On the 6th, all brigades made attempts to improve their positions by local attacks, but only minor adjustments at the cost of considerable casualties were achieved. Stopford now handed over his Corps Reserve, 33rd Brigade of the 7th Indian Division, to Grover who, on 7 May, used one of its battalions to attack Jail Hill, from which on previous days heavy and accurate machine-gun fire had hampered both 4th and 6th Brigades. The attack with great gallantry reached its objective, but was unable to dislodge the enemy from his deep bunkers, and we were again forced to abandon Jail Hill.

After four days' bitter fighting with heavy casualties, the assault had little to show. While the 31st Japanese Division certainly lacked initiative, it had all the enemy's fanatical stubbornness in defence. Our troops were again discovering that it was one thing to reach a Japanese bunker, another to enter it. Nor had artillery bombardment and accurate attacks by Hurricanes and Vengeance bombers on the limited areas engaged had much result. The most effective weapon proved to be the tank, firing solid shot at point-blank range; but the wooded terrain, its steepness, and the wet that made tanks churn everything into liquid mud, restricted their use. It was clear that the battle would be prolonged and savage.

During 8, 9 and 10 May, while its forward troops remained in close contact with the enemy, XXXIII Corps prepared to renew the attack. A main feature of the plan for the fresh attack, on which the corps commander insisted, was to be a generous use of smoke to screen the attacking troops from the enfilade and long-range machine-gun fire that had proved so damaging.

The main objectives in this attack, Jail Hill and the DIS, were allocated to 33rd Brigade of the 7th Division, but as both these were enfiladed from GPT and FSD Ridges, 4th and 6th Brigades of the 2nd Division were to clear the latter features before 33rd Brigade reached its objectives. The attack began on the night of 10/11 May, but that of the 2nd Division was only partially successful. When dawn came the enemy still held several bunkers on the reverse slopes of GPT Ridge and a strong-point on FSD Ridge. The main attack by 33rd Brigade fared

Above: Senior British commanders confer during the Kohima-Imphal battles. From left to right: Lieutenant-General Sir Montagu Stopford (1892-1971), commander of XXXIII Corps which reopened the Imphal road; General Sir William Slim, commander of the Fourteenth Army in Burma; and Major General C C Fowkes.

better. Probing forward in the darkness, a Punjabi battalion found Pimple Hill unoccupied and promptly dug in on it. The Queen's Regiment, after a stiff fight, was, soon after dawn, in possession of most of Jail Hill; and a second Punjabi battalion, although it suffered considerably, had cleared the DIS area. As the light strengthened, both these battalions were attempting to dig in on their gains, but were being greatly hampered, not only by fire from the front but by accurate enfilade from automatic weapons on GPT and FSD Ridges, not yet free of enemy. The situation of the two battalions, hanging on with great determination in the mud and rain but losing men fast, was relieved by a heavy smoke-screen put down at 8.45 a.m. by our artillery for several hours. The Japanese did not appear to have laid out any fixed lines of fire, and the effect of their machine-guns was reduced to such an extent that our men were able to dig in.

During the 11th, both battalions were reinforced, and after dark, with the help of Indian Sappers, they cleared a mine-field in the cutting between Jail Hill and the DIS area, which up to then had prevented tanks from joining them. The fight was resumed on the 12th, when in the afternoon, aided by tanks, further progress was made on Jail Hill and in the DIS area, but little elsewhere. At dawn on the 13th, in the face of our pressure, the surviving Japanese in both places fell back, and mopping-up was completed by midday. Seeing that the key-points of Jail Hill and the DIS area were lost, the enemy evacuated GPT Ridge, FSD Ridge and Kuki Piquet, which were occupied by units of the 2nd Division.

While this considerable action was going on, our other positions all along the front were being cleared up and extended by local operations. Typical of the Japanese resistance was the last phase of the prolonged struggle for the Deputy Commissioner's bungalow, where, although cut off, some enemy in deep bunkers continued to fight stubbornly. Sappers made a track up which a tank could climb and the Dorsets then attacked with its support. Each bunker was engaged in turn by the tank's 75-mm guns, whose effect at 30 yards was decisive. Japanese attempting to escape were bayoneted or shot; none tried to surrender. The few remaining bunkers were demolished by pole charges thrust through their loop-holes and, by the afternoon of 13 May, the Deputy Commissioner's bungalow, his garden and tennis court, which had acquired an almost ritual significance, were all finally in our hands at remarkably low cost in casualties.

Treasury Hill was the next objective of XXXIII Brigade. A Gurkha battalion was concentrated on Garrison Hill during the 14th for a deliberate attack next day, but from patrol reports the brigadier concluded that most of the enemy was pulling out and he ordered an infiltrating attack in the dark. By first light on the 15th, the Gurkhas, meeting practically no resistance, had occupied the whole of Treasury Hill.

The gains thus made in a few days since 10 May changed the whole picture around Kohima. The most satisfactory feature was the failure of the Japanese anywhere to counter-attack – evidence of their increasing disorganization under these heavy blows. There followed on this part of the battlefield a short lull while both sides regrouped themselves for a renewal of the struggle.

Meanwhile, on the Imphal front fighting as bitter but more diffuse had been claiming my attention. It was not without its moments of anxiety, for Scoones was being hard pressed.

Like unevenly spaced spokes of a wheel, six routes converged on to the Imphal plain to meet at the hub, Imphal itself:

(i) From the north, the broad Kohima road.
(ii) Also from the north, the footpath down the Iril River Valley.
(iii) From the northeast, the Ukhrul road.
(iv) From the southeast, the tarmac Tamu-Palel road.
(v) From the south, the rugged Tiddim highway.
(vi) From the west, the Silchar-Bishenpur track.

It was by these that the Japanese strove to break into the plain. The fighting all round its circumference was continuous, fierce, and often confused as each side manoeuvred to out-wit and kill. There was always a Japanese thrust somewhere that had to be met and destroyed. Yet the fighting did follow a pattern. The main encounters were on or near the spokes of the wheel, because it was only along these that guns, tanks, and vehicles could move. The Japanese would advance astride the route, attack our troops blocking it, and try to out-flank or infiltrate past them. We should first

hold, then counter-attack, and the struggle would sway a mile or two, one way and the other. All the time our airmen, who played so vital a part in these battles, would be daily in sortie after sortie delivering attacks at ground-level and hammering the enemy's communication right back into Burma. Gradually we should prevail, and, driven from the spokes of the wheel, the Japanese would take to the hills between them. Relentlessly we would hunt them down and when, desperate and rabid, they turned at bay, kill them. This pattern repeated itself along each of the spokes as, on one after the other, we passed from defence to outright offence.

Our casualties in this kind of fighting were not light. The infantry, as usual, suffered most and endured most, for this was above all an infantry battle, hand-to-hand, man against man, and no quarter. Our heaviest losses were among the officers, not only in the infantry who in this close fighting could not fail to be conspicuous, but among the artillery observation officers who to give accurate support pushed on with the leading troops, and among the young tank commanders who, regardless of safety, kept their turrets open or moved on foot so that they could guide their tanks through the jungle.

To deal briefly with the events on each spoke of the wheel is probably the clearest way to give a picture of this battle, but it should be remembered that encounters on all the spokes were going on simultaneously. At no time and in no place was the situation, either to commanders or troops, as clear even as I can make it now. Into Scoones's headquarters, from every point

Above: One of the Eastern Air Command's Hurricanes swoops down on a retreating Japanese column.

of the compass, day and night, streamed signals, messages, and reports, announcing successes, set-backs, appealing for reinforcements, demanding more ammunition, asking urgently for wounded to be evacuated, begging for air support. His was the task of meeting or withstanding these appeals, of deciding which at the moment was the place to which his by no means over-generous reserves should be allotted. It was impossible for him to satisfy all his commanders. It needed a tough, cool, and well-balanced commander to meet, week after week, this strain. Luckily Scoones *was* tough, cool and well-balanced.

To take first the actions on the Iril Valley and Ukhrul road spokes. By the beginning of April, the leading troops of the 5th Division, who had gone into action on the Ukhrul road almost straight from their aircraft, had with the remaining brigade of the 23rd Division pushed back the imminent threat on Imphal until the Japanese were held just west of Litan. But the enemy was now round Imphal on the north, and our troops on the Ukhrul road were menaced in the rear by a Japanese force which on 6 April attacked Nungshigum, a great hill which dominated the Imphal plain and gave direct observation over the main airstrip at a range of five or six miles. The fighting for this hill was typical of a hundred actions that went on at this stage round the edges of the plain.

Nungshigum has two peaks, a north and a south. The Japanese attack drove our men off the northern, but we clung to the southern. On 11 April, after several attempts, the enemy gained that too. On the 12th we retook the

southern summit, but lost it again. On the 13th, while Hurribombers, their guns blazing, dived almost into the tree-tops, and tanks, winched up incredible slopes, fired point-blank into bunker loopholes, our infantry stormed both peaks – and held them. The Japanese grimly defended their positions until the last men still fighting were bombed or bayoneted in their last foxholes.

In this fight, so difficult was the country and so dense the jungle that the tanks of the Carbineers had to go into action with turrets open if their commanders were to see enough to help the infantry. The young officer and NCO tank commanders unhesitatingly took this risk of almost certain death and, alas, a high proportion of them were killed.

When the 5th Division had secured Nungshigum, it was relieved by the 23rd Division of all responsibility for the Ukhrul road and proceeded to clear the Iril Valley. Between 16 April

Above: British infantry negotiate a hastily constructed roadblock during the advance from Kohima to Imphal in June 1944.

Left: A lone Grant tank pushes along the twisting road from Imphal to Ukhrul.

and 7 May there was heavy fighting to eject the Japanese from their positions on the big Mapao Spur which divides the Iril Valley from the Imphal-Kohima road and gives observation over the northwestern portion of the plain. Our attacks, which met fierce Japanese counter-attacks, were only partially successful. We drove the enemy from the southern parts of his position but he still held to the northern, though he no longer presented a serious threat to Imphal.

1st Brigade of the 23rd Division, having combed the hills to the south of the Ukhrul road and chased the headquarters of the 15th Japanese Division through the jungle, turned north and cleared the road to within 15 miles of Ukhrul. The enemy headquarters escaped, but to say the least its operational efficiency was not increased. 37th Brigade of the 23rd Division soon afterwards moved up the road and made contact with 1st Brigade. The division then, during the first half of May, kept up pressure on the enemy over the whole Ukhrul road front. By the middle of the month the situation both in the Iril Valley and on the Ukhrul road could be considered stabilized.

On the Palel road spoke of the wheel at the beginning of April, the 20th Division, having lost one brigade taken for Corps Reserve, was with the two remaining brigades, 80th and 100th, holding a 25-mile front running fom Tengoupal, ten miles southeast of Palel, through Shenam to Shuganu, 15 miles south-west of Palel. The country is a criss-cross of steep ridges and deep *nullahs*, all tree-covered, with in parts dense jungle. Gracey's troops could not, of course, maintain a continuous line; they had to content themselves by holding the most important heights and the passes by which the main road and the most usable tracks approached Palel and the Imphal plain. Between these tactical points they strove to dominate the country and prevent Japanese infiltration by constant and aggressive patrolling. In this, luckily, they had already obtained something of a mastery over the enemy, but it was a long and vulnerable front which, throughout this phase of the battle, was a source of some anxiety to Scoones.

The Japanese commander here, Major-General Yamamoto, was under great pressure from his superiors to break into the Imphal plain. The tanks and artillery which constituted a large part of his force were urgently wanted by Mutaguchi, the Army Commander, to reduce our defences around Imphal. So Yamamoto launched attack after attack to crash through the 20th Division defences on the Shenam Pass. These assaults, supported more heavily than usual for the Japanese by armour and artillery, were constant throughout April.

Some of the bitterest fighting was around Tengoupal which directly covered the main road up which Yamamoto was trying to blast

his way. Between 4 and 11 April the Japanese attacks were continuous and made some progress. On 11 April, a counter-attack in which the Devons distinguished themselves retook lost ground, but on the 15th and 16th fanatical enemy assaults on a young Indian battalion which had relieved the Devons regained portions of the position and were continued during the two succeeding nights. On the night of 19/20 April, three separate attacks with medium tanks were beaten off but our men, never very thick on the ground, were becoming exhausted from want of rest. On 22 April, after very heavy fighting, parts of our position were overrun; but the enemy had suffered too heavily to be able to continue and the attacks died down. Shenam, on the other side of the road, had not been heavily attacked, which was lucky, as part of the brigade here had to be sent to reinforce Shuganu, threatened by the reported approach of Japanese forces.

The Indian National Army's Gandhi Brigade was on this front, and towards the end of April, parties of Japanese, accompanied by Jiffs disguised as local inhabitants and as our sepoys, infiltrated towards Palel. There were numerous patrol clashes and we staged several successful ambushes, but it was impossible in such wild country to intercept every hostile group, and on the night of 29/30 April a small Japanese party actually attacked the Palel Keep. No damage

Below: The ruins of the District Commissioner's bungalow in Kohima, scene of bloody close-quarters fighting during the battle. Toward the end of the engagement, a tank was dragged into a position to blast the Japanese out of their trenches and bunkers at close range.

was done and the signal reporting the occurrence ended, 'enemy now being slain'. This attempt was a stout-hearted effort in contrast to the abortive 'attack' made on one of our positions by the Gandhi Brigade on the night of 2/3 May, in which a large party of Jiffs was ambushed and scattered as it approached. After this, considerable numbers of these unfortunate Jiffs appeared to be wandering about the country without object or cohesion. They had suffered a good many other casualties at the hands of our patrols and during May were surrendering in large numbers, but our Indian and Gurkha soldiers were at times not too ready to let them surrender, and orders had to be issued to give them a kinder welcome. The Gandhi Brigade took no further appreciable part in operations and what was left of it the Japanese in disgust used mainly as porters.

However, Japanese patrols were in the hills north and east of Palel, and their presence might interfere with the regular use of the airfield. This could not be risked, and Scoones sent 48th Brigade of the 17th Division between 6 and 7 May to comb that part of the country. When this brigade moved on to other tasks he replaced it by 1st Brigade of the 23rd Division which completed the comb-out and chased the headquarters of the Japanese 15th Division to the north over the Ukhrul road as already described.

This infiltration of Japanese parties to the area northeast of Palel coincided with a final effort by Yamamoto to break through on the main road. On the nights of 6/7 and 7/8 May fierce Japanese attacks on the Tengoupal front were repulsed, but on 8 May they broke into our positions. Counter-attacks, most gallantly supported by the RAF's fighter-bombers, failed to recover lost ground and we made a partial withdrawal. There were further Japanese attacks on the nights of 9/10 and 10/11 May during which we again lost some of our positions. A rather anxious situation was restored on the 12th by a most gallant counter-attack, and for the moment both sides were too exhausted to undertake further attacks or

counter-attacks. The 20th Division had successfully withstood very heavy assaults and continuous pressure for over two months, and to ease the strain on it Scoones now relieved it on the Palel front with Roberts's 23rd Division at its full strength of three brigades. On this spoke of the wheel, too, by mid-May we could consider the situation stablized.

It was along the Tiddim road and the Silchar-Bishenpur track, the southern and western spokes of the wheel, that some of the heaviest fighting of this Battle of Attrition took place. When the 17th Division reached Imphal after its withdrawal along the Tiddim road, Scoones left behind it, to hold off the Japanese 33rd Division which was pressing towards Imphal, two brigades, 37th and 49th, of Roberts's 23rd Division. 37th Brigade was quickly recalled to join its division, and 49th Brigade on 9 April was attacked in its positions south of Bishenpur at Milestones 30 and 35 on the Tiddim road. These attacks were repulsed and a Japanese detachment that had audaciously inserted itself between the forward battalion and the rest of the brigade was completely destroyed. In the short lull which followed, Scoones pulled out 49th Brigade so as to complete the 23rd Divi-

Above: A panoramic view of the Naga village area of the Kohima battlefield shows the scale of the destruction wrought in the battle.

Below: British troops attend a memorial parade on the tennis court of the District Commissioner's residence after the Japanese retreat from Kohima.

sion and replaced it by his Corps Reserve, 32nd Brigade of the 20th Division. The brigadier of 32nd Brigade, realizing the danger of encirclement from the west that threatened the old 49th Brigade position, decided to pull back to Bishenpur, where he commanded both the Tiddim road from the south and the Silchar track from the west.

It was well that he did so. Repulsed on the Tiddim road, the enemy, reverting to his favourite tactics, concentrated in the jungle west of the road, and made for the Bishenpur-Silchar track, hoping to break into the Imphal plain from the west. In the second week of April, Japanese patrols reached the track and encountered ours, but by then our 32nd Brigade was in position covering Bishenpur. On the night of 14/15 April the Japanese 33rd Division, which had now received reinforcements, attacked toward Bishenpur, but was again repulsed. While this attack was developing the enemy succeeded in blowing up the bridge at Milestone 51 on the Silchar track. This was a 300-foot suspension bridge over an 80-foot deep gorge and its destruction made a complete break in the track. The demolition was a typical Japanese suicide operation. While skirmishing was going on in darkness near the bridge, three Japanese eluded the engineer platoon guarding it and placed the explosive charges. One Japanese jumped to his death in the gorge; the other two went up with the bridge. Having failed to dislodge our troops covering Bishenpur, the enemy then attempted to pass a strong column into the plain round the northwest of the village. Heavy fighting lasting several days

resulted, and there were alarms and excursions throughout the area as Japanese detachments probed forward towards Imphal.

The threat from the west had caused Scoones to pull back the 17th Division, which had been operating north of Imphal, and give it the task of securing this line of approach. He also left under Cowan's command 32nd Brigade, now fully engaged and under heavy pressure. On 19 April, just in time, the leading troops of the 17th Division began to arrive and went straight into action northwest of Bishenpur. To the south of that village the enemy occupied the straggling hamlet of Ninthoukhong in force. A first attempt by 33rd Brigade to eject them failed on 23 April and so did a second by troops of the 17th Division two days later. In these

Above: Manning a Browning machine gun, two British infantrymen, part of IV Corps, man a forward gunpit on the perimeter of Imphal.

Above right: The Imphal battlefield; the fighting lasted from early April until the garrison was relieved on 22 June.

Left: Bren-gunners point out a Japanese position to two of their officers.

Right: A mortar in action during the Imphal battle.

attacks we suffered heavily and lost seven medium tanks. The valour of our troops had been equalled by the tenacity of the Japanese. Very bitter fighting continued and cost both sides many casualties; the Japanese advance into the plain was halted, but they held the village and remained a dangerous threat.

Again the fighting on the Silchar tracks west of Bishenpur flared up. The Japanese were under orders to break through at all costs and 32nd Brigade from the 20th Division were under equally emphatic orders to prevent them. The savage struggle surged backwards and forwards along the track and across it. Our casualties were alarmingly heavy, especially in British officers of the Indian Army who could not fail to be picked out in such close fighting. These officers, many of them in their early twenties, made me proud to belong to the same army. One young lieutenant-colonel, commanding a battalion that had already lost three-quarters of its officers and who had himself been severely wounded in the stomach by grenade fragments, was again hit while leading his men. When asked why at this second wound he had not gone back at least as far as the Field Ambulance to have his wounds properly dressed, he admitted the grenade in the stomach was a nuisance as it made getting about rather difficult, but he could still keep up with his men so there was no need to go back. As to the second wound, 'The bullet', he explained, 'has passed straight through my shoulder so it causes me no inconvenience!' No wonder the Japanese never broke through. When, a little time afterwards, I wished to promote this very gallant officer to command of a brigade, I found to my grief that he had been killed later in the battle.

Heavy attacks on 26 April were thrown back, although our forward troops remained cut off from Bishenpur for some time until the track was reopened. Fighting continued, and having failed in direct assaults, the enemy resorted to large-scale infiltration. In the first half of May, too, the Japanese Air Force made some of its rare appearances in strength. Besides bombing and strafing our airfields, about twenty-five Zeroes attacked Bishenpur on the 6th and again on 10 May. On the latter day our anti-aircraft guns took heavy toll and the visits were not repeated. The Japanese had managed to get into Potsangbam – the 'Pots and Pans' of the British soldier – only two miles south of Bishenpur, Potsangbam, like many villages in the plain, was intersected by high banks and belts of trees, which hampered tank movement and provided admirable positions for defence. Heavy fighting by 32nd and 63rd Brigade was needed, with lavish air support from the fighters of 221st Group and the bombers of Strategic Air Force, before our men were able on 15 May to winkle the enemy out. We lost twelve tanks and it was here for the first time the

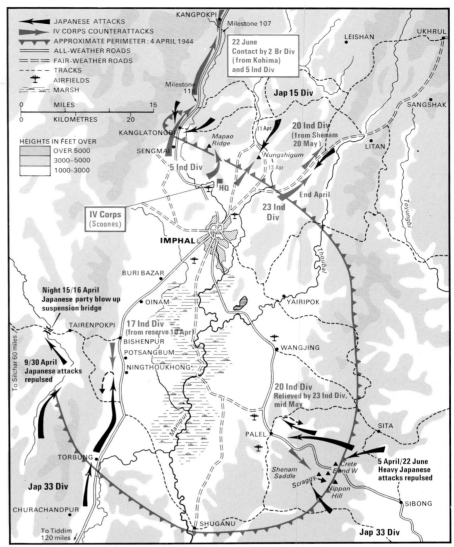

Japanese used their ten-inch mortars, one of which we captured. The situation around Bishenpur was still confused. The Japanese 33rd Division was living up to its reputation for being always dangerous, but it had suffered heavily. Deserters who came in reported that at the end of April one of its regiments was reduced from some 3,000 to a strength of only 800. The fact that even two or three deserters had appeared was a new and encouraging sign. We believed, however, that the divison had since received further reinforcements and would again attempt something. It was not possible to say here, as we could on other sectors of the Imphal front, that the situation was fully stabilized.

On the Imphal-Kohima road, the last and most important of the Imphal spokes, the Japanese 31st Division had cut the road 30 miles north of Imphal on 30 March. While some of the enemy turned north and moved on Kohima, a strong detachment of their 15th Division came south towards Kanglatongbi, where we had a large supply depot. 63rd Brigade of the 17th Division, newly arrived in Imphal, after its arduous withdrawal from Tiddim, was at once rushed up to the north to stop any further hostile advance. The depot was rather hurriedly evacuated but, on 9 April, a fighting patrol with armour escorted lorries removing arms and ammunition; then the Japanese occupied it and large quanities of such items as clothing fell into their hands. In a series of attacks between 11 and 15 April, in which our tanks, much to the surprise of the enemy, forced their way on to a steep narrow ridge covering Kanglatongbi, the Japanese pushed back, fighting all the time, and on 23rd April Kanglatongbi was raided. On 7 May the brigade was relieved by the 5th Division, as part of the re-sorting that Scoones was carrying out to reassemble his divisions with their original brigades, and joined its own 17th Division, to take part in the even harder fighting already described about Bishenpur.

Briggs as usual, wasted no time. His 5th Division now had with it 89th Brigade of 7th Division, which I had flown in to Imphal to compensate for his 161st Brigade that went so urgently to Dimapur. His original plan had been a wide right hook, with 123rd Brigade from the Iril Valley to cut the main Kohima road well behind the Japanese; but the continual rain caused heavy floods which held this up, and with his accustomed adaptability he abandoned it. Leaving 9th Brigade, on the east of the road, to hold Mapao Spur that had been such a hard nut to crack when he had attacked from the Iril Valley, he used 89th Brigade in a series of short hooks behind the enemy, while 123rd Brigade, brought in by the direct route, pushed north along the main road. After brisk fighting, the supply depot, with a great deal of its original contents, was finally retaken on 21

Above: Gurkhas take cover from a Japanese attack. Nepalese troops were among the best of the British forces in the Burma campaign and proved themselves to be formidable jungle fighters.

May and both brigades began to push north up the road. The situation on this spoke was well in hand.

By the middle of May 1944, therefore, my worst anxieties were over. At Kohima the Japanese had been thrown definitely on the defensive; on the Imphal-Kohima road the advance had begun; around Imphal, Scoones could feel assured that, unless the enemy was greatly reinforced, danger from the north and east was unlikely. The Japanese 15th Division had been well hammered and was losing cohesion. To the south and west, where the redoutable 33rd Japanese Division was being reinforced from both their 53rd and 54th Divisions, there was still the prospect of a last attempt by the enemy. Our command of the air over the whole battlefield was vitually unchallenged and, thanks to this and to the daring of our patrols, the enemy supply system was falling into confusion. Most significant, too, the monsoon was almost upon us.

The more satisfactory turn that events had taken did not pass unnoticed in other circles than Fourteenth Army. The number of visitors at my headquarters notably increased. In the opening stages of the battle most of my visitors

Below: British generals plan their next moves during the operations around Imphal.

had been rather gloomy, a state of mind perhaps understandable, as India was full of rumours of disaster. Now, except that they believed Imphal was starving, they tended to optimism. They were particularly anxious that I should 'relieve Imphal before it was too late'. Neither General Giffard nor I was as anxious as they appeared about Imphal's power to hold out; we knew that IV Corps would shortly take the offensive. The supply situation there, though tight – certain rations had already been reduced – would not become difficult until about the middle of June and not desperate until at least a month later. I therefore stuck to my date, the date I had consistently given for the opening of the road, the third week in June. There were not wanting suggestions from many sources as to how the relief of Imphal might be hastened. They did not all show a practical realization of the problem. One staff officer, not on my headquarters, proposed that I should push an armoured column, escorting supply lorries, rapidly along the road to replenish Imphal, 'as the Royal Navy had revictualled Malta'. I replied that to send a convoy of merchant-men, escorted by destroyers, down a canal both banks of which were held by the enemy and in which at frequent intervals there was no water – for the bridges on the road would be down – should not, I thought, appeal to naval tacticians, however gallant.

All the same, the time had now come for the Fourteenth Army to pass from the vigorous offensive-defensive it had been conducting to a full offensive on the Assam front. Although the road would have to be opened within the next five or six weeks, the immediate object of this offensive would be not so much the relief of

Imphal – that would be incidental – but the destruction of the Japanese Fifteenth Army. No one could have been more eager to launch this offensive than my two corps commanders.

The problem for Scoones was whether to make this offensive on all sectors of his front simultaneously or to strike first on one and then on another. He would have found it difficult to stage large-scale attacks all round the plain because, not only was he limited in ammunition and I had cut him heavily in petrol to save airlift, but the amount of animal transport that would be needed in such extensive operations could not be provided. The monsoon was also upon us. When this came, although it would handicap the enemy more than us, it would, as far as we were concerned, halve the rate of movement off the few main roads and make air supply hazardous. Our offensive could, therefore, be on only part of IV Corps' front. Scoones decided, with my full agreement, to launch it against the weakened Japanese 15th Division in the north and northeast, with his 5th and 20th Divisions. This plan had the advantage that not only did it attack the enemy in his weakest link, but by operating along the Kohima road it helped to reopen our line of communication to Dimapur.

On the Palel sector of IV Corps' front the relief of the 20th by the 23rd Division began on 13 May and continued, a battalion at a time, until the end of the month. During this time both divisions refrained from major undertakings, although 1st Brigade of the 23rd Division continued the clearing of the country east of Palel begun by the 20th Division. The 23rd Division had consolidated its positions, when, from 16 to 20 May, the Japanese fiercely

Left: Troops of the 9th
Royal Sussex Regiment
await orders to attack a
Japanese strongpoint
hidden among dense
jungle.

attacked the Shenam Pass in the Palel area. Some of our defences were temporarily lost, but counter-attacks regained them all. The enemy resumed his attacks from 9 to 12 June and lost heavily, for no appreciable gains. At Shuganu attacks and counter-attacks alternated, and, as a result, the 23rd Division advanced slightly and improved its positions. We had been considerably inconvenienced during the first half of May by the intermittent shelling of the Palel airfield by Japanese medium artillery. The advance of 1st Brigade, which combed the hills for ten miles to the east of Palel, put a stop to this nuisance. It also disposed finally of the Jiffs of the Gandhi Brigade, large numbers of whom, urged by leaflets dropped from the air, hastened to surrender. Minor activity continued throughout the area, but very few Japanese patrols managed to evade our forward troops. One enemy party of an officer and seven other ranks did, however, as late as the night of 3/4 July, succeed in reaching Palel airfield. As a farewell gesture they destroyed eight parked aircraft with magnetic mines and Bangalore torpedoes, and escaped unscathed – a very fine effort.

In mid-May, on the Bishenpur sector the 17th Division was fighting hard to hold the Silchar track with 32nd Brigade which it had borrowed from the 20th Division; its own 63rd Brigade had just captured Potsangbam. It was typical of our 17th and the Japanese 33rd Divisions that at this time each of them was plotting a bold surprise stroke against the other.

The Japanese plan was, by a series of sudden thrusts at night, to pierce deep into the defences of Bishenpur and then to disrupt the 17th Division from within. Cowan's plan, instead of penetration, was a wide turning movement with one brigade to come in on the Tiddim road behind the 33rd Division and crush it between this brigade and his two brigades in the north. 48th Brigade of the 17th Division had been taken as Corps Reserve and from 4 to 8 May had been engaged in cleaning up enemy parties which had infiltrated northeast of Palel. It was thus well placed, when Scoones returned it to Cowan, to begin the turning movement.

On 15 May, 48th Brigade set out. Moving rapidly across country, two days later it struck the Tiddim-Imphal road at Milestone 33 and dug in. During the 17th the Japanese hurriedly collected all available troops, including those of the administrative services, and twice attacked this road-block with tanks. They failed to dislodge our troops and suffered heavily. A more serious attack was delivered by troops of the 15th Japanese Division on the evening of the 19th, but this too was repulsed. In these attacks the enemy lost several tanks, three of which were captured and blown up, and left three hundred counted bodies in front of our positions, besides many more in the tall elephant grass. In accordance with the plan, 48th Brigade then moved north up the road to Moirang. The village was taken in two days' fighting and another road-block established it. It was now that the other two brigades of the 17th Division should have come south on a wide front and driven the Japanese 33rd Division against 48th Brigade. Unfortunately the Japanese counter-attack had already been delivered, and 32nd Brigade by itself failed to make enough progress. 48th Brigade was therefore ordered north and, fighting its way from village to village against considerable opposition, entered Potsangbam on 30 May and thus rejoined the 17th Division. This turning movement had inflicted many casualties on the enemy at comparatively light cost to itself, but it had failed in its object – the destruction of the Japanese 33rd Division.

The reason for this failure was that on the night of 20/21 May the enemy had launched his penetration attacks on our Bishenpur positions. One strong column pierced our defences and attempted to seize a hill only a few hundred yards from 17th Division Headquarters. A small Indian piquet on the hill held out for several hours against fanatical assaults. Cowan stoutly refused to move his headquarters, but was compelled to call on the 20th Division for help, and also to divert troops who should have been co-operating with the 48th Brigade's turning movement. Scoones hurriedly organized a small force, about a brigade in strength, under the headquarters of 50th Parachute Brigade, and with this reinforcement the enemy was first pinned down and then surrounded at the foot of the hill. In five days' hand-to-hand fighting they were almost annihilated, a few only escaping back into the hills to the west. Visiting the site of the battle a little later, I was struck by the way in which several Japanese gun crews had obviously been shot and bayoneted while serving their pieces in the open at point-blank range. While this was going on, another party of the enemy in darkness broke into 53rd Brigade area at Bishenpur and entrenched themselves in the mule lines. Our troops surrounded them and, with the help of tanks in several days' fighting, wiped them out. The slaughter of Japanese and of mules also was heavy. Bulldozers had to be employed to bury both.

It was here that some Gurkhas were engaged in collecting Japanese corpses from the corners inaccessible to bulldozers when one Japanese, picked up by a couple of Gurkhas, proved not to be as dead as expected. A Gurkha had drawn his *kukri* to finish the struggling prisoner when a passing British officer intervened saying, 'You mustn't do that, Johnny. Don't kill him!' The Gurkha, with *kukri* poised, looked at the officer in pained surprise, 'But, sahib,' he protested, 'we can't bury him *alive!*'

A third, but minor, Japanese attempt was made in a suicidal attack on our guns just north of Bishenpur. The enemy party was killed to a man. These penetration attacks were remarkable in their boldness and in the desperation with which the enemy fought to the death. They failed in their object – to break through the 17th Division into the Imphal plain – and they lost heavily, but they did prevent us from reaping the results of our turning movement. There can have been few examples in history of a force as reduced, battered, and exhausted as the 33rd Japanese Division delivering such furious assaults, not with the object of extricating itself, but to achieve its original offensive intention.

To turn now to those sectors of IV Corps' front, to the east and to the north, on which we passed to the offensive. On the Ukhrul road and in the Iril Valley, the 23rd Division had kept up its pressure on the Japanese, and under cover of this, the change-over with the 20th Division from the Palel sector was carried out during the second half of May, and the front taken over by 80th and 100th Brigades. 32nd Brigade of the 20th Division was still in the Bishenpur area with the 17th Division. No sooner were the troops of the 20th Division in their new positions covering Kameng and Nungshigum when it was discovered that the Japanese were building up their forces in the Sangshak area, with the obvious intention of launching further attacks astride the Ukhrul road. A considerable

Below: The crew of a carrier looks out over the valley carrying the road from Kohima to Imphal. The relief forces linked up with the town's garrison at Milestone 107 on 22 June.

concentration of mechanical and animal transport and increased movement was observed on their line of communication right back to the Chindwin. A good deal of sparring for position and heavy patrol activity now began on both sides. As part of the IV Corps offensive, on 3 June the 20th Division was ordered to advance with the object of destroying that part of the Japanese 15th Division east of the Iril River and of establishing a brigade group in Ukhrul.

The right wing of the division's offensive astride the Ukhrul road was at once counter-attacked by two reinforced regiments of the enemy 15th Division. The fight swung backwards and forwards as positions changed hands in local but severe fighting. Indeed at one time the Japanese pressure became so threatening that on 11 June the IV Corps reserve of two battalions was moved up. However, on the evening of that day, the 20th Division successfully retaliated, and by the 13th, all lost ground had been regained. During the following week our troops pushed back the enemy still farther and there were definite signs of his resistance cracking on both sides of the Ukhrul road.

Meanwhile the other brigade (80th) of the 20th Division had on 7 June struck out north from Nungshigum up the Iril Valley and, in spite of the difficulties of continuous rain, flooded streams, and deep mud that made all movement a desperate labour, had reached a point 20 miles north of Imphal. From there it raided the main east and west lateral communications of the enemy. These raids were most successful and increased the already evident dislocation of the Japanese 15th Division. By 20 June, 80th Brigade had pushed still farther north and was astride this enemy line of communication. The Japanese 15th Division had suffered heavily. Its supplies were dwindling rapidly, its replenishment routes were cut and now the monsoon made it impossible for the enemy to use other tracks. In this sector the IV Corps offensive was, at the end of May, going well and with increasing momentum.

On the other northern approach to Imphal, the main Kohima road, we had also made progress. Here the 5th Division, after retaking Kanglatongbi on 21 May, had pressed north on both sides of the road, aided by a series of short hooks coming in behind the Japanese positions. On 3 June IV Corps orders for intensifying the offensive were received, telling the 5th Division to destroy that part of the Japanese 15th Division west of the Iril River and to open the Kohima road to Karong, some 35 miles north of Imphal. Here we must leave the 5th Indian Division preparing in the rain and mud for a further push against the still stubborn but weakening Japanese 15th Division, and move to the other end of the road, to Kohima, where great things had been happening.

After our successes in mid-May and the short pause that followed for reorganization, the Kohima battle entered on its second phase. Although we now had the initiative, our situation was not a particularly good one. We had the town, or rather where the town had been, for the whole area in mud and destruction resembled the Somme in 1916; but the Japanese on the left were still holding the dominating Naga village position and the surrounding hills, while on the right they were along the great Aradura Spur. From both these, they commanded Kohima at close artillery range and, of course, dominated and closed the Imphal road. 4th and 5th Brigades of the 2nd British Division were, therefore, ordered to press on and capture the Japanese positions on both flanks. These were formidable tasks, but it was hoped that, after their defeat on 13 May, the enemy resistance would be crumbling. These hopes were dashed. The second phase of the battle was to be as hard fought as the first. The capacity of the ordinary Japanese soldier to take punishment and his fanatical will to resist were unimpaired. It was in the enemy higher control that weaknesses were first to appear.

During the five days of reorganization, units had some short periods of rest and 268th Indian Brigade took over part of the forward area. Patrolling and minor attacks by both sides were constant. On 19 May, 5th Brigade made their final attempt to clear Naga village. After initial

Below: Two comrades pay a visit to the site of Lance-Corporal Harman's grave at Kohima. Harman won a VC for his part in the battle.

Left: Members of A Company, 2nd Durham Light Infantry, link up with the 5th Indian Division on the Imphal-Kohima road, 22 June.

success the attack was held up by the usual skilfully concealed Japanese bunkers and by mortar fire from reverse slopes. Casualties were heavy and the attack was called off.

Meanwhile the headquarters of the 7th Indian Division, with its 114th Brigade, had arrived from Arakan and taken its own 33rd Brigade and 161st Brigade of the 5th Division, both already in the area, under its command. On 20 May, the division took over the left sector of the Kohima front, which included Treasury Hill and Naga village. 268th Brigade held Garrison Hill, leaving the main Kohima-Imphal road sector and all to its right to the 2nd Division. 33rd Brigade then took up the struggle for Naga village where the 2nd Division had left it. Between 24 and 30 May an Indian battalion delivered two attacks on the centre of the enemy defences. Twice they occupied them but suffered terribly and were unable to hold on. Medium artillery was then brought up to 1,500 yards' range while a Gurkha battalion infiltrated on to Gun Spur in the enemy's rear and dug in. At the same time a British battalion skilfully infiltrated in thick mist on to Church Knoll, the highest point in Naga village; the enemy, who still held positions on the reverse slopes, had little fight left in him and did not counter-attack. 33rd Brigade was then relieved by 114th Brigade which kept up the pressure until, on 2 June, the Japanese gave them best and abandoned Naga village, leaving large numbers of dead in the shattered bunkers and

foxholes. Meanwhile 161st Brigade, north of the village, had also made considerable gains against opposition. The northern half of the Japanese position at Kohima was in fact now in our possession.

On the southern sector, as the enemy outposts fell back before them, the 2nd British Division moved to the attack on the formidable Aradura Ridge. On 26 May, in spite of heavy rain, 6th Brigade reached a point half a mile west of the ridge. The next day 4th and 5th Brigades established themselves on a line running along the front of the northern face of the ridge to Milestone 48 on the main road, while 6th Brigade continued its climb to the Crest. During the afternoon, 4th and 5th Brigades came under very heavy fire from the reverse slope of Aradura Ridge and were compelled to withdraw to their start line. 6th Brigade under heavy fire had closed up by evening and were digging in south and west of the Crest. The advance up rain-sodden slopes for 3,000 feet had been almost as much an ordeal as the enemy fire. Here, owing to the desperate defence of the enemy, his well-sited and concealed positions, and the extreme difficulty of movement on these slippery, steep jungle slopes, a position of stalemate developed.

The corps commander in these circumstances decided to transfer the attack from the western and northern slopes of the Aradura Ridge to the eastern, a method now made possible by our capture of Naga village. The redispositioning of the troops for the new attack, and the necessary patrolling and reconnaissance, occupied some days. The attack proper began with an attempt by 5th Brigade to take Big Tree Hill, some 2,000 yards northeast of Aradura. This attack was held up towards evening, but was resumed next day with tank support and was successful. The whole brigade then advanced to the west of the road, cutting the Japanese supply routes to their troops high up on the Aradura Ridge. This was the end of the enemy resistance. As our troops advanced, the Japanese pulled out and the Aradura Ridge was ours.

The successes that the 2nd and 7th Divisions had been able to achieve in the last month had been helped in no small degree by the skilful and mobile operations of 23rd LRP Brigade in the very difficult and roadless Naga country on the left of XXXIII Corps. Through the jungle and over the hills, by tracks, passable only on foot or at the best by pack animals, the columns of the brigade, air-supplied, thrust round the enemy flank and struck at his communications from the Chindwin. Apart from the enemy resistance, the mere physical exertion of slip-

ping and sliding, heavily loaded, up and down these soaking tracks was a test that only tough, well-trained, and determined troops could have passed.

Columns circled the right flank of the Japanese main position and took Kharasom, a nodal centre of enemy supply tracks, about 25 miles due east of Kohima, against considerable opposition. The action of these columns achieved a threefold success. They cut the main northern Japanese supply route at the most awkward time for him, they constituted a threat to his rear whose strength he found it difficult to assess, and they stimulated the active support of the local tribesmen. These were the gallant Nagas whose loyalty, even in the most depressing times of the invasion, had never faltered. Despite floggings, torture, execution, and the burning of their villages, they refused to aid the Japanese in any way or to betray our troops. Their active help to us was beyond value or praise. Under the leadership of devoted British political officers, some of the finest types of the Indian Civil Service, in whom they had complete confidence, they guided our columns, collected information, ambushed enemy patrols,

Below: Gathering the fruits of the victories at Imphal and Kohima – a Sherman tank crosses the Irrawaddy River to the west of Mandalay, February 1945.

carried our supplies, and brought in our wounded under the heaviest fire – and then, being the gentlemen they were, often refused all payment. Many a British and Indian soldier owes his life to the naked, head-hunting Naga, and no soldier of the Fourteenth Army who met them will ever think of them but with admiration and affection.

It was clear now, at the beginning of June, that on the Kohima front the enemy was breaking and pulling out as best he could. While he still fought stubbornly as an individual, the cohesion of his units and the direction of his forces were obviously failing. The time had come to press on and destroy what was left of the 31st Japanese Division. The Supreme Commander, on 8 June, issued a Directive that the Kohima-Imphal road was to be opened not later than mid-July, and I was grateful to him for not being stampeded by more nervous people into setting too early a date. I intended that the road should be open well before mid-July, but I was now more interested in destroying Japanese divisions than in 'relieving' Imphal.

So was Stopford. His plan was for the 2nd Division, with the bulk of the corps artillery and tank support, as his main striking force, to push down the Imphal road. The 7th Indian Division was to advance southeast in pace with the 2nd Division through the country to the left of the road, thereby protecting the flank of the British division and cutting off any enemy attempting to disengage to the east. Simultaneously, 23rd LRP Brigade was called on for further exertions in an advance on Ukhrul.

This would exploit the special qualities of each formation; the hitting power of the 2nd Division group; the ability of the 7th Division to operate on pack transport away from roads, with little artillery support and on a lighter supply scale; and the extreme mobility of 23rd Brigade on air supply. It was hoped that 2nd Division would force the enemy off the road to their destruction at the hands of the 7th Division and 23rd Brigade. In any other type of country, this should have been easy. 33rd Corps now had superiority in numbers, artillery, and armour, and absolute domination in the air; but here the jungle, the hills, the single road, and over all, the monsoon clouds and pelting rain made the development of our strength slow and its employment difficult. Small rearguards were able to delay our advance while larger parties slipped away, but only in great disorganization and at the expense of much of their equipment.

On 6 and 7 June, the 2nd Division, after mopping up in the Aradura area, pushed on towards Milestone 55 on the Imphal road. There was some sharp fighting with Japanese rearguards before this was reached, and it is typical of the difficulties encountered that on the latter day the Royal Engineers with the leading troops had to clear three landslides and five road-blocks, pick up numerous mines, and replace two sizeable bridges. Luckily, in most instances the enemy, while he blew up the spans, neglected to destroy the abutments, and our engineers, who had shown the forethought to provide themselves with the original blueprints of all bridges, were able to calculate and

Below: British troops march past the body of a Japanese soldier killed during the push into Mandalay.

carry well forward what was required for replacement of the spans.

The first serious opposition was met at Viswema at about Milestone 60. Here the enemy held a strong rearguard position on a great ridge across the road, which was covered by minefields, artillery, and interlocking machine-guns. Our leading troops were held up, and, during the evening of 8 June, forced to fall back a little. Next day a strong flank-attack was directed against the ridge but, in the thick jungle, mist and rain, mistook one hill feature for another and missed its objective. The error, so close and broken was the country and so stiff the enemy resistance, was not discovered until 11 June. The attack was then reorientated and went in finally on the 14th. It was successful, and many enemy were killed as they attempted to withdraw. About four miles were gained along the road, but then delay was again caused by a blown bridge. This and another enemy rearguard slowed the advance and only a few miles were covered, so that, by the evening of the 16th, the leading troops were halted about a mile short of Mao Songsang.

Mao Songsang was the crest of the watershed between Kohima and Imphal. It offered another – the highest – of the ridges running roughly at right angles across the road. All our information was to the effect that the Japanese intended to hold this very strong position in a final attempt to bar the advance of XXXIII Corps on Imphal. Viswema had been a covering position to be held for some days while Mao Songsang was prepared. During 17 June, many enemy positions situated on the Mao Songsang ridge were heavily bombarded at night, while encircling movements round both the east and west flanks were launched. To everyone's surprise the enemy abandoned his positions and slipped away. This was, I think, the first time in the Burma campaign that such a position had been surrendered without a fight – a most significant change in Japanese mentality.

The 2nd Division pushed on hard at the heels of the enemy during the 18th and made its best advance up to that time – some 14 miles – but was then held up a few miles short of Maram as the Sappers rebuilding a bridge were heavily mortared.

Meanwhile the 7th Division had advanced on a wide front east of the road, meeting at first no opposition, but pressing hard on the retreating Japanese, who abandoned guns, mortars, and equipment of all kinds. Contact was regained on 6 June some ten miles southeast of Kohima, and, on the night of the 7th/8th, an indecisive attack was put in on a Japanese position on the Kekrima Ridge a few miles father east. After a number of encounters among the broken hills, a detachment managed, after a nightmare march of some days through pathless and dripping jungle, to outflank the position and the enemy, having delayed our advance until the

Above: A flotilla of DUKWs heads down the Chindwin in support of XXXIII Corps' drive on Mandalay.

13th, pulled out. On the 16th, the 7th Division reached and cut the main Japanese east-west supply route, the Tuphema-Khorasom-Somra track, at the same time threatening Mao Songsang from the rear. On the 17th they fought to within a mile of the village. There is no doubt that the action of the 7th Division decided the Japanese to abandon that position, which they could have expected to hold for a considerable time against attack from the north.

The maintenance of the 7th Division was now becoming a problem and, its immediate task completed, it was concentrated east of Mao Songsang to operate by fighting patrols against the remaining tracks used by the enemy and to round up stragglers. The main supply line of the division was first a 12-mile twisting ribbon of mud along which jeeps skidded and slithered, their wheels spinning, and then along a pack animal and porter track.

All this time, the columns of 23rd LRP Brigade had pushed on wide to the east. Mountains and rain were their chief opponents, but in a series of small, scattered encounters in dripping jungle they ambushed bewildered Japanese mule trains, inflicted casualties, took prisoners, still rather a novelty, and completely dislocated the enemy line of communication. Again, the contribution of 23rd Brigade to XXXIII Corps' advance was real and effective.

To my great annoyance at this time I was laid up in hospital in Shillong for some days, by an attack of malaria with some unpleasant complications. My annoyance was twofold. First, because I could not visit the front at this very interesting moment, and, second, because I had always preached that to get malaria was a breach of discipline. I had delivered what I felt to be some very effective exhortations to the troops on this theme and I felt now it would be a little difficult to repeat them. In fact, I had only proved on my own body the truth of my contention. Troops were forbidden to bathe after sunset and I had disobeyed my own orders. Returning very muddy and dirty late one evening I had washed in the open and been well and deservedly bitten by mosquitoes.

It was indeed going very well. Torrential rain was slowing up operations on all sectors of the Assam front, but in spite of it, by 18 June, IV Corps' 5th Division was, by attacks along the Kohima road and short hooks to each side of it, slowly approaching Kangpokpi. Although Scoones had ordered this division to advance to Karong, I had later told him not to let it go beyond Kangpokpi. I did this because reports were then coming in of considerable reinforcement of the Japanese forces south and east of Imphal. I expected, even at this stage, some further trouble from them, and I did not wish the 5th Division to get too far away from the 17th. Besides, XXXIII Corps was making satisfactory progress south. I should, I think, have been wiser instead to have urged Scoones to push on along the Kohima road as far and as fast as he could. I exaggerated the danger of renewed attacks on Imphal, and, by what was in effect slowing up the 5th Division, I allowed a considerable number of Japanese to escape between it and XXXIII Corps towards Ukhrul and the Chindwin. It was largely because of this that Ukhrul proved later to be so well defended.

By 18 June, the spearheads of my two corps were some 40 miles apart on the Kohima road,

the 2nd Division approaching Maram and the 5th nearing Kangpokpi. Athough he had given up the much stronger defences of Mao Songsang, the enemy attempted to hold against the 2nd Division another rearguard position at Maram, about eight miles farther south. The weight of our artillery preparations and airstrike, combined with the rapidity of the 2nd Division's deployment and infantry attack, was such that, instead of holding for the ten days ordered, this rearguard was overrun and mostly destroyed in a matter of hours. This was the last serious attempt the enemy made to delay the advance of XXXIII Corps. It was now evident that the 31st Japanese Division was disintegrating and the enemy higher command no longer controlled the battle. In Karong, for instance, our troops captured the almost complete equipment, maps, and documents of the 31st Divisional Infantry Headquarters, and at Milestone 92, the double-span bridge, although prepared for demolition, was rushed before the enemy Sappers could fire the charges.

On 22 June, after a brush with fleeing enemy at the Kangpokpi Mission Station – a Japanese headquarters as it had been mine two years before – the tanks of the 2nd Division met the leading infantry of the 5th Division at Milestone 109. A convoy, which was waiting for this moment, was at once sent through, and IV Corps had its first overland supply delivery since the end of March.

The Imphal-Kohima battle, the first decisive battle of the Burma campaign, was not yet over, but it was won.

Left: Men of the Dorset Regiment move up to the village of Ywathitgyi outside Mandalay to relieve the Royal Scots, late February 1945.

D-Day

by Omar Nelson Bradley

On 6 June 1944 the Allied Armies landed in Normandy and in ten weeks destroyed the German Seventh Army, 500,000 strong, and brought about the liberation of France after four years of cruel and humiliating subjection.

Operation Overlord was the greatest amphibious operation of all time, carried out in the teeth of formidable defences. The Allies enjoyed a tremendous superiority in the air and at sea, and altogether had a better balanced force. The fact remains that only eight divisions, three of them airborne, could be landed on D-Day.

The Allies broke the Atlantic Wall in a single day, at a cost of 9,000 casualties among the 156,000 men landed. It was a tremendous achievement by the British and American troops concerned. Here the story is told by the officer who commanded the US forces.

EDITOR

These pages: Heavily laden US troops make their way ashore during the first stages of D-Day, 4 June 1944.

Chronology

1943

Nov.   Rommel assumes command on the French Coast.

1944

Jan.   General Eisenhower takes command of the Allied European forces.

6 June   D-Day.

7-18 June   The beach-head consolidated.

19-22 June   The Great Storm.

27 June   Fall of Cherbourg.

9 July   British take Caen.

15 July   Rommel wounded.

18 July   Americans take St Lô.

20 July   The Bomb Plot. Hitler wounded.

30 July   Patton breaks out.

1 Aug.   Eisenhower takes command in France.

6/7 Aug.   The Germans' Avranches offensive.

15 Aug.   Allied landings in the south of France.

25 Aug.   Liberation of Paris.

1 Sept.   Canadians take Dieppe.

3 Sept.   British take Brussels.

4 Sept.   British occupy Antwerp.

At 9.30 on Sunday evening, 4 June, Eisenhower gathered his commanders once more at Portsmouth to discuss the weather reports. This time the forecast encouraged a flicker of hope. Rain squalls over the beaches were expected to clear in two or three hours. Visibility, it was thought, might hold up until Tuesday, 6 June. Meanwhile the winds were reported slackening, the cloud base lifting. But while the weather report held out hopes for improvement, it did not excite lively enthusiasm for the adventure. Instead it looked barely promising enough to tantalize Ike with the thought of taking a chance. For the clouds that were expected to close in again on 6 June might easily wash out air support and spoil spotting for the naval bombardment. Risky though it was, both Eisenhower and Smith welcomed this hazardous break in the weather. Almost anything would have been preferable, they thought, to the ordeal of another delay. Monty was for it. But Leigh-Mallory hung back and Tedder was not sure.

At 9.45 Eisenhower edged reluctantly into a decision. 'I'm quite positive we must give the order . . . I don't like it, but there it is . . . I don't see how we can possibly do anything else.'

The day for Overlord was now set, save for one last look at the weather at 4 a.m., 5 June, to make certain the choice need not be reversed.

Aboard the *Augusta* we awaited a postponement signal. But none came and by midnight we heard that Eisenhower had chosen to go. Overlord was underway; The Plan had taken over. For the next 24 hours the fate of the war in Europe was to ride not in the big-hulled command ships but in the wet flat-bottomed craft where many GIs were to be seasick on the slippery steel floors as they groaned through the choppy Channel.

'Ike has the forecasters and he undoubtedly knows what he's doing,' I confided to Kean, 'but by golly, the weather certainly looks lousy here.'

The decks were wet from the drizzle, a wind lashed at the canvas curtain to our war room. And the radar antenna on the tip of our foremast washed in and out of the overcast that hung low in the dark sky.

That evening as I fell into bed worrying about the weather, I was quite uneasy on three counts:

1. Unless the wind and surf abated they might swamp our DD tanks in their unsheltered run to Omaha Beach. We had bargained on the shock effect of those tanks. It would hurt badly to lose them.
2. If the overcast were to prevent spotter aircraft from directing naval gunfire, we might lose the effectiveness of our principal weapon in the initial assault. With but slight superiority in ground forces, we had banked heavily on this fire support to help break through the water's-edge defences. Fear of losing the naval gunfire worried me more than the likelihood of a washout in heavy-bomber missions.
3. The Channel could be distressingly cruel to GI stomachs. A heavy surf might defeat our troops with seasickness before they landed.

But these hazards, I reasoned, must have been equally apparent to Ike. He clearly must have had more pertinent weather forecasts than those available to us. Trusting to Ike's judgement, I went to sleep.

Below: A concrete observation post and tank-traps, part of the German defenses along the Atlantic Wall of northern Europe. Fortunately for the Allies the fortifications along the Normandy coast were far from complete or continuous.

General of the Army Omar Nelson Bradley (1893-1981)

Educated at the United States Military Academy, West Point, Bradley was commissioned in 1915, and attained the rank of lieutenant-colonel in 1936. During the Second World War he won swift promotion, commanding II United States Corps in Tunisia and Sicily. He commanded the US troops (First Army) in the invasion of Normandy and later the Twelfth Army Group, which comprised four American armies.

He was Chief of Staff of the US Army, 1948-9 and Chairman of the Joint Chiefs of Staff, 1949-53.

Eisenhower, who had a high opinion of Bradley dating back to their West Point days, speaks of 'his ability and reputation as a sound, painstaking, and broadly educated soldier'.

Confirmation came at dawn the following morning when a courier arrived from the *Achernar* with a teletype message from Portsmouth: '*D-Day stands as is, Tuesday, 6 June.*' Soon the waters of Plymouth harbour churned in a tangle of wakes as hundreds of ships turned obediently into line. As the columns uncoiled toward the Channel the *Augusta* put to sea, rapidly overtaking the awkward, slow-moving craft. On the eastern lip of the harbour a weathered pill-box squatted lonesomely on stilts offshore. From the gravelly beach behind it some half-dozen concrete blockhouses faced out across the Channel. They had been constructed as part of Britain's hasty preparations to repel a German invasion in 1940.

Thorson stared at the blockhouses. 'Well, after tomorrow Churchill can tear them down.'

'I hope he doesn't,' I answered. 'The British ought to leave them up to remind themselves and the world of the courage they showed when they built those things. That's something you can never take away from them.'

At an easy 15 knots the *Augusta* flanked the Utah-bound column out of Plymouth harbour and headed for the Isle of Wight. From the *Yoke* assembly point there, she would head with the Omaha forces through a mine-swept Channel to the Normandy coast. There she was to fire in support of the initial landing. As far as we could see both fore and aft, ships crowded the British coastline. Overhead their barrage balloons bucked in the wind. Fast destroyers screened us seaward.

Not until several weeks later could we calculate the significance of Eisenhower's decision to dare the Channel in dirty weather. Had he

delayed the attack two weeks to catch the tide on its next turn, his caution would have cost us a month's postponement. On 18 June an unseasonable summer storm raged through the Channel. It swamped hundreds of landing craft upon the beaches and taxed us more heavily in material than did the enemy guns on D-Day. In the face of this gale Eisenhower would have had no choice but to delay the invasion another two weeks until the favourable period of the July moon. And by then we would have had to contend with the enemy's V-1 bombardment, for the buzz-bomb campaign opened on 12 June when the first pilotless missile fell on London. Had they been aimed against our mounting ports on the eve of invasion, those V-1s might have seriously disarranged our preparations.

Even after gaining the continent, however, we would have been seriously hobbled by the month's delay. For it would have been August

Above: A German sentry stands guard in front of a massive gun emplacement. Such facilities suffered heavy air attack and naval bombardment prior to the Allied landings.

Left: A German tank-trap on a Normandy beach. The British created the 79th Armored Division of 'Funnies' – specially modified tanks – to deal with these obstacles.

Left: Transport ships of the US Coast Guard make the Channel crossing; barrage balloons provide a measure of protection from air attack.

before we could count on quantity tonnage through Cherbourg, September before we broke out. Instead of wintering on the Siegfried Line, we would have been lucky to have reached the Seine. And France rather than the Rhineland would have been ravaged during the winter campaign. But for the boldness of Eisenhower's decision, even Paris might have been reduced by artillery and air bombardment.

All afternoon, Monday, 5 June, the *Augusta* scudded past the Utah-bound convoys, heading for her rendezvous with the Omaha force. High above the cruiser's bridge a radar antenna rotated monotonously under the woolly sky. In the plotting room below an officer bent before the radar screen searching for the telltale pips that would signify enemy aircraft. But day passed and evening came without a bogey report.

'Seems hard to believe,' I said to Kirk, 'maybe we're going to have a Sicily all over again.' There, too, we had held our breaths in anticipation of air attacks against the convoys. Yet in Sicily the enemy had slumbered on until we piled up on his beaches. But in the narrow English Channel we could scarcely count on slipping through the enemy's alert without sounding an alarm. On a clear day, aircraft at 10,000 feet over Le Havre could look clear across to Southampton. Enemy radar fringed the French coast and E-boats patrolled offshore in regular night-time sorties. All that day we waited for signs of enemy recce from across the Channel. First the recce, then probing attacks. On D-Day we looked for the *Luftwaffe* to stage a mighty comeback with an attack against our

transports in their crowded anchorages offshore. At no time during the European campaign would Göring find a more congested and remunerative target.

We learned later it was nothing less than this dirty weather that spared us enemy detection and air attack. For the enemy could not believe we would venture into the stormy Channel in the face of those weather forecasts available to him. Lacking the weather stations we had established in Greenland and the North Atlantic, German meteorologists had failed to

Below: US troops go through a fitness routine before re-embarking on their landing craft for the Channel crossing.

pick up the prospective break that prompted Ike's decision. Because of the high winds and heavy overcast on 5 June, German naval patrols were cancelled and mine-layers restricted to ports. Even the ordinarily vigilant *Luftwaffe* recce lay grounded on its fields. In this capricious turn of the weather we had found a Trojan horse.

Even in June of 1944 the enemy was not especially alarmed over the imminence of invasion. Indeed there were Germans who viewed the Allied threat as an unlikely, if not impossible, hoax. Our concentration of coastwise shipping had failed to dent their composure and our tightening of the security belt was viewed as another move in the war of nerves. Rommel had returned to Germany for a command visit with Hitler and was now week-ending at his old home near Ulm. In their windowless bunkers on the Normandy coast, enemy troops waited in boredom as they had for so many months.

At 11 that evening I went below, unbuckled my Mae West, and fell into bed with my shoes on. Kirk remained on the bridge, buttoned up in his foul-weather gear, as the *Augusta* slipped quietly past the buoys that marked the mine-swept Channel. Only the lonely wind in the rigging and the wash of water past our sides broke the silence of the night. It was 3.35 a.m. when the clanking bell outside my cabin called the crew to battle stations. I reached for my helmet, scrambled into a Mae West, and hurried to Kirk's bridge. The moon hung misted in an overcast sky and the wind still lashed the Channel. According to the log the breeze had slackened but the change was not yet evident in the seas that washed by the *Augusta*. Off in the Cotentin Peninsula, almost 30 miles to the west, both airborne divisions had already been dropped. In its headquarters near the ancient terraced city of Le Mans, 40 miles behind the Normandy beaches, the German Seventh Army flashed an invasion alarm. But in the comfortable villa that Eisenhower was later to occupy in St Germain near Paris, von Rundstedt deferred judgement. He feared the airborne drop a diversion preparatory to a main Allied attack against the Pas de Calais.

A faraway roar echoed across the Channel and off our starboard bow orange fires ignited the sky as more than 1,300 RAF bombers swarmed over the French coastline from the Seine to Cherbourg. An enemy AA battery stabbed blindly through the night. A shower of sparks splintered the darkness and a ribbon of fire peeled out of the sky as a stricken bomber plunged toward the *Augusta*. It levelled off, banked around our stern, and exploded into the Channel. By 5.30, first light had diluted the darkness and three Spits whistled by overhead, the first sign of our umbrella. High above the overcast, relays of American fighters formed a second layer of air cover.

The *Augusta* closed in at five knots to its firing position offshore. High up on the cruiser's open bridge, I squinted toward the shore where it lay blurred in the morning mist. Zero hour had come for the DD tanks on Omaha Beach. They were to be launched from their mother craft at H minus 50 minutes and make their way ashore through paths cleared by demolition teams through the obstacle line. The infantry would swarm ashore on the heels of these DD tanks and inland under the cover of their fire.

Thorson stared at the heaving black Channel and shook his head.

'I don't like it, General. The DDs are going to have one helluva time in getting through this sea.'

'Yes, Tubby, I'm afraid you're right. But at this point there's nothing we can do.'

'Any sign of a let-up in the surf?'

'Not yet. Kirk tells me the DDs may be swamped in these seas if they're launched from the LCTs. Either the LCTs cart them ashore – or we'll have to count on getting along without them.'

The decision as to whether those tanks would swim or be carted ashore could not be made aboard the *Augusta*. It fell to the commanders of those tank detachments. By now Overlord had run beyond the reach of its admirals and generals. For the next few tortured hours we could do little but pace our decks and trust in the men to whom The Plan had been given for execution.

At 5.47 a message appeared on the G-2 journal. Fifteen German E-boats had left the harbour at Cherbourg to engage our fleet. Kean smiled and chewed on a piece of gum. Fifteen E-boats against our armada.

The *Augusta*'s eight-inch turrets were turned toward the shore. We plugged our ears with cotton. At 5.50 the ship shuddered as it opened fire upon its predesignated targets among the beach defences. The salvo coasted over the armada and we followed the pin-points of fire as they plunged down toward the shore. The targets had been painstakingly picked from thousands of aerial photos, by which each gun, trench, and pill-box was sited on a detailed map.

At 6.15 smoke thickened the mist on the coastline as heavy bombers of the Eighth Air Force rumbled overhead. Not until later did we learn that most of the 13,000 bombs dropped by these heavies had cascaded harmlessly into the hedgerows three miles behind the coast. In bombing through the overcast, air had deliberately delayed its drop to lessen the danger of spill-over on craft approaching the shore. This margin for safety had undermined the effectiveness of the heavy air mission. To the seasick infantry, bailing their craft as they wallowed through the surf, this failure in air bombing was to mean more casualties upon Omaha Beach.

Meanwhile, of the 332 DD tanks launched

off Omaha, 27 had foundered in the heavy surf. Our troops had not yet landed and already two critical supports for the assault had broken down. At 6.45, 15 minutes after H-Hour, word reached the *Augusta* that the first wave had clambered ashore. It was still too early for news from the beach. I choked down a scalding cup of coffee. By now it was daylight and because the sun was hidden in a haze overhead, a gray panorama opened about us. So far we had drawn no return fire from the enemy's coastal guns. 'I don't understand this lack of counterbattery,' Kean said. 'He's had time to get us in range.'

Thorson squinted toward a bluff that bulged on the shoreline. 'Maybe the Rangers have got in,' he said. The 2nd and 5th Battalions of Rangers were to knock out the battery of six 155-mm guns that covered our Omaha anchorage from the promontory at Pointe du Hoe.

No soldier in my command has ever been wished a more difficult task than that which befell the 34-year-old commander of this Provisional Ranger Force. Lieutenant-Colonel James E. Rudder, a rancher from Brady, Texas, was to take a force of 200 men, land on a shingled shelf under the face of a 100-foot cliff, scale the cliff, and there destroy an enemy battery of coastal guns. 'First time you mentioned it,' Rudder recalls, 'thought you were trying to scare me.' To prepare his troops for their mission, Rudder trained them on the stony cliffs of the Isle of Wight. There they experimented with mortar-propelled grapples designed by the British commandos to catapult scaling ropes over the cliffs. In addition to the ropes they trained with lightweight sectional steel ladders which could be quickly assembled and run up

the face of the cliff. To these British devices the Rangers then added a new wringle of their own. Four long extension ladders were borrowed from the Fire Department in London and mounted on platforms in DUKWs. The DUKWs were to scramble ashore over the shingle shelf and throw their extension ladders up the face of the cliff. In his plan Rudder proposed to lead the assault company ashore himself. Huebner objected, reminding Rudder that as commander of the Ranger force he bore responsibility for the operation. 'You can't risk getting knocked out in the very first round,' he said.

'I'm sorry, sir,' Rudder replied, 'but I'm going to have to disobey you. If I don't take it – it may not go.'

While Rudder assaulted the cliff, the remainder of his force was to wait offshore for the

Above: Smiling members of the US 2nd Ranger Battalion pose for the camera before sailing for France. The unit had one of the most difficult tasks of the whole operation – a cliff assault against a German coastal battery on the Pointe du Hoe to the west of Omaha Beach.

Left: Sherman tanks, part of the initial assault force destined to land on Omaha Beach, the objective of the US 1st Infantry Division, are prepared for the forthcoming battle. Many would flounder in the rough seas off the French beaches.

signal that Pointe du Hoe had been taken. If, after 30 minutes, the signal had not been fired, they were to land with the main Omaha assault force and make for the battery overland.

As Rudder closed in to Pointe du Hoe, 40 minutes behind schedule, enemy artillery raked his LCAs. The Rangers fired their mortars but many of the grappling hooks fell short as their wet ropes trailed sluggishly behind them. The shelf at the foot of the cliff had been pitted with bomb craters and there Rudder's ladder-carrying DUKWs were stalled. The mortar crews fired again and half a dozen ropes were catapulted over the edge of the cliff. But as the Rangers went up them hand over hand, the enemy dropped hand-grenades on their heads. A destroyer raced in and swept the top of the cliff with her guns. Within five minutes after they had landed at the base of Pointe du Hoe, the first Ranger had bellied over the top. Seconds later his companions swarmed up behind him.

There they found a desolate tableland bearing the scars of repeated bombings. The big guns, however, were missing; the quarry had skipped. Ranger patrols pushing inland found the guns in an apple orchard 1,200 yards from the cliff. They were mobile, long-barrelled French GPFs with a range of 20,000 yards and they had been sited to fire on both invasion beaches. Quantities of ammunition were stored at the gun sites but the weapons had not been fired. The Rangers killed those remnants of the gun crews that had not yet fled our naval bombardment and disabled the guns by blowing their breeches. By then, however, the enemy had counter-attacked on Pointe du Hoe. There the Rangers were to be cut off for two days while reinforcements struggled overland from Omaha to relieve them.

As the morning lengthened, my worries deepened over the alarming and fragmentary reports we picked up on the navy net. From these messages we could piece together only an incoherent account of sinkings, swampings, heavy enemy fire, and chaos on the beaches. By 8.30 the two assault regiments on Omaha had expected to break through the water's-edge defences and force their way inland to where a road parallelled the coastline a mile behind the beaches. Yet by 8.30, V Corps had not yet confirmed news of the landing. We fought off our fears, attributing the delay to a jam-up in communications. It was almost 10.00 before the first report came in from Gerow. Like the fragments we had already picked up, his message was laconic, neither conclusive nor reassuring. It did nothing more than confirm our worst fears on the DD tanks. 'Obstacles mined, progress slow . . . DD tanks for Fox Green swamped.'

Aboard the *Ancon*, Gerow and Huebner clung to their radios as helplessly as I. There was little else they could do. For at the moment

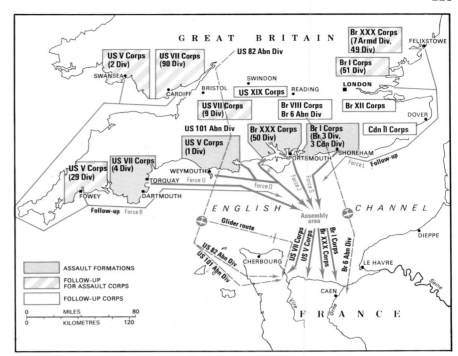

they had no more control than I did of the battle on the beaches. Though we could see it dimly through the haze and hear the echo of its guns, the battle belonged that morning to the thin, wet line of khaki that dragged itself ashore on the Channel coast of France. Alarmed over the congestion of craft offshore on Omaha Beach, Kirk ordered his gunnery officer in for a close-up view. I sent Hansen with him aboard a PT boat. They returned an hour later, soaked by the seas, with a discouraging report of conditions on the beach. The 1st Division lay pinned down behind the sea wall while the enemy swept the beaches with small-arms fire. Artillery chased the landing craft where they milled

Above: The Allied plan for Operation Overlord.

Below: The Allied High Command for D-Day – (sitting, left to right) Air Chief Marshal Sir Arthur Tedder, General Dwight Eisenhower and General Sir Bernard Montgomery; (standing, left to right) Lieutenant General Omar Bradley, Admiral Sir Bertram Ramsey, Air Chief Marshal Sir Trafford Leigh-Mallory and Lieutenant General Walter Bedell Smith.

offshore. Much of the difficulty had been caused by the underwater obstructions. Not only had the demolition teams suffered paralysing casualties, but much of their equipment had been swept away. Only six paths had been blown in that barricade before the rising tide halted their operations. Unable to break through the obstacles that blocked their assigned beaches, craft turned toward Easy Red where the gaps had been blown. Then as successive waves ran in toward the cluttered beachhead they soon found themselves snarled in a jam offshore.

When V Corps reported at noon that the situation was 'still critical' on all four beach exits, I reluctantly contemplated the diversion of Omaha follow-up forces to Utah and the British beaches. Scanty reports from both those sectors indicated the landings there had gone according to plan.

With the Omaha landing falling hours and hours behind schedule, we faced an imminent crisis on the follow-up force. There was due to arrive at noon in the transport area off Omaha Beach a force of 25,000 troops and 4,400 more vehicles to be landed on the second tide. However only a portion of the assault force of 34,000 troops and 3,300 vehicles had as yet got ashore. Unless we moved both forces ashore on D-Day, the whole intricate schedule of build-up would be thrown off balance. Whatever the improvisation, our build-up would have to be maintained if we were to withstand an enemy counter-offensive. Despite the setbacks we had suffered as the result of bad weather and ineffective bombing, I was shaken to find that we had gone against Omaha with so thin a margin of safety. At the time of sailing we had thought ourselves cushioned against such reversals as these.

Not until noon did a radio message from Gerow offer a clue to the trouble we had run into on Omaha Beach. Instead of the rag-tag static troops we had expected to find there, the assault force had run head-on into one of Rommel's tough field divisions.

In planning the assault, originally we had counted upon a thin enemy crust of two static divisions between Caen and Cherbourg. Rommel was known to have concentrated his better reserves behind the beach. Among them was the 352nd Division which had been assembled at St Lô.

Just before boarding the *Augusta* in Plymouth harbour, Dickson learned that the 352nd had been moved from St Lô to the assault beaches for a defence exercise. He promptly forwarded this information to V Corps and the 1st Division but was unable to give it to the troops already 'sealed' aboard their craft.

Had a less experienced division than the 1st Infantry stumbled into this crack resistance, it might easily have been thrown back into the

Left: Allied paratroopers land on French soil, the first members of the forces of liberation to get to grips with the German occupation forces.

Channel. Unjust though it was, my choice of the 1st to spearhead the invasion probably saved us Omaha Beach and a major catastrophe on the first landing.

Although the deadlock had been broken several hours sooner it was almost 1.30 p.m. when V Corps relieved our fears aboard the *Augusta* with the terse message: '*Troops formerly pinned down on beaches Easy Red, Easy Green, Fox Red advancing up heights behind beaches.*'

Behind Omaha the ground rose steeply up brush-covered slopes from 100 to 170 feet high. At four points along the 7,000-yard beach, lightly wooded draws indented these bluffs to provide exit routes inland. Here the enemy had concentrated his heaviest fortifications and here

Below: An A-20 Havoc of the 9th USAAF heads inland from the Normandy coast to bomb German troop and armor concentrations. Note the distinctive black-and-white invasion stripes on the aircraft's wings.

he had held out the longest. Only one draw was travelled by an improved road; the others contained nothing but cart tracks. Within days these cart tracks were to become the most heavily trafficked roads in Europe.

Reluctant to bank together on the laconic reports that trickled in from V Corps, I instructed Kean to go ashore, size up the beachfront congestion, and check on the advance inland that we might calculate our chances on landing a part of the follow-up force that night. With Hansen he sped off in a PT, closed to 1,000 yards offshore, and transferred to an LCVP for the final trip through the obstacles. High water had reached its mark and the tide was rolling out, leaving the LCTs and hundreds of craft dried out on the beaches. The *Augusta* had now closed in to within 4,000 yards of the beach and the waters about us were strewn with flotsam from the invasion.

Kean's report was more hopeful than I had dared wish for. Despite the congestion of vehicles on Omaha Beach, our troops had penetrated the enemy's defences between the well-guarded draws and to the east of Easy Red had pushed one mile inland to cut the first lateral road. Although the strategic draw at Easy Red had not yet been cleared of small-arms fire, bulldozers were already carving a path up its shoulder to the tableland on top of the bluff. And as the tide withdrew from the beach, engineers trailed after it through the debris, blowing new paths through the obstacles as they were uncovered by the Channel.

Despite the improved situation, however, Omaha had fallen seriously behind schedule. The beach was littered with stove-in craft, drowned-out vehicles, and burned-out tanks. Scores of bodies sprawled wet and shapeless in the shingle where they had fallen. Only the lightly wounded could be removed to hospital ships through the heavy surf. The more seriously wounded had been bedded down in slit trenches under the sea wall. And from one end of the beach to the other the tidal shelf was littered with the water-soaked debris that washes in with the surf in the wake of any amphibious invasion.

The enormous equipment losses on landing had left Omaha badly in need of replacements. 'What do they need most?' I asked Kean.

'Bulldozers,' he answered, 'bulldozers and artillery. They're badly pinched for both.'

Not only were bulldozers needed to clear the debris and obstacles in time for the second tide but without them our losses mounted as vehicles, ferried ashore on rhinos from the LSTs, mired in the soft, low-water sands. Of the 16 dozers that had been sent ashore that morning, only six reached Omaha Beach. Three of these were immediately knocked out by enemy artillery fire.

Although Omaha had squeezed through a crisis, she was still on the danger list. With

neither depth, artillery, nor tanks, we might easily be dislodged from our precarious footing and thrown back into the Channel by counterattack. I hurried off to see Gerow aboard the *Ancon*.

However desperate the situation, a senior commander must always exude confidence in the presence of his subordinates. For anxiety, topside, can spread like cancer down through the command.

While splashing toward the *Ancon* aboard a PT boat, I anticipated that Gerow and Huebner might have been unnerved by the prolonged struggle that morning. Both had gone under fire as senior commanders for the first time, and although neither could have averted the crisis, both bore an immediate responsibility for it. Thus while I was eager to check on the situation and push the follow-up ashore, I went partly to stiffen their confidence if confidence was what they needed. I found, however, that Gerow's map showed penetrations at five points on the Omaha Beach defences. The lateral road had been cut at Vierville and again at Colleville on the left. And a force was pushing toward Pointe du Hoe to relieve the dangers there. With that we hoisted our tails and went ahead with the original plan to land the follow-up force on Omaha Beach and put five regiments ashore by nightfall.

Huebner was planning to go in and take shore command of his 1st Infantry Division that evening.

'How about you, Gee?' I asked. 'When can you move V Corps headquarters ashore?'

'Early in the morning, Brad. We'll have our communications in by then.'

'To hell with your communications –'

Gerow grinned. 'We'll set up on the beach tonight.'

At 8.30 that evening V Corps opened its first CP in a ditch atop the bluffs behind Easy Red. I

Above: British troops cross 'Pegasus' bridge over the Orne canal on the east flank of the British beaches. In an epic gliderborne assault, British troops seized this vital bridgehead.

was anxious that Gerow get his teeth into the beach organization and speed up unloading of the 2nd Infantry Division on D plus 1.

Across the estuary that slashed into the Cotentin neck, our PT rammed through the surf for Utah Beach at full throttle. With two lookouts hugging the deck to warn him of floating mines, the skipper drove his egg-shelled craft through blinding spray. Inside the Utah anchorage we located the *Bayfield* by its topside antennae. As the PT boat pitched to the crest of a six-foot wave, I jumped for the rope net of the *Bayfield* and clambered up its high steel sides. In contrast to Omaha where the shadow of catastrophe had hung over our heads all day, the landing on Utah had gone more smoothly than during rehearsal five weeks before. As G-2 had predicted, the beach was held by second-rate static troops. Except for casemated artillery north of Utah, the resistance quickly collapsed. In tallying up G-1's reports almost a week later, I found that Collins had cracked the wall on Utah Beach at a cost of fewer than 350 casualties in his assault force. This was less than half of what he had lost in the rehearsal on Slapton Sands.

At the outset, however, Utah had got off to an unpromising start. In piloting the assault force ashore, the navy had missed its guide point and landed the lead regiment 2,000 yards south of its mark. Apparently Providence had put its hand to the helm. Not only were the underwater obstacles planted less thickly on these beaches but the shore defences proved less formidable than they were found to be farther north.

Ted Roosevelt, now a spare brigadier with the 4th Division, had volunteered to lead the assault units ashore in the first wave. With the skill and instinct of a veteran campaigner, he quickly improvised an attack to secure an exit across the lagoon that had caused us such anxiety in planning. As the lead regiment pushed across this marshland toward the lateral road three miles inland, it radioed reassuring reports to the 4th Division on the *Bayfield*. Collins promptly passed them on to Army. Thus while we struggled for a toe-hold on Omaha Beach, we were at least assured success on Utah. But the ease with which Collins had established his seaborne beach-head bore no similarity to the airborne struggle five miles inland where the Battle for France was already five hours old by the time VII Corps landed. By daylight, paratroopers from both the 82nd and 101st Divisions were fighting for their lives deep in the treacherous hedgerows and swamplands of the Cotentin.

The drop had gone awry almost as soon as the troop-carrier aircraft of the 101st Division made landfall on the west Cotentin coast after a midnight flight from England. Cloud banks forced the closely packed night-time formations to disperse. As the planes neared their drop zones now marked by pathfinder parties, enemy flak scattered the formations still farther apart. Although the drop concentration might have been judged remarkable in the light of our Sicilian episode, the 6,600 paratroopers of Taylor's division were scattered widely behind the causeways they had been ordered to secure. More than 60 plane-loads were dumped from eight to 20 miles beyond their drop zones. Others were scattered from Utah Beach through the lagoons. Nevertheless, remnants of the 101st struck smartly toward the causeways that led from Utah Beach while others headed south to seal off Carentan and block that path of enemy reinforcement.

Two-thirds of the 82nd Division was to have been dropped eight miles inland behind the Merderet River where it parallels Utah Beach. Here it could shield Collins' beaches from the west and harry the enemy in his reinforcement of Cherbourg. The remaining drop zone lay east of that river astride the principal route from Cherbourg to the beach-head. Here Ridgway would block from the north and 'establish a firm defensive base' in the village of Ste Mère Eglise.

Like the 101st, however, Ridgway's 82nd was badly scattered on landing, especially those elements scheduled to drop west of the Merderet. As a consequence, much of the division's effort on that first day was wasted in the difficult task

Above: A Catholic priest gives communion to US troops on Omaha Beach.

Below: Troops clamber aboard an infantry assault craft for the run in to the D-Day beaches. Calm weather, heavy fire support and total air superiority gave the Allies a key advantage during the first days of the invasion.

of assembling combat units. However the division did establish a base in Ste Mère Eglise from among the paratroopers who landed near that tiny dairying town. And like the 101st, it panicked the enemy in most rear areas during those first critical hours of the assault.

Shortly after noon on D-Day, Collins established contact with Taylor's 101st Division on the southernmost end of his beach-head. But the fate of the 82nd still lay obscured somewhere behind the miles of hedgerow that separated it from the beaches.

'No word from Ridgway?' I asked Collins.

'Nope – but I'm not worried about Matt. The 82nd can take care of itself. How's Gerow getting along? Has his situation over there cleared up?'

'It looks a lot better than it did at noon. But they've been hanging on all day by their fingertips. The 352nd gave us an awful jolt. But the worst seems to be over. Gee is going in tonight. He hopes to get the beach in shape and bring the 2nd in tomorrow.'

The commander of the 4th Division had gone ashore earlier that afternoon while Collins remained with his VII Corps staff aboard the *Bayfield* to keep a line on communications – and to hold down Admiral Moon. Alarmed over the loss of a few vessels in the assault, Moon had been persuaded by his staff to suspend nighttime unloading on Utah Beach. When Collins learned of Moon's decision, he objected strenuously and the Admiral was hastily dissuaded. 'Let the navy expend its ships,' I told Collins, 'if that's what it takes. But we've got to get the build-up ashore even if it means paving the whole damned Channel bottom with ships.'

I went over the rail of the *Bayfield* as dusk was falling. Below me the PT boat struck savagely at my legs atop each heavy swell. Finally as she reared, I leaped for her wet decks. On the bow, a sailor with a boathook grabbed wildly for balance, lost it, and toppled over the side. He fell into the white water that boiled between our boat and the *Bayfield* as the PT slammed its fenders against the merchantman's steel plates. While the skipper backed off to avoid crushing the man, we threw him a rope and hauled him aboard.

Late that evening as we closed in toward the anchorage off Omaha, a destroyer challenged us with a blinker through the darkness. Slipping into the Omaha anchorage from the estuary near Carentan, we might easily have been mistaken for a German E-boat.

'What in hell's the recognition signal!' the skipper bellowed below as he scrambled for a lantern. 'Give it to me quick, or we'll have the whole damn navy sweeping us with a broadside.'

'I hope he finds it,' I said to Hansen. 'This would be a helluva way for a doughboy to end

Left: Rangers scale the cliffs of the Pointe du Hoe. Although their losses were heavy and they were isolated for two days, the Rangers secured the position.

the war – skewered on the end of a five-inch shell in 15 fathoms of water.' The skipper got his proper signal and blinked back in reply.

Picking our way through the transport area, we located the *Augusta* just as a star shell broke in the sky. A line of tracers arced skyward. The enemy had come in for its nightly raid.

The skipper grabbed for his megaphone and hailed the *Augusta*.

'Ahoy – can we come aboard?'

'Lie off,' the deck called back, 'lie off until we get an all clear.'

I had confessed before to uneasiness in an air raid afloat. But if afloat we were to be, I preferred the 9,000-ton *Augusta* to this sea-going hot-rod. For 20 minutes we idled in a tight circle. When the raid appeared to slacken, we hove to the *Augusta* once more.

'Lie off,' the answer came back. 'Lie off.'

'But we've got passengers aboard,' our skipper shouted through the darkness.

'Prisoners?' the deck called; with a note of curiosity. 'Stand by to bring the prisoners aboard.'

I climbed a rope ladder up the *Augusta*'s side and crawled over the rail, cold, wet, hungry, and tired.

The crew pressed forward to see its 'prisoners'.

'Oh, hell,' a sailor grunted, 'it's only General Bradley.'

Despite the confusion that still existed in many of the smaller isolated units, our situation had materially improved by the morning of 7 June.

On the other hand, we were not yet out of danger. On the thin five-mile sliver of Omaha Beach, we had fallen far short of D-Day objectives. German artillery still pounded the beaches where traffic had congealed in the wreckage. And we had not yet reached the Caen-Carentan road that was to have strung our Allied landings together. Nevertheless we took some comfort in the fact that five regiments had been put ashore on Omaha by dawn, a miraculous achievement in view of the disordered condition of the beach. But to get them ashore we had sacrificed bulk tonnage. Had it not been for the 90 preloaded DUKWs that waded ashore on D-Day, we might have been hard put for ammunition.

However, the enemy had paid dearly for our delay on Omaha Beach. His 352nd Division had been mauled at the water's edge, depriving Rommel of one more field division. Meanwhile, during our first 12 perilous hours ashore, the enemy had failed to mount a single co-ordinated counter-attack against our beach-head. The omens were better than our progress.

On Utah, Collins had fared better than Gerow. Although unable to extend his beach to the north and overrun his D-Day objective, Collins had expanded to the south. There he anchored his landing tightly on the neck of the

Cotentin where we were to force a junction between both beach-heads. During the night he had finally linked up with Ridgway's 82nd Airborne Division.

It was still too early to evaluate the success of the airborne drop. The dispersal had so shaken our confidence in night-time airborne operations that we never again attempted a night-time drop. In the initial count casualties looked excessively high and some feared Leigh-Mallory might be vindicated in his prediction. But as 'lost' units trickled in through our lines, we discovered that airborne losses for the drop and the first day aground did not exceed 20 per cent. Not until we had turned the Utah force north toward Cherbourg did we learn how effectively those airborne troops had paralysed the enemy's rear.

On the morning of D plus 1 the enemy's high command in Berlin awaited word from Rommel that the Allied landing had been roped off and would soon be flung into the Channel. But with the passing of D-Day, the enemy had lost his best chance to destroy us. By the morning of D plus 1 we had not only got a tight grip on the beach-head, but Allied build-up was already beginning to swell.

I had long ago anticipated that the enemy would dash his *Luftwaffe* against our landing with every plane Göring could put into the sky. For it was while we were hanging precariously to a slender beach-head that we could have been most critically hurt by enemy air attack.

Throughout the daylight hours of 6 June only a few enemy *jabos* broke through our cordon of Allied fighter cover for ineffectual passes at the beach. And during the night-time raid

Above: HMS *Rodney* adds her weight of fire to the preliminary bombardment of the French coast.

that had stranded us aboard the PT, a meagre force was all that the *Luftwaffe* could muster against us. Not only had the Allied air force whittled the German down to 400 first-line aircraft in the west on D-Day, but the concentrated attack on his French fighter bases had driven him back to the German border. To conserve his fast-waning strength, Göring had flinched at the very moment a bold blow might have saved him.

Shortly after 6 a.m. on 7 June Montgomery came alongside the *Augusta* aboard a British destroyer. He was anxious that the Allied beaches be joined before Rommel could concentrate his forces against any single beach and there break through. While we perspired through the D-Day crisis, the British dashed ashore in their sector and quickly pushed inland for a penetration of seven miles near Bayeux. Their primary objective at Caen, however, had eluded them. Sensitive to the British attack against that vital communications centre, the enemy had attacked out of Caen in a panzer counter-offensive.

Eisenhower had signalled that he would arrive in the transport area at 11. Meanwhile, I had slipped ashore on Omaha to prod Gerow on Montgomery's order for an early link-up of the beaches. Gerow was to push Gerhardt's 29th to the right toward a juncture with Collins on the Cotentin neck while Huebner's 1st made contact with the British on their left.

V Corps had hidden its headquarters in a ditch behind the hedgerow on the exit road from Easy Red. I hitched a ride on a truck up a road still under construction. A column of infantrymen trudged up the hill, enveloped in dust from a line of trucks. On the flat top of the bluff engineers were already levelling an airstrip for the evacuation of wounded to England.

Gerow had gone forward to Huebner's CP and I went on to see him. The 1st Division had by-passed small enemy pockets in its advance on D-Day and was now rooting them out to prevent snipers from harrassing the rear.

'These goddam Boche just won't stop fighting,' Huebner complained. He was impatient to clean up the beach-head that he might drive inland and secure his immediate objectives. 'It'll take time and ammunition,' I told him, 'perhaps more than we reckon on both.'

As Admiral Ramsay's flagship manoeuvred into position abreast of the *Augusta*, the coxswain swung our LCVP under the ship's Jacob's ladder. I jumped for it and climbed aboard. Ike greeted me at the rail.

'Golly, Brad,' he exclaimed, grasping me by the hand, 'you had us all scared stiff yesterday morning. Why in the devil didn't you let us know what was going on?'

'But we did.' I was puzzled. 'We radioed you every scrap of information we had. Everything that came in both from Gee and Collins.'

Ike shook his head. 'Nothing came through until late afternoon – not a damned word. I didn't know what had happened to you.'

'But your headquarters acknowledged every message. You check it when you get back and you'll find they all got through.'

Aboard the *Augusta* 20 minutes later I

Above: Headquarters troops of the British 4th Special Service Brigade land in front of St Aubin-sur-Mer, a coastal village on the 'Nan' sector of Juno Beach.

Left: Members of 48 Royal Marine Commando land on Juno Beach.

double-checked our journals. Not only had the messages been sent but each had been properly acknowledged. Later I heard that the decoding apparatus had broken down at Montgomery's CP. So heavy was the D-Day radio traffic that code clerks fell 12 hours behind in deciphering the incoming reports.

However, Ike's vigil could not have been any more agonizing than the one we suffered aboard the *Augusta*. For the reports, if anything, were no less worrisome than the fears that are spun out of silence. A week later I confessed to Monty that I would never admit to Ike just how worried I was that morning we waited in the mist off Omaha Beach.

Later on the afternoon of 7 June Kirk ferried me to Utah aboard the *Augusta*. I hailed a lift ashore aboard a passing LCM draped with the coxswain's washing. Near shore we spotted a DUKW and I called the driver for a lift dry-shod to the beach.

'Sure, General,' he called, 'jump aboard.'

'Can you run me on to General Collins' head-quarters?' I asked.

The driver shook his head. 'Like nothing better, General,' he answered, 'but my captain would give me hell. He told me to hustle right back from this run.'

I did not dispute his captain's orders; on D plus 1 rank could not compete with the priority importance of tonnage. Pleased at having avoided a soaking in the surf, I jumped off on the beach and hitched a ride inland on a passing weasel amphibian.

Collins had established his VII Corps CP inside a walled Norman farmyard. He had gone forward leaving behind his deputy corps commander, Major-General Eugene M. Landrum. We checked the situation map in a stall in the barn. The 4th Division was pushing north to clear the beach of fire while the 101st shoved south for its link-up with V Corps. Although Ridgway had collected his 82nd east of the Merderet, units west of that river were still reported cut off.

'Heard anything from Matt today?'

Landrum showed me a typewritten situation report from the 82nd Division.

'Matt must be in pretty good shape. At any rate he's got a typewriter in action.'

Ridgway had organized a strong position north of Ste Mère Eglise. There, firmly astride the Carentan-Cherbourg road, he covered the left flank of the 4th Division.

On Friday, 9 June, army headquarters moved ashore from the *Achernar* to establish its first CP in an orchard behind Pointe du Hoe where the Rangers had tracked down the battery of French GPFs. With communications ashore there was no longer need for me to remain aboard the *Augusta*, and Saturday morning when I disembarked we closed down our floating CP. Kirk's bright young army aide, Lieutenant MacGeorge Bundy of Boston,

Massachusetts, reverted to his earlier eminence as the ranking army officer aboard the admiral's flagship. He reminded me the day I came aboard that I had usurped his position.

Monty had called a meeting that morning at the fishing village of Port-en-Bessin to co-ordinate First Army movements with those of the British Second Army. Dempsey had plotted an attack south of the unspoiled town of Bayeux, partly to extend his beach-head and partly to envelop Caen from the west. I found Monty waiting with Dempsey in a field where British MPs had been posted as out-guards. He wore a faded gabardine bush jacket, a grey turtleneck sweater, corduroy trousers, and a tanker's black beret. A map case had been spread on the flat hood of his Humber staff car. Two panzer divisions were dug in before Caen and Dempsey sought to outflank them in his attack from Bayeux. We were to parallel this British attack and drive south in the direction of Caumont. There Gerow was to establish a strong defensive outpost for V Corps. An attack on this end of the lodgement, we estimated, might also help divert enemy reinforcements from Collin's attack towards Cherbourg.

Monty was flying back to his headquarters in Portsmouth that afternoon.

'Anything I can bring you?' he asked.

'Why yes, sir, a newspaper – any one at all.' I felt strangely cut off from the news of the world without a paper at breakfast.

By Saturday morning, 10 June, Gerow had parlayed his original thin holdings on Omaha into a substantial beach-head. Not only had he linked forces with Dempsey but he had thrust beyond the lateral road that tied their landings together. On his right, the 29th Division had pushed through the burning streets of Isigny to reach the flatlands of the Carentan estuary. A few miles across the estuary, glider infantry manoeuvred in a move to outflank Carentan from the northeast. Meanwhile paratroopers of the 101st advanced toward that pivotal city down the highway that led south from Cherbourg to Carentan. The road ran through a vast marshland, flooded by the enemy in an effort to restrict us to the narrow roads.

'We've got to join up with Gerow just as quickly as possible,' I had told Collins, anticipating difficulty in those marshlands. 'If it becomes necessary to save time, put 500 or even 1,000 tons of air on Carentan and take the city apart. Then rush it and you'll get in.'

Later that afternoon word reached Army that Omaha and Utah had been joined together over a back-country route across the estuary. The company of glider infantry from Utah had forced its way to the village of Auville-sur-le-Vey where reconnaissance troops of the 29th Division waited a few miles beyond Isigny. With Hansen I drove down through Isigny to see if we could get through on this overland route to Collins.

A small dairying town of 2,800 known for its Camembert cheese, Isigny lay charred from its shelling the day before when the 29th called for naval gunfire to drive the enemy out of town. A few villagers searched sorrowfully through the ruins of their homes. From one, an aged man and his wife carried the twisted skeleton of a brass bed. And down the street, a woman carefully removed the curtain from a paneless window in the remaining wall of what had been the village café. For more than four years the people of Isigny had awaited this moment of liberation. Now they stared accusingly on us from the ruins that covered their dead.

Beyond the Vire we pulled up short of Auville-sur-le-Vey. In the intersection ahead an armoured car had engaged a sniper with its 37-mm gun. The ping of his rifle was lost in the crash of the car's cannon.

A jeep pulled up with Brigadier-General Edward J. Timberlake, Jr., commander of an AA brigade.

'You're crazy to go through, sir,' he said, 'The road may be mined. Let me go on in front.'

'Nope – but thanks anyhow,' I said. 'I'm not going to go through.'

As my driver wheeled the jeep around I turned back to Hansen.

'Be kinda silly to get killed by a sniper while out sightseeing,' I said. 'We'd better stick to the PT boat until Carentan is opened.'

By dawn on 12 June, Taylor's paratroopers had encircled Carentan in a brilliant pincer movement. At 6 a.m. that day they drove into the city's streets to open the main road between Omaha and Utah. On our seventh day ashore we had linked the Allied forces together in a beach-head 42 miles wide.

We would now force our way across the Cotentin and capture the port of Cherbourg.

Below: After the consolidation of the beach-head, US troops of the second assault wave push inland. Supply vessels wait offshore to unload their cargoes.

Leyte Gulf

by Douglas MacArthur

'The president of the United States ordered me to break through the Japanese lines and proceed from Corregidor to Australia for the purpose, as I understand it, of organizing the American offensive against Japan, a primary object of which is the relief of the Philippines. I came through and I shall return.'
GENERAL MACARTHUR on reaching Australia, 1942.

When on 11 March 1942 General MacArthur had left Corregidor for Australia he had vowed to return. In mid-1944 with Hollandia, Wake and Biak in his hands, it was in his power to fulfil his vow.

The assault on Leyte was preluded by fierce attacks on Formosa and Chinese airfields. Carrier-borne American aircraft destroyed 500 planes for a loss of 76. The invasion force for Leyte included 738 ships, of which 17 were carriers. The landing (20 October) did not meet with heavy opposition and by midnight on the 21st MacArthur had 132,000 men ashore.

Despite their recent heavy defeat in the Battle of the Philippine Sea (19/20 June) Admiral Toyoda was still seeking a decisive battle. He still had four carriers, but was very short of planes, since there had been no time to train new pilots since 'The Great Marianas Turkey Shoot' as the Philippine Sea battle was called. Admiral Ozawa, whose role was to lure Admiral Halsey northwards, came out into the Inland Sea with only 116 planes.   EDITOR

Chronology

1941
7 Dec.	Pearl Harbor.

1942
8 May	Battle of the Coral Sea.
4 June	Battle of Midway.

1944
6 June	Normandy landings.
19/20 June	Battle of the Philippine Sea.
18 July	Tojo cabinet resigns.
21 July–8 Aug.	Guam taken by Americans.
12-15 Sept.	Admiral Halsey's carriers raid the Philippines.
3 Oct.	First airfield ready on Moratai.
20 Oct.	Americans land on Leyte.
23-25 Oct.	Battle of Leyte Gulf.
24 Oct.	Bombing of Tokyo from Marianas begins.

1945
26 Feb.	Corregidor retaken.
4 March	Manila cleared.
8 May	Surrender of Germany.
26 May	British fleet joins the Americans in the Pacific.
6 Aug.	Atomic bomb dropped on Hiroshima.
8 Aug.	Russia declares war on Japan.
14 Aug.	Surrender of Japan.

These pages: The eight-inch guns of the USS *Portland* fire in support of the landings on Leyte of the US Sixth Army under Lieutenant-General Walter Kreuger, 20 October 1944.

The Philippine Islands had constituted the main objective of my planning from the time of my departure from Corregidor in March 1942. From the very outset I regarded this strategic archipelago as the keystone of Japan's captured island empire, and, therefore, the ultimate goal of the plan of operations in the Southwest Pacific Area . . .

As the Allies advanced westward along New Guinea and across the Central Pacific, a wide divergence of opinion developed among international planners and military strategists as to the methods of defeating Japan, but I never changed my basic plan of a steady advance along the New Guinea-Philippines axis, from Port Moresby to Manila. This plan was conceived as a forward movement of ground, sea, and air forces, fully co-ordinated for mutual support, operating along a single axis with the aim of isolating large Japanese forces that could be attacked at leisure or slowly starved into surrender. By choosing the route from Australia via New Guinea and the Halmaheras to the Philippines, I could constantly keep my lines protected, pushing my own land-based air cover progressively forward with each advance. My plan insured control of the air and sea during major amphibious operations, and was so designed that land-based air power, with its inherent tactical advantages, could be used to

the maximum extent. This remained my fundamental concept of operations as I moved my forces from Port Moresby and Milne Bay to Buna and Lae, through the Vitiaz Straits to the Admiralties, on to Hollandia and the Vogelkop, until they reached their final springboard at Morotai.

My plan, called 'Reno', was based on the premise that the Philippine archipelago, lying directly in the main sea routes from Japan to the source of her vital raw materials and oil in the Netherlands Indies, Malaya, and Indo-China, was the most important strategic objective in the Southwest Pacific Area. Whoever controlled the air and naval bases in the Philippine Islands logically controlled the main artery of supply to Japan's factories. If this artery were severed, Japan's resources would soon disappear, and her ability to maintain her war potential against the advancing Allies would deteriorate to the point where her main bases would become vulnerable to capture. Mindanao was selected as the tactical objective in the Philippines, and the flanks of my advance beyond the western tip of New Guinea would be safeguarded by the Central Pacific drive across the Pacific.

'Reno' enabled our forces to depart from a base closest to the objective, and advance against the most lightly organized positions of the enemy's defences, effecting a decisive penetration. The advance would be made by a combination of airborne and seaborne operations, always supported by the full power of land-based aviation, and assisted by the fleet operating in the open reaches of the Pacific. A penetration of the defensive perimeter along

General of the Army Douglas MacArthur (1880-1964)

MacArthur was educated at West Point and commissioned into the Engineers (1906). He served in France 1917-18 as Chief of Staff 42nd Division and was decorated. In 1925 he was promoted Major-General and given command of the 23rd Brigade, Philippine Division, later transferring to the armed service of that country and rising to the rank of Field Marshal, the only American citizen to do so. He retired from the American Army in 1937 with the rank of General.

In 1941, however, he was recalled and appointed Commander South Pacific, and in 1942 achieved fame by his stubborn defence of the Bataan Peninsula against the Japanese. Compelled to quit this last corner of the Philippines, he vowed 'I will return'. He did so in triumph in 1944 after a campaign of glittering brilliance which was to be crowned by his acceptance of the surrender of the Japanese armed forces abroad USS *Missouri* in Tokyo Bay, September 1945. After the war, he was appointed Supreme Allied Commander in Japan and effective ruler of that country which he guided towards democracy. In 1951, command of the UN forces devolved upon him. But his demands for a more ruthless prosecution of the Korean War, in particular for the bombing of China, brought conflict with the Government of the US and his dismissal by President Truman, 1951.

Below: A lone US destroyer lays a smokescreen to cover the landings on Leyte. American troops faced elements of the Japanese 16th Division during the initial landings on the island's east coast.

this line would result in by-passing extended, heavily defended areas that would fall, practically by their own weight, enabling us to perform mopping-up operations with a minimum of loss.

Other proposals were put forth, but 'Reno' finally met with general acceptance. Initial lodgements were to be effected in southern Mindanao on 15 November and at Leyte Gulf on 20 December. 'Musketeer II', as the plan was renamed, had as its major objective 'the prompt seizure of the Central Luzon area to destroy the principal garrison, command organization and logistic support of hostile defence for Japan'. The plan envisioned the full support of the United States fleet not only to secure a foothold on the eastern coast of the Philippine archipelago, but also to assist in the invasion of Central Luzon.

In conformity with this provision, carrier-based aircraft of Admiral Halsey's Third Fleet hit Mindanao on 9 and 10 September, and discovered unexpected and serious weakness in the enemy's air defences. Few Japanese planes were encountered, and further probing disclosed that Southwest Pacific land-based bombers, operating out of New Guinea fields, had caused severe damage to several enemy air installations.

On 12 and 13 September, carrier task groups of the Third Fleet hit the Visayas. Again enemy air reaction was surprisingly meagre, and heavy loss was inflicted upon Japanese planes and ground installations. It became apparent that the bulk of the mighty Japanese air force had been destroyed in the war of attrition incidental to the New Guinea operations.

Admiral Halsey suggested that Leyte should be seized immediately. At the time he radioed this suggestion, virtually the whole strategic apparatus of the United States government had moved to Quebec in attendance at the conference then being held between Mr Roosevelt and Mr Churchill. My views were requested on the proposed change of the invasion date for Leyte, and I cabled my assent to Halsey's proposal. Thus, within 90 minutes after Quebec had been queried as to the change in plans, we had permission to advance the date of our invasion of Leyte by two months.

The operation to take Leyte without a preliminary landing in Mindanao was a most ambitious and difficult undertaking. The objective area was located over 500 miles from Allied fighter cover. It was at the same time in the

Above: A landing craft fitted with rockets to bombard the shore supports the first US landings on Leyte.

Below: The Leyte Gulf invasion forces prepare to sail for the Philippines. The fleet comprises carriers, escorts, supply vessels and battleships.

centre of a Japanese network of airfields covering the Philippines. The islands would doubtless be defended to the limit of the enemy's capabilities, probably even at the risk of losing his heretofore husbanded navy, since a successful landing on Leyte would presage the eventual reoccupation of the entire Philippine area. The Japanese could reinforce their positions by bringing in troops and supplies from their lines, whereas, without airbases in the vicinity, the Allied forces would have to rely on naval aircraft to prevent enemy supply and reinforcement convoys from reaching the area. Again, as at Hollandia, Southwest Pacific forces would advance beyond the range of their own land-based fighter cover and put themselves under the protection of carrier planes for the assault phase. The success of the operation, even after a landing was secured, would depend on the ability of Allied naval forces to keep the enemy from building up a preponderance of strength on Leyte and adjoining Samar, and to prevent enemy naval craft from attacking shipping in the beach-head area.

Careful study preceded the selection of the landing beaches and the direction of the inland thrust on Leyte. The northeastern coastal plain of Leyte was chosen as most suitable for the assault. Seizure of the 18-mile stretch between Dulag and San Jose would permit the early capture of the important Tacloban airfield, and make possible the occupation and use of the airfield system under development at Dulag. It would permit domination of vital San Juanico Strait, and place the invading force within striking distance of Panaon Strait to the south. Intelligence reports indicated that the beach area would not be heavily defended, although some fortifications were being prepared along the inland road net.

I had no illusions about the operation. I knew it was to be the crucial battle of the war in the Pacific. On its outcome would depend the fate of the Philippines and the future of the war against Japan. Leyte was to be the anvil against which I hoped to hammer the Japanese into submission in the central Philippines – the springboard from which I could proceed to the conquest of Luzon, for the final assault against Japan itself. With the initiative in my hands, the war had reached that decisive stage where an important Japanese defeat would seal the fate of the Japanese Empire and a centuries-old tradition of invincibility.

The plan for the ground operations in the capture of Leyte comprised four main phases. Phase one covered minor preliminary landings to secure the small islands lying across the entrance to Leyte Gulf. Phase two included the main amphibious assaults on Leyte from Dulag to Tacloban, and called for the seizure of the airstrip, an advance through Leyte Valley, and the opening of San Juanico and Panaon Straits. The third phase consisted of the necessary over-

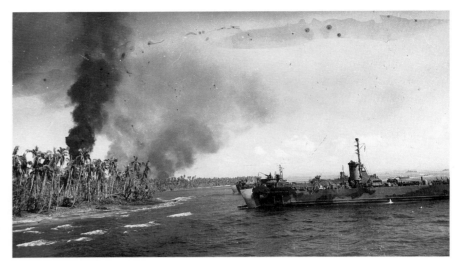

land and shore-to-shore operations to complete the capture of Leyte and the seizure of southern Samar. Phase four contemplated the occupation of the remainder of Samar and the further neutralization of enemy positions in the Visayas.

On 16 October, I left Hollandia and went aboard the *Nashville*, which was to serve as my flagship. On the waters around me lay one of the greatest armadas of history. America's rebuilt strength consisted of new battleships that replaced those lying at the bottom of Pearl Harbor, and many of the veteran ships that had survived that initial assault itself; of aircraft carriers, cruisers, and destroyers in massive array; of transports and landing craft of a type that had not even existed three years before. Altogether, there were 700 of these ships of war. They carried 174,000 of America's finest fighting men, veteran soldiers now a match for any warrior the world has ever known. The size of the land-

Above: Following the opening bombardment of the Japanese coastal defenses on Leyte, a pair of medium landing ships moves toward one of the two landing beaches chosen for the first assaults.

Right: The naval battles around Leyte Gulf, showing the movements of the rival fleets following the landings of 20 October.

Left: General Douglas MacArthur (1880-1964) had long cherished a triumphant return to the Philippines since their capture by the Japanese in March 1942.

Right: Their bow doors open, two landing ships prepare to disgorge their cargoes on the beaches of Leyte. The island was secured by January 1945.

ing force was equal to about half the Japanese strength in the islands, but the enemy was scattered. My force was concentrated. I intended my manoeuvre and surprise to bring a superior force to bear at the points of actual combat and, thereby, to destroy him piecemeal.

It is difficult even for one who was there to adequately describe the scene of the next two days. Ships to the front, to the rear, to the left, and to the right, as far as the eye could see. Their sturdy hulls ploughed the water, now presenting a broadside view, now their sterns, as they methodically carried out the zigzag tactics of evasion.

We came to Leyte just before midnight on a dark and moonless night. The stygian waters below and the black sky above seemed to conspire in wrapping us in an invisible cloak as we lay to and waited for dawn before entering Leyte Gulf. Phase one of the plan had been accomplished with little resistance. Now and then a ghostly ship would slide quietly by us, looming out of the night and disappearing into the gloom almost before its outlines could be depicted. I knew that on every ship nervous men lined the rails or paced the decks, peering into the darkness and wondering what stood out there beyond the night waiting for the dawn to come. There is a universal sameness in the emotions of men, whether they be admiral or sailor, general or private, at such a time as this. On almost every ship one could count on seeing groups huddled around maps in the ward-

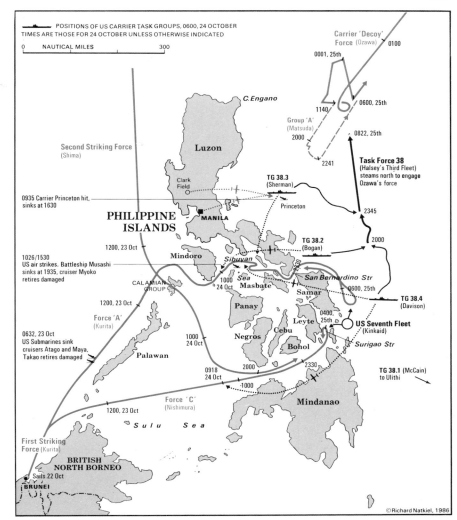

rooms, infantrymen nervously inspecting their rifles, the crews of the ships testing their gear, last-minute letters being written, men with special missions or objectives trying to visualize them again. For every man there were tons of supplies and equipment – trucks and vehicles of all kinds, and more than one ton of ammunition for every man who would storm those shores. Late that evening I went back to my cabin and read again those passages from the Bible from which I have always gained inspiration and hope. And I prayed that a merciful God would preserve each one of those men on the morrow.

The big guns on the ships opened fire at dawn. The noise, like rolling thunder, was all around us. The *Nashville*, her engines bringing to life the steel under our feet, knifed into Leyte Gulf. The ominous clouds of night still hung over the sea, fighting the sun for possession of the sky, but the blackness had given way to sombre grey, and even as we saw the black outlines of the shore on the horizon, the cloak of drabness began to roll back. On every side ships were riding toward the island. The battle for Leyte had already begun.

I was on the bridge with Captain C. E. Coney. His clear, keen eyes and cool, crisp voice swung the cruiser first to port, then to starboard as he dodged floating mines. An enemy periscope suddenly spouted up, only to be blotted out as destroyers closed in with roaring depth charges. And then, just as the sun rose clear of the horizon, there was Tacloban. It had changed little since I had known it forty-one years before on my first assignment after leaving West Point. It was a full moment for me.

Shortly after this, we reached our appointed position offshore. The captain carefully hove into line and dropped anchor. Our initial vantage point was two miles from the beaches, but I could cleary see the sandstrips with the pounding surf beating down upon the shore and, in the morning sunlight, the jungle-clad hills ris-

ing behind the town. Landings are explosive once the shooting begins, and now thousands of guns were throwing their shells with a roar that was incessant and deafening. Rocket vapour trails criss-crossed the sky and black, ugly, ominous pillars of smoke began to rise. High overhead, swarms of airplanes darted into the maelstrom. And across what would ordinarily have been a glinting, untroubled sea, the black dots of the landing craft churned toward the beaches.

From my vantage point, I had a clear view of everything that took place. Troops were going ashore at 'Red Beach', near Palo, at San Jose on 'White Beach' and at the southern tip of Leyte on tiny Panson Island. In the north, under Major-General Franklin C. Sibert, the X Corps, up of the 1st Cavalry and 24th Infantry Division; to the south, the XXIV Corps, under Major-General John R. Hodge, consisting of the 7th and 96th Infantry Divisions. In overall command of ground troops was Lieutenant-General Walter Kreuger of the Sixth Army.

At 'Red Beach' our troops secured a landing and began moving inland. I decided to go in

Above: MacArthur wades ashore on Leyte accompanied by US officers and officials of the exiled government of the Philippines.

Left: A scene from the Battle of the Sibuyan Sea, 24 October, the opening encounter of the naval struggle around Leyte. Despite the loss of one carrier and a cruiser, aircraft from two US carrier groups attacked Vice-Admiral Takeo Kurita's First Striking Force with some effect. Here, the Japanese battleship *Musashi* suffers a massive attack. Hits from 11 torpedoes and 19 bombs sealed the vessel's fate.

with the third assault wave. President Osmena, accompanied by General Basilio Valdez, the Philippine Army chief of staff, and General Carlos Romulo, my old aide, who had joined me on Bataan in 1942, had sailed with the convoy on one of the nearby transports. I took them into my landing barge and we started for the beach. Romulo, an old stalwart of the Quezon camp, was the resident commissioner for the Philippines in Washington. Noted for his oratorical ability, this popular patriot served on Bataan, and had been the radio 'Voice of Freedom' from Corregidor.

As we slowly bucked the waves toward 'Red Beach', the sounds of war grew louder. We could now hear the whining roar of airplane engines as they dove over our heads to strafe and bomb enemy positions inland from the beach. Then came the steady crump, crump of exploding naval shells. As we came closer, we could pick up the shouts of our soldiers as they gave the acknowledged orders. Then, unmistakably, in the near distance came the steady rattle of small-arms fire. I could easily pick up the peculiar fuzzy gurgle of a Japanese machine gun seemingly not more than 100 yards from the shoreline. The smoke from the burning palm trees was in our nostrils, and we could hear the continual snapping and crackling of flames. The coxswain dropped the ramp about 50 yards from shore, and we waded in. It took me only 30 or 40 long strides to reach dry land, but that was one of the most meaningful walks I ever took. When it was done, and I stood on the sand, I knew I was back again – against my old enemies of Bataan, for there, shining on the bodies of dead Japanese soldiers, I saw the insignia of the 16th Division, General Homma's ace unit.

Our beach-head troops were only a few yards away, stretched out behind logs and other cover, laying down fire on the area immediately inland. There were still Japanese in the undergrowth not many yards away. A mobile broadcasting unit was set up, and as I got ready to talk into the microphone, the rains came down. This is what I said:

'People of the Philippines: I have returned. By the grace of Almighty God, our forces stand again on Philippine soil – soil consecrated in the blood of our two peoples. We have come, dedicated and committed to the task of destroying every vestige of enemy control over your daily lives, and of restoring upon a foundation of indestructible strength, the liberties of your people.

'At my side is your President, Sergio Osmena, a worthy successor of that great patriot, Manuel Quezon, with members of his cabinet. The seat of your government is now, therefore, firmly re-established on Philippine soil.

'The hour of your redemption is here. Your patriots have demonstrated an unswerving and resolute devotion to the principles of freedom that challenge the best that is written on the pages of human history. I now call upon your supreme effort that the enemy may know, from the temper of an aroused people within, that he has a force there to contend with no less violent than is the force committed from without.

'Rally to me. Let the indomitable spirit of Bataan and Corregidor lead on. As the lines of battle roll forward to bring you within the zone of operations, rise and strike. Strike at every favourable opportunity. For your homes and hearths, strike! For future generations of your sons and daughters, strike! In the name of your sacred dead, strike! Let no heart be faint. Let every arm be steeled. The guidance of Divine God points the way. Follow in His name to the Holy Grail of righteous victory.'

President Osmena and I then walked off the beach, and picked our way into the brush behind the beach until we found a place to sit down. We had made our return and it was time to think of returning the government to constitutional authority. It was while we were finishing our discussion that the beach-head was subjected for the first time to an enemy bombing attack. It shook the log on which we sat, but that was all. As we finally got up to move, I noticed that the rain was no longer falling and that the only soldiers left near the beach were members of sniper patrols.

After inspecting the forward elements of our troops and the Tacloban airfield, I returned to the *Nashville*. That evening I ordered a coordinated attack by guerrillas all over the Philippines.

As I dropped off to sleep that night, the vision that danced before my tired eyes was not of bayonet, bullet, or bomb, but of an old, old man, a resident of Leyte, who stepped up to me amidst the shot and shell of the afternoon,

Top: Vice-Admiral Jisaburo Ozawa (1886-1966) led the Japanese Mobile Fleet at Leyte Gulf, where his vessels acted as decoys. He showed remarkable naval judgment in drawing Admiral Halsey's fleet away from the San Bernardino Strait on 24 October.

Above: Admiral Takeo Kurita (1889-1977) commanded the Close Support Force at Midway, but Leyte Gulf marked his debut as a senior officer in the Imperial Japanese Navy.

Left: The battleship *Yamato*, part of Kurita's force during the Battle of the Sibuyan Sea, is hit by a bomb. The damage was, however, light and the vessel survived to fight again. The strike was carried out by aircraft from the US Third Fleet which attacked the ship near the Tablas Strait.

welcoming me with outstretched arms. 'Good afternoon, Sir Field Marshal,' he said in his Visayan dialect. 'Glad to see you. It has been many years – a long, long time.'

The next two days our forces secured both the Tacloban area in the north and the Dulag area to the south, and continued to push inland in the face of increasing resistance. The airfields at Dulag proved to be unsuitable for immediate use because of numerous small swamps, the thick, sedimentary silt of the surrounding plain, and poor drainage. I established General Headquarters at Tacloban.

The Japanese recognized that we had made the most threatening move of the war to date. They knew, all too well, that if I succeeded, a half million of their best combat soldiers would be cut off to the south, without hope of support and with ultimate destruction at the leisure of the Allies a certainty. They placed in command of their Philippine forces their most distinguished general, Tomoyuk Yamashita. In 1942, General Yamashita had directed the brilliant drive down the Malayan peninsula to Singapore, and he was as confident of success in 1944 as he was then. He boastfully informed the world that 'the only words I spoke to the British Commander during negotiations for the surrender of Singapore were, "All I want to hear from you is yes or no". I expect to put the same question to MacArthur.' He was an able commander, much like those I had known in the Russo-Japanese war, but, unlike them, he talked too much.

In their desperation, the Japanese now prepared to stake their most valuable military asset, the Imperial fleet, on a gigantic gamble to

repel the invasion of Leyte and maintain their position in the Philippines. This determination to drive the Americans off the beaches was to very nearly succeed. It resulted in one of the great naval battles of modern times – actually four battles fought between 23 and 26 October 1944 – the Battle of Leyte Gulf.

The Japanese fleet had been in southern waters for many months, and Admiral Suemo Toyoda, its commander, maintained his flag at Singapore. As soon as he learned that the Americans had invaded Leyte in force, he assembled every ship in his command and set sail for his rendezvous with fate in the waters of Leyte Gulf.

As Admiral Toyoda later said in his memoirs:

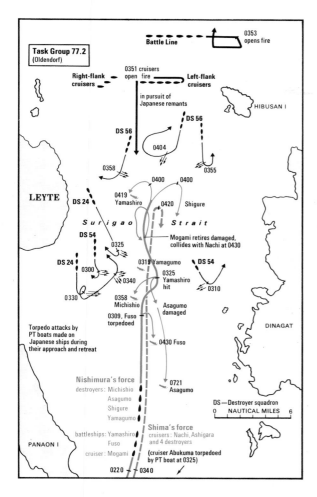

Map labels:
Task Group 77.2 (Oldendorf)

Battle Line
0353 opens fire

0351 cruisers open fire
Right-flank cruisers — Left-flank cruisers
in pursuit of Japanese remants

HIBUSAN I

DS 56
DS 56
0404
0358
0355

LEYTE
0419 Yamashiro
0400 0400
DS 24
0420 Shigure

Surigao *Strait*

DS 54
0325
Mogami retires damaged, collides with Nachi at 0430

DS 24
0319 Yamagumo DS 54
0300
0325 Yamashiro hit
0340
0310
0330
0358 Michishio
Asagumo damaged
0309, Fuso torpedoed

DINAGAT

Torpedo attacks by PT boats made on Japanese ships during their approach and retreat

0430 Fuso

0721 Asagumo

DS = Destroyer squadron
0 NAUTICAL MILES 6

Nishimura's force
destroyers: Michishio
Asagumo
Shigure
Yamagumo
battleships: Yamashiro
Fuso
cruiser: Mogami

Shima's force
cruisers: Nachi, Ashigara and 4 destroyers
(cruiser Abukuma torpedoed by PT boat at 0325)

PANAON I
0220 — 0340

Above: US destroyers take on Japanese vessels in the Surigao Strait. Some torpedo hits were scored against the Japanese: the battleship *Fuso* and three destroyers suffered mortal damage.

Above left: The night action in the Surigao Strait.

Force would pass through San Bernardino Strait north of Leyte, then set a course southward for Leyte Gulf. The Southern Force would pace its approach by way of the Mindanao Sea and Surigao Strait, so that both fleets in a co-ordinated pincer movement would converge simultaneously on the Allied flanks and attack the vulnerable 'soft shipping' unloading in Leyte Gulf. The Northern Force, in the Philippine Sea 300 miles north of San Bernardino Strait, was to decoy the powerful US Third Fleet from the protection of the entrance to Leyte Gulf.

'Since without the participation of our Combined Fleet [he stated] there was little possibility of the land-based forces in the Philippines having any chance against MacArthur, it was decided to send the whole fleet, taking the gamble. If things went well we might obtain unexpectedly good results, but if the worst should happen, there was a chance that we would lose the entire fleet, but I felt that that chance had to be taken. Should we lose the Philippine operations, even though the fleet should be left, the shipping lane to the south would be completely cut off so that the fleet, if it should come back to Japanese waters, could not obtain its fuel supply. If it should remain in southern waters, it could not receive supplies of ammunition and arms. There would be no sense in saving the fleet at the expense of the loss of the Philippines.'

Impressive and far-ranging, his plan was to deliver a paralysing blow at the US Navy and, with the strategic situation in his favour, to collapse my invasion of the beaches by the same attack. To manoeuvre their warships within firing distance of our troops and supply transports in the Leyte Gulf, the Japanese were ready to gamble the loss of their entire mobile fleet. They felt that one such chance would be decisive.

Admiral Toyoda divided the combined fleet into three distinct groups: a Central Force, under Admiral Takeo Kurita; a Southern Force (van) under Vice-Admiral Shoji Nishimura; and a Southern Force (rear) under Vice-Admiral Kiyohide Shima; a Northern Force, under Vice-Admiral Jisabuto Ozawa. The Central

Left: Vice-Admiral Marc Mitscher (1887-1947) commanded the US Task Force 38 during the Battle of Cape Engano, 25 October, which saw the destruction of Ozawa's carrier fleet.

In the crucible of the coming battle my own position was unique. The sweep of my forces along New Guinea had been consistently directed so that each operation would have available the full protection of my land-based air force. Every step forward had been governed by the basic concept of securing airfields no more than 200 or 300 miles apart from which to assure an 'air umbrella' over each progressive thrust into the enemy. By invading Leyte two months in advance of the original schedule, however, it became necessary to put my units on to beach-heads without my own guaranteed air protection. The US Navy, therefore, had a double responsibility. Initially, it had to assist the landing itself by its usual tasks of shore bombardment, convoy escort, and plane cover. In addition, it had the important mission of giving me further air support for a period of time beyond the landing date, until I could develop local airfields and stage my own air units forward from the south.

Should the naval covering forces allow either of the powerful advancing Japanese thrusts to penetrate into Leyte Gulf, the whole Philippine invasion would be placed in the gravest jeopardy. It was imperative, therefore, that every approach to the gulf be adequately guarded at all times, and that an enemy debouchment by way of either Surigao or San Bernardino Straits be blocked.

The naval forces protecting the Leyte invasion were disposed in two main bodies. The Seventh Fleet, under Vice-Admiral Thomas C. Kinkaid, protected the southern and western entrances to Leyte Gulf, while the stronger Third Fleet, under Admiral Halsey, operated off Samar to cover San Bernardino Strait and the approaches from the north and east. Admiral Halsey's immediate superior was Admiral Nimitz in Hawaii; Admiral Kinkaid was responsible to me, and was with me at Tacloban. While it was understood that such a division of command entailed certain disadvantages, it was theoretically, but wrongly, assumed in Washington that frequent consultation and co-operative liaison would overcome any difficulties in the way of proper co-ordination. The coming battle was to demonstrate the dangers involved in the lack of a unified command and the misunderstandings that can ensue during major operations in which the commander ultimately responsible does not have full control over all forces in the operation.

Up until 24 October, I had contented myself with daily expeditions ashore in order to keep in close touch with the action as it unfolded. I did not wish to add confusion on the beach-head in any way or to slow the flow of vital supplies ashore. The transportations of a large headquarters like my own, with all of its necessary communications and other equipment, was not imperative at that period. By 23 October, it had become apparent that the Japanese intended to commit their fleet. Admiral Kinkaid wanted to use the added firepower of the *Nashville* in the coming naval battle of the Seventh Fleet to the south. When we discussed this, I concurred. When word reached the Admiral that I intended to go along, he demurred. So did my staff. For some reason they felt that a 16-inch naval shell represented a greater peril to my person than all the tons of steel that the enemy was directing at the beach-head. All my life I had been reading and studying naval combat, and the glamour of sea battle had always excited my imagination. But Kinkaid was adamant. He said, 'I will not commit the *Nashville* as long as GHQ is aboard.' It was to be his fight, so I moved my headquarters ashore on the 24th, and the *Nashville* moved out to take its honoured position in the battleline.

For half a day on the 24th the Japanese Central Force under Admiral Kurita's command was under constant open attack by aircraft from the Third Fleet, while the enemy nervously threaded the dangerous reefs leading to San Bernardino. The *Musashi*, one of the newest and largest of Japan's battleships, mounting 18-inch guns, was sunk; its sister ship, the mighty *Yamato* was hit; one heavy cruiser was put out of action; other cruisers and destroyers were damaged. The increasing force of these aerial blows, together with the torpedoes of Seventh Fleet submarines, caused Admiral Kurita, who lacked air cover, to reverse his course for a time in order to reform his forces. This temporary withdrawal – executed at 3.33 in the afternoon – was later reported by hopeful airmen as a general retreat of Japanese Central Force. Admiral Kurita had no intention of abandoning his mission, however, and at 5.14 the force advanced again toward San Bernardino Strait. Shortly thereafter he received a message from Admiral Toyada in Tokyo: 'All forces will dash to the attack, trusting in divine assistance.'

In the meantime, Admiral Nishimura's

Below: One of the US torpedo boats that did so much to cripple the Japanese forces involved in the Surigao Strait action waits for the order to sail during the afternoon of 24 October.

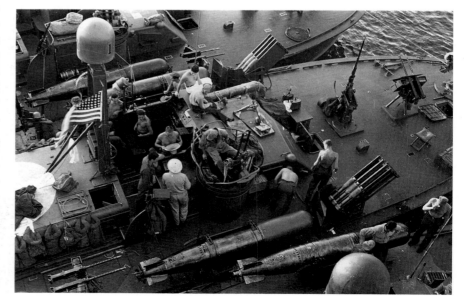

Far left: Vice-Admiral Shima, joint commander of the Japanese forces that received a mauling in the Surigao Strait.

Left: The USS *West Virginia* fires a broadside at the height of the Surigao Strait action.

Below: The Japanese battleship *Yamashiro*, accompanied by the cruiser *Mogami* attempts to avoid an air attack in the Sulu Sea. The *Mogami* was able to limp away badly damaged until she collided with the *Nachi*. The cruiser was sent to the bottom on the following day by aircraft from the Seventh Fleet.

Southern Force sailed doggedly on into the Mindanao Sea. Amply forewarned by sightings, Admiral Kinkaid had dispatched almost the whole of the Seventh Fleet's gunnery and torpedo force under Admiral Oldendorf to intercept and destroy the approaching Japanese fleet. Admiral Oldendorf deployed his PT squadrons at the entrance to Surigao Strait at a place where the Japanese would have to reform in columns to negotiate the narrow passage. Behind the torpedo boats, and covering the northern part of the strait, were posted the destroyer squadrons, cruisers and battleships to form a curtain of vast fire-power which the enemy would be forced to approach vertically as he moved forward.

The ambush worked perfectly. The Japanese fleet was practically annihilated. Only one lone destroyer escaped. The Japanese admiral went down with his flagship. This closed the southern entrance to Leyte Gulf.

In the late afternoon of the 24th, scout planes of the Third Fleet reported a large enemy task force, including several carriers, off the northeastern coast of Luzon, about 300 miles from San Bernardino Strait. Admiral Halsey apparently felt that Admiral Kinkaid's Seventh Fleet had ample strength with which to meet the Southern Force, and judging from his aviator's optimistic reports that the Central Force had been greatly damaged, had perhaps retired, and in all likelihood had been removed as a serious menace, estimated that the Northern

Force constituted the most potent danger to be met, and therefore decided to move his entire force northward to intercept it.

During the afternoon, Halsey had formed Task Force 34 as a strong surface force comprising four battleships, two heavy cruisers, three light cruisers, and fourteen destroyers. It was assumed that this task force would engage Admiral Kurita's force if it advanced. In the early evening Halsey informed Admiral Kinkaid and others of the position of the Japanese Central Force, and added that he was 'proceeding north with three groups to attack the enemy carrier forces at dawn'. Accordingly, on the evening of the 24th, he withdrew the battleships, carriers and supporting ships of the Third Fleet from San Bernardino Strait. It was a crucial decision, and no end of confusion and uncertainty followed his action. As the last battleships of the Third Fleet had been detached from the carrier groups and organized as Task Force 34, it was assumed that Task Force 34 was still guarding San Bernardino Strait. Although no definite statement had been made by Admiral Halsey, Admiral Kinkaid thought that the big battleships were standing by, awaiting the Japanese Central Force, and that Admiral Halsey was going after the Japanese Northern Force with carrier units. Actually, however, Admiral Halsey took his complete task groups on his run to the north, and left San Bernardino Strait open.

Unhampered movement through San Bernardino Strait was the kingpin of the enemy's strategy. Admiral Halsey did not know that Japan's carriers were to be deliberately sacrificed in a bold gamble to keep the Philippines from falling to the Allies. It was later revealed that the Northern Force of Admiral Ozawa, almost completely destitute of planes and pilots, had only one mission – to serve as a decoy and turn the most powerful units of the US fleet away from the Leyte area. It was expected that the Northern Force would probably be destroyed, but it was hoped that this desperate device would enable the Japanese Central Force to pass unmolested through the San Bernardino Strait and then move southward into Leyte Gulf.

To accomplish his mission, Admiral Ozawa continually sent out radio messages in an effort to advertise his position to the US fleet. An undetected fault in his transmission system, however, prevented the Third Fleet from intercepting these signals. Equally important to later operations, communication difficulties also prevented an exchange of information between the enemy's Northern and Central Forces.

During the night of the 24th Admiral Kurita led his warships through the treacherous passes of San Bernardino Strait in a dash that was a spectacular display of navigational skill. Shortly after midnight, he debouched into the

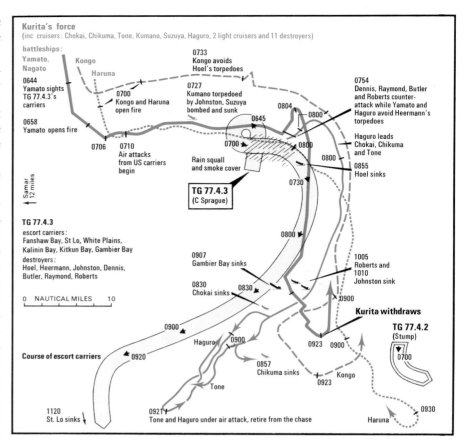

Philippine Sea. About 5.30 in the morning of the 25th, as he was coming down the coast of Samar, he received word of the disaster to the Southern Force of Admiral Nishimura. His was now the only Japanese force within striking distance of Leyte. The task of destroying the US invasion units rested solely in his hands.

At dawn on the 25th, a group of sixteen escort carriers, nine destroyers, and twelve destroyer escorts of the Seventh Fleet, under the command of Rear Admiral Thomas L. Sprague, was disposed east of Samar and Leyte Gulf. On a northerly course, they were directly in the path of Admiral Kurita's oncoming force. It soon became apparent that Halsey was

Above: The Battle of Samar, 25 October. The Japanese took a dangerously long time to savage the US escort carriers, allowing US reinforcements time to arrive on the scene. During the counter-attack three heavy cruisers (*Chokai, Chikuma* and *Suzuya*) were sunk; Kurita then withdrew.

Below: The flight-deck officer of a US carrier prepares for the launch of a F6F-3 Hellcat.

Left: Scene on the USS *Monterey* during the Leyte Gulf operations. The *Monterey* was part of Halsey's Third Fleet during the naval battles and fought in the Cape Engano encounter against the forces of Ozawa.

too far north to properly cover the Gulf of Leyte and so I radioed Nimitz asking him to drop Halsey back. This would not only protect my base, but would ensure his fleet being in the action, as the magnetic attraction of my point of landing would draw the enemy's fleet there. Three times I sent such dispatches, but without results. Nimitz repeated to Halsey, apparently without getting through, and then finally authorized me to communicate directly with Halsey, but it was then too late.

Through a series of fatal misunderstandings, directly attributed to divided command, ambiguous messages, and poor communications between the Third and Seventh Fleets, neither Admiral Kinkaid at Leyte Gulf nor Admiral Sprague off Samar realized that the exit from San Bernardino Strait had been left unguarded. During the night of the 24th, however, Admiral Kinkaid became uneasy concerning the actual situation at San Bernardino Strait and decided to check on the position of Task Force 34. At 4.12 a.m. on the 25th, he sent an urgent priority signal telling Admiral Halsey of the results in Surigao Strait and asking him the crucial question: 'Is Task Force 34 guarding San Bernardino Strait?' The reply was not dispatched until 7.04, by which time Admiral Kurita's battleships had opened fire off Samar. Admiral Halsey's answer said: 'Your 241912 negative. Task Force 34 is with carrier group now engaging enemy carrier force.'

It was a dramatic situation fraught with disaster. The forthcoming battle of Samar between the Seventh Fleet's slow and vulnerable 'jeep' carriers and the Japanese Central Force of

Below: A scene from the Battle of Samar, 25 October. US Task Group 77.4 under Rear-Admiral Sprague, was caught by ships under Kurita, and in the engagement the carrier *Gambier Bay* was sunk. Three other carriers, *Fenshaw Bay*, *Kalinin Bay* and *White Plains* were damaged.

greatly superior speed and firepower gave every promise of a completely unequal struggle. The light carriers of Admiral Sprague were no match for the great battleships and heavy carriers of the Japanese Central Force. Should the enemy gain entrance to Leyte Gulf, his powerful naval guns could pulverize any of the eggshell transports present in the area and destroy vitally needed supplies on the beach-head. The thousands of US troops ashore would be isolated and pinned down helplessly between enemy fire from ground and sea. Then, too, the schedule for supply reinforcement would not only be completely upset, but the success of the invasion itself would be placed in jeopardy. The battleships and cruisers of the Seventh Fleet were more than 100 miles away in Surigao Strait, their stock of heavy ammunition virtually exhausted by the preceding shore bombardment and the decisive early morning battle with the Japanese Southern Force. Halsey's Third Fleet was some 300 miles distant, still chasing the Northern Force, and could not possibly return in time to halt the progress of Admiral Kurita.

Ashore, all I had been able to do was call for carrier air cover over the Leyte beaches. Under the divided command set-up, I had no effective control over the Third Fleet. Having advanced beyond the range of my own land-based aircraft, I was completely dependent upon carrier planes for protection – a fact which I had emphatically made clear both before and during the planning for the invasion. In October, in discussion with Admiral Halsey, I had reiterated my conception of his mission by saying: 'The basic plan for this operation in which for the first time I have moved beyond my own land-based air cover was predicated upon full support by the Third Fleet; such land-based cover is being expedited by every possible measure, but until accomplished, our mass of shipping is subject to enemy air and surface raiding during this critical period. Consider your mission to cover this operation is essential and paramount.' Now I could do nothing but consolidate my troops on Leyte, tighten my lines of communication and wait the outcome of the impending naval battle around the island.

Admiral Kurita's Central Force had suffered considerable damage, yet it was still a powerful fleet. The main force was four fast battleships backed by nineteen smaller craft – eleven destroyers, and six heavy and two light cruisers. It was in quest of big game, its guns and shell hoists brimming with armour-piercing projectiles for use against our forces.

The battle was joined at 6.58 a.m. The *Yamato*'s 18-inch guns fired first, with the cruisers following as soon as they came within range. Never before had US warships been subjected to such heavy calibre fire. Admiral Kurita pressed the attack at full speed.

As soon as the enemy was sighted, Admiral Sprague's escort carriers changed course due east and began launching all available aircraft. Scarcely had the planes been sent aloft, when large-calibre shells began falling among the units of the formation. Admiral Kurita was closing rapidly, straddling the escort carriers with dye-marker salvoes which bracketed the area of their target with vivid splotches of red, yellow, green and blue. The situation was critical, and at 7.42 Admiral Kinkaid received a request for support. He promptly ordered Admiral Oldendorf 'to prepare to rendezvous his forces at the eastern end of Leyte Gulf'. The escort carriers' planes were sent the same order, and another dispatch was transmitted to Admiral Halsey requesting immediate aid.

Kurita's ships gradually closed, and his big batteries began to find the range. Along with these surface attacks, Japanese air units based

Above: One of the US escort carriers steams away from the battle against the Japanese forces of Kurita during the Samar action on 25 October. Despite their successes against the US carriers, the Japanese forces retired from the encounter, surrendering the initiative they had gained in the early stages of the engagement.

Below: Firefighters on the USS *Intrepid*, one of the eight carriers of the Third Fleet at Leyte, struggle to contain the fires started by a kamikaze attack.

in the Philippines launched a series of kamikaze strikes against the escort carriers. In his great distress, Admiral Kinkaid sent Admiral Halsey another dispatch: 'Urgently need fast battleships Leyte Gulf at once.' Meanwhile, the Third Fleet continued to steam northward in hot pursuit of the Japanese carrier group.

Admiral Sprague's escort carriers used every tactic of waterborne combat in their desperate struggle. Hit-and-run was the order of the day, heavy smokescreens were laid, temporary sanctuary sought in a providential rain squall. His destroyers and destroyer escorts fought back furiously. Interposing themselves between the carriers and their adversary, they boldly closed the range, and unleashed their fire with guns and torpedoes at cruiser and battleship targets. The planes from the escort carriers attacked continuously and put several cruisers out of action. They were gradually handicapped, however, by the damage inflicted on the carriers. The pilots seeing their carrier decks ripped open or their ships sunk, were forced to put down on Tacloban's already jammed airstrip. With General Kenney, I watched them with aching heart as, again and again, in endless stream they crashed in. Some also landed on the Dulag strip, while others were compelled at the last minute to ditch in Leyte Gulf.

With disaster staring him in the face, Admiral Kinkaid sent Admiral Halsey another urgent dispatch, which the latter received at nine o'clock: 'Our escort carriers being attacked by four battleships, eight cruisers plus others. Request Lee cover Leyte at top speed. Request fast carriers make immediate strike.' Admiral Lee commanded Task Force 34.

By this time ammunition aboard the escort carriers was running low; some of the destroyers had expended their torpedoes, and the torpedo planes were reduced to the dire expedient of making dummy runs on the enemy ships. Our losses had been very heavy. After two and a half hours of continuous battle, victory lay within Admiral Kurita's grasp.

In his desperation Admiral Kinkaid sent uncoded a last insistent plea to Admiral Halsey, this time in the clear: 'Where is Lee? Send Lee.' Back in Hawaii, thousands of miles away, Admiral Halsey's commander, Admiral Nimitz, had tried to contact the Third Fleet without success. He finally got through this

query almost simultaneously with Kinkaid's last message: 'The whole world wants to know where is Task Force 34.'

Then suddenly, Admiral Kurita broke off the engagement. His units had sustained much damage, and he was apparently unaware of the true battle situation. He ordered his forces to cease firing and to reassemble to the north. For the US carrier forces this retirement by the enemy meant a remarkable and completely unexpected escape. Admiral Sprague, in summing up the results of the battle shortly thereafter, stated: 'The failure of the enemy main body and encircling light forces to completely wipe out all vessels of this Task Unit can be attributed to our successful smokescreen, our torpedo counter-attack, continuous harassment of the enemy by bomb, torpedo and strafing air attacks, timely manoeuvres, and the definite partiality of Almighty God.'

The continuous and urgent dispatches from Admiral Kinkaid and the cryptic message from Admiral Nimitz caused Admiral Halsey to change course and direct the bulk of his fleet southward. He expected to arrive early next morning. His other units caught up with Admi-

ral Ozawa's fleet and in the battle of Cape Engano, inflicted much damage, but did not destroy it.

After regrouping his forces, Admiral Kurita decided to make one last attempt against Leyte Gulf. At 11.20, he ordered his ships to change course toward the target area to the southwest. He was *en route* approximately one hour, and was only 45 miles from his object, when he finally decided to give up the attempt. At 12.36, he ordered his ships about. He passed through San Bernardino Strait at 9.30 p.m. on 25 October. In the meantime, Admiral Halsey came racing down from the north with his big battleships. They were not to fire a shot, however, for when they arrived it was too late. Admiral Kurita had escaped.

I have never ascribed the unfortunate incidents of this naval battle to faulty judgement on the part of any of the commanders involved. The near disaster can be placed squarely at the door of Washington. In the naval action, two key American commanders were independent of each other, one under me, and the other under Admiral Nimitz 5,000 miles away, both operating in the same waters and in the same

Above: The Japanese carrier *Zuiho* takes evasive measures during the Battle of Cape Engano. Vice-Admiral Halsey caught Ozawa's Northern Force unprepared. Six waves of US aircraft destroyed four carriers, the *Chitose*, *Zuikaku*, *Zuiho* and *Chiyoda*, and damaged a light cruiser, the *Tama*, which was later sunk by a US submarine.

Right: A Japanese carrier turns to avoid an attack by aircraft from the USS *Enterprise*, 25 October.

Above: The *Zuikaku* bears the brunt of a US strike during the Battle of Cape Engano. Despite their success the forces of Halsey broke off their pursuit of Ozawa's fleet to attempt an attack on the vessels of Kurita.

Left: The Battle of Cape Engano, perhaps the decisive moment of the naval operations off Leyte.

battle. The Seventh Fleet to my force performed magnificently, as they always had, and always would, and Admiral Kinkaid wrote his name in this engagement among the greatest leaders in our naval annals.

To Admiral Nimitz I sent this message regarding the conduct of his units:

At this time I wish to express to you and to all elements of your fine command my deep appreciation of the splendid service they have rendered in the recent Leyte operations. Their record needs no amplification from me, but I cannot refrain from expressing the admiration everyone here feels for their magnificent conduct. All of your elements – ground, naval, and air – have alike covered themselves with glory. We could not have gone along without them. To you my special thanks for your sympathetic and understanding co-operation.

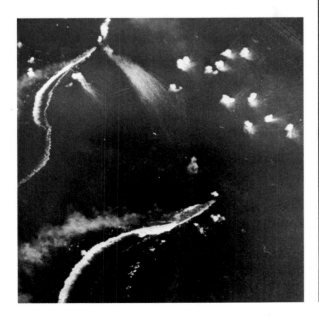

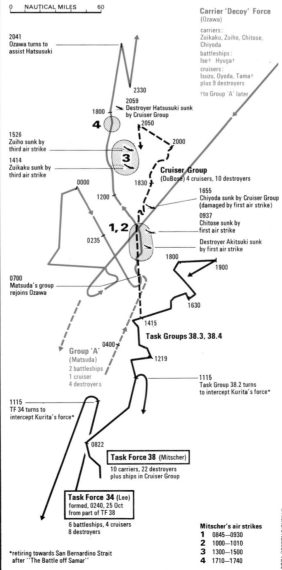

Carrier 'Decoy' Force (Ozawa)

carriers: Zuikaku, Zuiho, Chitose, Chiyoda
battleships: Ise†, Hyuga†
cruisers: Isuzu, Oyoda, Tama†
plus 9 destroyers
†to Group 'A' later

2041 Ozawa turns to assist Hatsusuki

2059 Destroyer Hatsusuki sunk by Cruiser Group

1526 Zuiho sunk by third air strike

1414 Zuikaku sunk by third air strike

Cruiser Group (DuBose) 4 cruisers, 10 destroyers

1655 Chiyoda sunk by Cruiser Group (damaged by first air strike)

0937 Chitose sunk by first air strike

Destroyer Akitsuki sunk by first air strike

0700 Matsuda's group rejoins Ozawa

Task Groups 38.3, 38.4

Group 'A' (Matsuda) 2 battleships 1 cruiser 4 destroyers

1115 Task Group 38.2 turns to intercept Kurita's force*

1115 TF 34 turns to intercept Kurita's force*

Task Force 38 (Mitscher)
10 carriers, 22 destroyers plus ships in Cruiser Group

Task Force 34 (Lee) formed, 0240, 25 Oct from part of TF 38
6 battleships, 4 cruisers 8 destroyers

*retiring towards San Bernardino Strait after "The Battle off Samar"

Mitscher's air strikes
1 0845—0930
2 1000—1010
3 1300—1500
4 1710—1740

©Richard Natkiel, 1986

Strategy 1944

by Dwight D. Eisenhower

One of the great controversies of the Second World War concerns the proper Allied strategy after the breakout from Normandy.

The Ardennes offensive of December may be taken as evidence that the Germans were not so spent as some thought.

Hitler's Germany was eventually ground to pieces before the upper millstone of the Russian armies and the nether millstone of the Western Allies. With the Russians the other side of the Vistula would it really have profited Eisenhower to get into the Ruhr? Would this really have shortened the war and saved thousands of Allied lives? In the nature of things we shall never know. Certainly to have launched the Arnhem operation *before* opening up the approaches to Antwerp seems strange strategy at a time when the Allies were being maintained over a long line of communications to the open beaches of Normandy. Neither Eisenhower nor Montgomery were men to treat logistical problems lightly, which makes the study of these events even more rewarding.   EDITOR

These pages: A US M10 tank-destroyer in position behind a relic from the campaign of 1940 – a smashed bunker on the Maginot Line.

Chronology

1944

6 June	D-Day.
7 June	Capture of Cherbourg.
9 July	Capture of Caen.
20 July	The Bomb Plot. Hitler wounded.
30 July	Patton breaks out of the Normandy beach-head.
1 Aug.	Eisenhower assumes command in France.
6/7 Aug.	The Germans' Avranches offensive.
15 Aug.	Operation Anvil. Allies land in south of France.
25 Aug.	Liberation of Paris.
28 Aug.	Capture of Marseilles.
3 Sept.	Liberation of Brussels.
4 Sept.	Fall of Antwerp.
17 Sept.	Operation Market Garden.
20 Oct.	Americans take Aachen.
8 Nov.	Fall of Walcheren.
28 Nov.	First Allied convoy reaches Antwerp.
16 Dec.	Ardennes offensive begins.

Pursuit and the Battle of Supply

During the period of the Battle of the Beachhead the enemy kept his Fifteenth Army concentrated in the Calais region. He was convinced that we intended to launch an amphibious attack against that fortress stronghold and as a result stubbornly refused to use those forces to reinforce the Normandy garrison. We employed every possible ruse to confirm him in his misconception; General McNair, for instance, was in the European theatre so that we could refer to him, semi-publicly, as an army commander, although his army was a phantom only. His name was kept on the censored list, but we took care to see that, in the United Kingdom, the secret was an open one. Thus any Axis agent would feel certain that knowledge of his presence was important information, to be passed promptly to the Germans, who, we hoped, would interpret his 'army's' mission to be an assault against the Pas de Calais front.

Finally the enemy began to obtain a clearer view of the situation; we quickly knew this. Identification of hostile units on the front is one of the continuous objectives of all battlefield intelligence activities. From this information we daily constructed, normally with remarkable accuracy, the 'Enemy Order of Battle', which revealed in late July that the Germans had started the divisions of the Fifteenth Army across the Seine to join in the battle. They were too late. Every additional soldier who then came into the Normandy area was merely caught up in the catastrophe of defeat, without exercising any particular influence upon the battle. In that defeat were involved, also, a number of divisions that the enemy had been able to spare from the south of France, from Brittany, from Holland, and also from Germany itself. When the total of these reinforcements had not proved equal to the task of stopping us, the enemy was momentarily helpless to present any continuous front against our advance.

When General Patton's Third Army Headquarters came into action on 1 August our ground organization expanded to four armies. On the right was the US Third Army under General Patton. Next to him the US First Army under General Hodges. These two, forming the US Twelfth Army Group, were under command of General Bradley. On the left was the British Twenty-first Army Group under General Montgomery. His group comprised the British Second Army under General Dempsey and the Canadian First Army under Lieutenant-General Henry D. G. Crerar. The British Air Force supporting General Montgomery's army group was commanded by Air Marshal Coningham. General Bradley's army group was supported by the US Ninth Air Force commanded by Major-General Hoyt S. Vandenberg. Subordinate to General Vandenberg were Major-General Otto R. Weyland, in charge of the tactical Air Command supporting General

---

General of the Army
Dwight D. Eisenhower
(1890-1969)

Born in Texas of a family of German Mennonites, who had emigrated in the 1730s, Eisenhower graduated from West Point in 1916, but saw no active service in the First World War. After serving on MacArthur's staff in the Philippines (1935-9) he held high staff appointments during the early years of the Second World War. He commanded the Allied Armies in North Africa, Sicily and Italy before being given command of the European invasion forces. He had a great gift for running a harmonious and co-operative Allied team. He had no battle experience at the tactical level, and there is no evidence that he was at home in this field. On the other hand he had a remarkable grasp of logistics and staffwork, as well as a good knowledge of the historical background of the profession of arms. He had men of strong character under him – Patton, Montgomery and Bradley – and needed firmness and tact as well as strategic insight to achieve final victory.

General Eisenhower was commander of the American Occupation Zone of Germany (1945); Chief of Staff US Army (1945-8); President of Columbia University (1948); Supreme Commander of the North Atlantic Treaty Forces in Europe (1950-2) and President of the United States (1953-61).

His publications include *Crusade in Europe, Mandate for Change, The White House Years* and *Waging Peace*, 1956-61.

Below: The partially burnt-out wreck of a Tiger tank belonging to the SS *Liebstandarte* Division lies amid the ruins of a Normandy village.

Patton's Third Army, and Major-General Elwood R. Quesada, who commanded the air units supporting Hodges' army.

In each of these armies and army groups the normal mission of the associated air forces was to carry out attacks requested by the respective ground commanders. However, all tactical air units were subordinated to Leigh-Mallory and consequently all, both American and British, could in emergency be employed as a mass against any target designated by SHAEF. A typical example of unified action was the work of the British air force in helping to defeat the German attack against Mortain in Bradley's sector. Owing to this flexibility in command, the Tactical Air Forces were also available, when needed, to support the big bombers, even when the bombers were proceeding to penetrations deep within Germany.

By the end of August the approximate strength of the Allied forces on the Continent was twenty American divisions, twelve British divisions, three Canadian divisions, one French, and one Polish division. There were no more British divisions available, but in the United Kingdom were an additional six American divisions, including three airborne. The operational strength of all available air forces was approximately 4,035 heavy bombers, 1,720 light, medium, and torpedo bombers, and 5,000 fighters. Added to all this was the Troop Transport Command, which, counting both American and British formations, numbered more than 2,000 transport planes.

Against a defeated and demoralized enemy almost any reasonable risk is justified and the success attained by the victor will ordinarily be measured in the boldness, almost foolhardiness, of his movements. The whole purpose of the costly break-through and the whirlwind attacks of the succeeding three weeks was to

produce just such a situation as now confronted us; we had been preparing our plans so as to reap the richest harvest from the initial success. But the difficulties of supply, once our columns began their forward race, was a problem that required effective solution if we were to gain our full battle profit.

Our logistic formations had been confined in a very restricted area during the entire Battle of the Beach-head. The only operating ports were Cherbourg and the artificial port on the British beaches near Arromanches. The repair of Cherbourg had presented many difficulties. The harbour and approaches had to be cleared of hundreds of mines, many of them of new and particularly efficient types. We began using the port in July, but it did not reach volume production until the middle of August. The artifi-

Above: General George Patton, commander of the US Third Army, Lieutenant Omar Bradley commander of the 12th Army Group, and General Bernard Montgomery, commander 21st Army Group, meet to discuss the breakout from Normandy, 7 July 1944.

Left: Members of the US 101st Airborne Division cautiously advance past the bodies of their comrades, victims of a well-hidden sniper, Carentan, 14 June 1944.

cial port on the American beaches had been completely demolished in the June storm. From Arromanches and Cherbourg we had not been able to project forward the roads, railways, and dumps as we would have done had our breakout line actually been as far to the southward as the base of the Cotentin Peninsula, where we originally expected it to be. All our marching columns, therefore, had to be supplied from stocks located near the beaches and over roads and railways that had to be repaired as we advanced.

These meagre facilities could not support us indefinitely and there was bound to be a line somewhere in the direction of Germany where we would be halted, if not by the action of the enemy, then because our supply lines had been strained to their elastic limit.

A reinforced division, in active operations, consumes from 600 to 700 tons of supplies per day. When battling in a fixed position, most of this tonnage is represented in ammunition; on the march the bulk is devoted to petrol and lubricants, called, in the language of the supply officer, POL.

With thirty-six divisions in action we were faced with the problem of delivering from beaches and ports to the front lines some 20,000 tons of supplies every day. Our spearheads, moreover, were moving swiftly, frequently seventy-five miles per day. The supply service had to catch these with loaded trucks. Every mile of advance doubled the difficulty because the supply truck had always to make a two-way run to the beaches and back, in order to deliver another load to the marching troops. Other thousands of tons had to go in advanced airfields for construction and subsequent maintenance. Still additional amounts were required for repair of bridges and roads, for which heavy equipment was necessary.

During the days that we were roped off in the beach-head we could not foresee the exact reaction of the enemy following upon a successful breakout on our right. His most logical move

appeared to be a swinging of his troops back toward the Seine, to defend the crossings of that river. If he had chosen to do this he could undoubtedly have made a stubborn defence of that obstacle until our advancing troops were able to outflank him and force evacuation.

If we had been compelled to fight a general battle on the Seine our lines of communications would have been relatively short and the logistic problem would have been solved gradually, conforming to the pace that our own troops could advance. However, when the enemy decided, under Hitler's insistence, to stand where he was and to counter-attack against the flank of our marching columns at Mortain the entire prospect was changed.

We grasped eagerly at the opportunity to swing in from the south against his rear in the attempt to accomplish a complete destruction of all his forces, because, if we were successful, then the intermediate battles that we had always calculated as possibilities on the Seine and the Somme would not be fought and our problem became a calculation of the furthermost line we could hope to reach before we completely outran supply.

Above: Sherman tanks, mounting a mixture of 75mm and 17-pounder guns, part of the East Riding Yeomanry, support the drive on Caen.

Left: A scene from the push out of the Normandy beach-head. British troops advance through a smokescreen to attack the village of Tilly-sur-Seulles, 26 June 1944.

Consequently, while General Bradley was swinging the mass of his forces in toward the German rear it became necessary for me to review our entire plan of campaign to determine what major changes this new development would indicate as desirable.

The two most hopeful probabilities then presented to us were the early capture of Marseilles, far in the south, and of Antwerp, in Belgium. Possession of this latter port, if usable, would solve our logistic problems for the entire northern half of our front. Not only was Antwerp the greatest port in Europe, but its location, well forward toward the borders of Germany, would reduce our rail and truck haulage to the point where supply should no longer be a limiting factor in the prosecution of the campaign, at least in the northern sectors.

We hoped for the early use of Marseilles because the Germans had already largely denuded that area of mobile divisions, and speedy capture should prevent extensive demolition. Final success in that region would afford the right flank of the Allies the best possible supply lines. Through that avenue would pour early reinforcements from the United States, and the capacity of the magnificent railway lines running up the valley of the Rhône was so great that after they were once operating we should have no great difficulty with the logistic support of any part of our lines south of the Luxembourg region.

To make full use of these two probabilities it was, of course, important that the right flank of our own armies join up as quicky as possible with General Devers' Sixth Army Group, which would be coming up from the south. At the same time we had thrust toward the north-

east with great strength. In this way we would, incidentally, quickly clear the area from which the V-1 and V-2 bombs had been consistently bombarding southern England. But the principal object was the early capture of Antwerp, with a line to the eastward thereof that would protect us in the use of that great port.

All this conformed to original plans except that the prospect of a speedy instead of a fighting advance promised early use of the ports further north and lessened our dependence upon the Brittany ports. But the problem remaining to be determined was whether or not our supply system, handicapped as it had been through all the first seven weeks of the battle, could support our movements up to and including the accomplishment of these purposes.

All units were certainly going to be short of supply. The task was to allot deficits so as to

Above: US infantry and armor move through the town of St Lô. The capture of this town allowed units of the US First Army to fan out for Brittany and Paris.

Left: Göring (fourth from left) surveys the devastation caused by the bomb explosion at Hitler's headquarters at Rastenberg on 20 July.

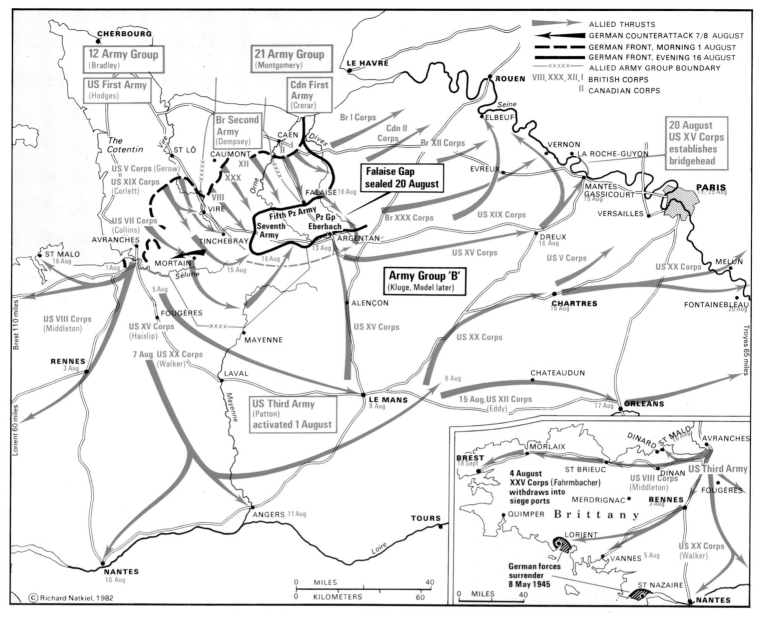

Map labels:

CHERBOURG
12 Army Group (Bradley)
US First Army (Hodges)
21 Army Group (Montgomery)
LE HAVRE
Cdn First Army (Crerar)
ROUEN
Seine
ELBEUF
The Cotentin
ST LÔ
Vire
CAUMONT
Br Second Army (Dempsey)
CAEN
Dives
Br I Corps
Cdn II Corps
Br XII Corps
VERNON
LA ROCHE-GUYON
US V Corps (Gerow)
US XIX Corps (Corlett)
XII
XXX
Orne
VIII
VIRE
Falaise Gap sealed 20 August
FALAISE 16 Aug
EVREUX
MANTES GASSICOURT 19 Aug
PARIS 19/25 Aug
20 August US XV Corps establishes bridgehead
US VII Corps (Collins)
AVRANCHES
TINCHEBRAY
Fifth Pz Army
Seventh Army
Pz Gp Eberbach
13 Aug
ARGENTAN
Br XXX Corps
US XIX Corps
VERSAILLES
ST MALO 16 Aug
MORTAIN
Sélune
16 Aug
15 Aug
Army Group 'B' (Kluge, Model later)
DREUX 16 Aug
US XV Corps
US V Corps
US XX Corps
MELUN
1 Aug
5 Aug
ALENÇON
FOUGÈRES
US VIII Corps (Middleton)
US XV Corps (Haislip)
MAYENNE
US XV Corps
US XX Corps
CHARTRES 16 Aug
FONTAINEBLEAU 20 Aug
Brest 110 miles
RENNES 3 Aug
7 Aug US XX Corps (Walker)
LAVAL
Mayenne
6 Aug
CHATEAUDUN
Troyes 65 miles
Lorient 60 miles
US Third Army (Patton) activated 1 August
LE MANS 8 Aug
15 Aug, US XII Corps (Eddy)
17 Aug
ORLEANS
ANGERS 11 Aug
Loire
TOURS
NANTES 10 Aug

MILES 0 40
KILOMETERS 0 60

Legend:
ALLIED THRUSTS
GERMAN COUNTERATTACK 7/8 AUGUST
GERMAN FRONT, MORNING 1 AUGUST
GERMAN FRONT, EVENING 16 AUGUST
xxxxx ALLIED ARMY GROUP BOUNDARY
VIII, XXX, XII, I BRITISH CORPS
II CANADIAN CORPS

Inset map (Brittany):
MORLAIX
DINARD ST MALO 16 Aug
AVRANCHES
BREST 18 Sept
ST BRIEUC
DINAN
US VIII Corps (Middleton)
US Third Army
4 August XXV Corps (Fahrmbacher) withdraws into siege ports
MERDRIGNAC
RENNES 3 Aug
FOUGÈRES
QUIMPER
Brittany
LORIENT
VANNES 5 Aug
US XX Corps (Walker)
German forces surrender 8 May 1945
ST NAZAIRE
NANTES

MILES 0 40

avoid stopping troops before they had accomplished their main objectives, and this in turn meant that no formation could get one pound of supply over and above that needed for basic missions.

When action is proceeding as rapidly as it did across France during the hectic days of late August and early September every commander from division upward becomes obsessed with the idea that with only a few more tons of supply he could rush right on and win the war. This is the spirit that wins wars and is always to be encouraged. Initiative, confidence, and boldness are among the most admirable traits of the good combat leader. As we dashed across France and Belgium each commander, therefore, begged and demanded priority over all others and it was undeniable that in front of each were opportunities for quick exploitation that made the demands completely logical.

In the late summer of 1944 it was known to us that the Germans still had disposable reserves within his own country. Any idea of attempting to thrust forward a small force, bridge the

Rhine, and continue on into the heart of Germany was completely fantastic. Even had such a force been able to start with a total of ten or a dozen divisions – and it is certain no more could have been supported even temporarily – the attacking column would have gradually grown smaller as it dropped off units to protect its flanks and would have ended up facing inescapable defeat. Such an attempt would have played into the hands of the enemy.

The more the entire situation was studied the more it became clear that the plan arrived at through weeks and months of earnest study was still applicable, even though the immediate conditions under which it would be executed did not conform to the detailed possibilities we had projected into the operation. Consequently I decided that we would thrust forward on our right to a point of junction with General Devers' forces, which we believed would be in the region of Dijon, while on the left Montgomery would be ordered to push forward as rapidly as possible, to make certain of securing a line that would adequately cover Antwerp. Bradley

Above: The Allied breakout from Normandy, August 1944. An estimated 50,000 men of the German Fifth and Seventh Armies were captured in the Falaise pocket.

directed Hodges' First Army to advance abreast of the British formations, roughly in the general direction of Aachen, so as to make certain of success on our left.

We hoped that this northeastward thrust would go so rapidly and that the collapse of the Germans would be so great that we might even gain, before the inevitable halt came about, a bridgehead over the Rhine, which would immediately threaten the Ruhr.

It was under this general plan that the battling of the succeeding weeks took place.

While affairs on the front of the Twelfth and Twenty-first Army Groups were proceeding in such satisfactory fashion, Lieutenant-General Alexander M. Patch's Seventh Army was achieving remarkable results in the south of France. At the conference of Allied war leaders at Teheran, in late 1943, the western Allies had informed Generalissimo Stalin that a secondary movement into the south of France would be an integral part of our invasion across the Channel to establish the second front in Europe. However, in early 1944 the Allies were waging one campaign in Italy and were planning for the great adventure of Overlord. During all the first half of 1944, therefore, it was impossible for General Wilson, commanding in the Mediterranean, to secure estimates of what might be available for the Dragoon attack.

My decision in January that the Overlord attack must be carried out on a front of five divisions had made it impossible to launch the Dragoon attack simultaneously with the Overlord landing, as had been originally planned. A vast amount of study and telegraphic correspondence subsequently developed between the Combined Chiefs of Staff, General Wilson, and my headquarters concerning the wisdom of persisting in the plan. From the beginning I had been an ardent advocate of this secondary attack and never in all the long period of discussion would I agree to its elimination from our plans. In this position I was supported by General Marshall.

All these arguments and discussion were now definitely things of the past and we were assured that very shortly there would be a force, to be constituted as General Devers' Sixth Army Group, of at least ten American and French divisions in southern France driving northward to join us and that these would be followed quickly by reinforcing divisions from the United States. There was no development of that period which added more decisively to our advantages or aided us more in accomplishing the final and complete defeat of the German forces than did this secondary attack coming up the Rhône Valley.

Because of the distance of General Patch's troops from my headquarters and the lack of communications, it had been arranged that General Wilson was to retain operational control of that force until it was possible for me to

establish the machinery for command. This date was estimated as 15 September. However, from the beginning of the southern invasion all battle fronts in France really became one, and all plans, both tactical and logistical, were devised upon the assumption that soon the whole would constitute one continuous order of battle. This we wanted to bring about quickly, and with the conclusion of the fighting on the Seine at the end of August, Bradley ordered Patton's Third Army to push eastward with a primary mission of linking up quickly with the Seventh Army to form a continuous front.

The remainder of the Allied forces continued their generally northeastern direction of advance to liberate Belgium, seize Antwerp, and threaten the Ruhr. This advance was conducted on a wide front and involved many

Above: A US patrol moves through the ruins of a French town. Note the extra turret armor on the knocked-out Panzer IV.

Below: A column of German horse-drawn artillery blasted by Allied ground-attack aircraft bears testimony to the scale of the Wehrmacht's losses in the Falaise pocket.

256

incidents of marches and battles that will be told only in detailed history. For example, the American VII and XIX Corps advanced so rapidly that in the vicinity of Mons, location of one of the great battles of the First World War, they trapped between them an entire German corps. After a fierce engagement 25,000 prisoners were taken. In ordinary times this would have been acclaimed as a great victory. But the times were far from ordinary and the incident passed almost unnoticed in the press.

The liberation of Paris on 25 August had a great impact on people everywhere. Even the doubters began to see the end of Hitler. By this time enemy losses were enormous. Since our landings three of the enemy's field-marshals and one army commander had been dismissed from their posts or incapacitated by wounds. Rommel was badly wounded by one of our strafing planes on 19 July. Some months later he committed suicide to escape trial for alleged complicity in the 20 July murder plot against Hitler. One army commander, three corps commanders, and fifteen division commanders had been killed or captured. The enemy had lost 400,000 killed, wounded, or captured. Half the total were prisoners of war, and 135,000 of these had been taken in the month subsequent to 25 July.

German matériel losses included 1,300 tanks, 20,000 other vehicles, 500 assault guns, and 1,500 pieces of artillery. In addition the German air force had suffered extensively. More than 3,500 of his aircraft had been destroyed and this in spite of the fact that the *Luftwaffe* had been seriously depleted before the invasion began.

There was a definite drop in enemy morale. So far as prisoners were concerned this was more noticeable among the higher officers because they, with professional training, could see the inevitability of final defeat. But the army as a whole had clearly not yet reached the stage of mass collapse and there was no question that the German divisions, given decent conditions, were still capable of putting up fierce resistance against our advance.

With the capture of Paris we were substantially on the line that had been predicted before D-Day as the one we would attain three to four months after our landing. Thus, in long-term estimate, we were two weeks ahead of schedule, but in the important particular of supply capacity we were badly behind. Because almost the entire area had been captured in the swift movements subsequent to 1 August, the roads, railway lines, depots, repair shops, and the base installations, required for the maintenance of continuous forward movement, were still far to the rear of the front lines.

When the German forces succeeded, in spite of defeat and disorder, in withdrawing significant numbers of their troops across the Seine, there still remained the hope of constructing

another trap for them before they could reorganize and present an effective defensive front. Portions of the German Fifteenth Army still remained in the Calais area, where they would provide a stiffening core for the retreating troops of the First and Seventh Armies. It was considered possible that some resistance would be attempted along one of the natural defences provided by the waterways of Belgium. A surprise vertical envelopment by airborne troops appeared to offer the best hope of encirclement if the enemy chose to make a stand.

As quickly as the defeat of the Germans on the Normandy front became certain, airborne forces were directed to prepare plans for drops in a number of successive positions, the appropriate spot to be selected when the developing situation should indicate the one of greatest promise. The mere paper planning of such operations was, while laborious, a simple matter. However, when actual preparation for a planned drop was undertaken, delicately

Above: Parisians scatter for cover as a German sniper opens fire on a large crowd celebrating the Allied liberation of the French capital, 26 August 1944.

Below: Members of the US 2nd Infantry Division prepare to move into the Brittany port of Brest. This vital city fell on 18 September after a heroic defense by its German garrison.

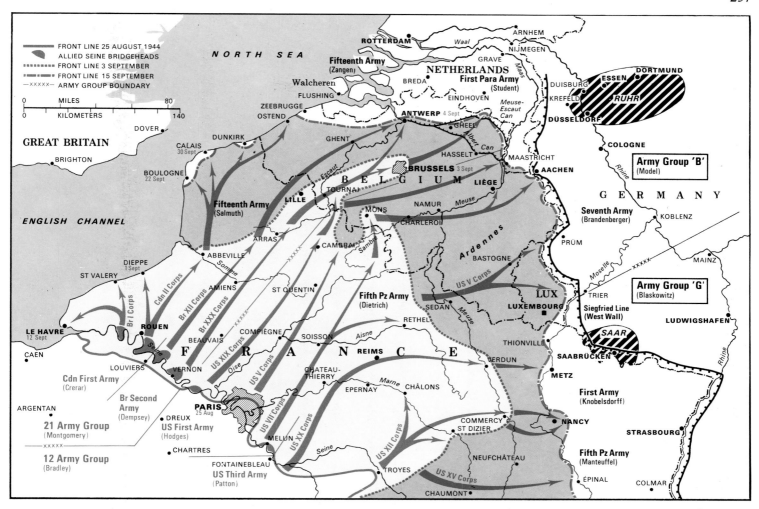

balanced alternatives presented themselves. Preparation for airborne attack required the withdrawal of transport planes from supply purposes, and it was difficult at times to determine whether greater results could not be achieved by continuing the planes in supply activity.

Unfortunately this withdrawal of planes from other work had to precede an airborne operation by several days, to provide time for refitting equipment and for briefing and retraining of crews. In late August, with our supply situation growing constantly more desperate, and with all of us eagerly following combat progress in the search for another prospect of cutting off great numbers of the enemy, the question of the Transport Command employment came up for daily discussion. On the average, allowing for all kinds of weather, our planes could deliver about 2,000 tons a day to the front. While this was only a small percentage of our total deliveries, every ton was so valuable that the decision was a serious one.

It appeared to me that a fine chance for launching a profitable airborne attack was developing in the Brussels area, and though there was divided opinion on the wisdom of withdrawing planes from supply work because of the uncertainty of the opportunity, I decided to take the chance. The Troop Carrier Command, on 10 September, was withdrawn temporarily

from supply missions to begin intensive preparation for an airborne drop in the Brussels area. But it quickly became clear that the Germans were retreating so fast as to make the effort an abortive one. Except with rearguards, the Germans made no attempt to defend in that region at all.

All along the front we pressed forward in hot pursuit of the fleeing enemy. In four days the British spearheads, parallelled by equally forceful American advances on their right, covered a distance of 195 miles, one of the many fine feats of marching by our formations in the great pursuit across France. By 5 September, Patton's Third Army reached Nancy and crossed the Moselle River between that city and Metz. Hodges' First Army came up against the Siegfried defences by the 13th of the month and was shortly thereafter to begin the struggle for Aachen. Pushed back against the borders of the homeland, the German defences showed definite signs of stiffening. On 4 September, Montgomery's armies entered Antwerp and we were electrified to learn that the Germans had been so rapidly hustled out of the place that they had had no time to execute extensive demolitions. Marseilles had been captured on 28 August and this great port was being rehabilitated.

These developments assured eventual solution of our logistical problem, which meant that within a reasonable time we would be in

Left: General Charles de Gaulle, leader of the exiled French authorities, marches in triumph down the Champs Elysées.

position to wage on the German border a battle of a scale and intensity that the enemy could not hope to match. However, there was much to be done before we could be in this fortunate position, and we had little remaining elasticity in our over-strained supply lines. On the south Patch's and Bradley's forces had to make a junction, and railway lines up the Rhône would have to be repaired. On the north we were faced by even greater difficulties.

Antwerp is an inland port connected with the sea by the great Scheldt Estuary. The German defences covering these approaches were still intact and before we could make use of the port we had the job of clearing out those defences.

The task on the north comprised three parts. We had to secure a line far enough to the eastward to cover Antwerp and the roads and railways leading out of it toward the front. We had to reduce the German defences in the areas lying between that city and the sea. Finally, I hoped to thrust forward spearheads as far as we could, to include a bridgehead across the Rhine if possible, so as to threaten the Ruhr and facilitate subsequent offensives.

On Montgomery's flank the question for immediate decision became the priority in which these tasks should be taken up. As a first requisite our lines had to be advanced far enough to the eastward to cover Antwerp securely, else the port and all its facilities would be useless to us. This had to be done without delay; until it was accomplished the other tasks could not even be started. Equally clear was the fact that, until the approaches to the port were

cleared, it was of no value to us. Because the Germans were firmly dug in on the islands of South Beveland and Walcheren, this was going to be a tough and time-consuming operation. The sooner we could set about it the better. But the question remaining was whether or not it was advantageous, before taking on the arduous task of reducing the Antwerp approaches, to continue our eastward plunge against the still retreating enemy with the idea of securing a possible bridgehead across the Rhine in proximity to the Ruhr.

While we were examining the various factors of the question, Montgomery suddenly presented the proposition that, if we would support his Twenty-first Army Group with all the supply facilities available, he could rush right on into Berlin and, he said, end the war. I am certain that Field-Marshal Montgomery, in the light of later events, would agree that this view was a mistaken one. But at the moment his enthusiasm was fired by the rapid advances of the preceding week and, since he was convinced that the enemy was completely demoralized, he vehemently declared that all he needed was adequate supply in order to go directly into Berlin.

Eisenhower and Montgomery met in Brussels on 10 September.

I explained to Montgomery the condition of our supply system and our need for early use of Antwerp. I pointed out that, without railway bridges over the Rhine and ample stockage of supplies on hand, there was no possibility of maintaining a force in Germany capable of penetrating to its capital. There was still a considerable reserve in the middle of the enemy country and I knew that any pencil-like thrust into the heart of Germany such as he proposed would meet nothing but certain destruction. This was true, no matter on what part of the front it might be attempted. I would not consider it.

It was possible, and perhaps certain, that had we stopped, in late August, all Allied movements elsewhere on the front he might have succeeded in establishing a strong bridgehead definitely threatening the Ruhr, just as any of the other armies could have gone faster and further, if allowed to do so at the expense of starvation elsewhere. However, at no point could decisive success have been attained, and, meanwhile, on the other parts of the front we would have got into precarious positions, from which it would have been difficult to recover.

General Montgomery was acquainted only with the situation in his own sector. He understood that to support his proposal would have meant stopping dead for weeks all units except the Twenty-first Army Group. But he did not understand the impossible situation that would have developed along the rest of our great front when he, having outrun the possibilities of maintenance, was forced to stop or withdraw.

I instructed him that what I did want in the north was Antwerp working, and I also wanted a line covering that port. Beyond this I believed it possible that we might with airborne assistance seize a bridgehead over the Rhine in the Arnhem region, flanking the defences of the Siegfried Line. The operation to gain such a bridgehead – it was assigned the code name Market Garden – would be merely an incident and extension of our eastward rush to the line we needed for temporary security. On our northern flank that line was the lower Rhine itself. To stop short of that obstacle would have left us in a very exposed position, particularly during the period when Montgomery would have to concentrate large forces on the Walcheren Island operation.

If these things could be done, we would engage in no additional major advances in the north until we had built up our logistics in the rear. But we could and would carry out minor operations all along the great front to facilitate later great offensives. Montgomery was very anxious to attempt the seizure of the bridgehead.

At the 10 September conference in Brussels Field-Marshal Montgomery was therefore authorized to defer the clearing out of the Antwerp approaches in an effort to seize the bridgehead I wanted. To assist Montgomery I allocated to him the 1st Allied Airborne Army, which had been recently formed under Lieutenant-General Lewis H. Brereton of the United States Air Force. The target date for the attack was tentatively set for 17 September, and I promised to do my utmost for him in supply until that operation was completed. After the completion of the bridgehead operation he was to turn instantly and with his whole force to the capture of Walcheren Island and the other areas from which the Germans were defending the approaches to Antwerp. Montgomery set about the task energetically.

All along the front we felt increasingly the strangulation on movement imposed by our inadequate lines of communication. The Services of Supply had made heroic and effective efforts to keep us going to the last possible minute. They installed systems of truck transport by taking over main-road routes in France and using most of these for one-way traffic. These were called Red Ball Highways, on which trucks kept running continuously. Every vehicle ran at least 20 hours a day. Relief drivers were scraped up from every unit that could provide them and the vehicles themselves were allowed to halt only for necessary loading, unloading, and servicing.

Railway engineers worked night and day to repair broken bridges and track and to restore

Below: Enthusiastic French civilians celebrate their new-found freedom after four years of German occupation.

the operational efficiency of rolling stock. Petrol and fuel oil were brought on to the Continent by means of flexible pipe-lines laid under the English Channel. From the beaches the petrol and oil were pumped forward to main distribution points through pipe-lines laid on the surface of the ground. Aviation engineers built landing strips at amazing speed, and throughout the organization there was displayed a morale and devotion to duty equal to that of any fighting unit in the whole command.

In the months succeeding the conclusion of hostilities I had many opportunities to review various campaigns with the leaders of the Russian Army. Not only did I talk to marshals and generals but on this subject I spent a considerable time with Generalissimo Stalin. Without exception, these Russian officers made one pressing demand upon me. It was to explain the supply arrangements that enabled us to make the great sweep out of our constricted beachhead in Normandy to cover, in one rush, all of France, Belgium, and Luxembourg, up to the very borders of Germany. I had to describe to them our systems of railway repairs and construction, truckage, evacuation, and supply by air.

They suggested that of all the spectacular feats of the war, even including their own, the Allied success in the supply of the pursuit across France would go down in history as the most astonishing. Possibly they were only being polite, but I nevertheless wished that they could have been heard by all the men who worked so hard during those hectic weeks to see that the front got every pound of ammunition, petrol, food, clothing and supplies.

Regardless, however, of the extraordinary efforts of the supply system, this remained our most acute difficulty. All along the front the cry was for more petrol and more ammunition. Every one of our spearheads could have gone farther and faster than they actually did. I believed then and believe now that on Patton's front the city of Metz could have been captured. Nevertheless, we had to supply each force for its basic missions and for basic missions only.

On our right we connected up near Dijon with Patch's advancing forces on 11 September, just twenty-seven days after the landing in southern France. From that moment onward the only thing standing in the way of the ample supply of all our forces south of Metz was the repair of the railways leading up the Rhône River valley. As a result of the junction with Patch's forces, a considerable number of Germans were trapped in southwestern France. These began to give themselves up by driblets except in one instance, when 20,000 Germans surrendered in a single body.

On the extreme left the attack against Arnhem went off as planned on the 17th. Three airborne divisions dropped, in column, from

north to south. The northernmost one was the British 1st Airborne Division, while farther southward were the American 82nd and 101st Airborne Divisions. The attack began well and unquestionably would have been successful except for the intervention of bad weather. This prevented the adequate reinforcement of the northern spearhead and resulted finally in the decimation of the British airborne division and only a partial success in the entire operation. We did not get our bridgehead but our lines had been carried well out to defend the important Antwerp base.

The progress of the battle gripped the attention of everyone in the theatre. We were inordinately proud of our airborne units but the interest in that battle had its roots in something deeper than pride. We felt it would prove whether or not the Germans could succeed in

Above: Tanks from the US First Army (General Courtney Hicks Hodges) drive through the Hürgten Forest. Hodges' troops would later play a key role in beating back the German offensive in the Ardennes.

Below: Smashed gliders, part of the Allied attempt to lay an airborne 'carpet' into northwestern Germany, lie in a Dutch field. The operation, codenamed Market Garden, failed to achieve its objectives but is best remembered for the heroic defense of the Arnhem bridge.

establishing renewed and effective resistance – on the battle's outcome we would form an estimate of the severity of the fighting still ahead of us. A general impression grew up that the battle was really a full-out attempt to begin, immediately, a drive into the heart of Germany. This gave a great added interest to a battle in which the circumstances were unusually dramatic.

When, in spite of heroic effort, the airborne forces and their supporting ground forces were stopped in their tracks, we had ample evidence that much bitter campaigning was still to come. The British 1st Airborne Division, in the van, fought one of the most gallant actions of the war, and its sturdiness materially assisted the two American divisions behind it, and the supporting ground forces of the Twenty-first Army Group, to take and hold important areas. But the division itself suffered badly; only some 2,400 succeeded in withdrawing across the river to safety.

It was now vital to avoid any further delay in the capture of Antwerp's approaches. Montgomery's forces were, at the moment, badly scattered. His front, in an irregular salient, reached to the lower Rhine. He had to concentrate a sizeable force in the Scheldt Estuary and still provide investing troops at some of the small ports holding out along the coast. To insure him opportunity to concentrate for the Scheldt operation we sent him two American divisions, the 7th Armored, commanded by Major-General Lindsay McD. Sylvester, and the 104th, commanded by Major-General Terry Allen, a veteran of the Sicilian campaign.

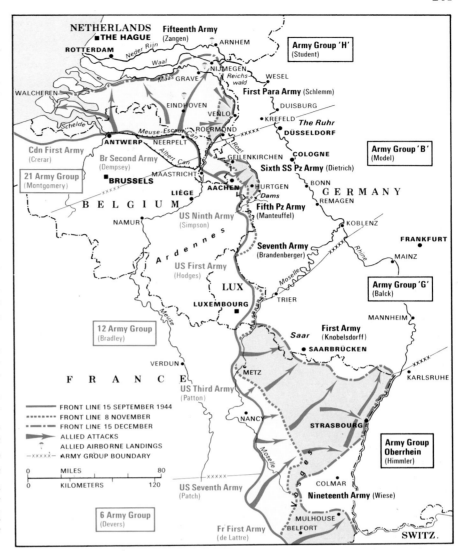

Above: Operation Market Garden and the Allied drive to the Rhine, September-December 1944.

Left: Into the Reich. Elements of the US 3rd Armored Division, including a bulldozer tank, break through a roadblock – part of the Siegfried Line – 15 September 1944.

The American First Army, at the end of its brilliant march from the Seine to the German border, almost immediately launched the operations that finally brought about the reduction of Aachen, one of the gateways into Germany. The city was stubbornly and fiercely defended but Collins, with his VII Corps, carried out the attack so skilfully that by 13 October he had surrounded the garrison and entered the city. The enemy was steadily forced back into his final stronghold, a massive building in the centre of the city. This was reduced by the simple expedient of draggng 155-mm 'Long Tom' guns up to point-blank range – within 200 yards of the building – and methodically blowing the walls to bits. After a few of these shells had pierced the building from end to end the German commander surrendered on 21 October, with the rueful observation: 'When the Americans start using 155s as sniper weapons, it is time to give up!'

As a tail-piece to this chapter it is only fair to give Field-Marshal Montgomery's views.

'The proper development of allied strategy north of the Seine will become one of the great controversies of military history. In the end it was the Germans who benefited from the argument. At the time, I was, and I remain, of the opinion that in September 1944 we failed to exploit fully the German disorganization consequent on their crushing defeat in the Battle of Normandy in August. The quickest way to end the German war was not merely to have the free use of Antwerp, as some have alleged. It was to act quickly in the middle of August, using the success gained in Normandy as a spring-board for a hard blow which would finish off the Germans and at the same time give us the ports we needed on the northern flank. To do these things we had to have a plan and concentration of effort; we had neither. I am still firmly convinced that had we adopted a proper operational plan in the middle of August, and given it a sound administrative and logistic backing, we should have secured bridgeheads over the Rhine and seized the Ruhr before the winter set in. The whole affair if properly handled would not only have shortened the war; it would also have held out possibilities of bringing it to an end in Europe with a balance very much more favourable to an early and stable peace than that which has actually emerged.

'Some have argued that I ignored Eisenhower's orders to give priority to opening up the port of Antwerp, and that I should not have attempted the Arnhem operation until this had been done. This is not true. There were no such orders about Antwerp and Eisenhower had agreed about Arnhem. Indeed, up to 8 October 1944 inclusive my orders were to gain the line of the Rhine "as quickly as humanly possible". On 9 October Antwerp was given priority for the first time – as will be seen from the orders quoted above.

'The trouble was that Eisenhower wanted the Saar, the Frankfurt area, the Ruhr, Antwerp, and the line of the Rhine. I knew how desperately the Germans had fought in Normandy. To get *all* these in one forward movement was impossible. If Eisenhower had adopted my plan

Below: German prisoners await transportation to the rear – part of the haul of men captured by the US forces involved in the capture of the Nijmegan bridges.

he could at least have got Antwerp and the Ruhr, with bridgeheads over the Rhine in the north, and would then have been very well placed. Or if he had adopted Bradley's plan he could have got the Saar and the Frankfurt area, with bridgeheads over the Rhine in the centre and south. But he was too optimistic. He compromised. He failed to get any of his objectives, and was then faced with a frustrating situation.

'I was, of course, greatly disappointed. I had hoped that we might end the German war quickly, save tens of thousands of lives, and bring relief to the people of Britain. But it was not to be.

'When I think back I am more and more convinced that the arguments, and difficulties of understanding, about the strategy after crossing the Seine have their origin in terminology. The matter has been argued under the labels "narrow versus broad front". My plan was described by Eisenhower as a "pencil-like thrust", and on another occasion as a "knife-like drive". But a strong thrust by forty divisions can hardly be described as "a narrow front"; it would represent a major *blow*. I was expounding the doctrine of the *single punch* against an enemy who was now weak on his pins. It was on the lines of the "left hook" of the desert battles, leading to the knock-out blow; after all I knew something about that sort of thing. Once we can disabuse ourselves of the word "narrow", all sorts of arguments go by the board, e.g. pencil-like, knife-like and so on.

'The dismal and tragic story of events after the successful battle in Normandy may be boiled down to one fundamental criticism. It is

this – whatever the decision, it wasn't implemented. In Normandy our strategy for the land battle, and the plan to achieve it, was simple and clear-cut. The pieces were closely "stitched" together. It was never allowed to become unstitched; and it succeeded. After Normandy our strategy became unstitched. There was no plan; and we moved by disconnected jerks.

'The rightness or wrongness of the decision taken is, of course, open to argument. But what cannot be disputed is that when a certain strategy, right or wrong, was decided upon, it wasn't directed. We did not advance to the Rhine on a *broad* front; we advanced to the Rhine on *several* fronts, which were uncoordinated. And what was the German answer? A single and concentrated punch in the Ardennes, when we had become unbalanced and unduly extended. So we were caught on the hop.'

Above: General Eisenhower meets members of the famous US 29th Infantry Division, the 'Blue and the Grey,' prior to the crossing of the Rhine.

Below: Part of the Allied operations to clear the strategically placed Dutch island of Walcheren. The fall of the island opened up the River Schelde to naval traffic, thus freeing the port of Antwerp for Allied use.

The Ardennes

by Omar Nelson Bradley

In December 1944 the end of the war in Europe seemed to most Allied soldiers to be in sight. Since July Hitler had been planning a mighty counter-offensive through the Ardennes. Unknown to the Allies he had massed 250,000 men and 1,100 tanks to launch against five understrength American divisions holding a seventy-mile front.

On 16 December 1944 Hitler launched the offensive on which hung the fate of the Third Reich. He hoped to capture Antwerp and to split the Allied front. Perhaps he dreamed of a second Dunkirk.

However, the American forces put up a stronger defence than the French had done in 1940. General Eisenhower, unlike Gamelin, had a reserve – albeit a small one – and launched it in good time.

The 101st Airborne Division made a valiant stand at Bastogne, which seriously delayed the Fifth Panzer Army.

By this time a salient – 'the Bulge' – had developed in the American line. Eisenhower (20 December) placed Montgomery in command of the troops north of the salient, leaving Bradley – much to the latter's indignation – only those to the south. Bad though this may have been for Bradley's *amour-propre* it certainly made it easier for Eisenhower to co-ordinate the well-planned counter-attacks which followed once the momentum of the German onslaught was spent. With his HQ at Luxembourg it was not possible for Bradley to control the northern half of his Army Group, now that a wedge had been driven deep into the US First Army.

Montgomery had already deployed 30th

Corps (General Horrocks) to ensure that the Germans should not cross the Meuse. In a press conference on 7 January he explained the battle as he saw it:

'Then the situation began to deteriorate. But the whole Allied team rallied to meet the danger; national considerations were thrown overboard; General Eisenhower placed me in command of the whole northern front. I employed the whole available power of the British Group of Armies; this power was brought into play very gradually and in such a way that it would not interfere with the American lines of communication. Finally it was put into battle with a bang, and today British divisions are fighting hard on the right flank of the First US Army. You have thus the picture of British troops fighting on both sides of American forces who have suffered a hard blow. This is a fine Allied picture.'

The well-planned Allied counter-attack drove the Germans back beyond the Ardennes. They had suffered 70,000 casualties as well as 50,000 prisoners, 500-600 tanks and 1,600 planes. The battle cost the Allies 76,980 casualties.

Speaking of his press conference Montgomery wrote in his memoirs:

'Distorted or not, I think now that I should never have held that press conference. So great was the feeling against me on the part of the American generals, that whatever I said was bound to be wrong. I should therefore have said nothing. Secondly, whatever I said (and I was misreported) the general impression I gave was one of tremendous confidence. In contradistinction to the rather crestfallen American command, I appeared, to the sensitive, to be triumphant – not over the Germans but over the Americans. This was a completely false picture . . .

'What I did *not* say was that, in the Battle of the Ardennes, the Allies got a real "bloody nose", the Americans had nearly 80,000 casualties, and that it would never have happened if we had fought the campaign properly after the great victory in Normandy, or had ensured tactical balance in the dispositions of the land forces as the winter campaign developed. Furthermore, because of this unnecessary battle we lost some six weeks in time – with all that that entailed in political consequences as the end of the war drew nearer.'

The Ardennes campaign was the last strong German reaction to the slow but relentless advance of the Allies into Germany. In it Hitler spent his last reserves.   EDITOR

These pages: The crew of a US 105mm M3 howitzer, an easily portable weapon much favored by Allied airborne troops, bring their gun into action.

Chronology

1944

6 June	D-Day.
25 Aug.	Liberation of Paris.
3 Sept.	Liberation of Brussels.
17 Sept.	Operation Market Garden (Arnhem).
20 Oct.	Americans take Aachen.
28 Nov.	First Allied convoy reaches Antwerp.
16 Dec.	German offensive begins.
18 Dec.	101st Airborne Division reaches Bastogne.
19 Dec.	Sixth Panzer Army held up.
21 Dec.	Germans take St Vith. Weather improves.
22 Dec.	Bastogne summoned to surrender.
23 Dec.	Weather clears.
24 Dec.	High-water mark of German advance.
25 Dec.	German spearhead crushed near Dinant.
30 Dec.	Patton and Manteuffel clash round Bastogne.

1945

3 Jan.	Hodges counter-attacks.
8 Jan.	Hitler permits limited withdrawals.
9 Jan.	Patton breaks out of Bastogne.
(12 Jan.	Opening of Russian winter offensive.)
13 Jan.	Hitler orders a retreat on the Western front.
16 Jan.	Patton and Hodges meet at Houffalize.
28 Jan.	End of the battle.

Counter-Offensive

The Ardennes sector in which von Rundstedt had struck was held in the north by two fledgling divisions and in the south by two veteran divisions, both of them badly mauled after a month in Huertgen Forest. Those dispositions, however, were not unintentional. Since Middleton's sector comprised the only quiet front on our line, we used it as a combined training ground and rest area. Altogether those four divisions held a lonely wooded front of 88 miles. Behind them an inexperienced armoured division had been parked in reserve.

South of the Ardennes, Third Army had broken into the Siegfried Line where it barricaded the far shore of the Saar River. And to its right, the Seventh Army extended that Saar River line eastward to the Rhine near Karlsruhe. Elsewhere Devers' Sixth Army Group had closed to the Rhine opposite the Black Forest except in the region of Colmar where a substantial enemy pocket had been by-passed this side of the river.

Three days before, on 13 December, Hodges had resumed his attack against the Roer dams after having failed to break those giant earthen structures with blockbusters dropped by the RAF. Rather than approach those dams again through the Huertgen Forest, Hodges had moved this time to outflank them from the south through the hills of the Schnee Eifel. Farther to the north, Hodges' front swelled out beyond Aachen to join Simpson's Ninth Army on the banks of the Roer. From there it dropped back into Montgomery's sector where it followed the Meuse downstream before turning sharply westward to the North Sea.

Of the 63 Allied divisions deployed the length of that 400-mile Western front, 40 were American, and of those 31 were assigned to 12th Army Group. Montgomery's two Armies comprised 15 divisions while Devers accounted for 17 more.

The 230-mile front of 12th Army Group had been subdivided among three US Armies. In the middle, Hodges' First Army straddled the lion's share of that front with a sector of 115 miles. Two-thirds of this First Army front stretched across the wooded Ardennes where Hodges had committed the four divisions of Middleton's VIII Corps. In the vicinity of Aachen Hodges had concentrated his remaining ten US divisions for the Rhineland offensive. North of the First Army sector, Simpson had concentrated the seven divisions of his Ninth Army into a narrow 18-mile front. Thus our combined forces north of the Ardennes totalled 17 US divisions. When added to Monty's British forces they equalled approximately half of all Allied strength in the West.

To the south of the Ardennes, Patton had deployed ten divisions the width of his 100-mile Third Army front, from the Moselle where it formed the Luxembourg border, past Saarbrücken halfway to the Rhine.

While startled by the suddenness of von Rundstedt's offensive, I was even more astonished that he should choose so unremunerative an objective. For in calculating our risks on that lightly held Ardennes front, I had discussed with Middleton the likely inducements that might tempt an enemy to strike there.

'First,' I said, 'when anyone attacks, he does

Right: Adolf Hitler confers with Heinrich Himmler, one of the men behind the Ardennes offensive.

Below: A German self-propelled gun mounted on a Panzer IV chassis comes out of hiding. Total Allied air superiority forced the Germans to conceal their armor during daylight hours.

it for one of two reasons. Either he's out to destroy the hostile forces or he's going after a terrain objective. If it's terrain he's after then he feels he must either have it himself or deny it to the other fellow.'

Neither objective could be attained in the Ardennes, for nowhere were we more thinly dispersed than across that wooded front and nowhere along the length of our Allied line was a sector more devoid of industrial resources, transportation facilities, and worthwhile or significant terrain objectives.

When I queried Troy on his chances of blunting an enemy attack through that unpromising front, he showed me the hilly, wooded terrain and drove me over the narrow black-top roads that twisted through his sector. 'If they come through here,' he said 'we can fall back and fight a delaying action to the Meuse. Certainly we could slow them down until you hit them on the flanks.'

I reported this reconnaissance to Ike who acknowledged the risks but accepted them as part of the price to be paid for resumption of the winter offensive.

'Why even if the Germans were to bust through all the way to the Meuse,' I said, 'he wouldn't find a thing in the Ardennes to make it worth his while.'

We were not unmindful that in 1940 Hitler had broken through this same unlikely Ardennes front to overrun France. But if, as some critics say, that precedent should have forwarned us, they would have us ignore, as perhaps Hitler did, a striking change in Allied dispositions between 1940 and 1944.

As a result of the artificial division of nation states in Europe, France is poorly defended by natural geographic barriers from invasion in the east. Yet of the many pathways that lead to France, the least penetrable is through the Ardennes. For there the roads are much too scarce, the hills too wooded, the valleys too limited for manoeuvre.

However, in 1940, of the four paths for invasion then available to Hitler, the Ardennes was the one least securely blocked. Across the Rhine from the Black Forest; French guns commanded these river crossings. Farther north where the Lorraine hills rolled up to the Saar, the Wehrmacht dared not trifle with the casemated guns of the Maginot Line. And high above the Ardennes where the lowlands of Belgium formed an open path into France, the Belgian Army and the British Expeditionary Force waited behind the Meuse.

This left only the Ardennes, north of where the unfortified frontier of Luxembourg paralelled the Siegfried Line. When the enemy struck in the Ardennes and forced a penetration, the static French fortress troops on both sides of that gap lacked the mobility and armour to stab back with a counter-attack into the enemy's flanks.

Although lightly held in contrast to those sectors in the north and south where we had massed for the winter offensive, the Ardennes was nevertheless defended by more than 70,000 troops. But of far greater significance was the mobility of our heavily armed strength on the shoulders of the Ardennes. For this was the key factor Hitler had overlooked when he planned his second Ardennes offensive. He had forgotten that this time he was opposed not by static troops in a Maginot Line but by a vast mechanized US Army fully mounted on wheels. In accepting the risk of enemy penetration into the Ardennes, we had counted heavily on the speed with which we could fling this mechanized strength against his flanks. While Middleton absorbed the enemy's momentum in a rearguard withdrawal, Hodges' and Patton's Armies would clamp the invader in a vice.

To the south Patton's Third Army consisted of a quarter-million troops, with its tanks and supporting guns. To the north, the remainder of Hodges' First Army numbered another quarter-million men. Both were equipped with sufficient trucks for speedy redeployment.

Above: Field Marshal Walter Model (1891-1945) commanded Army Group B in the Ardennes operation. He was renowned for his ability to snatch victory from the jaws of defeat. He committed suicide after the Allies crossed the Rhine in April 1945.

When news of the German offensive reached me at SHAEF, I first thought it a spoiling attack assembled by von Runstedt to force a halt on Patton's advance into the Saar. For George had hurt the enemy severely in his month-long winter offensive and now, after reclaiming Lorraine for the French, he was about to break through the Siegfried Line.

'The other fellow knows that if he's to hold out much longer,' I said, 'he must lighten the pressure that Patton has built up against him in the Saar. If by coming through the Ardennes he can force us to pull Patton's troops out of the Saar and throw them against his counter-offensive, he will get what he's after. And that's just a little more time.'

Not until after the war when interrogators tracked down the origins of this Ardennes counter-offensive, did we learn how grossly I had underrated the enemy's intentions in thinking the offensive a spoiling attack.

Instead of the tactical diversion I had accused von Rundstedt of staging as an antidote to Patton's advance in the Saar, the German counter-offensive had been marshalled as a master stroke that was to regain the initiative in the West. Antwerp was to be the primary objective, for the enemy reasoned that if he could sever our major supply lines from that port, he would have isolated four Allied armies north of the Ardennes. Though he did not delude himself with dreams of victory in the West, he nevertheless anticipated abundant rewards in Allied losses and disorganization. If successful in the Ardennes counter-offensive, the enemy might stall our Western drive long enough to strike the Red Army then massing on the Vistula.

Moreover, it was thought that the psychological effect of a German offensive might stave off the despair that by now had infected so many Germans. For as the Allied armies neared those cities already devastated by air, the German people began more clearly to comprehend the catastrophe that came with defeat. But it was not primarily for morale that the enemy had devised this Ardennes counter-attack. Instead he had chosen to gamble his dwindling resources on the slender chance of achieving a strategic upset.

Bradley goes on to give an outline of the German plan which is omitted here.

Initially, the enemy had contemplated a counter-attacking force of between 25 and 30 divisions. But by 16 December he had amassed a surprising total of 36 in all four armies. Of these, four were crack SS Panzer divisions assigned to Sepp Dietrich's Sixth Army. General Hasso von Manteuffel's Fifth Panzer Army to the left included three ordinary panzer divisions and four more of infantry. Altogether von Rundstedt had accumulated 600 tanks for the attack.

In the face of this astonishing German build-up, I had greatly underestimated the enemy's offensive capabilities. My embarrassment however was not unique, for it was shared not only by the Army commanders but by Montgomery and Eisenhower as well. Early in December intelligence had counted ten panzer divisions parked behind the Roer; an eleventh together with six more infantry, down opposite the Ardennes. Although the Ardennes concentration was far heavier than von Rundstedt required for the security of that front, we were too much addicted to the anticipation of counter-attack on the Roer to credit the enemy with more fanciful or ambitious intentions. For

Above: A Panzergrenadier inspects an abandoned US half-track. Surprise and the speed of the opening assault caught the US forces off balance. In the first stage of the attack six American divisions were swamped by 25 German divisions, the latter including 11 armored formations.

Left: German troops are hailed as liberators as they move into a German town to the south of Belgium.

a while we acknowledged the enemy's capability for a knockdown battle there, we could not believe he possessed sufficient resources for a strategic offensive. And unless he sought such strategic objectives as Antwerp and Liège, there was little profit to be gained by his venturing into the Ardennes. On the other hand, if a spoiling attack were to be the limit of his ambitions, we estimated that we could sucessfully contain it without serious damage or dislocation to our front.

Although we had erred in evaluating the enemy's *intentions*, this estimate of his *capabilities* at the time was nearer right than wrong. For as events in subsequent weeks proved, von Rundstedt lacked the resources necessary to succeed in a strategic offensive against so powerful a force as ours. Instead, he squandered his reserves so recklessly in the Ardennes that two months later when he was charged with defence of the Rhine, he found himself too weak to hold that river line. In his anxiety to stave off for a few more months the disaster that shadowed him in the West, Hitler unwittingly hastened the war to an earlier end.

Earlier that fall von Rundstedt had reached the same conclusion as we on the inadequacy of German forces for the strategic offensive envisioned by Hitler. When the latter disclosed his grandiose plan, von Rundstedt offered a counter-proposal. He would attack toward Aachen and restore the Siegfried Line. The dodge, however, failed. Hitler curtly rejected von Rundstedt's substitution, contending that it lacked a strategic objective.

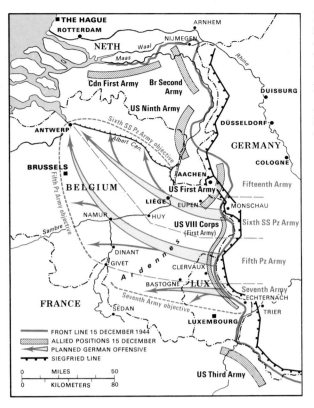

Left: The plan of attack for the Ardennes campaign. German forces were supposed to smash through the weakly held Ardennes sector and then break out for the port of Antwerp, gathering fuel from captured Allied dumps as they advanced.

But if the enemy's resources fell far short of Hitler's aspirations, they also admittedly exceeded our conservative estimates on German strength. Representative of the Allied outlook at this time was the Montgomery estimate of German offensive capabilities published at 21st Army Group on 16 December. Had I been preparing an estimate of my own on the same day, I would not have changed a word of Monty's,

Below: A squad of infantry rushes across a Belgium road. Burning US artillery and half-tracks, victims of an ambush, litter the picture.

for his appraisal was identical to my own:

'The enemy is at present fighting a defensive campaign on all fronts; his situation is such that he cannot stage major offensive operations. Furthermore, at all costs he has to prevent the war from entering on a mobile phase; he has not the transport or the petrol that would be necessary for mobile operations, nor could his tanks compete with ours in the mobile battle.

The enemy is in a bad way; he has had a tremendous battering and has lost heavily in men and equipment. On no account can we relax, or have a 'stand still', in the winter months; it is vital that we keep going, so as not to allow him time to recover and so as to wear down his strength still further. There will be difficulties caused by mud, cold, lack of air support during periods of bad weather, and so on. But we must continue to fight the enemy hard during the winter months.'

Just as soon as the enemy fell back behind his Siegfried Line, Allied intelligence suffered from a lack of secret-agent reports. No longer, as in France, was the German fighting in a hostile land where French patriots reported his movements and shielded our agents behind his lines. Within the Reich he was at home among his own people where the only informers were traitors and there were far too few of them. As a result, the flow of information from behind German lines thinned to a trickle. More and more we were forced to depend upon PW interrogation, front-line intelligence, and aerial observation.

Since success was predicated largely upon surprise, in massing his troops for the Ardennes offensive the enemy invoked his most rigid security precautions of the war. Pledges were required of all commanders briefed on the operation. Radio communication on the operation was forbidden; correspondence was ordered carried only by trusted couriers and anyone with a knowledge of the offensive was prohibited from flying west of the Rhine. Troops

Above: The onset of winter made conditions difficult for both sides, but the poor weather did confer one priceless advantage on the German forces – the ability to move in daylight without having to suffer the attentions of Allied bombers and ground-attack aircraft.

were to be staged in their final assembly areas only at the eleventh hour, and then only at night. Meanwhile, all non-German soldiers were evacuated from the front line. To conceal these elaborate preparations, armies were to maintain their existing CPs and fake a routine radio traffic. And a complete dummy headquarters was established opposite Simpson's army to divert our attention up north.

When the time came for the enemy's movement of reserves into position for the offensive, the weather on which von Rundstedt had counted closed down on the Western Front. For days the sun shone only fitfully and air reconnaissance found its cameras blinded by cloud cover. Meanwhile, the agents that we slipped through the enemy's lines disappeared into the winter and were never heard from again.

In spite of these handicaps, however, intelligence had detected some slight sign of an enemy build-up in the Ardennes. Unfortunately those indications in themselves were not conclusive. What did they mean? Intelligence

Left: The victors and the vanquished. US troops trudge into captivity while a German armored column, led by a King Tiger, pushes deeper into southern Belgium.

asked. And what should we do about them? Admittedly, there was nothing disquieting, nothing alarming about troop movements in the Eifel. The enemy was using that sector, as we were, to rest his battleweary divisions and to blood the new ones. For this reason the Eifel might easily echo with more movement than one would ordinarily expect on so 'quiet' a front.

In the absence of more conclusive evidence of the enemy's intentions, there were two deductions that could be drawn from this night-time activity in the Eifel. Either it could be part of an enemy build-up for counter-attack behind the Roer, or it could mean the beginning of an enemy threat in the Ardennes. The first conclusion seemed the more rational one, even though it was far riskier for us.

For by chancing the danger of an enemy surprise attack in the Ardennes, we could push on with the winter offensive, secure the Roer dams, and thus force the enemy to commit his reserves in a battle west of the Rhine. But if we were inclined to play it safe by preparing for trouble in the Ardennes, we should have to call off the winter offensive, strengthen Middleton's VIII Corps front, and brace him with reinforcements to meet this danger of counter-attack. Clearly there were not enough troops for both a winter offensive and a secure defence everywhere else on the Allied line. To push on in the attack – or bed down until the spring: these were the alternatives we faced.

At that moment nothing less than an unequivocal indication of impending attack in the Ardennes could have induced me to quit the winter offensive. And that did not come until 5 a.m. on 16 December when the enemy opened his artillery barrage.

Our failure to foresee that those signs pointed to an attack through the Ardennes ironically enough spared us heavier casualties when it came. For had we doubled our divisions across Middleton's thin VIII Corps front, we could not have withstood the weight of von Rundstedt's powerful offensive. With the 24 divisions he was to throw into the Bulge, the enemy could have broken a hole anywhere in our line. He may not have been able to advance as far as he did had he dragged through heavier defences, but he would have undoubtedly inflicted more casualties upon Middleton's troops in the effort.

In the next few pages Bradley offers some reflections on how he came to be surprised by the German offensive. He suggests that as he commanded 750,000 men it was 'impossible for me even to scan the intelligence estimates of subordinate units' – a view that would not have commended itself to a Napoleon (or even a Montgomery). To General Marshall he wrote: 'I do not blame my commanders, my staff or myself, for the situation that resulted. We had taken a calculated risk and the

German hit us harder than we anticipated he could.'

Stubbornly he asserts: 'Time has not altered that opinion.' He concludes: 'I would rather be bold than wary even though wariness may sometimes be right.' This last cautious comment hardly deserves to rank with the maxims of the Great Captains.

When the blow fell on 16 December, von Rundstedt caught us fully committed without a division in Army Group reserve. This plight was not uncommon. Against an enemy as badly

Above: A valuable prize lost to the Germans due to the prompt action of American troops – empty five-gallon fuel cans.

Below: US troops dig in along the edge of a wood; one GI lies dead, a victim of sniper fire. As the Germans advanced, isolated pockets of resistance fought stubbornly to slow their progress.

Left: A Greyhound armored car leads a US reconnaissance patrol through a ruined town.

'I hate like hell to do it, George, but I've got to have that division. Even if it's only a spoiling attack as you say, Middleton must have help.' Within a few minutes Patton issued the orders.

I then phoned Lev Allen at *Eagle Tac* to tell him of my orders to Patton. At the same time I instructed him to have Simpson turn the 7th Armoured Division over to Hodges that it, too might be used like the 10th Armoured to hit von Rundstedt on his flank.

Meanwhile Major General Raymond O. Barton had already begun to worry over the wobbly position of his 4th Division on the right end of the Luxembourg line. We had not yet replaced the losses he had suffered in Huertgen Forest, and at the time of attack his division was critically under-strength. The following morning as the enemy swarmed across the Sauer River, Barton rushed his cooks, bakers, and clerks into the line. 'But we're not stopping them,' he warned Lev Allen, 20 miles to the rear in Luxembourg. 'If the 10th Armoured doesn't get up here soon, Army Group had better get set to barrel out.'

Below: The main street of Bastogne. The town was the focal point of several roads in southern Belgium and its defense by the US 101st Airborne Division was one of the decisive factors in the outcome of the offensive.

beaten as we imagined the Germans to be, I could not conscientiously withhold in reserve divisions better utilized on the offensive. At no time did my Group 'reserve' consist of anything more than a few divisions assigned to one or another of the Armies where they could be employed only with Group's consent.

SHAEF's strategic reserve consisted of two airborne divisions, the 82nd and the 101st. Both had been assembled at Reims for refitting after Arnhem. After having been loaned to Monty for what SHAEF anticipated would be a 48-hour commitment until relieved by British armour, both divisions were held in the line for 58 days in Holland.

Just as soon as I learned of the Ardennes attack on the afternoon of 16 December, I telephoned Patton at Nancy from Eisenhower's office. George's 10th Armoured Division, now out of the line, was in reserve near Thionville just south of the Luxembourg-French border. I wanted to use that armour to stab into the enemy's southern flank in the event he broke through on Middleton's front.

'George, get the 10th Armoured on the road to Luxembourg,' I told him, 'and have Morris report immediately to Middleton for orders.'

Patton objected, as I anticipated he would. One less armoured division meant lessening his chance of breaking through into the Saar. 'But that's no major threat up there,' George balked. 'Hell, it's probably nothing more than a spoiling attack to throw us off balance down here and make us stop this offensive.'

Patton might have been right; it was too soon yet to tell. But I had decided that we couldn't afford to take chances. The risk we had knowingly taken in the Ardennes had been calculated partly upon our ability to counter-attack.

On Sunday morning, 17 December, I awakened early in the handsome stone villa Ike occupied at St Germain-en-Laye. The weather had not yet lifted for air flight and I was anxious to get to my headquarters just as soon as I could. It was mid-afternoon when we sped into Verdun on the road from Paris. The night before the Germans had dropped parachutists behind our lines to cut the roads leading into the north flank of their penetration. The drop had miscarried as most night drops do and enemy paratroopers had been scattered widely behind our lines. A machine-gun jeep was waiting at Verdun to escort me the rest of the way.

On the road into Luxembourg a giant American flag hung from the roof of a modest stone cottage.

'I hope he doesn't have to take it down,' I said, pointing it out to Hansen.

'You mean we'll stay put in Luxembourg –'

'You can bet your life we will. I'm not going to budge this CP. It would scare everyone else to death.'

Eisenhower later challenged the wisdom of that resolution. Fearful that we might lose control should the enemy drive us out and destroy our communications, he recommended that we play safe and pull *Tac* back to Verdun. I balked but not for pride. Any hint of withdrawal by Army Group, I told him, might easily alarm the command. It might also incite panic in Luxembourg, cause refugees to jam the roads at the very time they were needed for troop movements. A parallel system of Army Group communications tied in Verdun where *Eagle Main* was located. Even if *Tac* were to be turned out of Luxembourg at gun point, the switch-over could be made without a break in our vital communications.

We drove directly to the brownstone state railway building in which *Tac* was located and there found Lev Allen brooding over a map in the war room. G-2 was posting enemy divisions identified in the attack. Already they totalled 14, and half of them were panzers. I scanned the map in dismay. 'Pardon my French, Lev, but just where in hell has this sonuvabitch got all his strength?'

By the following morning, 18 December, the centre of our line in the Ardennes had been crushed but the shoulders were holding firm. Sepp Dietrich's main thrust had been blocked by First Army to Malmedy. A few miles south of that ridge line the 7th Armoured raced into St Vith to nose out the SS panzers driving hard for that intersection on the road to Liège. Although Barton had been forced to give ground on our right, the timely arrival of the 10th Armoured Division had steadied his position and the shoulder now appeared secure.

In the centre, Manteuffel's panzers had smashed through the 28th Division to overrun Middelton's reserves and head for Bastogne almost midway between the city of Luxembourg and Liège. To the north of the unlucky 28th, two regiments of the 106th had already been encircled in position. The remainder of that newly arrived division was fighting for its life at St Vith.

My decision to hold Bastogne, at all costs, had been anticipated by Middleton even as his front was crumbling to pieces. When I called Troy to give him the order to hold that crucial road junction, he replied that he had already instructed his troops there to dig in and hold. Elements of the 10th Armoured Division raced north to Bastogne to reinforce tanks of the 9th Armoured in their defence of that key position. That evening the 101st Airborne Division roared into Bastogne after a wild truck ride from Reims while the 82nd Airborne continued on north to blunt the pincer that had forced its way between Malmédy and St Vith.

If we could limit von Rundstedt's penetration to the 35-mile gap between Malmédy and Bastogne while holding firm on the shoulders, we might force the enemy to funnel his strength due west into the Ardennes where the terrain would sponge it up. Between those two points only three mediocre roads meandered westward toward the Meuse.

On the evening of 18 December, I had intended to run up through Bastogne to Spa until Hodges' aide telephoned to suggest that I come instead by air. English-speaking Germans in captured American ODs had infiltrated our lines in a brash attempt to panic our rear areas. Captured enemy orders for the recruitment of those 'reconnaissance' units had fallen into our hands two weeks before. Volunteers were to be selected and trained by the notorious Lieutenant-Colonel Otto Skorzeny, the airborne privateer who the year before had snatched Mussolini out of the Italian hotel in which he had been imprisoned following his fall from power. Most of these GI-uniformed enemy troops were cut down before they reached the

Above: Brigadier General Anthony McAuliffe, the deputy commander of the 101st Airborne Division during the fighting around Bastogne.

Below: Two GIs who fought their way back to friendly lines after their unit was cut off in the early stages of the German attack. The man on the right cradles an M1 carbine with a spare ammunition pouch on the stock.

Left: A Panther tank undergoes running repairs deep in the forests of the Ardennes. Note the ridges of anti-magnetic mine paste applied to the glacis plate of the Panzer V.

Right: Paratroopers of the 101st Airborne Division clear rubble to free some of their comrades trapped after a German artillery bombardment on Bastogne.

Below: Frightened Belgian refugees negotiate the war-torn streets of Bastogne, heading west to escape the advancing German forces.

Meuse but not until a half-million GIs played cat and mouse with each other each time they met on the road. Neither rank nor credentials nor protests spared the traveller an inquisition at each intersection he passed. Three times I was ordered to prove my identity by cautious GIs. The first time by identifying Springfield as the capital of Illinois (my questioner held out for Chicago); the second time by locating the guard between the centre and tackle of a line of scrimmage; the third time by naming the then current spouse of the blonde named Betty Grable. Grable stopped me but the sentry did not. Pleased at having stumped me, he nevertheless passed me on.

Within two days it was apparent the enemy had mounted more than a spoiling attack. In an order of the day to his troops, von Rundstedt had declared, 'We gamble everything now – we cannot fail.' At Army Group we concluded his target lay in the swollen dumps of Liège. I

could not yet believe that his ambitions stretched beyond Liège to Antwerp.

As Hodges thinned his Roer River front to fend off the panzers on the right of his line and dig in on a defensive position between the Bulge and the Meuse River, I made ready to call off Patton's offensive in the Saar. While First Army rolled with the Germans' Bulge offensive in the north, Third Army would slash into its underbelly by wheeling up from the Saar. George was dismayed at the prospect of abandoning his toe-hold in the Siegfried Line. 'But what the hell,' he shrugged, 'we'll still be killing Krauts.'

I walked out with him to his jeep when he left Luxembourg for Nancy that day. 'We won't commit any more of your stuff than we have to,' I said, 'I want to save it for a whale of a blow when we hit back – and we're going to hit this bastard hard.' George grinned and pulled his parka tightly under his chin.

To free Patton for the underbelly offensive it became necessary for Eisenhower to widen Devers' 6th Army Group front and spill Third Army on the Saar. To co-ordinate this change-over between Army Group, Eisenhower called a council at *Eagle Main* in Verdun on 19 December. He drove into the chilly caserne from Versailles in a heavy bullet-proof car. CIC had insisted on the precaution after reports reached SHAEF that Skorzeny had dispatched a squad of assassins to hunt down the Supreme Commander. Patton was to pull two of his three corps out of the line in the Saar for the Bulge counter-attack while Devers thinned out his front and side-slipped off to the left into Third Army's sector. Like Patton, Devers disliked the need for relinquishing his 6th Army Group offensive to help pull our chestnuts out of the Ardennes. But he, too, had resigned himself to the strategic realignment.

Meanwhile Patton, who in Sicily had brushed off supply as a bothersome detail, demonstrated how well he had learned his lesson during the September drought by stuffing his Third Army dumps with engineer bridging equipment to be used in spanning the Rhine.

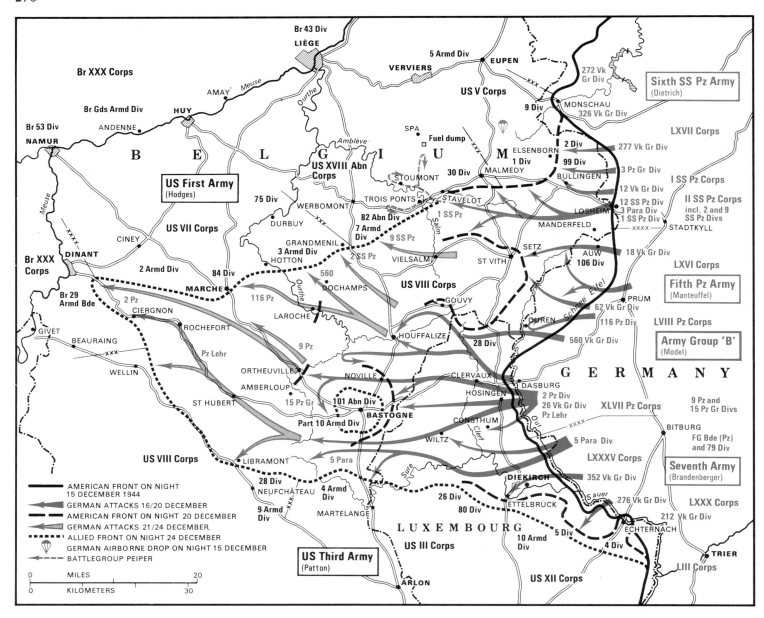

The offensive in the Ardennes. German columns were checked at St Vith, Houffalize and Bastogne. In the north Kampfgruppe Peiper was responsible for the massacre of US prisoners at Malmédy, one of the worst atrocities committed in the battle for northern Europe.

Fearful lest Devers ransack that hoard should it fall into his hands on the Army Group shift, George insisted that in rearranging his boundary we keep those dumps within his sector. Two months later that foresight paid off when George took the Rhine on the run and jumped Third Army across it on those bountiful engineer stores.

In the chilly squad room of the Verdun caserne where a lone pot-bellied stove helped ease the chill of the moist December, we quickly agreed to an overall plan for spearing the enemy Bulge on its flanks. Eisenhower had already approved the shift of Third Army; the conference had been called primarily to draft Devers' resources in it. No one proposed an alternative line of action, for the only 'alternative' would have involved withdrawal to a winter line on the Meuse. Even the theorists of G-3, whose duty it was to explore the alternatives open to us, shunned withdrawal as too unthinkable to merit consideration.

Although I would have preferred to clamp the Bulge in simultaneous attacks from both

shoulders, it was clear that Hodges could not mount an offensive until first he checked the enemy's advance. And on 19 December, the harried First Army was too preoccupied in stemming the German offensive to think about a retaliatory blow. Had Hodges been able to gather a force behind his shoulder at Malmédy and strike south from there to St Vith, he might have narrowed the neck and greatly foreshortened the Bulge. But as fast as he pulled divisions out of the Roer, he was forced to commit them piecemeal to prevent a break-through to the Meuse. As the enemy drove deeper into the Ardennes searching for an unblocked road north to the Meuse, Hodges extended his line in a frantic effort to contain him. If Sepp Dietrich's panzers were to break through that wall and drive on to Liège, Hodges would probably have been compelled to slacken his grip on the Malmédy shoulder. And it was there that he saved First Army by holding the enemy's main force to a draw.

But if Hodges could not strike back into the enemy's northern flank, there was nothing to

deter Patton from counter-attacking against the Bulge from the south. Indeed the plight of First Army had become so grave that unless Patton soon hurried to its aid with a diversion, we feared Hodges' lines might crack, enabling the enemy to pour across the Meuse.

Meanwhile our situation at the cross-roads of Bastogne was rapidly shaping into a major crisis. Manteuffel's Fifth Panzer Army, in the centre of von Rundstedt's line, had spilled past that isle of resistance to cut its north and south exit roads. With the encirclement of Bastogne foredoomed, I nevertheless ordered Middleton's VIII Corps to hold on to that vital objective. Even though it could well cost us heavy casualties in the airborne division and the two armoured combat commands that had reached that outpost I could not afford to relinquish Bastogne and let the enemy widen his Bulge. But though I did not minimize the ordeal we inflicted upon its defenders, I was confident that the 101st could hold with the aid of those tankers from the 9th and 10th Amoured Divisions. They could hold out I thought at least until Patton's Third Army broke through to relieve them. The relief of Bastogne was to be the priority objective in Patton's flanking attack.

'How soon will you be able to go, George?' I asked, knowing how difficult his movement would be over the limited roadnet that connected Luxembourg with his Alsatian front. George estimated 48 hours; any other commander would have held his breath and believed himself taking a chance on 98.

Now totally reconciled to an indefinite postponement of his Saar offensive, George was itching to start the counter-attack. He lighted a fresh cigar and pointed to the Bulge where it pierced the thin blue lines of our war map.

'Brad,' he exclaimed, 'this time the Kraut's stuck his head in a meat grinder.' With a turn of his fist he added, 'And this time I've got hold of the handle.'

Within two days George had made good on the start of his attack. A week later von Rundstedt dragged to a halt on the high-water mark

of his offensive. Patton's brilliant shift of Third Army from its bridgehead in the Saar to the snow-covered Ardennes front became one of the most astonishing feats of generalship of our campaign in the West. Even before he left Verdun for Nancy on 19 December, George had touched off the movement by phone. Two days later, on 21 December, he was attacking towards Bastogne with an armoured and infantry division. By Christmas those original two had been joined by four more. Within less than a week Patton had switched the bulk of his Third Army, with its guns, supply and equipment from 50 to 75 miles north into the new offensive. More than 133,000 tanks and trucks joined that round-the-clock trek over the icy roads. From the windows of my office overlooking the gorge where the medieval dungeons and battlements of Luxembourg had been cut into the rock, I could count the double-banked columns as they crossed the arched stone bridge. In heavy greatcoats still caked with the

Above: A vital airdrop, made possible by the improving weather, brings much-needed supplies to a frontline Allied unit.

Below: General Eisenhower (left) congratulates Lieutenant-General George Patton, commander of the US Third Army during the counter-attack in the Ardennes. Lieutenant-General Omar Bradley, commander of the US Twelfth Army, looks on.

mud of the Saar, troops huddled against the wintry cold that knifed through their canvas-topped trucks. In the turrets of their Shermans, tank commanders had wrapped their faces in woollen scarves as they guided their awkward vehicles through the streets of the city. Day and night those columns rattled over the cobble-stoned pavements until on 21 December a new carpet of snow muffled their passage and they glided through like ghosts.

The speed with which Third Army turned its forces north astonished even those of us who had gambled in the Ardennes on the mobility of our army. When movement orders were tele-phoned to the 5th Infantry Division on 20 December, two regiments were engaged in an attack against the enemy in Sauerlautern while the third held a defensive sector north of that bridgehead. Twenty-four hours later, two regi-ments had closed in an assembly area northeast of Luxembourg, while the third was awaiting relief preparatory to moving north.

Until the Battle of the Bulge I did not share George's enthusiasm for his Third Army staff which unlike those of both the First and Ninth Armies, lacked outstanding individual per-formers. Indeed, I had once agreed with the observation of another senior commander who said, 'Patton can get more good work out of a mediocre bunch of staff officers than anyone I ever saw. His principals were almost without exception hold-overs from the Sicilian cam-paign where their performance could be most charitably described as something less than per-fect. However, five months in Europe had sea-

soned that staff and the greatly matured Patton succeeded in coaxing from it the brilliant effort that characterized Third Army's turnabout in the Bulge.

Although Patton had been understandably reluctant to relinquish his 10th Armoured Divi-sion during the first day of the Bulge offensive, this remarkable switch-over on his front had caused George very little worry. For despite the enormous complexity of the manoeuvre, he handled it almost entirely by telephone, impro-vising from day to day to stretch the capacity of his roads.

While mobility was the 'secret' US weapon that defeated von Rundstedt in the Ardennes, it owed its effectiveness to the success of US Army staff training. With division, corps, and

Above: An American officer studies a piece of German graffiti. It reads: 'Behind the last battle of this war stands our victory.'

Below: Sherman tanks of the US Third Army are used as artillery to bombard German positions on the other side of a nearby hill.

Army staffs schooled in the same language, practices, and techniques, we could resort to sketchy oral orders with an assurance of perfect understanding between US commands. Those orders, in turn, were transmitted easily over the most valued accessory of all: the elaborate telephone system we carried with us into the field. From my desk in Luxembourg I was never more than 30 seconds by phone from any of the Armies. If necessary, I could have called every division on the line. Signal corps officers like to remind us that 'although Congress can make a general, it takes communications to make him a commander'. The maxim was never more brilliantly evidenced than in this battle for the Ardennes.

Although Hodges was fighting a touch-and-go battle on the evening on 19 December, I was not perturbed so long as he held tightly to the Malmédy shoulder. Sepp Dietrich had already shattered four first-rate divisions against that position before diverting his *main* effort south through the road centre at St Vith. There, where five principal highways intersected in the centre of that small Belgian town, Hodges blocked the German advance with his 7th Armoured Division. Dietrich's unwieldy columns piled up in a jam behind. As his panzers forked north and south in an effort to avoid that intersection, they soon lost their precious momentum on the muddy secondary roads that made the Ardennes so treacherous a vehicle trap.

Von Rundstedt had gambled on speed in his offensive, knowing that unless he could score a quick break-through, time would react in favour of our motorized Armies as we threw reinforcements in against his flanks. After four days of violent attack the enemy had not yet loosened Hodges' grip on the shoulder at Malmédy nor had he driven the outnumbered 7th Armoured Division out of St Vith. The schedule on which the German had banked his offensive had gone awry and though we could not yet be certain, it looked as though Hodges had already tipped the scales of the Bulge in our favour. Having failed to secure a break-through to the Meuse by 19 December, the enemy should have despaired of the Bulge and withdrawn his forces.

Although First Army headquarters had been chased out of its CP at Spa when an enemy column approached to within 2,000 yards of that resort city, this threat was dented by the timely arrival of tanks from the 3rd Armoured Division. Before quitting its CP, however, First Army had removed more than a million gallons of motor fuel from the enemy's reach. Another 124,000 gallons were ignited to prevent their capture. And a third dump of 2,225,000 gallons was in the process of being removed to the rear. The acute fuel shortages that had followed destruction by air of the enemy's petroleum industry had forced von Rundstedt to mount his attack without adequate gasoline reserves. Without captured American fuel his offensive could not succeed.

Before quitting the office late that evening of 19 December for my billet at the Alfa, I called Middleton at his VIII Corps headquarters.

Left: A column of dejected German prisoners is sent to the rear, watched by an armored convoy waiting to head up to the front line. By Christmas Eve 1944, the German offensive was running out of steam.

Troy estimated that his corps, though shattered by the offensive, had cost the enemy far more delay than he could afford. For despite the overwhelming weight and surprise of his first day's attack, von Rundstedt had spent four valuable days getting to Bastogne.

Troy was entitled to pride in the VIII Corps, for his divisions had rallied nobly in a furious delaying struggle that emphasized the resourcefulness of the American soldier. Though surprised and disorganized, part of the 106th fell back to the crossroads of St Vith. There it was joined by the 7th Armoured Division in the defence of that road junction. In tactical importance that road centre was even more valuable than Bastogne itself. On the south end of Middleton's line, where Luxembourg bulges into the vineyards of the Moselle Valley, Barton's 4th Division had buckled but it did not break. In valour, however, neither had outshone the broken and bruised 28th. Though overrun by the first wave of Germans that moved out of the mists of the Eifel, the 28th split into a forest full of small delaying units. For three sleepless days and nights the embattled troops of that division backed grudgingly toward Bastogne buying time for the reinforcement of that anchor position. During the first week of that Ardennes offensive, almost one-fourth of the entire division had been reported killed, wounded, or missing.

Although Eisenhower had evidenced no sign of uneasiness during the conference at Verdun on 19 December, his staff at SHAEF had shown symptoms of what we at Group diagnosed as an acute case of the shakes. This uneasiness soon spread to the Scribe Hotel in Paris where newsmen accredited to SHAEF echoed the nervousness that came out of Versailles. So exaggerated were their tales of our plight in the Ardennes that I afterward asked Ike's permission to open a press camp at *Eagle Tac* where they might get a better picture of the front than they were getting in Paris.

The first evidence of SHAEF's anxiety came in a TWX cautioning us to make certain that no bridge over the Meuse fell into the enemy's hands. 'What the devil do they think we're doing,' Lev Allen complained, 'starting back for the beaches?'

The big blow-up, however, came in a telephone call from Bedell Smith on the evening of 19 December.

'Ike thinks it may be a good idea,' Bedell said, 'to turn over to Monty your two Armies on the north and let him run that side of the Bulge from 21st Group. It may save us a great deal of trouble, especially if your communications with Hodges and Simpson go out.'

This was my first intimation of the change in command that was to put both Hodges and Simpson under Montgomery; the former for a month, the latter until after we crossed the Rhine. Eisenhower had not raised the issue

during our meeting at Verdun early that morning nor had he shown any concern over my communications to the north. Our lines through Bastogne had been cut but an auxiliary circuit had been run across the western tip of the Ardennes. Still another was being strung for safety's sake behind the Meuse. As long as the enemy was contained within the Meuse, it seemed unlikely that we would lose all our long lines to either the First or Ninth Armies. And as a matter of fact we never did.

The suddenness of Bedell's proposal made me turn it hurriedly over in his mind. 'I'd question whether such a change-over's necessary,' I said. 'When we go to drive him out of the Bulge, it'd be easier to co-ordinate the attack from here.' If Montgomery were to come into the picture as Bedell had suggested, co-ordination between both Army Groups would have to be directed from SHAEF.

But Smith was for the change-over. 'It seems the logical thing to do,' he said. 'Monty can take care of everything north of the Bulge and you'll have everything south.'

'Bedell, it's hard for me to object,' I told him. 'Certainly if Monty's were an American command, I would agree with you entirely. It would be the logical thing to do.' In this moment of decision I could not tell him that what I feared most was the likelihood that this forced change-over would discredit the American command.

For no one could dispute that the change-over would not have been a logical one; there was ample justification for the Army Group on the north taking *temporary* command of all Armies on that side of the penetration. Furthermore, if von Rundstedt were to force the Meuse behind both our US Armies, Montgomery would find his 21st Group seriously jeopardized by the offensive. To protect himself he would undoubtedly want to establish a reserve on that right flank. Yet if his command were to include

Below: The twisted remains of a German tank-destroyer based on a 38t chassis; a victim of direct hits from several anti-tank rounds fired at close quarters.

the US Armies and be extended all the way down to the Bulge, he would probably employ that British reserve against the enemy threat to the Meuse.

'There's no doubt in my mind,' I admitted to Smith, 'that if we play it the way you suggest, we'll get more help from the British in the way of reserves.'

I asked if the change-over was to be a *temporary* one. Bedell agreed that it was and that it would last only as long as the Bulge.

With this assurance that the change-over was to be temporary, my only other objections revolved around the question of face. For unless the change-over were clearly explained by SHAEF, it could be interpreted as a loss of confidence by Eisenhower in me – or more significantly in the American command. If, as a result of the shift, the public were to lose confidence in me, Eisenhower could quickly remedy that situation by sending me home. But if his action were taken to mean repudiation of the American command, if it were inferred that we were bailed out by the British, the damage could be irreparable to our future role in the war.

Although these objections seemed rational enough, I nevertheless distrusted them, fearing they might be too much involved in my concern for my career. Eisenhower had resolved to fight us together as an Allied command. If there were to be no distinctions between Allies, then I questioned my right to wave the flag for prestige in this particular crisis.

The change-over was to be made at noon on 20 December. With this acquisition of the First and Ninth US Armies, Montgomery's command would then be expanded to four. I was to be left *temporarily* with only Patton's Third.

Had the senior British field commander been anyone else but Monty, the switch in command could probably have been made without incident, strain or tension. Certainly it would never have touched off the Allied ruckus it subsequently did. But Montgomery unfortunately could not resist this chance to tweak our Yankee noses. Even Freddy de Guingand, his chief of staff, was later to chide Montgomery for the manner in which he behaved. And while Eisenhower held his tongue only by clenching his teeth, he was to admit several years after the war that had he anticipated the trouble that was to be caused by it, he would never have suggested the change. Fortunately, the mischief was delayed until after our crisis in the Bulge had passed.

Above: Sherman tanks of 40th Tank Battalion, 7th Armored Division, fire on enemy positions beyond the town of St Vith, 29 January 1945. This unit was part of the US First Army (General Courtney Hodges) which held the northern part of the 'Bulge'.

Below: Members of the 325th Glider Regiment, 82nd Airborne Division, drag supplies through heavy snow on their way to attack the town of Herresbach.

Although Montgomery did not commit more than a *single* brigade of British troops against the Bulge offensive, he backed the First Army's flank with four British divisions. While those British reserves encouraged Hodges to throw everything into the Ardennes, I afterwards questioned whether this bargain was worth the misunderstanding that came with the change in command.

Almost as soon as the change-over brought Hodges' and Simpson's Armies under his 21st Group, Montgomery hurried a liaison officer down to the Meuse to ascertain in a first-hand report whether the enemy had anywhere crossed it. Hodges could readily have told him the Germans had not. The 7th Armoured still held to its salient at St Vith, and to the north on the Malmédy shoulder the veteran 1st, 2nd, and 9th Divisions had dug in on that critical shoulder. At the Belgian farm village of Stavelot, only twenty-two miles southeast of Liège, the 30th Division once more heeled in with the doggedness it had shown at Mortain. Now as the Bulge spilled harmlessly westward through the empty Ardennes, Hodges gathered his VII Corps on the flank in preparation for a counterattack.

The remarkable regroupment of First Army while under attack equalled even the astonishing performance of Third Army. On 17 December alone, it put 60,000 men and 11,000 vehicles in motion on the realignment. During the first nine days of von Rundstedt's offensive, First Army cleared 196 convoys of 48,000 vehicles and 248,000 troops. When during the First World War, Marshal Foch raced his famous 'taxi-cab' army to halt the Kaiser's troops on the Marne, he shuttled a bare 4,985 troops a distance of twenty-eight miles in 1,200 Paris cabs.

On the eve of Patton's attack towards the US redoubt at Bastogne, Montgomery radioed that he was planning to delay the companion attack from the north for which Hodges had massed Collins' VII Corps. He had chosen instead to 'tidy up' the defences on his front before undertaking a counter-offensive. As a result, the divisions that had been gathered for Collins' attack were dispersed on a retaining wall and the enemy continued to hold the initiative on the northern edge of the Bulge. It was not until 3 January, 12 days later, that Montgomery completed his primping and attacked.

Meanwhile, the enemy now acknowledged that his main effort had been thwarted on the shoulder at Malmédy where Hodges had fought Sepp Dietrich to a draw. Gone was the element of surprise; von Rundstedt had gambled on

Above: Tanks and infantry of the US 6th Armored Division advance in open order across exposed ground on their way to Bastogne. The town was relieved on 26 December.

Right: A snow-covered Sherman advances in pursuit of the retreating Germans. The 'Bulge' was finally eradicated in late January 1945; Hitler had already ordered a series of limited withdrawals on the 8th.

speed and lost. Now faced with a major battle instead of the break-through he had planned to the Meuse, von Rundstedt shifted the main force of his drive to Manteuffel's Fifth Panzer Army. At the same time he committed his remaining reserves in the gap that had been opened north of Bastogne and attacked due westward. Thus after having been repelled in his advance towards Liège, von Rundstedt, now with no worthwhile objective, could only spend his strength against the Ardennes.

Two days before Christmas the grey cloud blanket that had hung so long over our front lifted for the first time in eight days and a blaze of sunlight silhouetted the enemy against the Ardennes snows.

Prior to this, each morning our gloom had deepened as the Ninth Air Force's youthful meteorologist opened the daily briefing with his dismally repetitious report. And each morning Vandenberg, in a chair next to mine, pulled his head a little tighter into his leather flying jacket. On more than 100 socked-in airfields from Scotland to Brussels, an Allied air force of more than 4,000 planes waited for the end of von Rundstedt's conspiracy with the weather.

On the morning of 23 December, Vandenberg's meteorologist hurried into the *Tac* war room with a forecast for good weather across the entire front. Within an hour the air began to pulse with a mighty roar of engines as aircraft swarmed high over Luxembourg to join the attack. Even as von Rundstedt continued to push his famished columns towards the Meuse, he could no longer support the offensive as long as we could pound him from the air. On that first clear day air flew a total of more than 1,200 sorties. The following day 2,000 bombers escorted by more than 800 fighters went after 31 tactical targets with 4,300 tons of bombs. Fighter-bombers splayed out through the Ardennes hunting the enemy where he waited

helplessly in clotted columns. At Bastogne where three enemy divisions were attacking that brave pocket, 241 troop-carrier aircraft pin-pointed a low-level drop of food, medical supplies, and ammunition.

From Luxembourg we could see the contrails of the heavies as they droned overhead bound for the busy marshalling yards of Trier behind the German border.

Back at SHAEF where the gloom thickened as red tabs marking von Rundstedt's Armies moved across their war maps, G-3 fretted again over the security of those bridges across the Meuse between Namur and Dinant. While not denying that von Rundstedt might yet extend his Bulge to that river, I disputed his ability to cross it even with light reconnaissance forces. The enemy had previously destroyed those bridges during his rout to the Siegfried Line. None had been repaired in that unimportant

Above: Belgian civilians look on as the commander of the relief force is greeted by the commander of the 'Battered Bastards of Bastogne,' December 1944.

Below: German troops captured by the US 82nd Airborne Division at Hierlot. Defeat in the Ardennes cost the German Army 70,000 casualties and 50,000 prisoners. Material losses ran to over 500 tanks and 1,600 aircraft. The US victory marked the beginning of the collapse of the German forces in the western European theater.

crook of the river and our pontoon substitutes could be demolished with the stroke of a detonator box. I suggested to Allen that we radio SHAEF to keep its shirt on.

Assured by Patton that he would soon break through to relieve Bastogne, I was eager to have Montgomery hit the enemy from the north. I therefore begged Ike to prod Montgomery in an effort to speed up that counter-attack. But Mongomery would not be hurried. Rather than pinch off the enemy at the middle as Patton and I were eager to do, Monty preferred to halt him by denting the nose of his advance. Elsewhere across the flank, Monty was still preoccupied in the task of 'tidying up' his front. The 82nd Division had been ordered back from its salient on the river line behind St Vith following the 7th Armoured's withdrawal from that position. But when Montgomery proposed a further withdrawal that would have widened the Bulge at that point, both Collins and Ridgway objected so heatedly that Montgomery promptly backed down. In a letter to Hodges I wrote that although he 'was no longer in my command, I would view with serious misgivings the surrender of any more ground' on his side of the Bulge.

On Christmas Eve Montgomery suggested I fly up to 21 *Tac* the next day and there coordinate our respective Group plans for reducing the Bulge. Patton's tanks had now forced an alley to within two and a half miles of Bastogne. North of that city a 25-mile corridor sep rated it from the First Army. We could now in t with artillery the three second-class roads that carried the enemy's lifeline through that narrowing gap.

Fearful that a detachment of Skorzeny's assassins might have penetrated the city of Luxembourg, Sibert had tucked me under an elaborate security wrap. As part of his security precautions, Sibert evacuated my C-47 from the Luxembourg airport where it had been parked, to a night-fighter base, forty minutes by car to the rear at Étain. To save time on the flight to Montgomery's CP, I instructed Robinson to fly the plane from Étain and pick me up at Luxembourg, only two minutes' flying time from the German line. His crew was to join him there. But, when Sibert got wind of these plans, he protested so strenuously that I abandoned the idea and hurried after the pilot down the road to Étain. Rather than wait for the crew then marooned on the Luxembourg airfield, we took off from Étain in the *Mary Q* on a tree-level course across the corner of the Ardennes. While Robinson piloted, Hansen and I conned the course from a map. An hour later we landed at St Trond in Belgium, where Hodges' aide, Major William C. Sylvan of Columbia, South Carolina, was waiting with a car. *En route* to the modest Dutch house in which Montgomery had established his CP, I munched on an apple for lunch.

In the villages through which we sped, the sidewalks were filled with Hollanders in holiday dress.

'What's happening today?' I asked.

'It's Christmas, General –' Hansen replied.

Although I had hoped Montgomery would soon join our counter-attack with one from the north, I found him waiting expectantly for one last enemy blow on that flank. Not until he was certain the enemy had exhausted himself, would Montgomery plunge in for the kill. Disappointed at the prospect of further delay, I headed back to St Trond.

As Robinson revved his engine, the control tower called, 'You can't make it before dark –' the dispatcher warned, 'you'd better not take off.' Pretending that he had misunderstood, Robinson called back into the mike, 'Downwind? Thank you, I'll take off downwind.' We shot down the runway and climbed into the dusk at full throttle. In the failing light we hedgehopped over the slag piles of Belgium's coal fields, straining to pick up the dim checkpoints. It was dark when we skimmed into Étain. The field lighted its oil torches and we touched down to a feathery landing. That evening Sergeant Dudley sent a plate of turkey up to my room.

It was on 26 December that the Bulge reached its high-water mark seventeen miles from where the picturesque city of Dinant

Above: US combat engineers make repairs to a bridge to facilitate the pursuit of the retreating Germans near the town of Houffalize.

guards the rocky gorge of the Meuse. There Ernie Harmon threw his 2nd Armoured Division across the path of von Rundstedt's 2nd Panzer Division to bring the last enemy thrust to a standstill. For three days those divisions hammered each other without respite. In this head-on clash, Harmon left eighty-one enemy panzers smoking in the hills. And he halted von Rundstedt's advance.

In reporting to me on the battle several days later, Harmon wrote with characteristic brevity: 'We got in front of the 2nd Panzer Division on December 23, 24 and 25 and polished them off. Attached is a list of the spoils we took – including 1,200 prisoners. Killed and wounded some 2,500. A great slaughter.'

The 'spoils' he had listed included 405 of the enemy's fast-dwindling trucks and 81 artillery pieces. After that single historic meeting with its opposite number in the American army, the 2nd Panzer limped back with 1,500 frostbitten grenadiers and a handful of surviving Panthers – all that was left of the division that had sallied towards the Meuse.

At 4 o'clock that afternoon Patton called to report that his 4th Armoured Division had broken through to relieve Bastogne and end the seven-day siege of that city. At a cost of 482 killed, 2,449 wounded, Tony McAuliffe had withstood the attacks of three German divisions while memorializing the epoch with his single-word rejection of the enemy's demand for complete surrender.

I telephoned Eisenhower that evening to urge that he now goad Montgomery into an attack against the Bulge on its north flank. However, Eisenhower had headed for 21st Group and I spoke to Bedell Smith instead.

'Dammit, Bedell, can't you people get Monty going on the north? As near as we can tell this other fellow's reached his high-water mark today. He'll soon be starting to pull back – if not tonight, certainly by tomorrow.'

But Bedell disputed this optimistic appraisal, for SHAEF had been surfeited with the apprehensive estimates of 21st Group. 'Oh no, Brad, you're mistaken,' he said. 'Why they'll be across the Meuse in 48 hours.'

'Nuts,' I answered, plagiarizing McAuliffe for the lack of any other retort. It was apparent that SHAEF totally lacked our feel of the situation. For by then the enemy's plight was clear. We had all but destroyed his leading division and were holding firmly everywhere on the flanks. Patton's broad advance from the south had joined up at Bastogne and the enemy's three remaining east-west roads were under artillery interdiction.

For two days the enemy held without renewing his advance. On the third day he began to fall back. The following day I drove to Versailles with a plan for resuming the offensive once we had flattened the Bulge. Ike jubilantly declared he would reward me with the rarest

Left: A member of the 26th Infantry Division, part of Patton's Third Army, eats cold rations during a lull in the fighting.

treasure in all France. A waiter came in with two steaming bowls. In a pool of rich cream there floated a half-dozen oysters from Chesapeake Bay. I ate them without confessing his treasure gave me the hives.

The New Year began more brightly than the old one had ended when Montgomery reported that he would attack into the north side of the Bulge on 3 January. When on New Year's Eve, Bill Walton, a parachutist correspondent for *Time*, toasted the old year out with the doleful farewell, 'Never was the world plagued by such a year less worth remembering,' I could have added, '– especially the last fifteen days.' Another fifty-three days were to pass before we jumped across the Roer to resume the winter offensive that had been halted by German attack. But if our afflictions were heavy, we could take comfort in the knowledge that the enemy's outweighed our own. None of those divisions in the Bulge was ever effective again.

Below: Troops of a German Volksgrenadier Regiment line up for interrogation after their capture. Signs of battle fatigue are evident in their faces.

Index

  Twentyfifth Army *68*
  DIVISIONS
  5th 74-83 *passim*, 85-7, 88, 91
  15th 181, 200, 201, 204, 205, 206,
    208
  16th 237
  18th 73, 75-83 *passim*, 85-90
    passim
  31st 181, 182, 186, 188, 189, 191,
    193, 197, 211, 213
  33rd 180, 184, 201, 202, 204, 206,
    207
  53rd, 54th 204
  Konoe Imperial Guards 74-5, 76,
    79-80, 81, 82, 85, 86, 87
  in Assam/Burma *186-7*, *194*
  in Malaya/Singapore *70-91*
  named regts 77, 78, 88, 89
Japanese navy 68, 87, 96
  at Leyte Gulf *237-9*, 238-9
  at Midway 96-7, 98-105, *102*
Jervis, HMS 56, 58, 63
Jeschonnek, Maj-Gen 39, 46
Joint Air Force Anti-Submarine
  School 149
Juin, Gen Alphonse P 165, 171, 172

Kaga, carrier 97, 100, 104
kamikaze attacks *244-5*, 245
Kawamura, Maj-Gen 94
Kenny, Gen George 245
Kesselring, FM Albert 32, 46, 160,
  164, 169
Keyes, Geoffrey 165
Khopko, Major S N 137
Khrushchev, N S 138, 140
Kinkaid, Vice-Adm T C 240-47
  passim
Kirchner, General 13
Kleist, Gen E von 12, 13, 14, 16, 17,
  21, 22, 23, 27
Klimov, G T 127, 129
Kohima battle 180, 182, map 184,
  186-98, *190*, *200-201*, 204,
  208-9, 208-11
Kondo, Vice-Admiral N 105
Korfes, Maj-Gen Otto 144
Kretschmer, Otto *149*
Kreuger, Lt-Gen Walter 236
Krylov, Gen N I 130-37 *passim*, 141,
  144
Kurita, Admiral T *237*, 239, 240,
  242, 244, 245-6
Kusaka, Rear Admiral 100-101

Landrum, Maj-Gen Eugene M 228
Lee, Rear Admiral W A 245
Lee-Barber, Lt-Cdr J 62
Leeb, Col-Gen Ritter von 30
Leese, Gen Sir Oliver 108
Leigh-Mallory, ACM Sir Trafford
  216, *221*, 226, 251
Leyte Gulf 231, 233-5, 242-3
  landings *232-5*, 236-8, 240
  sea battles 7, *236-7*, 238-47, *242-7*
  maps 235, 247
Liebenstein, Lt-Col Freiherr von 20
List, Col-Gen W von 11, 22, 23
Littorio class battleship *54*, 57
Lörzer, Gen 13, 16, 17, 18
Lucas, Maj-Gen J P 160, *163*
Luftwaffe 13, *15*, 16-18, *17*, 26-8,
  35-6, 122-5 *passim*, 127, 132,
  134, *135*, *138*, *150*, 219, 266-7,
  256
  Battle of Britain 32-51, *34*, *36-7*,
    41-2, *44*, *46*, *48*
  fighter tactics 36-7, 41-2
Lumsden, Gen Herbert 108

MacArthur, Gen Douglas 231,
  232-47, *236*
McAuliffe, Brig-Gen A *273*, 285
Mack, Capt Philip 58, 62-3
McCreery, Gen R L 165, 172
McNair, Lt-Gen L J 250
Maginot Line 10, *15*, 18, 19, *249*, 267
Majdalany, Fred 170, 177
Manstein, Gen E von 10, 12, 22, 123
Manteuffel, Gen Hasso von 268,
  273, 277, 283
Marshall, Gen G C 255, 271

Marshall-A'Deane, Cdr W R 62
Matsui, Lt-Gen 82, 84
Middleton, Maj-Gen Troy H 266-7,
  271, 272, *273*, 277, 279-80
Midway *96*, 96-105, maps 100, 104
Mitscher, Vice-Admiral Marc *239*
Model, FM Walter 267
Mogami, cruiser 105, *105*, *241*
Mölders, Werner 37, 43, 44, 49, 50,
  51
Monterey, USS *243*
Montgomery, Gen Sir B L 6, 106-7,
  108-21, *113*, 216, *221*, 227-8,
  248, 250, 251, 254, 257, 258-9,
  261, 262-3, 264-5, 266, 268,
  269-70, 280-82, 284, 285
Moon, Admiral 225
Morrison, Samuel E 96, 158, 159
Morshead, Lt-Gen Sir L *121*
Mountbatten, Adm Lord Louis 187
Musashi, battleship *236*,
  240
Mutaguchi, Lt-Gen R 81-2, 89-90,
  93, 200

Naga, cruiser 97, 100-102
Naga tribesmen *191*, 210-11
Nagumo, Vice-Admiral C 96, 97,
  98, *98*, 100-102
Nashville, USS 236, 237, 240
Nautilus, US submarine 97, 104
Nettuno *see* Anzio landing
New Zealand forces 170, *170-71*, 177
  NZ Corps 165, 171, 172, 173
  2nd NZ Div 108, 111, 112, 114-20
Nicholson, Brigadier 27
Nimitz, Admiral Chester W 96, 240,
  243, 245-7
Nishimura, Vice-Adm S 239, 241,
  242
Normandy *216-17*
  landings 214, *214*, map 221, *222-3*
  Juno Beach *227*
  Omaha 7, 216, 219-26, *224*, 228
  Utah 217, 222, 224, 226, 228
  break-out 251, 253-7, 260, 262
  maps 254, 257
Nubian, HMS 56, 58

O'Connor, Gen Sir Richard 52
Offa, HMS 157, 158
Okumiya, Masatake 98-105
Oldendorf, Rear-Adm J *238*, 241,
  244
Operation Sealion 33, 35, *35*
Oribi, HMS 154, 158
Orion, HMS 56
Osmena, President Sergio 237
Oster, General 168
Ozawa, Vice-Admiral J 231, *237*,
  239, 242, 246

Paris, liberation of 256, *256*, *258*
Patch, Lt-Gen A M 255, 258, 260
Patton, Maj-Gen G S 250-51, *251*,
  255, 257, 260, 266, 267, 268,
  270, 274-8 *passim*, *277*, 282,
  284, 285
Paulus, Gen F von 122-3, *126*, 137,
  140, 144, *144*
Pearl Harbor 97, 98, *99*
Percival, Lt-Gen A E 66-7, 76, *82*,
  89, 91-3, 94
Pfeffer, Lt-Gen 144-5
Philante convoy training 149
Philippine Islands 232-47
Philippine Sea battle 231
Philipps, A C 172, 173
Pink, HMS 156, 158
Pola 59, 62-3, 64, 65
Polish forces 160, *173*, 251
Power, Commander 55, 60
Power, Rear Admiral A J 57
Pownall, Gen Sir Henry 68
Pozharski, General 138-9
Pridham-Wippell, Vice-Admiral 56,
  57, 58, 59, 62, 63
Prince of Wales, HMS 68, *71-2*
Princeton, USS, light carrier 7
Prittwitz, Colonel von 19, 25

Quesada, Maj-Gen E R 251

Raffles, Sir Stamford 68, 93
Ramsey, Adm Sir Bertram *221*, 227
Ranking, Maj-Gen R P L 189, 190,
  191
Reinhardt, General G H 19
Repulse, HMS 34, 68, *70*
Richards, Col H U 188, 194
Richthofen, Manfred von 41, 44
Ridgway, Mak-Gen Matthew B 224,
  226, 228, 284
Roberts, Maj-Gen Ouvry 183, 201
Rodimtsev, Maj-Gen A I 135, 138,
  141, 143
Rodney, HMS 226
Rommel, Gen Erwin 6, 52, 110, 117,
  118, 121, 219, 222, 226, 227, 256
Romulo, Gen Carlos 237
Roosevelt, President F D 108, 233
Roosevelt, Brig Gen Theodore 224
Roskill, Capt S W 159
Rotterdam, bombing of *20*
Royal Air Force 19, *81*, 219, 250
  Assam/Burma 182, 183, 184, 187,
    193, 194, *198*, 201, 203
  in Atlantic 146, 149, 155, 156, *156*,
    159
  Battle of Britain 32, *32*, 36-8, *43*,
    44-5, *45*, 47-9
  Coastal Command 146, *159*
  fighter control 37, *39*
  in N Africa 111, 117, 119, 120
Royal Canadian Air Force 159
Royal Marines, 48 Commando *227*
Royal Navy 146
  Mediterranean Fleet 52, 54-65
  see names of individual ships
Rudder, Lt-Col James E 220-21
Rundstedt, Col-Gen G von 9, 10, 12,
  14, 19, 22, 29, 219, 266, 268-80
  passim, 283-4, 285

St Lô, USS, escort carrier 245
Samar battle *242-3*, 243-3, 243-4,
  244
San Bernardino Strait 239, 240, 242,
  243
Sarayev, Colonel 126, 136-7, 138
Sato, Lt-Gen K *188*, 191, 193, 194
Schaal, General 13, 15, 20, 27
Schmidt von Altenstadt, Col 167
Scoones, Lt-Gen Sir G 180, 182, 184,
  186, 189, 193, *196*, 198-202
  passim, 204, 205, 207, 213
Senger und Etterlin, Gen F von 160,
  162-77, *171*
Seydlitz-Kurzbach, Lt-Gen von
  144-5
Sherwood, Lt-Cdr R E 157, 159
Shima, Vice-Adm K 239, *241*
Shoho, carrier 97, *98*
Sibert, Maj-Gen F C 236, 284
Sibuyan Sea battle 7, *236-7*
Siegfried Line 218, 257, 266, 267,
  268, 270
Simpson, Lt- Gen W H 266, 270,
  272, 280, 282
Singapore *70-71*, *84-5*, *89*, *92-5*
  battle for 6, 66, *67*, 67-95
  map 80
Singapore Volunteer Corps *83*
Skorzeny, Lt-Col O 273, 275, 284
Slim, Gen Sir W 6, 178, 180-213, *197*
Smith, Lt-Gen W Bedell 216, *221*,
  280-81, 285
Snowflake, HMS 153, 154
Sodenstern, General von 10
Soryu, carrier 97, 100, 104
South African forces 112
  1st South African Div 115, 116, 117
Soviet Army 122-3, *133*, 134-7,
  137-41, 248
  62nd Army 126, 130-45
  13th Guards Div 134-7 *passim*,
    140, 141, 143
  112th, 229th Inf Divs 124
  Siberian Division 122
Sperrle, General Hugo 16, 18, 32
Sprague, Rear Adm T L 242, 243-6
Spruance, Rear Adm R A 96
Stalingrad 6, 45, *122*, 125-45 maps
  126, 128, *127-44*, 177
Stauffenberg, Count 167
Steinmetz, General 162
Stephenson, Adm Sir Gilbert 148
Stillwell, Lt-Gen J W 186

Stopford, Lt-Gen Montague 188,
  191-2, 193-5, 196, 197, *197*, 211
Stuart, HMS 56, 62
Stumpf, Gen H A 46
Stutterheim, General von 15
Sunflower, HMS 148, 152, 154
Surigao Strait action *238-9*, 241, *241*,
  243, 244
Sylvester, Maj-Gen L McD 261

Tanaka, Admiral Raizo *102*
Taranto raid 52, 53, 54, *56*
Tay, HMS 149, 151-4 *passim*, 157,
  158, 159
Taylor, Gen Maxwell D 224, 225,
  229
Tedder, ACM Sir Arthur 216, *221*
Timberlake, Brig Gen E J Jr 229
Torrens Spence, Lt F M A 64
Toyoda, Adm S 231, 238-9, 240
Tsuji, Col Masanobu 6, 66-7, 68-95

U-boats 146, *148-9*, *151-9*, *153*, *157*,
  159
  named boats 151, *151*, 153, 156,
    158, 159, *159*
Udet, Ernst 39
United States Army
  Sixth Army Group 253, 255, 266,
    275
  Twelfth Army Group 250, 255,
    264, 266, 273
  ARMIES
  First 228, 250, 251, 257, *260*, 262,
    264-7 *passim*, 273, 274, 276-82
    passim
  Third 250, 251, 255, 257, 266,
    267, 274-8 *passim*, *278*, 281, 282
  Fifth 165, *167*, 171
  Sixth 236
  Seventh 255, 266
  Ninth 266, 278, 280-81
  CORPS
  II 165
  V 221, *222-3*, 227, 228
  VII 224-5, 228, 256, 262, 282
  VIII 266, 271, 277, 279-80
  X 236
  XIX 256
  XXIV 236
  DIVISIONS
  1st Cavalry 236
  1st Inf 221, 222, 223, 227, 282
  2nd Armored 285
  2nd Inf 224, *256*, 282
  3rd Armored *261*, 279
  4th 224, 225, 228, 272, 280, 285
  5th Inf 278
  6th Armored *282*
  7th Armored *261*, 272, 273, 279,
    280, *281*, 282, 284
  7th Inf 236
  9th Armored 273, 277, 282
  10th Armored 272, 273, 277, 278
  24th Inf 236
  26th Inf *285*
  28th 273, 280
  29th Inf 227, 228-9, *263*
  30th 282
  34th 162, 165, 171
  36th Inf 162, 165, 171
  82nd Airborne 224-5, 226, 228,
    260, 272, 273, *281*, 284
  96th 236
  101st Airborne 224-5, 228, 260,
    264, 272, 273, *275*, 277
  104th 261
  106th 273, 280
  REGIMENTS
  2nd Rangers *220*, 220-21, 225
  5th Rangers 220-21
  in Ardennes *272-3*
  across France 255, *263*, 265
  in Italy *162*, *167*, *169*
  Normandy *214*, *218*, *220*, 229
United States Army Air Force 156
  Ninth Air Force 250, 283
  in Burma/Assam 187, 203
  in Italy *167*, *174*
  over Normandy 219, *222*,
    224-5 passim
United States Navy
  Third Fleet 233, 239-45
  Seventh Fleet 240-41, 242-4, 247

Acknowledgments

I am indebted to the following for
permission to reproduce copyright
material:
  Sir Basil Liddell Hart and Michael
Joseph Ltd, for permission to
reproduce excerpts from *Panzer
Leader* by Heinz Guderian; Methuen
Ltd, for permission to reproduce
excerpts from *The First and the Last*
by Adolf Galland; Hutchinson & Co,
and A P Watt for permission to
reproduce excerpts from *El Alamein
to the River Sangro* by Viscount
Montgomery of Alamein and for
excerpts from *A Sailor's Odyssey* by
Viscount Cunningham of
Hyndhope; Constable & Co Ltd, for
permission to reproduce excerpts
from *Singapore* by Masanobu Tsuji;
Hutchinson Publishing Group Ltd,
for permission to reproduce excerpts
from *Midway* by Mitsuo Fuchida
and Masatake Okumiya, also
reproduced by permission from
Midway copyright © 1955 by US
Naval Institute, Annapolis,
Maryland; Macgibbon & Kee Ltd,
for permission to reproduce excerpts
from *The Beginning of the Road* by
Marshal Vasili Chuikov; Cassell &
Co Ltd, for permission to reproduce
excerpts from *Convoy Escort
Commander* by Vice-Admiral Sir
Peter Gretton; Macdonald & Co
Ltd, for permission to reproduce
excerpts from *Neither Fear Nor Hope*
by General von Senger und Etterlin;
Cassell & Co Ltd, and David
Higham Associates Ltd, for
permission to reproduce excerpts
from *Defeat into Victory* by Field-
Marshal Sir William Slim; Laurence
Pollinger Ltd, for permission to
reproduce excerpts from *A Soldier's
Story of the Allied Campaign from
Tunis to the Elbe* by General Omar
Nelson Bradley; William
Heinemann Ltd, for permission to
reproduce excerpts from
Reminiscences by General Douglas
MacArthur, and for excerpts from
Crusade in Europe by General
Dwight D Eisenhower; Macmillan &
Co Ltd, for permission to reproduce
excerpts from *The Last Enemy* by
Richard Hillary.

In addition I wish to acknowledge
the help of my friend and colleague
Antony Brett-James, who gave me
much valuable advice. Herbert van
Thal, by helping to organize this
work, has put me much in his debt.
The publishers would also like to
thank David Eldred for designing
the book, Melanie Earnshaw for the
picture research and Ron Watson for
compiling the index.

**All illustrations supplied courtesy
of the Trustees of the Imperial
War Museum.** (Prints for
illustrations credited to the Imperial
War Museum are for sale on
application to its Department of
Photographs, Lambeth Road,
London, SE1 6HZ. The Visitor's
Room is open to the public by
appointment).

Except for the following:

AKG, Berlin: pages 2-3, 130
(below), 131, 134 (both)
Bison Books: pages 6, 8-9, 14
(both), 15 (both), 17 (both), 18
(both), 19, 25 (below), 28, 29
(below), 30, 35 (top), 39, 44 (left),
50 (top & below left), 60 (below),
64, 86 (top), 92 (both), 109 (top
left), 113 (top right). 118 (both), 124,
125 (all 3), 126 (top right), 132
(below), 133, 135, 143, 155 (top),
156(both), 157 (below), 158 (right),
163 (top), 169 (both), 175 (below),
216, 217 (top), 229, 234 (below), 238
(both), 239 (both), 253, 259, 266
(top), 267 (below), 268 (both), 270
(both), 274, 278 (top), 279, 280, 283
(below right), 285 (below)
Camera Press: page 141 (below)
Robert Hunt Picture Library: pages
23, 26, 29 (top), 35 (below), 37
(below), 38 (top), 41 (top), 43
(both), 52-53, 54, 55, 56 (both), 60
(top), 62 (both), 68-69, 69 (top), 73
(both), 76, 81, 82 (below), 83, 84, 85
(both), 91, 93, 95 (both), 98, 100
(top), 102 (below right), 110, 115
(below), 116 (top), 120 (both),
122-123, 126 (below), 127, 129
(both), 130 (top), 132 (top), 145
(top), 146-147, 149 (top), 150, 151
(right), 153 (below), 158 (left), 163
(below), 165 (below), 166 (below),
167 (below), 171 (top) 177 (below),
186, 187 (both), 188 (top), 192 (top),
202 (below), 211, 218 (both), 221
(below), 222 (both), 224 (top), 226,
237 (both top), 241 (top left), 250,
256 (below), 258, 262, 271 (below),
277 (top), 278 (below), 281 (below),
284
The Keystone Collection: pages 45
(right), 59, 78, 80, 86 (below), 88,
90, 128, 136 (below), 137 (left), 142
(right), 145 (below), 155 (below), 157
(top), 160-161, 166 (top), 167 (top),
177 (top), 184, 185, 204 (below),
214-215
MARS: pages 36, 37 (top), 41
(below), 44 (below right), 148
(below), 149 (below), 151 (left), 175
(top), 176 (top)
MARS/Musée de l'Armée: pages 11
(top), 25 (top)
MARS/US National Archive; pages
224 (below), 225, 253
MARS/Fujiphotos, Tokyo: pages
66-67, 74 (below), 75
**MARS/Royal Engineers Officers
Mess:** page 113 (below)
MARS/US Navy: pages 102 (top),
246, 247 (top)
MARS/IWM: pages 51 (both), 195,
203 (below), 205, 223, 227 (both),
283 (below left)
Peter Newark's Historical Pictures:
pages 245 (top)
Novosti Press Agency: pages 136
(top), 137 (right), 139 (below), 140,
144
Spaarnestad Archiv, Haarlem:
pages 70 (below), 77, 79 (both)
TRH: pages 220 (both), 242 (below)
US Air Force: pages 174 (below)
US Army: pages 251 (below), 255
(top), 256 (below), 261, 263, 272
(both), 275 (both), 277 (below), 283
(top), 285 (top)
US National Archive: pages 1,
96-97, 99 (both), 105 (below), 165
(top), 237 (below), 240, 241 (below),
243 (top), 244 (below), 251 (top), 281
(top)
US Navy: pages 7 (below), 101
(top), 102 (below left), 103 (below),
230-231, 232, 233 (both), 234 (top),
235 (below), 241 (top right), 243
(below)
Weidenfeld Archive: pages 63, 87,
103 (top), 138 (both), 183, 189, 247
(below), 269, 273